4:1 - 5:1
5:2 - 6:3
me 6:4 - 7:9

SONG OF SONGS

The Old Testament Library

GENESIS, A Commentary. Revised Edition. BY GERHARD VON RAD
THE BOOK OF EXODUS, A Critical, Theological Commentary. BY BREVARD S. CHILDS
LEVITICUS, A Commentary. BY ERHARD S. GERSTENBERGER
NUMBERS, A Commentary. BY MARTIN NOTH
DEUTERONOMY, A Commentary. BY RICHARD D. NELSON
DEUTERONOMY, A Commentary. BY GERHARD VON RAD
JOSHUA, A Commentary. BY RICHARD D. NELSON
JUDGES, A Commentary. BY SUSAN NIDITCH
JUDGES, A Commentary. BY J. ALBERTO SOGGIN
RUTH, A Commentary. BY KIRSTEN NIELSEN
I & II SAMUEL, A Commentary. BY HANS WILHELM HERTZBERG
I & II KINGS, A Commentary. BY MARVIN A. SWEENEY
I & II CHRONICLES, A Commentary. BY SARA JAPHET
EZRA-NEHEMIAH, A Commentary. BY JOSEPH BLENKINSOPP
ESTHER, A Commentary. BY JON D. LEVENSON
THE BOOK OF JOB, A Commentary. BY NORMAN C. HABEL
THE PSALMS, A Commentary. BY ARTUR WEISER
PROVERBS, A Commentary. BY RICHARD J. CLIFFORD
ECCLESIASTES, A Commentary. BY JAMES L. CRENSHAW
SONG OF SONGS, A Commentary. BY J. CHERYL EXUM
ISAIAH, A Commentary. BY BREVARD S. CHILDS
ISAIAH 1–12, A Commentary. Second Edition. BY OTTO KAISER
ISAIAH 13–39, A Commentary. BY OTTO KAISER
ISAIAH 40–66, A Commentary. BY CLAUS WESTERMANN
LAMENTATIONS, A Commentary. BY ADELE BERLIN
JEREMIAH, A Commentary. BY LESLIE C. ALLEN
EZEKIEL, A Commentary. BY WALTHER EICHRODT
DANIEL, A Commentary. BY NORMAN W. PORTEOUS
HOSEA, A Commentary. BY JAMES L. MAYS
JOEL AND OBADIAH, A Commentary. BY JOHN BARTON
AMOS, A Commentary. BY JAMES L. MAYS
THE BOOK OF AMOS, A Commentary. BY JÖRG JEREMIAS
JONAH, A Commentary. BY JAMES LIMBURG
MICAH, A Commentary. BY JAMES L. MAYS
NAHUM, HABAKKUK, AND ZEPHANIAH, A Commentary. BY J. J. M. ROBERTS
HAGGAI AND ZECHARIAH 1–8, A Commentary. BY DAVID L. PETERSEN
ZECHARIAH 9–14 AND MALACHI, A Commentary. BY DAVID L. PETERSEN

EXILE AND RESTORATION: A Study of Hebrew Thought of the Sixth Century B.C. BY PETER R. ACKROYD
A HISTORY OF ISRAELITE RELIGION IN THE OLD TESTAMENT PERIOD, Volumes I and II. BY RAINER ALBERTZ
INTRODUCTION TO THE OLD TESTAMENT. Third Edition. BY J. ALBERTO SOGGIN
JEWISH WISDOM IN THE HELLENISTIC AGE. BY JOHN J. COLLINS
OLD TESTAMENT THEOLOGY, Volumes I and II. BY HORST DIETRICH PREUSS
OLD TESTAMENT THEOLOGY, Volumes I and II. BY GERHARD VON RAD
THEOLOGY OF THE OLD TESTAMENT, Volumes I and II. BY WALTHER EICHRODT

J. Cheryl Exum

Song of Songs

A Commentary

WESTMINSTER
JOHN KNOX PRESS
LOUISVILLE · KENTUCKY

THE OLD TESTAMENT LIBRARY

Editorial Advisory Board

© 2005 J. Cheryl Exum

Originally published in hardback in the United States by Westminster John Knox Press in 2005.

2011 paperback edition
Published by Westminster John Knox Press
Louisville, Kentucky

Research for this commentary was supported in part by a grant from the Arts and Humanities Research Board (now the Arts and Humanities Research Council) in the United Kingdom.

"my love". Copyright 1923, 1951, © 1991 by the Trustees for the E. E. Cummings Trust. Copyright © 1976 by George James Firmage, from *Complete Poems: 1904–1962* by E. E. Cummings, edited by George J. Firmage. Used by permission of Liveright Publishing Corporation.

"Bella" ["Beauty"] is copyright © Brian Cole, 1994; used by permission.

Book design by Jennifer K. Cox

This book is printed on acid-free paper that meets the American National Standards Institute Z39.48 standard. ♾

11 12 13 14 15 16 17 18 19 20—10 9 8 7 6 5 4 3 2 1

Library of Congress Cataloging-in-Publication Data is on file at the Library of Congress, Washington, D.C.

ISBN 978-0-664-23841-4 (paper edition)

CONTENTS

COMMENTARY

ABBREVIATIONS

AB	Anchor Bible
ABD	*Anchor Bible Dictionary*. Edited by David Noel Freedman. 6 vols. New York: Doubleday, 1992
AJSL	*American Journal of Semitic Languages and Literatures*
AnBib	Analecta biblica
ANET	*Ancient Near Eastern Texts Relating to the Old Testament*. Edited by James B. Pritchard. 3rd ed. with Supplement. Princeton, 1969
AOAT	Alter Orient und Altes Testament
ATD	Das Alte Testament Deutsch
BAR	*Biblical Archaeology Review*
BASOR	*Bulletin of the American Schools of Oriental Research*
BBB	Bonner biblische Beiträge
BDB	Brown, F., S. R. Driver, and C. A. Briggs. *A Hebrew and English Lexicon of the Old Testament*. Oxford, 1907
BBET	Beiträge zur biblischen Exegese und Theologie
BHS	*Biblia Hebraica Stuttgartensia*. Edited by K. Elliger and W. Rudolph. Stuttgart, 1983
Bib	*Biblica*
BibInt	*Biblical Interpretation*
BibOr	Biblica et orientalia
BSac	*Bibliotheca Sacra*
BKAT	Biblischer Kommentar: Altes Testament
BN	*Biblische Notizen*
BTB	*Biblical Theology Bulletin*
BZ	*Biblische Zeitschrift*
CBQ	*Catholic Biblical Quarterly*
COS	The Context of Scripture. Edited by W. W. Hallo. 3 vols. Leiden, 1997–
DCH	*The Dictionary of Classical Hebrew*. Edited by David J. A. Clines. Sheffield, 1993–
DJD	Discoveries in the Judaean Desert

EncJud	*Encyclopaedia Judaica*
ETL	*Ephemerides theologicae lovanienses*
FAT	Forschungen zum Alten Testament
FOTL	Forms of the Old Testament Literature
GCT	Gender, Culture, Theory
GKC	*Gesenius' Hebrew Grammar.* Edited by E. Kautzsch. Revised and translated by A. E. Cowley. Oxford, 1910
HALOT	Koehler, L., W. Baumgartner, and J. J. Stamm. *The Hebrew and Aramaic Lexicon of the Old Testament.* Translated and edited under the supervision of M. E. J. Richardson. 4 vols. Leiden, 1994–1999
HAR	*Hebrew Annual Review*
HAT	Handbuch zum Alten Testament
HThKAT	Herders Theologischer Kommentar zum Alten Testament
IB	*Interpreter's Bible*
JAAR	*Journal of the American Academy of Religion*
JAOS	*Journal of the American Oriental Society*
JB	Jerusalem Bible
JBL	*Journal of Biblical Literature*
JNES	*Journal of Near Eastern Studies*
Joüon-Muraoka	Joüon, P. *A Grammar of Biblical Hebrew.* Translated and revised by T. Muraoka. 2 vols. Subsidia biblica 14/1–2. Rome, 1991
JPOS	*Journal of the Palestine Oriental Society*
JPS	Jewish Publication Society Version
JQR	*Jewish Quarterly Review*
JSNTSup	*Journal for the Study of the New Testament,* Supplement Series
JSOT	*Journal for the Study of the Old Testament*
JSOTSup	*Journal for the Study of the Old Testament,* Supplement Series
JSS	*Journal of Semitic Studies*
JTS	*Journal of Theological Studies*
KAT	Kommentar zum Alten Testament
KHAT	Kurzer Hand-Kommentar zum Alten Testament
KJV	King James Version
LXX	Septuagint
MT	Masoretic Text
NAB	New American Bible
NCB	New Century Bible
NEB	New English Bible
NIB	*The New Interpreter's Bible*

NICOT	New International Commentary on the Old Testament
NIV	New International Version
NIVAC	New International Version Application Commentary
NJB	New Jerusalem Bible
NJPS	New Jewish Publication Society Version
NRSV	New Revised Standard Version
OBO	Orbis biblicus et orientalis
PEQ	*Palestine Exploration Quarterly*
REB	Revised English Bible
RSV	Revised Standard Version
SBB	Stuttgarter biblische Beiträge
SBLWAW	Society of Biblical Literature Writings from the Ancient World
SEÅ	*Svensk exegetisk årsbok*
VT	*Vetus Testamentum*
WBC	Word Biblical Commentary
ZAW	*Zeitschrift für die alttestamentliche Wissenschaft*
ZBAT	Zürcher Bibelkommentare: Altes Testament

SELECT BIBLIOGRAPHY

Commentaries in Series

Bergant, Dianne. *The Song of Songs*. Berit Olam. Collegeville, MN: Liturgical Press, 2001.

Budde, Karl. *Das Hohelied*. KHAT 17. Freiburg im Breisgau: Mohr, 1898.

Carr, G. Lloyd. *The Song of Solomon: An Introduction and Commentary*. Tyndale Old Testament Commentaries. Leicester, England: Inter-Varsity Press, 1984.

Delitzsch, F. *Proverbs, Ecclesiastes, Song of Solomon*. Translated by James Martin. Commentary on the Old Testament VI. Grand Rapids: Eerdmans, 1980 [1872].

Garrett, Duane. *Song of Songs*. WBC 23B. Nashville: Word, 2004.

Gerleman, Gillis. *Ruth. Das Hohelied*. BKAT 18. Neukirchen-Vluyn: Neukirchener Verlag, 1965.

Haller, Max. *Ruth, Hoheslied, Klagelieder, Esther*. HAT 18. Tübingen: Mohr, 1940.

Harper, Andrew. *The Song of Solomon with Introduction and Notes*. Cambridge Bible for Schools and Colleges. Cambridge: Cambridge University Press, 1907.

Keel, Othmar. *The Song of Songs*. Translated by Frederick J. Gaiser. Minneapolis: Fortress Press, 1994 [German original: *Das Hohelied*. ZBAT 18. Zurich: Theologischer Verlag, 1986].

Krinetzki, Günter (=Leo). *Kommentar zum Hohenlied: Bildsprache und theologische Botschaft*. BBET 16. Frankfurt am Main: Peter Lang, 1981. [All references to Krinetzki are to the 1964 monograph below unless otherwise noted.]

————. *Hoheslied*. Neue Echter Bibel. Würzburg: Echter Verlag, 1980.

Longman, III, Tremper. *The Song of Songs*. NICOT. Grand Rapids: Eerdmans, 2001.

Meek, Theophile J. "The Song of Songs: Introduction and Exegesis." *IB* 5 (1956): 91–148.

Müller, Hans-Peter. *Das Hohelied*. ATD 16/2. Göttingen: Vandenhoeck & Ruprecht, 1992.

Murphy, Roland E. *The Song of Songs: A Commentary on the Book of Canticles or the Song of Songs.* Hermeneia. Minneapolis: Fortress Press, 1990.

Pope, Marvin H. *Song of Songs: A New Translation with Introduction and Commentary.* AB 7C. Garden City, NY: Doubleday, 1977.

Provan, Iain W. *Ecclesiastes, Song of Songs.* NIVAC. Grand Rapids: Zondervan, 2001.

Ringgren, Helmer. *Das Hohe Lied.* ATD 16. Göttingen: Vandenhoeck & Ruprecht, 1967.

Rudolph, Wilhelm. *Das Buch Ruth, Das Hohe Lied, Die Klagelieder.* KAT XVII, 1–3. Gütersloh: Gerd Mohn, 1962.

Snaith, John G. *The Song of Songs.* NCB. Grand Rapids: Eerdmans, 1993.

Weems, Renita J. "The Song of Songs: Introduction, Commentary, and Reflections." *NIB* 5 (1997): 361–434.

Würthwein, Ernst. *Ruth, Das Hohe Lied, Esther.* HAT 18. Tübingen: Mohr, 1969.

Zakovitch, Yair. *Das Hohelied.* HThKAT. Freiburg: Herder, 2004.*

Books and Monographs

Abu-Lughod, Lila. *Veiled Sentiments: Honor and Poetry in a Bedouin Society.* Berkeley: University of California Press, 1986.

Alexander, Philip S. *The Targum of Canticles: Translated, with a Critical Introduction, Apparatus, and Notes.* Aramaic Bible 17A. Collegeville, MN: Liturgical Press, 2003.

Ayo, Nicholas. *Sacred Marriage: The Wisdom of the Song of Songs.* Words by Nicholas Ayo and paintings by Meinrad Craighead. New York: Continuum, 1997.

Black, Fiona C. "The Grotesque Body in the Song of Songs." Ph.D. dissertation, University of Sheffield, 1999 [=1999a].

Bloch, Ariel, and Chana Bloch. *The Song of Songs: A New Translation with an Introduction and Commentary.* New York: Random House, 1995.

Bloom, Harold. *The Anxiety of Influence: A Theory of Poetry.* Oxford: Oxford University Press, 1973.

Brenner, Athalya. *The Intercourse of Knowledge: On Gendering Desire and 'Sexuality' in the Hebrew Bible.* Biblical Interpretation Series 26. Leiden: Brill, 1997.

Brenner, Athalya, and Fokkelien van Dijk-Hemmes. *On Gendering Texts: Female and Male Voices in the Hebrew Bible.* Biblical Interpretation Series 1. Leiden: Brill, 1993.

*I regret not having been able to include discussion of this important commentary, which appeared after I had submitted my manuscript to the publisher.

Brenner, Athalya, ed. *A Feminist Companion to the Song of Songs*. The Feminist Companion to the Bible 1. Sheffield: JSOT Press, 1993.

Brenner, Athalya, and Carole R. Fontaine, eds. *The Song of Songs: A Feminist Companion to the Bible (Second Series)*. Sheffield: Sheffield Academic Press, 2000.

Brooks, Peter. *Body Work: Objects of Desire in Modern Narrative*. Cambridge: Harvard University Press, 1993.

Cook, Albert. *The Root of the Thing: A Study of Job and the Song of Songs*. Bloomington: Indiana University Press, 1968.

Dahood, Mitchell. *Ugaritic-Hebrew Philology*. BibOr 17. Rome: Pontifical Biblical Institute, 1965.

Elliott, M. Timothea. *The Literary Unity of the Canticle*. Frankfurt: Peter Lang, 1989.

Falk, Marcia. *Love Lyrics from the Bible: A Translation and Literary Study of the Song of Songs*. Sheffield: Almond Press, 1982.

———. *The Song of Songs: A New Translation and Interpretation*. Illustrated by Barry Moser. San Francisco: HarperSanFrancisco, 1990. [All references to Falk are to this book, unless otherwise noted.]

Foster, John L. *Hymns, Prayers, and Songs: An Anthology of Ancient Egyptian Love Poetry*. SBLWAW. Atlanta: Scholars Press, 1995.

———. *Love Songs of the New Kingdom Translated from the Ancient Egyptian*. New York: Charles Scribner's Sons, 1974.

Fox, Michael V. *The Song of Songs and the Ancient Egyptian Love Songs*. Madison: University of Wisconsin Press, 1985.

Ginsburg, Christian D. *The Song of Songs and Coheleth*. Prolegomenon by Sheldon H. Blank. New York: Ktav, 1970 [1857, 1861].

Gordis, Robert. *The Song of Songs and Lamentations: A Study, Modern Translation and Commentary*. Rev. and augmented ed. New York: Ktav, 1974.

Goulder, Michael D. *The Song of Fourteen Songs*. JSOTSup 36. Sheffield: JSOT Press, 1986.

Grossberg, Daniel. *Centripetal and Centrifugal Structures in Biblical Poetry*. SBLMS 39. Atlanta: Scholars Press, 1989.

Harding, Kathryn. "The Song of Songs and the Construction of Desire in the Hebrew Bible." Ph.D. dissertation, University of Sheffield, forthcoming.

Heinevetter, Hans-Josef. *"Komm nun, mein Liebster, Dein Garten ruft Dich!": Das Hohelied als programmatische Komposition*. BBB 69. Frankfurt: Athenäum, 1988.

Jacobsen, Thorkild. *The Harps That Once . . . : Sumerian Poetry in Translation*. New Haven: Yale University Press, 1987.

———. *The Treasures of Darkness: A History of Mesopotamian Religion*. New Haven: Yale University Press, 1976.

Keel, Othmar. *Deine Blicke sind Tauben: Zur Metaphorik des Hohen Liedes.* SBB 114/115. Stuttgart: Katholisches Bibelwerk, 1984.

Kramer, Samuel Noah. *The Sacred Marriage Rite: Aspects of Faith, Myth, and Ritual in Ancient Sumer.* Bloomington: Indiana University Press, 1969.

Krinetzki, Leo (= Günter). *Das Hohe Lied: Kommentar zu Gestalt und Kerygma eines alttestamentarischen Liebesliedes.* Düsseldorf: Patmos, 1964. [All references to Krinetzki are to this monograph unless otherwise noted.]

LaCocque, André. *Romance She Wrote: A Hermeneutical Essay on Song of Songs.* Harrisburg, PA: Trinity Press International, 1998.

Landy, Francis. *Paradoxes of Paradise: Identity and Difference in the Song of Songs.* Sheffield: Almond Press, 1983. [All references to Landy are to this monograph unless otherwise noted.]

Leick, Gwendolyn. *Sex and Eroticism in Mesopotamian Literature.* London: Routledge, 1994.

Lichtheim, Miriam. *Ancient Egyptian Literature, Vol. II: The New Kingdom.* Berkeley: University of California Press, 1976.

Loretz, Oswald. *Das althebräische Liebeslied.* AOAT 14/1. Neukirchen-Vluyn: Neukirchener Verlag, 1971.

―――. *Gotteswort und menschliche Erfahrung: Eine Auslegung der Bücher Jona, Rut, Hoheslied und Qohelet.* Freiburg im Breisgau: Herder, 1963. [All references are to the 1971 version, which is more extensive.]

Mariaselvam, Abraham. *The Song of Songs and Ancient Tamil Love Poems.* AnBib 118. Rome: Pontifical Biblical Institute, 1988.

Marsman, Hennie J. *Women in Ugarit and Israel: Their Social and Religious Position in the Context of the Ancient Near East.* Leiden: Brill, 2003.

Meyers, Carol. *Discovering Eve: Ancient Israelite Women in Context.* New York: Oxford University Press, 1988.

Moldenke, Harold N., and Alma L. Moldenke. *Plants of the Bible.* Chronica Botanica 28. Waltham, MA: Ronald Press, 1952; repr. New York: Dover Publications, 1986.

Müller, Hans-Peter. *Vergleich und Metapher im Hohenlied.* OBO 56. Freiburg, Schweiz: Universitätsverlag; Göttingen: Vandenhoeck & Ruprecht, 1984.

Munro, Jill M. *Spikenard and Saffron: A Study in the Poetic Language of the Song of Songs.* JSOTSup 203. Sheffield: Sheffield Academic Press, 1995.

Perles, Felix. *Analekten zur Textkritik des Alten Testaments (NF).* Leipzig: Gustav Engel, 1922.

Robert, A., and R. Tournay, with A. Feuillet. *Le Cantique des Cantiques.* Paris: J. Gabalda, 1963.

Sefati, Yitschak. *Love Songs in Sumerian Literature: Critical Edition of the Dumuzi-Inanna Songs.* Ramat Gan: Bar-Ilan University Press, 1998.

Simpson, William Kelly, ed. *The Literature of Ancient Egypt.* New Haven: Yale University Press, 1973.

Stadelmann, Luis. *Love and Politics: A New Commentary on the Song of Songs.* New York: Paulist Press, 1992.

Tournay, Raymond Jacques. *Quand Dieu parle aux hommes le langage de l'amour: Études sur le Cantique des Cantiques.* Paris: J. Gabalda, 1982 [ET = *Word of God, Song of Love: A Commentary on the Song of Songs*, trans. J. Edward Crowley. New York: Paulist Press, 1988].

Walsh, Carey Ellen. *Exquisite Desire: Religion, the Erotic, and the Song of Songs.* Minneapolis: Fortress Press, 2000.

Wolkstein, Diane, and Samuel Noah Kramer. *Inanna, Queen of Heaven and Earth: Her Stories and Hymns from Sumer.* New York: Harper & Row, 1983.

Wyke, Maria, ed. *Gender and the Body in the Ancient Mediterranean.* Oxford: Blackwell, 1998.

Young, Ian. *Diversity in Pre-Exilic Hebrew.* FAT 5. Tübingen: Mohr, 1993.

Zohary, Michael. *Plants of the Bible.* Cambridge: Cambridge University Press, 1982.

Articles and Chapters in Books

Albright, William F. "Archaic Survivals in the Text of Canticles." In *Hebrew and Semitic Studies Presented to G. R. Driver*, ed. D. Winton Thomas and W. D. McHardy, 1–7. Oxford: Clarendon, 1963.

Alster, Bendt. "The Manchester Tammuz." *Acta Sumerologica* 14 (1992): 1–46.

Alter, Robert. "The Garden of Metaphor." In *The Art of Biblical Poetry*, 185–203. New York: Basic Books, 1985.

Angénieux, J. "Le Cantique des Cantiques en huit chants à refrains alternants." *ETL* 44 (1968): 87–140.

———. "Les trois portraits du Cantique des Cantiques." *ETL* 42 (1966): 582–86.

———. "Structure du Cantique des Cantiques." *ETL* 41 (1965): 96–142.

Arbel, Daphna V. "'My Vineyard, My Very Own, Is for Myself.'" In Brenner and Fontaine (eds.) 2000: 90–101.

Barbiero, Gianni. "Die Liebe der Töchter Jerusalems: Hld 3,10b MT im Kontext von 3,6–11." *BZ* 39 (1995): 96–104.

———. "Die 'Wagen meines edlen Volkes' (Hld 6, 12): eine strukturelle Analyse." *Bib* 78 (1997): 174–89.

Bekkenkamp, Jonneke. "Into Another Scene of Choices: The Theological Value of the Song of Songs." In Brenner and Fontaine (eds.) 2000: 55–89.

Bekkenkamp, Jonneke, and Fokkelien van Dijk. "The Canon of the Old Testament and Women's Cultural Traditions." In Brenner (ed.) 1993: 67–85.

Benzen, Aage. "Remarks on the Canonisation of the Song of Solomon." In *Studia Orientalia Ioanni Pedersen*, 41–47. Copenhagen: Munksgaard, 1953.

Bergant, Dianne. "'My Beloved Is Mine and I Am His' (Song 2:16): The Song of Songs and Honor and Shame." *Semeia* 68 (1994): 23–40.

Black, Fiona C. "Beauty or the Beast? The Grotesque Body in the Song of Songs." *BibInt* 8 (2000): 302–23 [=2000a].

———. "Nocturnal Egression: Exploring Some Margins of the Song of Songs." In *Postmodern Interpretations of the Bible—A Reader*, ed. A. K. M. Adam, 93–104. St. Louis: Chalice Press, 2001.

———. "Unlikely Bedfellows: Allegorical and Feminist Readings of Song of Songs 7.1–8." In Brenner and Fontaine (eds.) 2000: 104–29 [=2000b].

———. "What Is My Beloved? On Erotic Reading and the Song of Songs." In *The Labour of Reading: Desire, Alienation, and Biblical Interpretation*, ed. Fiona C. Black, Roland Boer, and Erin Runions, 35–52. Semeia Studies. Atlanta: Society of Biblical Literature, 1999 [=1999b].

Black, Fiona C., and J. Cheryl Exum. "Semiotics in Stained Glass: Edward Burne-Jones's Song of Songs." In *Biblical Studies/Cultural Studies: The Third Sheffield Colloquium*, ed. J. Cheryl Exum and Stephen D. Moore, 315–42. JSOTSup 266, GCT 7. Sheffield: Sheffield Academic Press, 1998.

Boer, Roland. "Night Sprinkle(s): Pornography and the Song of Songs." In *Knockin' on Heaven's Door: The Bible and Popular Culture*, 53–70. London: Routledge, 1999.

———. "The Second Coming: Repetition and Insatiable Desire in the Song of Songs." *BibInt* 8 (2000): 276–301.

Boyarin, Daniel. "The Song of Songs: Lock or Key? Intertextuality, Allegory and Midrash." In *The Book and the Text: The Bible and Literary Theory*, ed. Regina M. Schwartz, 214–30. Oxford: Blackwell, 1990.

Brenner, Athalya. "Aromatics and Perfumes in the Song of Songs." *JSOT* 25 (1983): 75–81.

———. "'Come Back, Come Back the Shulammite' (Song of Songs 7.1–10): A Parody of the *waṣf* Genre." In Brenner (ed.) 1993: 234–57. Repr. from *On Humour and the Comic in the Hebrew Bible*, ed. A. Brenner and Y. T. Radday, 251–76. Sheffield: Almond Press, 1990 [=1993a].

———. "'My' Song of Songs." In Brenner and Fontaine (eds.) 2000: 154–68.

———. "To See Is to Assume: Whose Love Is Celebrated in the Song of Songs?" *BibInt* 1 (1993): 265–84 [=1993b].

———. "Women Poets and Authors." In Brenner (ed.) 1993: 86–97 [=1993c].

Broadribb, Donald. "Thoughts on the Song of Solomon." *Abr-Nahrain* 3 (1961–62): 11–36.

Brown, John Pairman. "The Mediterranean Vocabulary of the Vine." *VT* 19 (1969): 146–70.

Budde, Karl. "The Song of Songs." *The New World* 3 (1894): 56–77.

Burrus, Virginia, and Stephen D. Moore. "Unsafe Sex: Feminism, Pornography, and the Song of Songs." *BibInt* 11 (2003): 24–52.

Buss, Martin J. "Hosea as a Canonical Problem: With Attention to the Song of Songs." In *Prophets and Paradigms: Essays in Honor of Gene M. Tucker*, ed. Stephen Breck Reid, 79–93. JSOTSup 229. Sheffield: Sheffield Academic Press, 1996.

Butting, Klara. "Go Your Way: Women Rewrite the Scriptures (Song of Songs 2.8–14)." In Brenner and Fontaine (eds.) 2000: 142–51.

Buzy, T. R. Denis. "Un chef-d'œuvre de poésie pure: Le Cantique des Cantiques." In *Mémorial Lagrange*, 147–62. Paris: Gabalda, 1940.

Byington, Steven T. "Brief Communications." *JBL* 39 (1920): 77–82.

Carr, David M. "Gender and the Shaping of Desire in the Song of Songs and Its Interpretations." *JBL* 119 (2000): 233–48.

———. "The Song of Songs as a Microcosm of the Canonization and Decanonization Process." In *Canonization and Decanonization*, ed. Arie van der Kooij and K. van der Toorn, 173–89. Leiden: Brill, 1998.

Civil, M. "The 'Message of Lú-dingir-ra to His Mother' and a Group of Akkado-Hittite Proverbs." *JNES* 23 (1964): 1–11.

Clines, David J. A. "Why Is There a Song of Songs and What Does It Do to You If You Read It?" In *Interested Parties: The Ideology of Writers and Readers of the Hebrew Bible*, 94–121. JSOTSup 205, GCT 1. Sheffield: Sheffield Academic Press, 1995.

Cooper, Jerrold S. "New Cuneiform Parallels to the Song of Songs." *JBL* 90 (1971): 157–62.

———. "Sacred Marriage and Popular Cult in Early Mesopotamia." In *Official Cult and Popular Religion in the Ancient Near East*, ed. Eiko Matsushima, 81–96. Heidelberg: Winter, 1993.

Dahood, Mitchell. "Canticle 7,9 and *UT* 52,61." *Bib* 57 (1976): 109–10.

Dales, George F. "Necklaces, Bands and Belts on Mesopotamian Figurines." *Revue d'assyriologie et d'archéologie orientale* 57 (1963): 21–40.

Davidson, Richard M. "The Literary Structure of the Song of Songs *Redivivus*." *Journal of the Adventist Theological Society* 14 (2003): 44–65.

Deckers, M. "The Structure of the Song of Songs and the Centrality of *nepeš* (6.12)." In Brenner (ed.) 1993: 172–96.

Dirksen, P. B. "Song of Songs III 6–7." *VT* 39 (1989): 219–25.

Dorsey, David A. "Literary Structuring in the Song of Songs." *JSOT* 46 (1990): 81–96.

Driver, G. R. "Birds in the Old Testament II. Birds in Life." *PEQ* 87 (1955): 129–40.

———. "Hebrew Notes." *ZAW* 52 (1934): 51–56.

———. "Hebrew Notes on 'Song of Songs' and 'Lamentations.'" In *Festschrift A. Bertholet*, ed. Walter Baumgartner, 134–46. Tübingen: Mohr, 1950.

———. "Problems and Solutions." *VT* 4 (1954): 225–45.

————. "I. Studies in the Vocabulary of the Old Testament." *JTS* 31 (1929–30): 275–84.

————. "Studies in the Vocabulary of the Old Testament II."*JTS* 32 (1930–31): 250–57.

————. "Studies in the Vocabulary of the Old Testament VI."*JTS* 34 (1933): 375–85.

————. "Studies in the Vocabulary of the Old Testament VII."*JTS* 35 (1934): 380–93.

————. "Supposed Arabisms in the Old Testament." *JBL* 55 (1936): 101–20.

Emerton, J. A. "Lice or a Veil in the Song of Songs 1.7?" In *Understanding Poets and Prophets: Essays in Honour of George Wishart Anderson*, ed. A. Graeme Auld, 127–40. JSOTSup 152. Sheffield: Sheffield Academic Press, 1993.

Emmerson, Grace I. "The Song of Songs: Mystification, Ambiguity and Humour." In *Crossing the Boundaries: Essays in Biblical Interpretation in Honour of Michael D. Goulder*, ed. Stanley E. Porter, Paul Joyce, and David E. Orton, 97–111. Leiden: Brill, 1994.

Eslinger, Lyle. "The Case of an Immodest Lady Wrestler in Deuteronomy XXV 11–12." *VT* 31 (1981): 269–81.

Exum, J. Cheryl. "Asseverative ʾ*al* in Canticles 1:6?" *Bib* 62 (1981): 416–19.

————. "How Does the Song of Songs Mean? On Reading the Poetry of Desire." *SEÅ* 64 (1999): 47–63 [= 1999a].

————. "In the Eye of the Beholder: Wishing, Dreaming, and *double entendre* in the Song of Songs." In *The Labour of Reading: Desire, Alienation, and Biblical Interpretation*, ed. Fiona C. Black, Roland Boer, and Erin Runions, 71–86. Semeia Studies. Atlanta: Society of Biblical Literature, 1999 [= 1999b].

————. "A Literary and Structural Analysis of the Song of Songs." *ZAW* 85 (1973):47–79.

————. "Seeing Solomon's Palanquin (Song of Songs 3:6–11)." *BibInt* 11 (2003): 301–16.

————. "Seeing the Song of Songs." In *Cultural Industry: The Bible and the Arts*. Sheffield: Sheffield Phoenix Press, forthcoming.

————. "Ten Things Every Feminist Should Know about the Song of Songs." In Brenner and Fontaine (eds.) 2000: 24–35.

————. "'The Voice of My Lover': Double Voice and Poetic Illusion in Song of Songs 2.8–3.5." In *Reading from Right to Left: Essays in Honour of David J. A. Clines*, ed. J. Cheryl Exum and H. G. M. Williamson, 146–57. JSOT-Sup 373. Sheffield: Sheffield Academic Press, 2003.

Falk, Marcia. "The Song of Songs." In *Harper's Bible Commentary*, ed. James L. Mays, 525–28. San Francisco: Harper & Row, 1988.

Fisch, Harold. "Song of Solomon: The Allegorical Imperative." In *Poetry with a Purpose: Biblical Poetics and Interpretation*, 80–103. Bloomington: Indiana University Press, 1988.

Fontaine, Carole R. "The Voice of the Turtle: Now It's *My* Song of Songs." In Brenner and Fontaine (eds.) 2000: 169–85.

Goitein, S. D. "*Ayumma Kannidgalot* (Song of Songs VI.10)." *JSS* 10 (1965): 220–21.

———. "Women as Creators of Biblical Genres." *Prooftexts* 8 (1988): 1–33.

Good, Edwin M. "Ezekiel's Ship: Some Extended Metaphors in the Old Testament." *Semitics* 1 (1970): 79–102.

Goodspeed, Edgar J. "The Shulammite." *AJSL* 50 (1934): 102–4.

Gordon, Cyrus H. "New Directions." *Bulletin of the American Society of Papyrologists* 15 (1978): 59–66.

Görg, Manfred. "'Kanäle' oder 'Zweige' in Hld 4,13?" *BN* 72 (1994): 20–23.

Greenfield, Jonas C. "Ugaritic *mdl* and Its Cognates." *Bib* 45 (1964): 527–34.

Grossberg, Daniel. "Canticles 3:10 in the Light of a Homeric Analogue and Biblical Poetics." *BTB* 11 (1981): 74–76.

Hallo, William W. "'As the Seal upon Thy Heart': Glyptic Roles in the Biblical World." *Bible Review* 1 (1985): 20–27.

Hansen, Eric. "The Hidden History of a Scented Wood." *Aramco World*, November/December 2000: 3–11.

Haupt, Paul. "The Book of Canticles." *AJSL* 18 (1902): 193–245 [=1902a].

———. "The Book of Canticles." *AJSL* 19 (1902): 1–32 [=1902b].

Hicks, R. Lansing. "The Door of Love." In *Love and Death in the Ancient Near East: Essays in Honor of Marvin H. Pope*, ed. John H. Marks and Robert M. Good, 153–58. Guilford, CT: Four Quarters, 1987.

Hirschberg, Harris H. "Some Additional Arabic Etymologies in Old Testament Lexicography." *VT* 11 (1961): 373–85.

Holman, Jan. "A Fresh Attempt at Understanding the Imagery of Canticles 3:6–11." In *"Lasset uns Brücken bauen . . ." Collected Communications to the XVth Congress of the International Organization for the Study of the Old Testament, Cambridge 1995*, ed. Klaus-Dietrich Schunck and Matthias Augustin, 303–9. Frankfurt: Peter Lang, 1998.

Honeyman, A. M. "Two Contributions to Canaanite Toponymy." *JTS* 50 (1949): 50–52.

Isserlin, B. S. J. "Song of Songs IV, 4: An Archaeological Note." *PEQ* 90 (1958): 59–61.

Jacob, Irene, and Walter Jacob. "Flora." *ABD* II: 803–17.

Keefer, Kyle, and Tod Linafelt. "The End of Desire: Theologies of Eros in the Song of Songs and *Breaking the Waves*." *Journal of Religion and Film* 2 (1998). Available at http://www.unomaha.edu/~wwwjrf/endofdes.htm.

Krauss, Samuel. "The Archaeological Background of Some Passages in the Song of Songs." *JQR* 32 (1941–42): 115–37.

Kuhn, Gottfried. "Erkärung des Hohen Liedes." *Neue Kirchliche Zeitschrift* 36 (1926): 501–10, 521–72.

Landsberger, Franz. "Poetic Units within the Song of Songs." *JBL* 73 (1954): 203–16.

Landy, Francis. "On Metaphor, Play, and Nonsense." *Semeia* 61 (1993): 219–37.

———. "Perversity, Truth, and the Readerly Experience." In *Autobiographical Biblical Criticism: Between Text and Self*, ed. Ingrid Rosa Kitzberger, 60–78. Leiden: Deo Publishing, 2002.

———. "The Song of Songs." In *The Literary Guide to the Bible*, ed. Robert Alter and Frank Kermode, 305–19. Cambridge: Belknap Press, 1987.

Lavoie, Jean-Jacques. "Festin érotique et tendresse cannibalique dans le Cantique des Cantiques." *Studies in Religion/Sciences Religieuses* 24 (1995): 131–46.

Lemaire, André. "*Zāmīr* dans la tablette de Gezer et le Cantique des Cantiques." *VT* 25 (1975): 15–26.

Linafelt, Tod. "Biblical Love Poetry (. . . and God)." *JAAR* 70 (2002): 323–45.

Livingstone, Alasdair. "Love Lyrics of Nabu and Tashmetu." *COS* 1.128: 445–46.

Long, Gary Alan. "A Lover, Cities, and Heavenly Bodies: Co-text and the Translation of Two Similes in Canticles (6:4c; 6:10d)." *JBL* 115 (1996): 703–9.

Mackintosh-Smith, Tim. "Scents of Place: Frankincense in Oman." *Aramco World*, May/June 2000: 17–23.

May, Herbert G. "Some Cosmic Connotations of *Mayim Rabbîm*, 'Many Waters.'" *JBL* 74 (1955): 9–21.

Merkin, Daphne. "The Women in the Balcony: On Rereading the Song of Songs." In *Out of the Garden: Women Writers on the Bible*, ed. Christina Buchmann and Celina Spiegel, 238–51. New York: Fawcett Columbine, 1994.

Meyers, Carol. "Gender Imagery in the Song of Songs." *HAR* 10 (1986): 209–23.

———. "Returning Home: Ruth 1.8 and the Gendering of the Book of Ruth." In Brenner (ed.) 1993: 85–114.

———. "'To Her Mother's House': Considering a Counterpart to the Israelite *Bet ʾab*." In *The Bible and the Politics of Exegesis: Essays in Honor of Norman K. Gottwald on His Sixty-fifth Birthday*, ed. David Jobling, Peggy L. Day, and Gerald T. Sheppard, 39–51. Cleveland: Pilgrim Press, 1991.

Moore, Stephen D. "The Song of Songs in the History of Sexuality." In *God's Beauty Parlor and Other Queer Spaces in and around the Bible*, 21–89. Stanford, CA: Stanford University Press, 2001.

Murphy, Roland E. "Dance and Death in the Song of Songs." In *Love and Death in the Ancient Near East: Essays in Honor of Marvin H. Pope*, ed. John H. Marks and Robert M. Good, 117–19. Guilford, CT: Four Quarters, 1987.

Nissinen, Martti. "Love Lyrics of Nabû and Tašmetu: An Assyrian Song of Songs?" In *"Und Mose schrieb dieses Lied auf": Studien zum Alten Testament und zum Alten Orient (Festschrift Oswald Loretz)*, ed. Manfried Dietrich and Ingo Kottsieper. AOAT 250. Münster: Ugarit-Verlag, 1998.

Ohler, Annemarie. "Der Mann im Hohenlied." In *Der Weg zum Menschen: Zur philosophischen und theologischen Anthropologie, für Alfons Deissler*, ed. Rudolf Mosis and Lothar Ruppert, 183–200. Freiburg im Breisgau: Herder, 1989.

Ostriker, Alicia. "A Holy of Holies: The Song of Songs as Countertext." In Brenner and Fontaine (eds.) 2000: 36–54.

Pardee, Dennis. "'As Strong as Death.'" In *Love and Death in the Ancient Near East: Essays in Honor of Marvin H. Pope*, ed. John H. Marks and Robert M. Good, 65–69. Guilford, CT: Four Quarters, 1987.

Pardes, Ilana. "'I Am a Wall, and My Breasts like Towers': The Song of Songs and the Question of Canonization." In *Countertraditions in the Bible: A Feminist Approach*, 118–43. Cambridge: Harvard University Press, 1992.

Pelletier, Anne-Marie. "Le Cantique des cantiques: Un texte et ses lectures." In *Les nouvelles voies de l'exégèse: En lisant le Cantique des cantiques*, ed. Jacques Nieuviarts and Pierre Debergé, 75–101. XIXe congrès de l'Association catholique pour l'étude de la Bible (Toulouse, septembre 2001). Paris: Éditions du Cerf, 2002.

Phipps, William E. "The Plight of the Song of Songs." *JAAR* 42 (1974): 82–100.

Polaski, Donald C. "'What Will Ye See in the Shulammite?' Women, Power and Panopticism in the Song of Songs." *BibInt* 5 (1997): 64–81.

Pope, Marvin H. "A Mare in Pharaoh's Chariotry." *BASOR* 200 (1970): 56–61.

———. "Metastases in Canonical Shapes of the Super Song." In *Canon, Theology, and Old Testament Interpretation: Essays in Honor of Brevard S. Childs*, ed. Gene M. Tucker, David L. Petersen, and Robert R. Wilson, 312–28. Philadelphia: Fortress Press, 1988.

Rogerson, John W. "The Use of the Song of Songs in J. S. Bach's Church Cantatas." In *Biblical Studies/Cultural Studies*, ed. J. Cheryl Exum and Stephen D. Moore, 343–51. JSOTSup 266, GCT 7. Sheffield: Sheffield Academic Press, 1998.

Rowley, H. H. "The Interpretation of the Song of Songs." In *The Servant of the Lord and Other Essays on the Old Testament*, 197–245. 2nd ed., revised. Oxford: Blackwell, 1965.

———. "The Meaning of 'The Shulammite.'" *AJSL* 56 (1939): 84–91.

Rundgren, Frithiof. "אַפִּרְיוֹן 'Tragsessel, Sänfte.'" *ZAW* 74 (1962): 70–72.

Sæbø, Magne. "On the Canonicity of the Song of Songs." In *Texts, Temples, and Traditions: A Tribute to Menahem Haran*, ed. Michael V. Fox, Victor Avigdor Hurowitz, Avi Hurvitz, Michael L. Klein, Baruch J. Schwartz, and Nili Shupak, 267–77. Winona Lake, IN: Eisenbrauns, 1996.

Sefati, Yitschak. "Dumuzi-Inanna Songs." *COS* 1.169: 540–43.

Sasson, Jack M. "A Further Cuneiform Parallel to the Song of Songs?" *ZAW* 85 (1973): 359–60 [=1973a].

———. "A Major Contribution to Song of Songs Scholarship." Review of Michael V. Fox, *The Song of Songs and the Ancient Egyptian Love Songs*. *JAOS* 107 (1987): 733–39.

———. "On M. H. Pope's *Song of Songs* [AB 7c]." *Maarav* 1/2 (1978–79): 177–96.

———. "The Worship of the Golden Calf." In *Orient and Occident: Essays Presented to Cyrus H. Gordon on the Occasion of His Sixty-fifth Birthday*, ed. Harry A. Hoffner Jr. AOAT 22 (1973): 151–59 [=1973b].

Shea, William H. "The Chiastic Structure of the Song of Songs." *ZAW* 92 (1980): 378–96.

Sonnet, Jean-Pierre. "Le Cantique: La fabrique poétique." In *Les nouvelles voies de l'exégèse: En lisant le Cantique des cantiques*, ed. Jacques Nieuviarts and Pierre Debergé, 159–84. XIXe congrès de l'Association catholique pour l'étude de la Bible (Toulouse, septembre 2001). Paris: Éditions du Cerf, 2002.

Soulen, Richard N. "The *Waṣfs* of the Song of Songs and Hermeneutic." *JBL* 86 (1967): 183–90.

Stephan, St. H. "Modern Palestinian Parallels to the Song of Songs." *JPOS* 2 (1922): 199–278.

Tanner, J. Paul. "The History of Interpretation of the Song of Songs." *BSac* 154 (1997): 23–46.

Trible, Phyllis. "Love's Lyrics Redeemed." In *God and the Rhetoric of Sexuality*, 144–65. Philadelphia: Fortress Press, 1978.

Tuell, Steven S. "A Riddle Resolved by an Enigma: Hebrew נלגש and Ugaritic GLṮ." *JBL* 112 (1993): 99–104.

Van Beek, G. W. "Frankincense and Myrrh." *BAR* 2 (1960): 99–126.

Viviers, Hendrik. "The Rhetoricity of the 'Body' in the Song of Songs." In *Rhetorical Criticism and the Bible*, ed. Stanley E. Porter and Dennis L. Stamps, 237–54. JSNTSup 195. London: Sheffield Academic Press, 2002.

Waldman, Nahum M. "A Note on Canticles 4:9." *JBL* 89 (1970): 215–17.

Watson, Wilfred G. E. "Love and Death Once More (Song of Songs VIII 6)." *VT* 47 (1997): 385–87.

———. "Some Ancient Near Eastern Parallels to the Song of Songs." In *Words Remembered, Texts Renewed: Essays in Honour of John F. A. Sawyer*, ed. Jon Davies, Graham Harvey, and Wilfred G. E. Watson, 253–71. JSOTSup 195. Sheffield: Sheffield Academic Press, 1995.

Webster, Edwin C. "Pattern in the Song of Songs." *JSOT* 22 (1982): 73–93.

Wendland, Ernst R. "Seeking the Path through a Forest of Symbols: A Figurative and Structural Survey of the Song of Songs." *Journal of Translation and Textlinguistics* 7 (1995): 13–59.

Westenholz, Joan Goodnick. "Love Lyrics from the Ancient Near East." In *Civilizations of the Ancient Near East*, vol. 4, ed. Jack M. Sasson, 2471–84. New York: Charles Scribner's Sons, 1995; repr. Peabody, MA: Hendrickson Publishers, 2000.

———. "The Seven Species, the First Fruits of the Land." In *Sacred Bounty Sacred Land: The Seven Species of the Land of Israel*, ed. Joan Goodnick Westenholz, 13–55. Jerusalem: Bible Lands Museum, 1998.

Whedbee, J. William. "Paradox and Parody in the Song of Solomon: Towards a Comic Reading of the Most Sublime Song." In *The Bible and the Comic Vision*, 263–77. Cambridge: Cambridge University Press, 1998.

Winandy, Jacques. "La litière de Salomon (Ct. iii 9–10)." *VT* 15 (1965): 103–10.

INTRODUCTION

" Explores the nature of love"

1. A Love Poem

The Song of Songs is a long lyric poem about erotic love and sexual desire—a poem in which the body is both object of desire and source of delight, and lovers engage in a continual game of seeking and finding in anticipation, enjoyment, and assurance of sensual gratification. A love poem. The poem's genius lies in the way it shows us as well as tells us that "love is strong as death" (8:6), and in the way it explores the nature of love. It looks at what it is like to be in love from both a woman's and a man's point of view, and it relies exclusively on dialogue, so that we learn about love through what lovers say about it.

> To me my lover is a sachet of myrrh,
> > lying all night between my breasts.
> To me my lover is a cluster of henna blossoms
> > in the vineyards of En-gedi.
> > > > (1:13–14)

> Rise up, my friend, my fair one,
> > and come away . . .
> Let me see you,
> > let me hear your voice,
> for your voice is sweet,
> > and you are lovely.
> > > > (2:13–14)

> You have captured my heart, my sister, bride,
> > you have captured my heart with one glance of your eyes,
> > with one pendant of your necklace.
> > > > (4:9)

> His form, like Lebanon,
> > distinguished as the cedars.
> His mouth is sweet,
> > and all of him desirable.
> This is my lover; this, my friend . . .
> > > > (5:15–16)

Turn your eyes away from me,
   for they overwhelm me.
             (6:5)

On my bed nightly,
   I have sought my soul's beloved.
   I sought him but I did not find him.
I will rise now and go about the city,
   in the streets and in the squares;
I will seek my soul's beloved.
             (3:1–2)

I place you under oath, women of Jerusalem:
   if you find my lover,
what will you tell him?
   That I am faint with love.
             (5:8)

Come, my love, let's go out to the open field,
   spend the night among the henna blossoms.
Let's go early to the vineyards,
   we'll see if the vine has budded,
if the grape blossoms have opened,
   if the pomegranates have bloomed.
There I will give you my love.
          (7:11–12 [12–13 H])

Such, the Song proclaims, are the cadences of love.

But it is not just the lovers who speak. A third speaking voice belongs to a group, the women of Jerusalem, a kind of women's chorus who function as an audience within the poem and whose presence facilitates the reader's entry into the lovers' intimate world of eroticism.

2. Love and Death

Only once does the poet offer an observation about the nature of love in general, and it is of the utmost importance for understanding the Song of Songs. Like everything else that is said in the poem, it appears in the mouth of one of the speakers (not as the voice of the poet) and it is addressed to another character in the poem (and not directly to the reader, though its readers are the poem's ultimate audience).

Place me like a seal on your heart,
   like a seal on your arm,
for love is strong as death . . .
         (8:6)

love is as strong as death! (as long as the poem is read)

Here for the first time, the woman speaks to her lover not about their love, but about love itself. Though death is mentioned only once, and that near the poem's end, everything in the poem converges upon and serves to illustrate the affirmation that love is as strong as death. The proof is the poem. Perhaps all literature is a defense against mortality; certainly the Song of Songs is. The desiring subject of Song 8:6 may be a character in the poem, but it is also the poet, whose desire to preserve a particular vision of love gives rise to the poem. Real lovers die, but the love that is celebrated here lives on, preserved on the page. It still seems fresh and alive centuries after it was written down, because it is love in progress, not a story about famous lovers of the past. The Song is too engrossed in how glorious it is to be alive and in love to voice bitterness or melancholy about death. Ever discovering their pleasure anew and ever rejoicing in each other and in the sights, sounds, smells, tastes, and tangibility of the world around them, the textual lovers and the vision of love they embody live on so long as the poem is read.

3. Controlling Poetic Strategies

By "controlling poetic strategies" I refer to how the poetry of desire works, the tactics and techniques it employs, and the effects it produces; in other words, to the way the poet shows us, as well as tells us, that love is as strong as death. In poetry in general, and certainly in the Song, the medium is the message, as the saying goes. We cannot understand the Song, much less appreciate how it succeeds as a love poem, without paying attention to the *way* it presents its vision of love, to its emotional sequences in time and the accompanying shifts in technical management. Attention to the Song's guiding poetic strategies, therefore, forms a major part of this commentary, and the reader is referred to the Commentary section (especially the general introduction to each section of the Song) for a fuller discussion of them in context. These codes of structure and meaning in the text belong to its translatable structure; that is to say, they are reproducible in English, unlike many of the Song's other aesthetic features such as assonance, alliteration, and wordplay (see under "A Masterpiece of Pure Poetry," pp. 30–33). Employed across the space of the poem, these manifold and interconnected strategies are the means by which the poet strives to make present, through language, what cannot be captured on the page: the lovers whose multiple identities enable them to stand for all lovers and, ultimately, love itself.

The Illusion of Immediacy

The most striking and successful way in which the Song of Songs immortalizes the love it celebrates is by creating the illusion of immediacy, the impression that,

*1. Concrete —
we are the observer
(dialogue technique)*

far from being simply reported, the action is taking place in the present, unfolding before the reader. It does this through the exclusive use of direct speech; unlike other biblical texts, there is no narrative description. Voices that seem to reach us unmediated lend the illusion of immediacy to what is actually reported speech, a written text whose author/narrator is brilliantly effaced. The poem presents its readers with a vision of love, not in the abstract but in the concrete, through showing us what lovers do, or, more precisely, by telling us what they say. By presenting the lovers in the act of addressing each other, the poem gives us the impression that we are overhearing them and observing their love unfold.

The key to this unfolding is the dialogue. The dialogue format, though not unique, is certainly unusual. Most love poetry is written from a single point of view, with the poet or narrator implicitly or explicitly speaking to or about the object of her or his desire. Even in the closest parallel to the Song of Songs from the ancient world, the Egyptian love poems, there is no dialogue such as we find in the Song of Songs, only soliloquies or monologues or, in some of the longer songs, "double monologues," where a monologue of one lover is joined to that of the other (Fox 263–65). The Song is a dialogue between a man and a woman (and occasionally the women of Jerusalem). It represents itself as offering both points of view, a woman's and a man's. This is part of its supreme artifice and artistry, for a moment's reflection tells us the Song is not a transcription of a lovers' tryst. Nor is it likely that the Song is a joint composition in which a woman wrote the woman's words and a man, the man's, or that someone recorded from memory a lovers' conversation.

The voices that seem unmediated are the voices of lovers created for us by the poet. As is the case with any good writer, their voices seem authentic. Perhaps the poet writes from personal experience, influenced and inspired by a distinguished succession of poetic precursors (see "Literary Context: Ancient Near Eastern Love Poetry," pp. 47–63). Conceivably the dialogue format of the Song reflects performance (cf. Fox 247–50) or even cultic ritual—for what do all poets work with, if not their cultural heritage? Surely the poet responsible for *shir hashirim*, "the best of songs," is a strong poet in Harold Bloom's sense,[1] one who has overwritten the tradition with a fresh vision of desire. Whatever its irretrievable sources of inspiration, the Song as we now have it is a written text, an artistic creation, and the man and woman who appear in it are literary personae. This commentary takes seriously the implications of this fact for interpretation, asking not only what the lovers are like but also how the poet presents them to us (cf. Fox 253).

The illusion of immediacy in the Song might be compared to the situation John Keats describes upon observing figures on a Grecian urn:

1. Harold Bloom, *The Anxiety of Influence: A Theory of Poetry* (Oxford: Oxford University Press, 1973).

> Fair youth, beneath the trees, thou canst not leave
>   Thy song, nor ever can those trees be bare;
>   Bold Lover, never, never canst thou kiss,
>   Though winning near the goal—yet, do not grieve;
>   She cannot fade, though thou hast not thy bliss,
>   For ever wilt thou love, and she be fair!
>   (John Keats, "Ode on a Grecian Urn")

Like Keats's lovers, those of the Song are captured in language on the brink of attaining their bliss (though they also—through double entendre and the blurring of distinctions between wishing and having, longing and fulfillment—achieve their heart's desire; see "Blurring Distinctions between Anticipation and Enjoyment of Love," pp. 9–11). The love that unfolds before us in the Song as the lovers speak is a love that is being celebrated in the present. The poem is not a recollection in tranquility of bygone days of romance, nor a fantasy about what it might be like to obtain that obscure object of desire. Here the lovers are always taking their pleasure or just about to do so. The erotic imperative—the call to love by means of grammatical imperatives, jussives, and cohortatives—lends urgency to the moment: "draw me after you," "let us run" (1:4), "tell me" (1:7), "rise up," "come away" (2:10, 13), "turn" (2:17), "open to me" (5:2), "let me hear" (2:14; 8:13). The Song begins with the erotic imperative ("let him kiss me," 1:2) and ends with it ("take flight . . . be like a gazelle or young deer," 8:14). Not least, the climactic affirmation of love in 8:6–7 is grounded in the erotic imperative: "place me like a seal on your heart, for love is strong as death." Because love is strong as death, the woman wants to be a seal on her lover's heart—a mark of ownership and sign of intimate identification.

Coupled with imperatives, vocatives strengthen the impression of the lovers' presence at the moment of utterance: "my soul's beloved," "my sister, bride," "my dove, my perfect one," "most beautiful of women." The present moment is also vividly captured by participles: the man is approaching, bounding over hills, standing, knocking—his activity arrested in time and space (2:8–9; 5:2). Someone or something is coming up from the wilderness (3:6; 8:5). The illusion is that we are watching along with the speaker, our eyes riveted upon the apparition just entering our field of vision, poised between the wilderness and the unspecified location of the speaker.

Always in progress, love also unfolds as the poem progresses. The progression is not linear, however, for the Song is a lyric, not a dramatic, poem. Sudden temporal shifts are characteristic of the Song and strengthen the impression of immediacy (see, e.g., the Commentary under 3:1–5; 5:2; 5:3; 5:4; cf. Munro 117–42). In the garden of eroticism and the realm of the senses, both time and place collapse. Past events are of the recent past ("the king has brought me to his chambers," 1:4b) and the future is about to be realized ("we will delight and rejoice in you," 1:4c). The lovers move effortlessly over the poetic landscape—vineyards, gardens, palaces, houses, rocky cliffs, the wilderness, Lebanon—finding pleasure wherever they materialize. One moment the woman is in the king's chambers, the next, the lovers are in their pleasure garden. The immediacy arising from the sensation of desire on the verge of gratification precludes the melancholy that we find in Keats's poem, with its consciousness of the fragility and transience of the physical world. Not that a reader could not supply it by reflecting on the voice as something ephemeral (love is strong as death, and conversely death is strong as love). But absent in the Song is the interfusion of joy and sadness we find not only in Keats (expressed often through oxymoron, as in "sweet pain," "aching pleasure") but in numerous other love poems as well. Whereas Keats longs to retreat to a visionary world of unmingled bliss, the Song gives the impression that the lovers already inhabit such a world. This is not to say the Song's world is completely idyllic, but, like all besotted lovers, its lovers do not let the weariness, the fever, and the fret of the world around them intrude upon their bliss.

Conjuring

"Conjuring you up and letting you disappear, that's the game I'm always playing," writes a poet about her lover.[2] It is the game the Song's lovers are always playing too. The Song casts a spell with words: through seductively beautiful poetry the lovers materialize and dematerialize in a continual play of seeking and finding. The man conjures his lover up repeatedly by describing her bit by bit, in densely metaphorical language, until she materializes before us, a body clad in metaphor (4:1–5, 12–15; 6:4–10; 7:1–6 [2–7 H]). The woman calls her lover forth through her poetic powers of representation only to let him disappear so that she can conjure him up again (see under 2:8–17; 3:1–5; 3:6–11; 5:2–6:3). She is a consummate conjurer, for she also puts words in his mouth (2:10–14; 5:2). She imagines what he says to her, whereas he does not imagine her words. In 5:2–6:3, for example, she conjures him up as a suitor begging entry to her chamber (she is the narrator of these events; he speaks as a character in her story), and, seemingly, she lets him disappear. Then, by means of the language of praise, which she uses to describe his body in extravagant detail to the women of Jerusalem, she conjures him up again. Elsewhere she conjures him up as a Solomonic figure, approaching from the desert in a magnificent sedan chair (3:6–11).

The lovers are always present for each other because they are always speaking or being spoken about; in other words, they are continually desiring and desired. Throughout the Song, speech embodies desire by calling bodies into

---

2. "Dich hinzaubern und vergehen lassen, / Immer spiele ich das eine Spiel" (Else Lasker-Schüler, "Siehst du mich" ["Do you see me"]).

being and playing with their disappearance in an infinite deferral of presence. Conjuring seeks to make immanent through language what is absent, to construct the lovers as "real" (that is, present before us) and endow them with meaning.

This is how it all begins, with the woman conjuring up her lover: "Let him kiss me with the kisses of his mouth, for your caresses are better than wine" (1:2). She begins by speaking of "him" and "his mouth" as if he is not there with her, and in the next breath she addresses him directly, "your caresses." One might think of "let him kiss me with the kisses of his mouth" as an incantation, and the shift from "let *him* kiss me" to "*your* caresses" an act of conjuring. As if in response to articulated desire, the lover materializes, brought into being, as he is elsewhere (2:8–3:5; 5:2–6:3), by poetic imagination.

The Invitation to the Reader

For the poet's vision of love to live on, the poem must be read. For readers, however, a certain element of voyeurism is involved in being privy to the intimate exchanges of lovers. Presenting the lovers as aware of and in conversation with an audience is a poetic strategy that makes the relationship between the lovers less private, less closed (and the Song less voyeuristic), and thus facilitates the reader's entry into the lovers' seemingly private world of erotic intimacy. The audience, the women of Jerusalem (see under 1:5–6), are sometimes addressed directly (1:5; 2:7; 3:5, 10–11; 5:8, 16; 8:4) and sometimes speak (5:1, 9; 6:1; 8:5; and perhaps 1:8; 6:13 [7:1 H]). At times their presence is simply assumed. When the woman says, for example, "Listen! My lover! Look! He's coming!" (2:8) or "What is this coming up from the wilderness?" (3:6), to whom is she speaking? In the world of the poem, her audience is the women of Jerusalem, but ultimately, of course, it is the poem's readers. At other times, we are reminded of the women's presence when the lovers seem to be enjoying the most intimate pleasures (2:4–7; 3:4–5; 5:1ef; 6:1–3; 8:3–4).

The lovers do not view the presence of these women as either intrusive or embarrassing, and, by addressing them, the woman invites their active participation. The invitation to the women of Jerusalem to participate in the lovers' bliss is also an invitation to the reader. The women's presence is always a reminder that what seems to be a closed dialogue between two perpetually desiring lovers is addressed to us, for our pleasure and possibly our enlightenment. The poem needs us in order to be actualized here and now, in the acts of reading and of appreciation. And so the poem encourages its readers to join the women in their approbation of the lovers, and, by showing us how marvelous it is to be in love, invites us to become lovers too: "Eat, friends, drink yourselves drunk on caresses!" (5:1). Readers bring the lovers to life when, by overhearing them, they observe their love unfold and when they answer the poem's invitation to participate in the lovers' joy.

The invitation to the reader is a poetic strategy; obviously nothing compels readers to accept the poem's invitation or to accept it on the poet's terms. To judge from the admiration, and even adoration, it has elicited over the centuries, the Song is very effective in seducing most readers with its poetic vision of desire, though recently the number of resistant readers seems to be increasing. We might ask, how can a poem about desire not arouse readerly desire? Readerly desire, of course, can take as many forms as there are real readers (see "The Song of Songs and Its Readers," pp. 73–86).

The Lovers as Representing All Lovers

Who are the lovers of the Song of Songs? They are identified neither by name nor by association with any particular time or place (except for the vaguest connections to Solomon and Jerusalem; see the Commentary under 1:1). The Song's lovers are archetypal lovers—composite figures, types of lovers rather than any specific lovers. In the course of the poem, they take on various guises or personalities and assume different roles. The man is a king and a shepherd; the woman is a member of the royal court and an outsider who tends vineyards or keeps sheep. She is black (1:5), as well as like the white moon and radiant sun (6:10), with a neck like an ivory tower (7:4 [5 H])—an impossible combination in one person according to many commentators.

By providing access only to the voices of the lovers, to what they say not who they are, the poet is able to identify them with all lovers. Their love is timeless. All this makes it easier for readers to relate the Song's lovers' experience to their own experience of love, real or fantasized. Consider, for example, the difference it would make if the Song were specifically about King Solomon and, say, the queen of Sheba or, as the old dramatic theory had it, a country maiden (see under "The Dramatic Theory," pp. 78–79). Would readers be as likely to identify so readily with its protagonists as readers have done throughout the centuries? I doubt it (and it would have made allegorical interpretation more difficult as well). The woman is addressed once as "Shulammite," and some interpreters use this appellation for her, though it is not a personal name (see under 6:13 [7:1 H]). I have not provided her with a name in this commentary, because to name her would be to particularize her (and Shulammite is only one of her multiple identities), whereas the figure in the poem is universal.

Although they are types, representatives of all lovers rather than identifiable individuals, the lovers seem to take on distinct personalities as we get to know them. For this reason, I speak of them in this commentary in the singular, as "the woman" and "the man." They are consistent in the way they each talk about their love and in the way love makes them behave—she seeking him (3:1–5; 5:2–8), he courting her (2:8–17; 5:2–4) and praising her charms (4:1–15; 6:4–10; 7:1–8 [2–9 H])—and this encourages us to feel we know them and enables us to build a picture of them. In particular, the poet's remarkable sensitivity to differences between women and men gives the Song's lovers psychological depth (see "Gendered Love-Talk and the Relation of the Sexes," pp. 13–28). Love is, after all, a many-faceted emotion. The longing for union, blissful oblivion in the other, is simultaneously a desire to absorb the other. Desire, even when gratified, triggers anxieties—fear of loss of self, of rejection or disappointment. The poet's characterization of the lovers allows us to see their vulnerability, perhaps even their insecurities—her anxiety created by his absence (1:7; 3:1–5; 5:2–8), his anxiety created by the powerful effect her presence has on him (4:1–9; 6:4–5; 7:5 [6 H])—as well as their confidence, mutual enchantment, and sheer delight in each other. If the lovers created for us by the poet emerge as "real" flesh-and-blood lovers, we can also construct a kind of loose plot, revolving around the pleasure they take in each other and their efforts to overcome the obstacles that keep them apart (see "Lyric Poetry and Reading for the Plot," pp. 42–45).

The lovers are not to be confused with the poet, who presents them to us both as explorers discovering the delights of intimacy and as knowing all there is to know about love. On the one hand, the Song gives the impression that its lovers are young lovers. Often they appear to be courting, and love seems to take them by surprise, so amazed are they by its power. On the other hand, the Song is not about young love only; its lovers are experienced and conversant in the art of love. They know that society's rules and regulations (8:1, 8–9), angry brothers (1:6), cruel city guards (5:7), and unspecified terrors of the night (3:8) are no real obstacles to love—only death is. In choosing to portray love in progress, unfolding, the poet captures the sense of discovery and the excitement of being in love as though for the first time—the way that being in love makes one feel young (as in the lyrics of the popular song "you make me feel so young, you make me feel like spring has sprung") and the romance and nostalgia associated with first love (a feeling William Butler Yeats effectively appeals to in a poem entitled "A Dream of Death," by praising a woman as "more beautiful than thy first love").

Blurring Distinctions between Anticipation and Enjoyment of Love

How much of the Song of Songs is wishing for the beloved, as opposed to anything explicitly sexual happening? Kissing, for example, is wished for, but not represented as taking place ("let him kiss me," 1:2; "If only you were my brother . . . I would kiss you," 8:1). The woman invites her beloved to come out to the countryside, where she will give him her love (8:11–13), but this is something yet to occur. He takes her to the house of wine (2:4); she takes him to her mother's chamber (3:4). But do they consummate their love there? Or anywhere else in the poem? Yes, on the figurative level.

In the Song sexual union is represented through the indirection of language, through innuendo, double entendre, and metaphor. This aspect of the Song is discussed in detail by Cook (1968). As he perceptively points out, "coition, the center of desire in the poem, is veiled by circumlocution, by metaphor, or by roundabout description of the delights of love play" (110).[3] The man is an apple tree whose fruit is sweet to his lover's taste (2:3). The woman is a lily (2:1) and a garden (4:12–5:1), and her beloved goes down to his garden to feed among the lilies (6:2–3). In 4:11–14 he speaks of honey and milk under her tongue and her body as a pleasure garden of choice fruits and spices. Has he tasted the milk and honey and sampled the garden's fruit? If not, how would he know about them? One could say that he simply assumes he will find his fantasy gratified. So is sexual intimacy represented or not? The sexual suggestiveness of this particular encounter between the lovers becomes even stronger when she invites him to come to his garden and eat its choicest fruits (4:16). It is surely a rare reader who would mistake the sexual innuendo in his reply as describing a light snack alfresco:

> I come to my garden, my sister bride;
>   I gather my myrrh with my spice,
> I eat my honeycomb with my honey,
>   I drink my wine with my milk.
>
> (5:1)

But what form intimacy takes here and elsewhere, though it may be strongly suggested, is never literally described. Moreover, an imaginative reader can find sexual innuendo and double entendre everywhere. Like beauty, double entendre is in the eye of the beholder. While recognizing it as a reader's conundrum, I treat it also as a feature of the text: a poetic quality of the Song that allows it to be read as both very explicitly and very delicately erotic. A love poem like the Song encourages reading for sexual meanings. "Love poets tease us with sexual double entendre. Sexual innuendoes, not to mention explicit sexual references, start us looking for more of the same until we begin seeing them everywhere" (Fox 298). Sexuality is pervasive in the Song, even though we may disagree where and how, exactly, it gets expressed or what correspondence there may be between a suggested image and its possible sexual referents. Double entendre is an important feature of the Song's erotic lyricism; encoded in the text, it is activated by the reader.[4] A particularly good example of double entendre and its indeterminacy is Song 5:2–6, which manages not simply to be

3. Thus I do not agree with Walsh (2000: 29, 34–35 *et passim*) that love is not represented as consummated in the Song.

4. Cf. Terry Eagleton, *Literary Theory: An Introduction* (Minneapolis: University of Minnesota Press, 1983), 119–20: "Homer did not anticipate that I personally would read his poems, but his language, by virtue of the ways it is constructed, unavoidably offers certain 'positions' for a reader, certain vantage-points from which it can be interpreted. To understand a poem means grasping its

suggestive but to reflect sexual union at the same time that, for all appearances, it tells about a missed encounter (see the Commentary). Less elaborate cases can be crucial for interpretation. In the last verse of the Song ("Take flight, my love, and be like a gazelle or young deer upon the mountains of spices") is "mountains of spices" a double entendre for the woman herself, so that she seems to be sending her lover away but is also calling him to her?

It is surely an artistically sophisticated poem that can be read as both delicately erotic and sexually overt at the same time. The Song is roundabout, insinuative, but not coy. Double entendre gives the impression of gratification taking place even as it is longed for. Desire in the Song is always on the brink of fulfillment, and has an urgency about it (come! tell me! make haste!). Fulfillment is simultaneously assured, deferred, and, on a figurative level, enjoyed. The slippage from one mode to another, the blurring of distinctions between the more literal level of wishing and desiring and the figurative level of consummation is central to the Song's poetic artistry and erotic persuasiveness.

The boundaries between anticipation and experience are already blurred in the temporal slippage of the opening lines ("let him kiss me . . . the king has brought me . . . we will rejoice"), where wishing, experiencing, and anticipating coalesce. Why does she want kisses? Because, she avers, his love play is better than wine. Does this not assume some prior knowledge of his lovemaking on her part? Either his lovemaking is imagined as something that will be deliciously stimulating or it is known to be. Here at the beginning, as throughout the poem, we cannot disentangle the lovers' experience of each other from their wishes and desires.

Love Forever in Progress: Repetition and Resistance to Closure

The Song of Songs is lyric poetry; its progression, as noted above, is not linear but rather meandering. It surges forward and circles back upon itself, continuously and effortlessly repeating its acts of conjuring and reissuing its invitation to the reader. Just as the harmony of the male and female voices represents, on the poetic plane, their sexual union, so the poetic rhythm of the Song, ever forward and then returning, reflects the repetitive pattern of seeking and finding in which the lovers engage, which is the basic pattern of sexual love: longing–satisfaction–renewed longing–and so on. The prolonging of desire and

---

language as being 'oriented' towards the reader from a certain range of positions: in reading, we build up a sense of what kind of effects this language is trying to achieve ('intention'), what sorts of rhetoric it considers appropriate to use, what assumptions govern the kinds of poetic tactics it employs, what attitudes towards reality these imply." Eagleton goes on to point out that "none of this need be identical with the intentions, attitudes and assumptions of the actual historical author at the time of writing," and offers the book of Isaiah as an example.

of fulfillment stretching across the span of the poem plays an essential part in the Song's effectiveness—its power—as a love poem.

Variations played upon themes and images establish echoes across the time and space of the poem, as, for example, in 4:10–11, when the man uses the same language and imagery to describe the woman's caresses that she used of his in 1:2–4, incrementing the images she uses by adding spices to the perfumes she speaks of and milk and honey to the wine. These verses are antiphonal across the space of the poem in much the same way as the couplets, "Like a lily among thistles, so is my friend among women / Like an apple tree among the trees of the forest, so is my lover among men" (2:2–3), are antiphonal. Further associations are created among parts of the poem by variations in the refrain of mutual possession, "my lover is mine and I am his" (2:16), which later becomes "I am my lover's and my lover is mine" (6:3), and then "I am my lover's and his desire is for me" (7:10 [11 H]).

Repetition occurs within and among poetic units, creating interlacing patterns; for instance, in the nighttime longing for and seeking of the lover in 3:1–4 and 5:2–6:3, in the repeated descriptions of the woman's body, or in the call to hear her voice in 2:14 and 8:13. Refrains echo across the poem ("I place you under oath, women of Jerusalem," "until the day breathes and the shadows flee," "his left hand is under my head and his right hand caresses me," "who is this coming up from the wilderness," "I sought him but I did not find him"), and certain images stamp themselves upon the imagination because they keep cropping up (the voice of the loved one, the gazelle and young deer, feeding on lilies, bringing the beloved to the house or chamber). The effect is cumulative, a gradual unfolding and a denouement, which is achieved by a returning at the end of the poem to some of the themes of the beginning, such as the vineyard, its keepers, and the companions.

There is, however, no real closure to this poem about desire. In the last verse of the Song, the woman seems to be sending her lover away and calling him to her in the same breath:

> Take flight, my love, and be like a gazelle
>   or young deer
>   upon the mountains of spices.

Its resistance to closure is perhaps the Song's most important strategy for immortalizing love. Closure would mean the end of desiring, the silence of the text, the death of love.[5] Resistance to closure is an attempt to keep love always

---

5. Brooks (1993: 20) writes about "the way in which narrative desire simultaneously seeks and puts off the erotic dénouement that signifies both its fulfillment and its end: the death of desiring, the silence of the text." See also Landy (1983: 113): "The tension in the Song between the desire of the lovers to unite and the inevitability of their parting is that also between their voice and the silence into which it vanishes, and between love and death—the ultimate parting, the unbroken silence."

in progress on the page before us. Moreover, not only does the Song end without closure, it begins *in medias res*, "let him kiss me"—a design that makes the Song, in effect, a poem without beginning or end. Like the love it celebrates, the Song of Songs strives to be ongoing, never-ending (cf. Fox 226; Munro 89). The last verse, because it signals both the lovers' separation and their union, suspends their love in time. As an analogy, we might consider the activity captured in time on a Grecian urn, like that described by Keats, mentioned above. Where does the urn's "story" begin and end? We could name a particular point as the beginning, but the movement portrayed circles back upon itself. Even if we perceive an end to the activity portrayed, it begins again where it left off. We might imagine the Song as something like a verbal Grecian urn. Only when the woman sends her lover away can the poem begin again, with the longing and the search for him. In answer to the man's request for her voice—his imperative "let me hear it!"—the woman's voice at the end of the Song brings the poem round full circle to desire's first articulation, "let him kiss me," desire that is never sated because it folds back upon itself.

4. Gendered Love-Talk and the Relation of the Sexes

In considering the relationship between the sexes in the Song of Songs, it is important to keep in mind that we are dealing with love poetry, where the boundaries between the conventional and unconventional are unpredictable, and not with a description of actual gender relations of a particular time and place. The Song of Songs is a priceless resource not so much for what it tells us about relations between the sexes in ancient Israel, for it tells us very little, but for what it reveals about the construction of desire in ancient Israelite culture. Without the Song, we could be tempted to conclude from the rest of the Bible that desire in Israel was constructed as male, and as dangerous, something to be repressed or controlled (cf., e.g., the laws governing sexual relations, the advice of Proverbs to young men, and the "lessons" taught by the examples of such heroes as Samson and David, led astray by desire). Because we possess the Song of Songs, we know that a romantic vision of love was available in ancient Israel, a vision that recognized both desire and sexual pleasure as mutual and that viewed positively a woman actively seeking to gratify her desire. Romance is more than sexual gratification. Romance transforms the way lovers look at the world around them; suddenly the whole world becomes more beautiful, more vibrant, more wonderful. This is what happens to the Song of Songs lovers. Nature in all its glory reflects and participates in their mutual delight. And everything is experienced more intensely, from the thrill of watching a lavishly outfitted palanquin approach from a distance (3:6–11) to the pleasure derived from the intimate contemplation of the beloved's attributes (4:1–6; 5:10–16; 6:4–7; 7:1–5 [2–6 H]), from the anguish caused by the beloved's absence (3:1–3), to the joys found in an exotic pleasure garden fit for a king

(4:11–15). If we did not possess the Song, we might safely assume that people in ancient Israel fell in love, as people do, but we would not know how they felt about it, or dreamed about it, or envisioned its possibilities.

Different Ways of Speaking about Love

The dialogue format of the Song enables the poet to explore the nature of love and longing from both points of view, a woman's and a man's. On the one hand, the female and male voices are in complete accord, both desirous, both rejoicing in the pleasures of sexual intimacy; they merge into one, creating the poetic equivalent of their sexual union. On the other, the poet has given the lovers distinct perspectives. The differences in the way the poet portrays the female and male lovers reveal the poet's remarkable sensitivity to differences between women and men—differences that, in turn, reflect cultural assumptions about gender differences and roles (which is not to say the poem does not challenge certain of these assumptions as well).

There are differences in emphasis in the way the male and female lovers talk about love. They do not look at love or at each other in quite the same way. She expresses her desire and explores her feelings for him, and his for her, through stories, stories in which she and he both play roles, as themselves (2:8–17; 3:1–5; 5:2–6:3) or in fantasy guises (3:6–11). Her stories have a narrative movement and a sense of closure, a tension and a resolution. They are the only parts of the Song that display narrative development or what one might call a plot. For example, she tells two stories in which her lover comes courting: in one, he invites her to join him outside to enjoy the springtime (2:8–17), and in the other, which takes place at night, he asks to be admitted to her chamber (5:2–7). Twice she recounts how she goes out in the city streets searching for him: the first time, she is immediately successful in finding him; the second, she encounters a distressing setback before achieving her goal (3:1–4; 5:6d–6:3).

The man does not tell stories. His way of talking about love is to look at her and tell her what he sees and how it affects him. He describes what he sees metaphorically (4:1–5; 6:4–10; 7:1–9 [2–10 H]). Her effect on him is captivating ("You have captured my heart, my sister, bride," 4:9; "the hair of your head is like purple; a king is held captive by the tresses," 7:5 [6 H]). He finds her awesome (6:4), and, when her gaze meets his, he is overwhelmed ("Turn your eyes away from me, for they overwhelm me," 6:5).

The difference in the way the man and woman talk about love extends to a contrast on the poetic level between sight and speech. The man constructs the woman, creates a picture of her for us, through the gaze. We follow his gaze as he progressively builds up a metaphorical picture of her, bit by bit, until she materializes before us. The woman constructs the man primarily through the voice. She quotes him speaking to her (2:10–14; 5:2), but he never quotes her.

Through putting words in his mouth when she tells stories in which he courts her, she controls the way we view him. We see him as a lover who comes courting by day and by night, who woos her with sweet words—and as a somewhat elusive lover she must seek, but one who is never difficult to find. She looks at him too, but when she describes him she pictures his body differently from the way he depicts hers (see "Speaking Metaphorically about the Female and Male Body," pp. 17–22).

(She) (He) Lovesick and Awestruck

The lovers describe differently what it is like to be in love. The difference is subtle, for both feel wondrously overwhelmed by the other. The woman speaks about herself, about being in love and how she experiences it: "I am faint with love" or "I am lovesick" (2:5; 5:8). Her condition, lovesickness, is a malady to which lovers are prone, a state of intense longing that feeds on love and leaves one languid and in need of the sustenance only love can bring. In Song 2:5, she is lovesick when he is with her. He has brought her to the house of wine, which is also the house of love, where she calls for raisin-cakes and apples (as if they would help), because she is lovesick. She is also lovesick when they are apart. After a missed encounter, when she goes seeking him in the streets at night, she calls on the women of Jerusalem to tell him of her condition, since he is both the cause and the cure: "if you find my lover, tell him that I am lovesick" (5:8).

The woman tells others, the women of Jerusalem, what *love* does to her; the man speaks to the woman about what *she* does to him. He thinks in terms of conquest, of power relations: "*you* have captured my heart" (4:9). Unlike the woman, who expresses her feelings subjectively, he does not say, "I am overwhelmed," but rather describes the way *he* feels as something *she* has done to him. Similarly, in 6:5 he says, "Turn *your eyes* away from me, for *they* overwhelm me." It appears that, in ancient Israelite culture as in many others, autonomy is part of the dynamic of male eroticism. As a man, he is used to feeling in control. But love makes him feel as though he is losing control. He is powerless to resist; his autonomy is challenged. He welcomes this, to be sure, but these feelings are new and surprising and thus disconcerting. He is—and he admits it—awestruck: "You are beautiful, my friend, like Tirzah, lovely as Jerusalem, as awesome in splendor as they" (6:4).

He is awestruck; she is lovesick. As a woman, she is used to a world in which men are in control, and to a version of love according to which women surrender to men. Whereas he speaks of being captured by her, she speaks of surrender to him (8:10). Her autonomy is not challenged, because she does not have the kind of autonomy a man has (even though she is the most autonomous of all biblical women). She is not in awe of him; she is in need of him. She longs passionately for him and cannot do without him. From her woman's point of

view, he may sometimes seem elusive (1:7; 3:1–3; 5:6–8). The corollary, for
him, is that she at times appears inaccessible (2:14; 4:8; 5:2–3; 6:13 [7:1 H]).

It is interesting to note that *she* does not think of him as being in awe of her.
In her version of love, he thinks of her as shy and reticent.

> Rise up, my friend, my fair one,
>> and come away,
> my dove in the clefts of the rock,
>> in the covert of the cliff.
> Let me see you,
>> let me hear your voice,
> for your voice is sweet,
>> and you are lovely.
>
>   (2:13–14)

When she puts words in his mouth, he calls her "my dove in the clefts of the
rock, in the covert of the cliff," an image that suggests shyness. But when he
speaks for himself, he imagines her as dwelling among lions and leopards on
remote mountaintops.

> With me from Lebanon, bride,
>> come with me from Lebanon.
> Come forth from the peak of Amana,
>> from the peak of Senir and Hermon,
> from the dens of lions,
>> from the lairs of leopards.
>
>   (4:8)

He does not associate her with the domestic security of the house, as she had
presented him doing in 2:8–17, but rather with formidable wild animals whose
inhospitable abode she shares. Both these images convey the idea that he perceives her as inaccessible, but her inaccessibility seems vastly more daunting
in his version.

The lovers' emotional states, feelings of lovesickness and awe, are aspects
of their characterization that reveal their vulnerability. She suffers from the anxiety that his absence causes ("I sought him but I did not find him," 3:1; 5:6),
and she deals with it by seeking him until she finds him, taking a risk in seeking him in the city streets at night. The outcome, as far as the poet is concerned,
is assured—for just as she let him disappear, she can conjure him up again (see
"Conjuring," pp. 6–7)—but one hears in her words the anxiety of the moment
as she tells the women of Jerusalem about her plight (5:2–8). He is vulnerable
too—conquered by a glance (4:9), overwhelmed by her gaze (6:5), a king held
captive by her tresses (7:5 [6 H]). He finds the power she has over him—which
is the power he has given her—most unsettling. He deals with his anxiety about

her effect on him by distancing himself from the whole person through the breakdown of her body into parts—eyes, hair, teeth, lips, mouth, cheeks, neck, and breasts in 4:1–5; eyes, hair, teeth, lips, cheeks in 6:5–7; feet, thighs, navel, belly, breasts, neck, eyes, nose, head, hair in 7:1–5 [2–6 H]—and by lingering over the details of her body, investing each part with meaning so that they become familiar and less threatening (see, further, under 4:1–5).

Many love poems present us with a familiar lover's anxiety, the uncertainty of "loves me, loves me not," or the thought that one loves more than one is loved. This is often the case because love poems typically present only one person's point of view.[6] The dialogue format of the Song, in which the lovers tell each other about their passion and devotion, militates against such anxiety on the part of its protagonists. Such worries, however, are a common experience in love, and it could be argued that, as realistic literary creations, the Song's lovers are not exempt from them (Landy 1983, ch. 2 *et passim*; Black 2000a: 320; Harding, forthcoming). The dominant mood, however, is one of exuberance and assurance: "my lover is mine and I am his" (2:16; cf. 6:3; 7:10 [11 H]). The lovers' devotion never wavers, and their desire, which they express freely, never abates. This assurance undergirds the poet's vision of love as "strong as death."

Speaking Metaphorically about the Female and Male Body

Looking in the Song, like desire, is constructed as mutual. His "Look at you! You are beautiful" (1:15) is echoed by her "Look at you! You are beautiful" (1:16). Lovers love with their eyes, and often they rely on metaphor to describe what they see. Striking and unusual metaphorical descriptions of the body are not at all uncommon in love poetry, though for some reason they seem to be a stumbling block for literal-minded commentators on the Bible's only love poem. Do the critics who have difficulty with the body imagery in the Song lack sensitivity and imagination? Are we too far removed culturally to appreciate the poetic conventions that influenced the choice of metaphors and the meanings these metaphors would have had for their original hearers? Was the poet not very good at selecting similes to describe body parts? The choice of imagery to describe the lovers' bodies in the Song may be difficult and challenging for contemporary readers, but so is that of many other love poems from various ages and places. Some relevant ancient Near Eastern examples are discussed below and in the Commentary. Further afield, Mariaselvam compares the Song with ancient Tamil love poetry. Closer to home, Sasson cites the following example from one of e. e. cummings's poems, entitled "Orientale," and observes, "Notice how useless it would be to concretize cummings' imagery by brandishing measuring sticks

6. See, e.g., though it is not a poem, Roland Barthes, *A Lover's Discourse: Fragments*, trans. Richard Howard (London: Vintage, 2002).

(Pope), by appealing to twentieth-century iconographic remains (Keel, supported by R. Murphy's symposium remarks) or, for that matter, by taking refuge in clever terminology (Fox)" (1987: 737):

> my love
> thy hair is one kingdom
>   the king whereof is darkness
> thy forehead is a flight of flowers
>
> thy head is a quick forest
>   filled with sleeping birds
> thy breasts are swarms of white bees
>   upon the bough of thy body
> thy body to me is April
> in whose armpits is the approach of spring
>
> thy thighs are white horses yoked to a chariot
>   of kings
> they are the striking of a good minstrel
> between them is always a pleasant song
>
> my love
> thy head is a casket
>   of the cool jewel of thy mind
> the hair of thy head is one warrior
>   innocent of defeat
> thy hair upon thy shoulders is an army
>   with victory and with trumpets
> thy legs are the trees of dreaming
> whose fruit is the very eatage of forgetfulness
>
> thy lips are satraps in scarlet
>   in whose kiss is the combining of kings
> thy wrists
> are holy
>   which are the keepers of the keys of thy blood
> thy feet upon thy ankles are flowers in vases
>   of silver
>
> in thy beauty is the dilemma of flutes
>
>   thy eyes are the betrayal
> of bells comprehended through incense

Although I discuss in the Commentary some of the issues and more common proposals for understanding the imagery in the Song, my observations there are not intended to explain the meaning of the images in any definitive sense, for it is not the case that there is only one correct way to approach them. Soulen (1967) rightly claims that the images are meant to convey to the reader the emotions the speaker experiences upon beholding the loved one. But that cannot be all. Falk (130–31) and Fox (272–77) are also correct when they claim that the one-to-one correspondences between the images and their referents are precise and meant to convey some particular aspect of each body part. Images are matched in some way to their referents and are not interchangeable. As Fox observes, a flock of goats winding down the mountainside is said to be like the woman's hair, not her eyes (275). But what exactly the images are meant to convey is not always apparent. Words and images are never simply denotative, and in poetry they are excessively connotative. Much of the power of metaphoric language, and the source of our pleasure in it, derives from its plurisignificance, from its ability to be suggestive of multiple meanings. Poetic metaphor cannot be reduced to prose paraphrase. And as if this did not make the commentator's job of discussing the Song's metaphoric descriptions of the body hard enough, the task is further complicated by the presence in these verses of numerous *hapax legomena* and rare words whose meaning is uncertain.

The Song's profuse metaphors are not just artistic flourishes that challenge the commentator and trigger the imaginations of its readers. Like everything else in the Song, metaphor is employed in the service of the poet's vision of love as mutual desire and gratification, as strong as death, as transforming the world.

> As the poem proceeds, the images, given an importance independent of their referents, combine to form a cohesive picture of a self-contained world: a peaceful, fruitful world, resplendent with the blessings of nature and the beauties of human art. That world blossoms in a perpetual spring. Doves hide shyly, sit near water channels, and bathe in milk. Spices give forth their fragrance. Springs flow with clear water. Fruits and winds offer their sweetness. Mounds of wheat are surrounded by lilies. Ewes, white and clean, bear twins and never miscarry. Goats stream gently down the mountainside. Proud and ornate towers stand tall above the landscape. Nor are there lacking silver and gold, precious stones, and objects of art: a rich and blessed world. . . . [S]ince that world comes into being and is unified only through the lovers' perception of each other, the imagery reveals a *new* world—one *created* by love. (Fox 329–30)

Metaphor, too, is play (see Landy 1993). The lovers in the Song are playing with compliments, leading up to love play.

There are numerous occasions in the Song where the lovers use arresting imagery to describe each other (e.g., 1:9–10, 13–14; 2:1–3, 9). Of particular interest where looking is concerned are the descriptions that construct the lovers' sexuality through a series of metaphors for various body parts, for it is here that the issue of the relation between gender and the gaze is crystallized: 4:1–5 [or 1–7? 9–16?]; 5:10–16; 6:4–7 [+8–10?]; 7:1–9 [2–10 H] [or 7:1–5? or

beginning in 6:13?]. These passages are often referred to in the scholarly literature as *wasfs* (after a genre of descriptive praise of the body in Arabic poetry)
or as "Praise Songs" or "Description Songs" or *Beschreibungslieder* (a form-
critical category). I do not use these labels, since they do not really aid us in
understanding the passages in question, and, more important, because the bodily descriptions are not separable from their contexts. Indeed, as is indicated by
the verses in brackets above, the extent of the unit that constitutes a *wasf* or
"description of praise" is open to question and there is no scholarly consensus
on the matter.

   On the one hand, the descriptions are intimate, suggestive, and even explicit.
On the other, the metaphors function as much to hide the body as to display it.
"Your belly is a heap of wheat encircled by lilies" (7:2 [3 H]). "Your eyes are
doves behind your veil" (4:1). How much does this reveal about the woman's
body? "His lips are lilies, dripping flowing myrrh" (5:13). "His hands are rods
of gold, inlaid with Tarshish stones" (5:14). Does this tell us something about
his lips or his hands, or is it about the way she experiences them? For discussion of the relation between metaphors and their referents, see the Commentary
 under 4:1–5; Keel 1994: 25–29; Falk 1990: 127–35; Murphy 1990: 70–74, and
the detailed treatments of Müller 1984 and Keel 1984. One might also raise the
question of perspective. Is the poet envisioning the body from a particular perspective (standing? lying down? dancing?) when describing it? (see the discussion under 4:4 and 7:1–5 [2–6 H]).

   Metaphor follows metaphor in the bodily descriptions in quick succession,
building an ever more complex metaphoric picture. "The initiator of the litany
of praise cannot say everything at once, and hence there is a piece-by-piece presentation of the body of the beloved in a visual cornucopia" (Ayo 1997: 183).
The man pictures the woman's body part by part three times, describing her from
her head downwards in 4:1–5 and 6:4–7, and from her feet to her head in 7:1–5
[2–6 H], as well as offering a particularly erotic extended metaphor of her body
as a pleasure garden in 4:10–15. She describes his body in a similar fashion only
once (5:10–16), but the fact that she too owns the gaze is an extraordinary feature of the Song, for traditionally women are looked at and men do the looking
(Brenner 1997: 39–43, 168–70). Important in the poet's vision of love is the
 mutual pleasure in visualizing the beloved's body—even though the lovers look
at each other differently, in what seem to be gender-determined ways.

   Some commentators find what the woman says about the man's body more
static, less imaginative, and less sensuous than what he says about hers. Landy,
for example, calls the description of the man "stiff and tense" compared to
his descriptions of her (71). Richard Soulen (1967: 183–90) attributes the differences to "the limited subject matter" in 5:10–16, and possibly even "the
difference in erotic imagination between poet and poetess" (184 n. 6, naively
assuming that because a woman is pictured as looking then a woman is the

author of these verses). Fiona Black discusses the bodily imagery used for the lovers in terms of the grotesque, for which the body is hybrid, exaggerated and mutable, in process, and thus comic, hideous, disconcerting, and unsettling. Both bodies are grotesque, she concludes, but differently so, with the woman's somehow more amenable to grotesquerie (2000a).

Whatever the differences, it is reasonable to assume that the poet will have represented the different ways men and women might speak about each other in terms of the prevailing cultural ideals of male and female beauty and desirability. The woman draws on images of hardness and solidity, as well as value, to describe the firm muscular body she treasures: rods of gold for his hands, an ivory bar for his torso, marble pillars on gold pedestals for his legs. The man favors nature imagery and images of tasty delicacies to be consumed to picture her as a bountiful source of erotic pleasures. Consumption, in ancient Israel as elsewhere in the ancient Near East, is a typical way of representing male sexual activity. But the woman enjoys the man's body too: the sweet taste of his fruit (2:3), the scent of his face (5:13), the taste of his kisses (5:13, 16).

If his imagery is more vivid and animated than hers, hers is more relational than his (see the Commentary under 5:10–16). Both lovers' faces are animate focal points of the body (4:1–3; 5:11–13, 16; 6:5–7; 7:4–5 [5–6 H]), not surprisingly, since faces convey so much of a person's individuality, and even their character. The fact that he describes her body more often than she describes his has something to do with the way he speaks about love (looking at her and describing her effect on him) and may reflect a cultural convention of reticence about depicting the male body (Brenner 1997: 31–43). But before one concludes that she seems more reticent than he, more discrete—not to mention less imaginative and less sensuous—one should allow for double entendre in her description (see the Commentary under 5:14–15; 5:14; and 5:15).

Each lover delights in the other's body. Each describes the loved one part by part, organizing the body in an effort to know it, and investing each part with meaning through a simile or metaphor whose import cannot be reduced to prose paraphrase. An important difference is that, unlike his descriptions of her, her description of him is textually motivated. She describes him in answer to a question raised by the women of Jerusalem, who ask, "What distinguishes your lover from other lovers?" His descriptions, in contrast, are represented by the poet as spontaneous outbursts inspired by the sight of her (for subtle differences in the way he talks about looking each time he describes her, see under 6:4–7:9 [10 H] and 6:4–7). She is not looking at him when she pictures his body. Her description is based not on looking but, presumably, on having looked, and this may help to explain why her reaction to his body is different from his to hers. She is not so unsettled by his body as he is by hers. He deals with her body in parts to cope with her devastating presence. She treats his by parts to cope with his absence and to conjure him up through the evocative power of language.

Other viewers are also included in the gazes of the lovers. The woman invites other women to share her intimate gaze at the man's body in 5:10–16; however, they are not allowed to look directly but only through her eyes. If he is the speaker of 6:13 [7:1 H], he invites others to look with him at her, as he describes her in intimate terms. The gaze in 7:1–9 [2–10 H] appears more direct, and the female body thus seems more vulnerable to the look, but in this case too we see the body through a lover's eyes. Though the poet treats the male and female bodies differently in terms of their availability to the gaze within the poem, we, the readers, see the man in the same way that we see the woman, through an inventory of body parts described metaphorically.

Only the woman is concerned with self-description. Is this particularly or necessarily a woman's concern; for example, in 1:5–6, where, by calling herself lovely, she raises the issue of her appearance and how others might perceive her, and 8:10, where she describes herself in the context of societal expectations? It does have the effect of making her seem more introspective than he is, an impression strengthened by the fact that he does not express his feelings about what it is like to be in love as directly as she does when she says simply "I am lovesick" (see "Lovesick and Awestruck," pp. 15–17).

A cultural notion of woman as other may have some bearing on the different status the woman and the man have with respect to the gaze. On the basis of what we can construct from the rest of the Bible, in ancient Israel the male body was considered the norm. It is not therefore an occasion for anxiety. The female body is other, mysterious, and thus provokes a more complex response. What is often described as the more static nature of the woman's description of the man may be due to a reticence to describe the male body any more explicitly. Thus the man's descriptions are more visual, whereas hers are relational. In 4:1–5 he invites her to see herself through his eyes, to share his visual pleasure ("Look at you . . . ,"4:1; cf. 1:15). She, too, invites him to see himself through her eyes, but without an inventory of body parts. Instead, as in her longer description, she is most interested in what he means to her: "Look at you! You are beautiful, my love, and delightful too" (1:16).

Erotic Look or Voyeuristic Gaze?

The privileged place given to looking in the Song can be construed as a sign of the desire to know the body and possess it. We might ask, is this looking loving, or is it objectifying and controlling, or something of both? While not presuming that this commentary can answer this question, I prefer to distinguish between the gaze as voyeuristic, looking that intrudes upon that which is seen, and the look as erotic, looking that participates in that which is seen. Being looked at is not necessarily objectifying. Nor is the one who looks, the subject of the gaze, automatically in a position of power over the one seen (we need only recall that

looking at his lover makes the man feel he has lost control). The look is objectifying when the one seen is expected to reveal intimate secrets and to become
fully accessible to a viewer who remains invisible and inaccessible. But this is
not what happens in the Song, where the erotic look preserves the mystery, the
otherness, of the other through figuration. Not only is looking reciprocal but,
when the man looks at the woman, he participates in what is seen. He always
puts himself in the picture (4:6–9; 6:5; 7:8–9 [9–10 H]). Putting himself in the
picture he constructs of her is not unlike her telling stories in which both he and
she are characters. Neither lover constructs the other without being affected
themselves—without becoming part of the story or entering the picture.

If the look in the Song is erotic and not voyeuristic (and readers will make up
their own minds on this score), still one might ask how lovingly and positively
those who look feel about what they see. Most writers on the Song assume that
the lovers have only praise for each other, but recently some critics have argued
that ambivalence is expressed in the way both the man's and, especially, the
woman's bodies are represented. The imagery has been variously described as
parodic (Brenner 1993a), comic (Whedbee 1998), and grotesque (a word frequently used but whose theoretical value has been explored only by Black 1999a,
2000a, 2000b). That the lovers mean their metaphoric flights of fancy to be complimentary seems obvious. He frames his descriptions of her with exclamations
about how beautiful she is (4:1, 7; 6:4, 10; 7:6). She declares that he stands out
among all other men and that "all of him is desirable" (5:16). Even so, in addition to producing the feelings of well-being and euphoria that give rise to such
exuberant outbursts, love involves the possibility of being hurt or disappointed.
In portraying a man and woman in love so realistically—in making their speech
so "authentic" (Falk 1990: 118)—the poet confers upon them subjectivity, thus
making it possible for us to imagine how a lover's unconscious drives and
impulses, desires and anxieties, may also contribute to the picture. The fact that
the lovers' beauty is communicated primarily by metaphor is, of course, an artistic decision, but it conveys more than the lovers' delight in each other's body. It
also reveals the poet's sensitivity to the vulnerability of lovers, a point particularly well argued by Black (1999a: 263–66 *et passim*; 2000: 320) and Harding
(forthcoming). The lovers protect themselves by distancing themselves from the
object of their desire, using imagery to obscure the reality of the beloved (Landy
1983: 176), even while they mean to erase any distance.

How do those who are looked at feel about being seen? Only the woman is
represented as being looked at by others besides her lover. In 1:5 she invites the
Jerusalem women's gaze ("black am I, and lovely") but seems ambivalent about
it as well ("pay no heed that I am black," 1:6). In 6:13 [7:1 H], where she is
called upon to return "that we may gaze upon you," it is not clear from her reply
whether she wishes to avoid this shared gaze, is ambivalent to it (as in 1:5–6),
or takes pleasure in the rapt visual attention she receives from her lover (see the

Commentary). Having one's body appreciated by one's lover may not be intrusive or embarrassing. Here, however, we are dealing with a text, where looking and intimate love-talk are not private. The question thus becomes, how does the poet negotiate looking and manage the reader's gaze?

I described above how the Song invites the reader to enter the lovers' intimate erotic world and, at the same time, keeps us out (see "The Invitation to the Reader," pp. 7–8). By presenting the lovers in the act of looking and describing what they see, the poet seeks to convey this pleasure concretely to the reader. We follow the lovers' gazes downward or upward as they enumerate details about each other's body that progressively build up a fuller picture. In this way the Song offers its readers poetic access to the pleasure of looking at and knowing the body. Seen through images and not seen in their entirety, the Song's lovers are both available to the gaze (each other's and that of others) and not available, in the sense that they defy representation. The bodies of the lovers are created through the way in which each is imagined by the other and in relation to the other—and through our gaze, when we read the Song, which actualizes the lovers' gazes.

The Song also keeps us out of the garden of eroticism. It renders our looking less voyeuristic, and our pleasure more aesthetic than erotic, by clothing the lovers' bodies in metaphors, which never quite gives access to the body being described.[7] The images may be strongly visual, but they are literary, part of a text not a picture. Metaphor may be commonplace, but in the hands of the poet it is a sophisticated literary technique for managing the reader's gaze.

The women of Jerusalem, the audience within the poem who also look and whose look the lovers are aware of, authorize the reader's look (see "The Invitation to the Reader," pp. 7–8). How successful this strategy is in making the Song seem less voyeuristic is a question only a reader can answer. One person's erotic look may be another person's voyeuristic gaze. Moreover, one might, for any number of reasons, want to resist the Song's invitation to look, or one might choose to look differently, or even perversely (see, e.g., Boer 1999, 2000; Black 2000a; Burrus and Moore 2003). Readers of this commentary will no doubt draw their own conclusions as to whether the body as it is presented in the Song is the object of the voyeuristic gaze or the erotic look (or something in between) and whether the imagery is complimentary or not (or something more complex). And readers will decide for themselves how they feel about looking, both the characters' looking and their own looking at the characters in this love poem.

7. See Brooks 1993: 123. Although Brooks's subject is modern narrative, many of his insights can be applied mutatis mutandis to an ancient love poem like the Song. His first chapter sketches an interesting, though brief and highly selective, history of the representation of the body in literature. He also makes a move I consider important: he views the body as both a cultural construct and as something outside language that language struggles to be embodied in. In my view, this struggle captures something of the erotic dynamic of the Song.

The Song and Conventional Gender Relations

In exploring love from both points of view, the Song offers a sustained focus on the woman as well as the man. Their speeches are fairly evenly divided, which is the poet's way of affirming the mutuality of desire. The attention the woman receives is unique in the Bible and so too is her characterization. For one thing, her behavior does not conform to the social norms one can construct from the rest of the Bible. A woman initiates sexual encounters; she roams the streets looking for her lover; she speaks openly about her desire. She expresses her sexuality as freely as he does; there is no indication that the man and woman are married, yet they are lovers, at least on the level of erotic suggestiveness or double entendre. For another, there is no other female character in the Bible whom we get to know so well through her intimate and innermost thoughts and feelings.

Not only does the Song focus on the female lover as much as on the male, it foregrounds other women characters as well, perhaps as a result of its attention to the woman. Besides the lovers, the only other speaking voice identified in the Song is that of women, the "daughters of Jerusalem." Both the woman's mother and the man's mother are mentioned, and, whereas the mother is referred to seven times (1:6; 3:4, 11; 6:9; 8:1, 2, 5), there is no mention of the father. It is to her "mother's house" that the woman wants to bring her lover. The woman's brothers are not accorded an identity in their own right: instead of calling them "brothers" she refers to them as "the sons of my mother" (1:6). Even 8:8–9 does not identify those responsible for their sister's future. Men's roles in the family seem to be pushed into the background. No wonder so many critics see in the Song an anodyne to biblical patriarchy (see under "Feminist Criticism," pp. 80–81).

A literary work might challenge its culture's traditional gender roles and expectations, but it could hardly be expected to be free from their influence. We should thus not be surprised to find in the Song evidence of societal attitudes characteristic of a patriarchal culture like that of ancient Israel. The man's chastity, for example, unlike the woman's, is not an issue (1:6; cf. 8:8–10). He enjoys a freedom of movement and social autonomy she does not share. She is subject to control by her brothers (1:6), and social restraints on her freedom to display her affection are indicated by her wish that her lover were like a brother, whom she could kiss openly without censure (8:1). There is no restriction on the man's movement. He comes from afar to woo his love (2:8–17) and just as quickly disappears into the night (5:2–6). But when she goes out in the streets to search for him, she is apprehended and mistreated by the city's watchmen (5:7). This may be a cultural expression of love as willing to undergo suffering. Nevertheless, it is a woman whom the poet represents as abused by men in a role of authority. Her lover does not undergo suffering for her sake, and, even if the poet had portrayed him as braving hardship for love's sake, it is hard to imagine a man experiencing the kind of treatment she is subjected to. Here too the situation seems to reflect the social mores and expectations of the poet's society, in which men enjoyed a social freedom that women could not expect to share.

In the Song's vision of romance, where desire is represented as mutual, female eroticism is paradoxically celebrated and controlled, but it does not ever seem to be successfully controlled either by the woman's angry brothers, who make her tend the vineyards ("my own vineyard I did not keep," she tells us) or by the watchmen who beat her when she goes out looking for her lover (since, undeterred, she continues her search and eventually finds him). Social control of female sexuality and society's investment in marriage arrangements are represented in 8:8–9:

> We have a little sister
> who has no breasts.
> What shall we do for our sister
> on the day she is spoken for?
> If she is a wall,
> we will build upon it a silver tier.
> And if she is a door,
> we will panel it in cedar.

I take these verses as well as v. 10 as the woman's speech, in which she addresses a topic of concern for women in a culture where before marriage women were under the control of their fathers or other male relatives, where marriages were usually arranged, and where the virginity of the bride was an important issue. In such circumstances, what role do matters of the heart play? She avers that such familial and societal concerns as these do not apply to her, since she has already reached womanhood and offered herself in surrender to her lover (8:10). Not surprisingly, in 8:11–12, the companion piece to these verses, the man also speaks along gender-specific lines. The imagery he uses is drawn from the domain of economic livelihood—vineyards and their care, hired workers, and payment—and he thinks in terms of competition with other men: he alone will tend his vineyard, which is worth more than Solomon's.

Conventional as well as unconventional behavior can be seen in the way both lovers take the initiative in love. The man's role as suitor is what we would expect in this culture. Three times he comes courting, petitioning the woman either to come to him (2:8–17; 4:6–8) or to admit him to her chamber (5:2), and on two of these occasions she is inside the house, where we might expect a woman to be, when he comes calling. Whereas he takes the initiative, the decision whether or not to join him outside or let him in is hers. She clearly desires him, and she can take the initiative too. Less conventional in terms of gender relations in ancient Israel as portrayed elsewhere in the Bible, though not unusual in love poetry, is the image of the woman going out in the streets to seek her lover (see under 5:2–6:3). On one of these occasions the initiative is hers (3:1–5); on the other, she acts in response to an encounter he sought to initiate (5:2–6). But her search for him has an air of unreality about it that leads some commentators to call it a dream (in contrast to the man's visits, which seem "natural"; see "Fantasy, Reality, and Poetic Imagination," pp. 45–47).

If the man seems at times to be an elusive lover (cf. also 1:7–8), perhaps it is because we see him from her point of view, going where he pleases, while she is more often associated with a domestic setting (but cf. 4:8). Her anxiety about seeking him and not being able to find him might be attributed to the fact that traditionally the discourse of absence is carried on by women, who wait at home while men venture out into the world.[8] We are not told where she is when she invites her lover to the vineyards for lovemaking in 7:11–13. Her fondest wish is to get the man inside, to seize him and bring him to her mother's house, the woman's domain. She does this in 3:1–5 (for discussion of these verses against the background of courtship and an envisioned outcome in marriage, see the Commentary under 3:6–11). In 8:2 she also speaks of bringing her lover to her mother's house and goes on to describe love in patently erotic terms as something she will give and he (by implication) will take: "I'll have you drink spiced wine, the nectar of my pomegranate."

Conventional roles for men and women respectively seem to inform the picture of love as something she gives and he takes. The woman is a garden whose fruits are ripe for the plucking and a vineyard to be tended. She invites her lover to come to his garden, an image in which she assumes the role of recipient, waiting for his visit. He comes to his garden and takes what is offered. Entering the garden, gathering, eating, and drinking its produce symbolize male sexual activity (as does tending the vineyard, 8:11–12, or spoiling vineyards in 2:15). He is poised to take what he desires in 7:7–8, where he likens her to a date palm he will climb and her breasts to clusters he will lay hold of. But he takes what he desires only by invitation. Just as the decision whether or not to respond to his overtures in 2:8–17 and 5:2–6 is hers, so too is the decision whether or not and when to offer her love: "Let my lover come to his garden and eat its choice fruits!" (4:16). In 7:11–13 she invites him to lovemaking in words reminiscent of those he used in 2:10–13: "Come, my love, let's go out to the open field. . . . Let's go early to the vineyards. . . . There I will give you my love." Here, too, even when the initiative is hers, love is pictured as something she gives and he takes.

---

8. See Barthes, *A Lover's Discourse: Fragments*, 13–14, who also suggests that a man who discourses upon absence is feminized. Cf., regarding 8:7, Landy's observation that a man is shamed only if he surrenders himself to love (1983: 226).

Some interpreters see the application of conventional male imagery of warfare and architecture to the woman as a sign of the woman's power. The question is, what kind of power? Meyers (1986; 1988: 177–81) takes the imagery as evidence that women exercised power in the domestic sphere in ancient Israel. It is hard to see how the Song can be used to support such a claim. Landy rightly perceives that the power the woman has in the Song is erotic (1983: 74–78, 87). It is the kind of power the Bible conventionally ascribes to women, though outside the Song it is usually viewed with suspicion, as power that makes men lose their heads and thus leads to their undoing[9] (no wonder the male lover of the Song is a bit anxious). It is the irresistible attraction of sex, and the Song celebrates it.

5. Poetic Composition and Style

The most important aspects of composition, the Song's controlling poetic strategies, are discussed above, and, as that discussion also reveals, this commentary approaches the Song as a single poem. But the view of the Song as an artistic whole is not shared by all commentators, and the issue of the Song's unity, whether compositional or redactional, as well as other features of the Song's literary style and artistry merit attention at this point.

Text and Translation

The Hebrew text (MT) as it has been transmitted presents no major problems and is generally supported by the ancient versions and the few fragments of the Song from Qumran. Places where emendation of MT seems to be in order are discussed in the notes to the Translation and the Commentary. Song 6:12 is hopelessly corrupt, and 7:9 [10 H] has also suffered some damage in the process of transmission. Neither of these verses is contained in the fragments from Qumran, and the difficulties of MT are already reflected in the translations of the versions.

The manuscripts of the Song found at Qumran are only partially preserved and consist of the following fragments: Song 3:4–5; 3:7–4:6; 4:7; 6:11?–7:7 (4QCant[a]);[10] 2:9–3:2; 3:5, 9–4:1a; 4:1b–3, 8–11a; 4:14–5:1 (4QCant[b]); 3:7–8 (4QCant[c]); and 1:1–7 (6QCant). The manuscripts from Cave 4 are dated to the first century BCE and the manuscript from Cave 6 to the mid-first century CE. These texts display minor differences from MT, mainly orthographic. An interesting difference is that 4QCant[a] reverses the order of image and referent in the

9. See, e.g., J. Cheryl Exum, *Fragmented Women: Feminist (Sub)versions of Biblical Narratives* (Valley Forge, PA: Trinity Press International, 1993), 61–93, 170–201.

10. As mentioned above, 6:12 is not attested. For 6:11–12, only one word *prḥ(h?)*, "budded," and possibly three letters of another word, "chariot," are preserved.

metaphoric descriptions of Song 4:1–2. 4QCant[b] contains a number of scribal errors and shows Aramaic influence, and 4QCant[c] is only a tiny fragment. Based on the reconstruction, there are omissions of segments of the text in 4QCant[a] and 4QCant[b] that lead Tov, the editor of these texts, to describe them as abbreviated texts. Where the two overlap, however, they are shorter at different points: part of the section lacking in 4QCant[a] is witnessed in 4QCant[b] (viz., 4:8–11a and 4:14–5:1), and QCant[a] contains 3:7–8 and 4:4–7, omitted in 4QCant[b]. Either, as Tov proposes, sections of the text were deliberately left out (why, one can only speculate) or the Qumran fragments represent a different textual tradition from that represented in MT and the versions. For detailed discussion, see Tov, DJD XVI: 195–219 on 4QCant, and Baillet, DJD III: 112–14 on 6QCant. For a survey of the characteristics of the ancient versions and their relation to MT, see Murphy.

Although the text itself is sound, the Song is notoriously difficult to translate. *Hapax legomena*, words that appear only once in the Bible, account for 9.2 percent of its vocabulary, and 11.3 percent of its vocabulary is unique to the Song (as compared to 11.1 percent and 13.3 percent in Job, also known for its difficult vocabulary). Many rare and obscure terms, whose meaning is all too often uncertain, occur as well. The poetry is sonorous, but it is difficult, and often impossible, to reproduce sound patterns, wordplay, and other poetic devices in translation. Even word order, which can be quite significant, does not translate well; where it is especially important for appreciating the force of a passage, I have tried to show it (e.g., in 3:3, "My soul's beloved—have you seen him?"). The translation I offer seeks to be fairly literal without being wooden. Fortunately the Song's guiding poetic strategies—the means by which the poet shows us, as well as tells us, that love is strong as death—belong to the translatable structure. And the luxurious, sensual imagery, with its appeal to all the senses, comes across well in translation.

For the most part, it is not difficult to determine who is speaking in the poem. Whether the speaker is the man or the woman is usually immediately apparent in the Hebrew text, because Hebrew uses different forms for masculine and feminine nouns, adjectives, verbs, pronouns, and pronominal suffixes. Epithets (she calls him "my lover" and "my soul's beloved"; he calls her "my friend, my fair one," "my sister bride," "my dove, my perfect one") and the contents of the speeches also provide reliable indications of a speaker's identity. After much deliberation, I have chosen to identify speakers in the Translation by means of notations within brackets < >, as an aid to the reader. Although it could be argued that such notations disrupt the flow of the poem, identifying the speakers seemed, in the end, the best procedure, since the Hebrew text effectively does this by means of grammatical forms. The practice is witnessed in some early Septuagint manuscripts: Alexandrinus identifies the speakers and Sinaiticus has further dramatic notations.

A Masterpiece of Pure Poetry

A masterpiece of pure poetry—*un chef-d'œuvre de poésie pure*—is what Denis Buzy calls the Song of Songs, proposing that words used in the Song are chosen for their musical quality and suggestiveness (1940). Goethe, in the notes to his *West-Östlicher Divan*, famously praised it as "the most tender and inimitable expression of passionate yet graceful love that has come down to us."[11] In its opening lines we encounter some of the most exquisite verses in all of Hebrew poetry. I reproduce them here in the Hebrew, in a transliteration that aims to illustrate sound patterns more clearly than the scientific transliteration, and, finally, in English translation.

יִשָּׁקֵנִי מִנְּשִׁיקוֹת פִּיהוּ   כִּי מוֹבִים דֹּדֶיךָ מִיַּיִן
לְרֵיחַ שְׁמָנֶיךָ מוֹבִים   שֶׁמֶן תּוּרַק שְׁמֶךָ
עַל כֵּן עֲלָמוֹת אֲהֵבוּךָ
מָשְׁכֵנִי אַחֲרֶיךָ נָרוּצָה   הֱבִיאַנִי הַמֶּלֶךְ חֲדָרָיו
נָגִילָה וְנִשְׂמְחָה בָּךְ נַזְכִּירָה דֹדֶיךָ מִיַּיִן
מֵישָׁרִים אֲהֵבוּךָ

1:2 yish-sha-ké-ni min-ne-shi-qót pí-hu
     ki to-vím do-dé-ka miy-yá-yin
1:3 le-ré-ah she-ma-né-ka to-vím
     shé-men tu-ráq she-mé-ka
     al-kén a-la-mót a-he-vú-ka
1:4 ma-she-ké-ni a-ha-ré-ka na-rú-tsa
     he-bi-á-ni ha-mé-lek ha-da-ráv
     na-gí-la ve-nis-me-há bák
     naz-kí-rah do-dé-ka miy-yá-yin
     me-sha-rím a-he-vú-ka

1:2 Let him kiss me with the kisses of his mouth
     for better (*ṭôbîm*) are your caresses than wine!
1:3 The fragrance of your perfumes is good (*ṭôbîm*),
     perfume poured out is your name,
     for this women love you.
1:4 Draw me after you; let us run!
     The king has brought me to his chambers,
     we will rejoice and delight in you,
     we will savor your caresses above wine;
     rightly they love you.

11. S. M Prem (ed.), *Goethes ausgewählte Werke in sechzehn Bänden*, vol. 3 (Leipzig: Max Hesses Verlag, [1895]), 111.

"Let him kiss me with the kisses of his mouth." Ten words in English are needed to render only three in Hebrew (*yiššāqēnî minnĕšîqôt pîhû*). The first two Hebrew words are forms of the word "kiss," and the third and final word of the stich is *pîhû*, the mouth, the source of the longed-for kisses. In vv. 2–3, alliter-ation of sibilant *sh*-sounds (*yiššāqēnî, minnĕšîqôt, šĕmānêkā, šemen, šĕmekā*), punctuated with plosives *p, t,* and *d* (*pîhû, ṭôbîm, dōdêkā, ṭûraq*), prevails up to the final stich, where the alliteration of a-sounds in *ʿal-kēn ʿălāmôt ʾăhēbûkā* brings us to the caesura. *Ṭôbîm,* used of the lover's embraces in v. 2, is taken up in v. 3 to describe the fragrance of his perfumes (*šĕmānêkā*). The form is the same in the Hebrew (*ṭôbîm*), though it is used as a comparative the first time ("better") and as a positive ("good") in verse 3. "Perfume" (*šemen*) is repeated in the second stich of v. 3 in paronomasia with *šĕmekā,* "your name." Twice (vv. 2 and 4) the lover's caresses are compared to wine (*dōdêkā miyyāyin*), and twice (at the end of vv. 3 and 4) the woman tells him that all women love him (*ʾăhēbûkā*). Each time the love he inspires is emphasized through the position of *ʾăhēbûkā* (they love you) as the last word in an unparalleled stich. Sense and sound work together to produce an aesthetic effect that cannot be captured in translation.

Among the many poetic features that go into making the Song the beautiful poem it is, we may include assonance, alliteration, sound play (paronomasia), parataxis, enjambment, and ellipsis. Structuring devices, such as chiasmus, inclusio, and other complex patterns, contribute to the Song's symmetry and circularity (see "Love Forever in Progress: Repetition and Resistance to Clo-sure," pp. 11–13, and "Literary Arrangement and Its Significance," pp. 37–41). Such devices, some of which appear in these first two verses, contribute sub-stantially to the success of the Song as a poem. But they can be trying, if not boring, to read about. I deal with them in the Commentary when they seem rel-evant or significant, but not as a matter of course separate from interpretation of the poem. Readers who wish to know more about particular poetic devices can find them treated in greater detail elsewhere. Landy's poetic analysis of major sections of the Song in his 1983 study is exemplary. Grossberg offers a useful discussion of a range of poetic features, as does Sonnet (2002), who treats such features as repetition, intensification, focalization, and concretiza-tion, in addition to exploring the Song's figurative language. Metaphor receives an insightful treatment by Alter (1985). Murphy discusses poetic devices with an attentiveness to their literary quality that leads him to conclude: "[T]he mul-tifaceted rhetorical structures of the Song contribute in substantial measure to its aesthetic beauty as well as to a strong sense of its literary coherence" (1990: 85–91 [91]). Mariaselvam offers a catalogue of various literary features, includ-ing sound patterns and rhetorical and poetic devices (1988: 56–69). Krinetzki, in his 1964 commentary, gives detailed and perceptive attention to literary pat-terning, especially sound patterns (though it is questionable whether the latter carry the meaning he attributes to them). Attention to literary patterns, especially chiasmus and inclusio, can also be found in Bergant's commentary.

A distinguishing feature of Hebrew poetry that does come through in translation is couplet, and sometimes triplet, composition, often referred to as parallelism (couplets and triplets are indicated in the Translation by indentation). The effect is to set up an internal relationship within a couplet. A couplet typically has an A line and a B line (or an A, B, and C), where B will repeat, emphasize, extend, or modify A.[12] For example:

> A   His left hand is under my head,
> B   and his right hand caresses me.
>
> (2:6; 8:3)

Here B balances and completes the thought of A.

> A   Sixty queens there are,
> B   and eighty concubines,
> C   and countless women—
> A   unique is she, my dove, my perfect one,
> B   unique is she to her mother,
> C   splendid is she to her who bore her.
>
> (6:8–9)

Here two triplets nicely balance and extend each other. Murphy, in his discussion of prosody, offers further examples of this phenomenon, which he calls "basic units of stichometry" or "patterned lineation of segmentation" (1990: 86–91).

But what about the opening lines considered above?

> A   Let him kiss me with the kisses of his mouth
> B   for better are your caresses than wine;
> A   the fragrance of your perfumes is good;
> B   perfume poured out is your name;
> C   for this women love you.

In a typical couplet (if there is such a thing), I would expect A to be matched in B somewhat like this:

---

12. Terminology for describing lines or couplets or units of poetry differs widely, and my brief discussion greatly simplifies the question of the nature of balance, or couplet composition, or parallelism in Hebrew poetry. The subject has been much discussed; see especially, David J. A. Clines, "The Parallelism of Greater Precision: Notes from Isaiah 40 for a Theory of Hebrew Poetry," in *New Directions in Hebrew Poetry*, ed. Elaine R. Follis (Sheffield: JSOT Press, 1987), 77–100; James L. Kugel, *The Idea of Biblical Poetry: Parallelism and Its History* (New Haven: Yale University Press, 1981); Adele Berlin, *The Dynamics of Biblical Parallelism* (Bloomington: Indiana University Press, 1985); W. G. E. Watson, *Traditional Techniques in Classical Hebrew Verse* (Sheffield: Sheffield Academic Press, 1994).

A   Let him kiss me with the kisses of his mouth,
B   let him caress me with the caresses of his hands.

But B in Song 1:2 goes in a different direction altogether. And the next couplet complements the previous one with a new development; here too, though "perfume" is repeated in line B, B extends A rather than repeating or modifying it. And C develops the idea further in another new direction. It is interesting to note how rarely the Song appears in the standard discussions of Hebrew poetry. I suspect the reason may be that the poetry of the Song is more lyrical, less regular or neatly balanced than any other part of the Hebrew Bible (except perhaps Deutero-Isaiah). Couplets and triplets in the Song seem to rush forward, spilling over each other, as though impelled by the desire they communicate. This is not unrelated to the subject matter. The poetry seems impatient, like desirous lovers, and full of erotic energy.

One Poem or Many?

Whether the Song is a collection of love lyrics or a unified work is a vexed issue about which biblical scholars are not likely to reach a consensus. Those who see it as an anthology or collection draw attention to the abrupt shifts of scene, speaker, subject matter (e.g., songs of admiration, songs of longing, banter, descriptions of experience),[13] and sometimes of mood, and the lack of any apparent structural organization or narrative development (i.e., the absence of progression or plot). The many similarities of theme and imagery and the repetitions among various parts of the Song are explained as conventional language characteristic of the genre of love poetry, and the refrains (adjuration, mutual possession, etc.) are typically treated as the result of editorial intervention, linking the various poems by supplementing one with lines taken from another. Doublets could be the result of smaller collections of love poems having been combined. Among scholars who approach the Song as a collection, there is no agreement about the number and extent of the individual poems that comprise it (e.g., Longman has 23, Gordis 29, Rudolph, Würthwein, and Loretz 30, Falk 31, Zakovitch 31 [some of which are only fragments], Gerleman 34, Müller 39, Keel 42). This lack of consensus is often used to criticize their position.

Those who see the Song as a unified work, on the other hand, point out that there are no superscriptions within the Song or other indications of composite status, as we have, for example, in the Psalms. They view the repetitions and

13. These and other form critical categories are treated at length in Roland Murphy, *Wisdom Literature: Job, Proverbs, Ruth, Canticles, Ecclesiastes, and Esther*, FOTL 13 (Grand Rapids: Eerdmans, 1981) and more briefly in his commentary. In spite of claims made for its importance, form criticism has done little to shed light on the composition of the Song, or its *Sitz im Leben*, or its meaning.

similarities among parts of the Song as an indication of thematic and literary unity. Too many correspondences appear, with verbal and thematic echoes and repetitions appearing too regularly among all the parts of the book, to be serendipities or a matter of convention. What constitutes the sort of difference in subject matter or mood that would mark off a unit as an individual poem is a matter of opinion; thematic shifts are not in themselves evidence of disunity. Moreover, the springtime setting is the same throughout (Fox 217; Elliott 1989: 237). Since there are only three clearly identifiable speaking voices in the Song (a man's, a woman's, and a group of women called "daughters of Jerusalem"), there is no reason to posit other speakers. The Song offers no clue that the male and female speaking voices belong to different men and women—indeed, some view the consistency of character portrayal as a sign of unity (e.g., Murphy 80–85; Fox 217; Elliott 1989: 252–53). Equally, it is difficult to imagine distinct sets of women called "daughters of Jerusalem" acting as a chorus in unrelated love songs. Nor should one expect a lyric poem to conform to the conventions of narrative and offer a clearly developed plot.

Some scholars who advocate unity have argued that a conscious artistic design can be discerned in the Song (e.g., Broadribb 1961–62, Exum 1973, Shea 1980, Webster 1982, Elliott 1989, Dorsey 1990, Deckers 1993, Wendland 1995, Davidson 2003, Garrett).[14] No agreement exists among them, however, as to how it is arranged, or the number, extent, and relation of the parts that comprise it, and this lack of consensus is often used to criticize the position that the Song is a unity. The questions of the Song's unity and its structure are different, though related. A structure may be more or less intricate and more or less formal, and may even be created from originally unrelated poems because of similarity of theme, key words, and other common features. Unity is created by an artistic vision—in this case, a distinct and consistent attitude toward love—and by continuity of character portrayal, which leads us to posit the same protagonists throughout and see everything that happens in the poem as happening to them. In a unified literary creation, the meaning of the whole is more than the sum of its parts. Some scholars therefore affirm the unity of the Song without proposing a detailed structural or schematic design (e.g., Murphy, Fox), and I include myself among this group.

The question of unity is often confused with unity of authorship, but they are not the same thing. An author might create a more or less unified work. A compiler or redactor could give unity to a collection of love songs. Unless one concludes that the editing is haphazard (Pope 54, cf. 41) or extremely loose (e.g., simply connecting poems on the basis of catchwords; so Rudolph 97–100; Keel 17), one may recognize either some general principles of arrangement that

---

14. The attempt by Angénieux (1965, 1966, 1968) to find a structure in the Song relies upon a rearrangement of the text that distorts the Song almost beyond recognition.

lend coherence to the Song or a plan so thoroughgoing that the editor or redactor deserves to be deemed the "author" of the final product (Fox 220). If the Song exhibits cohesiveness, homogeneity, consistency of character portrayal, and a distinctive vision of love—and I believe it does—is there any need to posit an editor at all? Perhaps the Song was composed by a single author, working within a poetic tradition, and was only lightly edited in the process of its transmission. If the Song is an anthology of love poems, one might reasonably expect it to feature different protagonists and exhibit different attitudes toward love, sex, and the body. But this is by no means apparent. If it is a loose or haphazard collection, why are there no songs about unrequited love, or laments over love lost or unattainable, or a song of a jealous lover who has a rival, or a complaint that the loved one is unfaithful, such as one finds among the Egyptian and Mesopotamian love poems?

Excellent discussions of the issue of unity versus disunity, leading to a decision in favor of unity, are offered by Murphy (62–91) and Fox (202–26). Murphy finds "at least a contrived unity" in the dialogue arrangement of the Song, and draws attention to a number of features that strengthen the impression of unity, such as coherence of literary style and language, the presence of formulae and literary topoi, consistency of character portrayal, and a characteristic perspective on human love (67). Because of this "overall coherence," Murphy leans toward the idea of "common authorship of most if not all of the major units" (85).[15]

Fox makes a particularly strong case for the unity of the Song. Not only does he point out the weaknesses in the various arguments for disunity, he also challenges the assumption that the lack of a comprehensive design proves a book to be an anthology. "If there are other unifying factors," he writes, "a poet can create a single, cohesive poem without organizing its parts in sequential, hierarchical, or symmetrical designs" (205). Because the Song has come to us as a unity, he contends, the burden of proof rests with those who assert disunity. Using the Egyptian love poems as an analogy, Fox proposes five criteria that one might use to argue that the Song is a loose anthology that has undergone only superficial editing (205; the references are to his translations of the Egyptian love poems):

1. Lack of systematic structure or sequential development, when this lack is conjoined with consistent variations in style.
2. Protagonists who cannot be identified with one another as one person. The boy in the [*sic*] "The Crossing," for example, who achieves

---

15. He has problems with 3:6–11 and 8:6–14, which he considers problematic in their context (62 n. 277 *et passim*). Of 8:5–14 he says, "These verses exhibit little coherence and lend support to the claim that the Song is simply a collection of disparate love poems" (66).

his desire, is different from the boy in "Seven Wishes," who only yearns for his beloved. (The two poems can be separated on this basis even though they are probably by the same author.)

3. Contradictions in facts or events. A boy sailing to Memphis (no. 5) and a girl sailing to Heliopolis (no. 8), for example, will not meet each other in the same song.

4. Doublets that differ in style, especially when there are a number of doublets that, when separated, can be grouped into internally consistent series. (This criterion was significant in the separation of the Pentateuchal sources because the duplicated stories there are cast in distinctly different styles.)

5. Two or more blocks of material in sequence, each with its distinctive content and form, and with no cross-references among the blocks (e.g., groups A and B of Harris 500).

Most, if not all of these criteria would need to be met to make a strong case for disunity, but Fox doubts, and I concur, that any one of them could be effectively applied to the Song. In fact, he notes, the Song possesses a degree of homogeneity and consistency of character portrayal unmatched by either the Egyptian or the Mesopotamian love poems (where, for example, the central characters Inanna and Dumuzi are portrayed differently in different poems). He concludes that "[t]he most likely explanation of these qualities [the Song's cohesiveness and stylistic homogeneity] is that the Song is a single poem composed, originally at least, by a single poet. The poet may have used earlier materials, and later singers and scribes may have made changes of their own, but the result is a unified text" (220).

Where does this leave us as far as interpretation of the Song is concerned? The important issue is what the implications for interpretation are of unity (either compositional or redactional) or disunity. A persuasive interpretation of the Song as a collection of unrelated poems ought to foreground differences and aim to show the distinctiveness of the various poems that makes it difficult to accommodate them into a coherent whole. But commentators who describe the Song as a collection generally do not do this. They tend, rather, to speak of "the man" and "the woman" throughout, without distinguishing among the lovers portrayed in the miscellaneous poems, and when they discuss the attitude toward love, it seems to be the same in all the parts. An important exception is Keel, who, because of his systematic attention to difference, offers what is in my opinion the strongest case for reading the Song as a collection of discrete poems.

In contrast to what one might wish for in a reading of the Song as a collection, an interpretation of the Song as a unity should, ideally, draw out the relationships among the parts, showing how the parts fit together and serve to expound the poet's vision of love. Fox's commentary, with its attention to dramatic modes of presentation, major themes, and aspects of the poet's vision of love, offers an excellent example of this type of approach.

My intention when I began writing the present commentary was to interpret the Song both as a unity and as a collection of disparate poems, in what I hoped would be a creative tension.[16] I began by asking how each (sub)unit could be interpreted on its own, as an independent poem, and also as part of a unified literary work. The further I got into the book, however, the more difficult it became to isolate independent units, on the one hand, and, on the other, to find genuine difference or distinctiveness among the smaller units. There were only two places where this approach seemed to work (1:2–4 and 3:6–11). I therefore abandoned, fairly early on, the attempt to read the parts as discrete poems. Whether commentators see the whole or only the parts when they read the Song may be largely a matter of temperament; for my part, I have become increasingly convinced that an inspired poetic vision of love has guided the composition of the Song. The present commentary assumes that only by reading it as a whole can we do justice to its poetic accomplishment.

Literary Arrangement and Its Significance

We might ask why, if the Song is an artistic unity, scholars cannot agree on the precise shape it takes. Among those who argue for a particular formal design, the lack of agreement on detail may well be due, as Francis Landy astutely observes, to the fact that, far from being structureless, the Song offers a superabundance of structural clues.[17] One problem encountered by formalistic approaches that seek evidence of a conscious poetic design in the strategic repetitions of key words, motifs, and in other formal patterns, such as chiasmus and inclusio, is that there are too many structural features one could isolate and find meaningful. Relying on different formal features and correspondences to isolate different poetic building blocks, different interpreters perceive different structural patterns.

The extremely complex patterning posited by most structural analyses exposes another limitation of the formalistic approach: it fails to take adequately into account what differences the elaborate patterns and microstructures make to the reading process. Do real readers perceive the formal intricacies—

---

16. J. Cheryl Exum, "Developing Strategies of Feminist Criticism/Developing Strategies for Commentating the Song of Songs," in *Auguries: The Jubilee Volume of the Sheffield Department of Biblical Studies*, ed. D. J. A. Clines and S. D. Moore, JSOTSup 269 (Sheffield: Sheffield Academic Press, 1998), 230: "In the commentary I am writing, I intend to argue for the validity of both views of the Song—a collection and a unity—as against the necessity of choosing one, and to follow both interpretive paths, since both are well established."

17. Francis Landy, Review of M. Timothea Elliott, *The Literary Unity of the Canticle*, Bib 72 (1991): 571.

the chiasms, inclusios, and other structural devices—that some scholars find in the Song? Perhaps, on a subliminal level, the way we perceive the structural intricacies of a musical composition, even if we cannot read the score. What readers will recognize, however, is the presence of repetition within and among larger and smaller units, and the sense of balance it produces.

Some patterns stand out more than others. For instance, narrative development gives the woman's stories a unity. A description that starts at the head comes to an end at some point lower down the body. Thus there is some agreement on the general contours of the Song. Commentators, whether they think the Song is a unity or collection, typically treat Song 5:2–6:3 as a unit, and the coherence of 2:8–17, 3:1–5, and 3:6–11 is widely recognized. The latter part of the Song poses the most difficulties, with the result that the arrangement of material after 6:4 is the subject of the greatest disagreement. When one takes into account the possibility of dividing or combining some of the subunits, the following sample of schemes shows overlap at a number of points or differences only in the placement of a single verse (references to ch. 7 are to the English versification); see the table on the facing page. It is interesting to note that Bergant, though she accepts the view that the Song is a collection, divides it into six poetic units identical to those of Elliott, who argues for its structural unity. This is similar to the arrangement followed by Robert, Krinetzki, Carr, Dorsey, Murphy, and Wendland, and to the one I adopt in this commentary.

My division of the Song into parts in this commentary is a practical division based on sense and sometimes (as in 5:2–6:3) structural clues. Where one unit ends and another begins is not particularly important, since the lovers speak antiphonally throughout the Song, always responding to each other, with urgent invitations to love and desire eager for satisfaction. What matters is how one sees the relation of the parts to each other. I see no problem, for example, in saying that 2:8–17, 3:1–5, and 3:6–11 are all parts of a long speech by the woman. Clearly they are different: the mood changes, the scene changes, and in the case of 3:6–11 the topic seems to be a new one. But there is no reason why such shifts cannot take place within the same speech, for this is a poem, not a description of actual events happening at different places and at different times.

Although I would not argue for any particular structural organization for the Song, I do discern a pattern in the overall arrangement of the parts. Since dialogue is what determines the poetic development of the Song, I read a speech as continuing until there is good evidence to see it as coming to a close and something new beginning. Thus I view the Song as composed of two cycles of long speeches, in which the woman speaks first and then the man. These are framed by sections in which the voices of the woman, the man, and, occasionally, the

Robert (1963)
1:2–4
1:5–2:7
2:8–3:5
3:6–5:1
5:2–6:3
6:4–8:5a
8:5b-7
8:8–14

Krinetzki (1964)
1:2–2:7
2:8–3:5
3:6–5:1
5:2–6:3
6:4–12
6:13–8:4
8:5–14

Exum (1973)
1:2–2:6
2:7–3:5
3:6–5:1
5:2–6:3
6:4–8:3
8:4–14

Shea (1980)
1:2–2:2
2:3–17
3:1–4:16
5:1–7:9
7:10–8:5
8:6–14

Webster (1982)
a five-section chiasmus,
with 2 units in each
except the central one
1:2–2:6 and 2:7–3:5
3:6–11 (interlude)
4:1–7 and 4:8–15
4:16–6:3
6:4–10 and 6:11–7:9
7:10–8:3 and 8:4–14

G. L. Carr (1984)
1:2–2:7
2:8–3:5
3:6–5:1
5:2–8:4
8:5–14

Elliott (1989)
1:2–2:7
2:8–3:5
3:6–5:1
5:2–6:3
6:4–8:4
8:5–14

Dorsey (1990)
1:2–2:7
2:8–17
3:1–5
3:6–5:1
5:2–7:10
7:11–8:4
8:5–14

Murphy (1990)
1:2–6
1:7–2:7
2:8–17
3:1–5
3:6–11
4:1–5:1
5:2–6:3
6:4–12
6:13–8:4
8:5–14

Wendland (1995)
1:2–2:7
2:8–17
3:1–5
3:6–5:1
5:2–6:3
6:4–7:10
7:11–8:4
8:5–14

Bergant (2001)
1:2–2:7
2:8–3:5
3:6–5:1
5:2–6:3
6:4–8:4
8:5–14

Davidson (2003)
12 macrounits in a
14-member pattern
1:2–2:7
2:8–17
3:1–5
3:6–11
4:1–7
4:8–15
4:16
5:1
5:2–8
5:9–6:3
6:4–12
6:13–7:9
7:10–8:2
8:3–14

Table Showing Units into Which the Song Is Divided by Various Commentators

women of Jerusalem intermingle; speakers change frequently; and their speeches are short. The woman has her first long speech in 2:8–3:5. Since she is, in my opinion, the speaker of 3:6–11, we could see her speech as encompassing all of 2:8–3:11. A long speech by the man follows in 4:1–5:1. Then the woman has a second long speech (5:2–6:3), followed by the man's second long speech (6:4–7:9 [10 H]). I use the term "long speech" loosely, for speech in these sections is never exclusively that of the woman or the man. Nevertheless, when other voices do make themselves heard—be it the women of Jerusalem or the voice of the loved one—they are integrated into the poetic fabric of the lovers' long speeches in a way that the voices at the beginning and end of the Song are not integrated.

Since Song 7:10–13 [11–14 H] is the woman's invitation to lovemaking in response to the man's passionate exclamation of desire in the preceding verses, these verses are intimately connected to his speech in 6:4–7:9, and are best seen as completing the second cycle of speeches. The situation is similar to that in 4:16, where her invitation to lovemaking is incorporated into his first long speech. One might, however, choose to read 7:10–13 separately or with the verses that follow (see the Commentary), for the Song now begins to return to the format with which it commenced, with speeches that are shorter, less intricate, and loosely connected. In 1:2–2:7 and 8:1–14, surrounding the long speeches of the lovers, we find a kind of montage, with alternating voices highlighting various aspects of love.

The balance of speech between the woman and the man—two long speeches each—affirms their mutuality. When, in the course of the lovers' long speeches, other voices are heard (5:1ef, 9; 6:1, 11–12 [?]; 6:13 [7:1 H]), they constitute only brief interludes in the speech in question (and sometimes we cannot be sure to whom these voices belong). Significantly, the long speeches of each of the lovers open up to include the voice of the other, a feature that further underscores the lovers' mutuality. The man speaks in both of the woman's long speeches when she quotes him; that is, when she, as narrator of stories in which he comes courting, puts words in his mouth (2:10–14; 5:2). At the end of each of the man's long speeches, where they reach an erotic crescendo, the woman breaks in to invite him to lovemaking (4:16 and 7:10–13). It is as if she is so excited by his fervor that she cannot wait any longer to tell him that her desire matches his.

The long speeches of the lovers show a remarkable degree of consistency, along with differences that make them more intricate and interesting. In each of her speeches, the woman tells a story in which her lover comes to woo her, and then goes on to recount her experience of seeking and finding him. Her success in finding him is more drawn out the second time: she suffers a serious setback when the city watchmen, whom she also encountered on her first search, mistreat her, but, undeterred, she engages in a dialogue with the women of Jerusalem by means of which she "finds" her lover by praising his charms until she has successfully conjured him up. The most striking difference in her second speech is that she adopts the man's characteristic mode of speaking about love and describes his body metaphorically.

Whether or not one includes 3:6–11 as part of the woman's first long speech is, as indicated above, less important than how these verses relate to that speech. Since nothing like 3:6–11 occurs in the woman's second speech, perhaps these verses should be accorded separate status. On the other hand, since the speaker has not changed since 2:8, all of 2:8–3:11 could be read as a continuous speech by the woman, in which she begins with a "story" of courtship and ends with a description of marriage (see the Commentary under 3:6–11).

The man's first long speech contains two metaphoric descriptions of his lover's body: first he uses a striking simile or metaphor for each body part described, followed by an intimate extended metaphor of her body as a pleasure garden of exotic plants and abundant waters. Nothing like this elaborate pleasure-garden metaphor occurs in his second speech. Rather, in his second long speech, he praises her physical charms in detail, not once but twice (6:4–10 and 7:1–9 [2–10 H]). Here, as in his first speech, the second description is more intimate. In between these two metaphoric descriptions, there appears a short, rather cryptic first-person narrative about a visit to the nut garden (6:11–12). The identity of the speaker here is open to question (it may be the man but more likely is the woman), and part or all of 7:1 belongs to a voice, or voices, other than the man's. Because these verses are only a brief interlude before the man resumes his praise of the woman, I take the entire section 6:4–7:9 as the man's second long speech.

Each of the man's long speeches leads to an invitation to lovemaking issued by the woman and to the promise of consummation to which the poem is always striving. In 5:1, at her invitation, he enters the garden of eroticism. In 7:8 he expresses his intention to climb the palm tree, to which he has likened her, and take hold of its branches. Here too his speech—in which he hungers for breasts like vine clusters, apple-scented breath, and kisses like wine—gives rise to her invitation to lovemaking in the vineyards (7:10–13 [11–14 H]).

There is no need for another, third cycle of long speeches in which the woman speaks and then the man, for what would it be but yet another variation on their previous speeches? (As an analogy we might consider whether or not a fourth cycle of speeches between Job and his friends would be meaningful.) Instead the poem draws to an end, but without a sense of closure. We hear the climactic affirmation that love is strong as death (8:6–7) at a point in the Song where the speeches of the lovers are growing shorter, as at the beginning. But it is not the final word about love because, I suspect, if it appeared at the end of the Song, it might seem too much like closure.

Lyric Poetry and Reading for the Plot

The Song is a poetic text of great lyrical power and beauty. When we read lyric poetry, which is essentially a discontinuous form, we revel in words and images, and we normally do not expect the kind of linear unfolding of events that produces a plot. Indeed, sudden shifts of speaker and topic and the fact that the Song repeats both longer and shorter poetic units, ever returning to the same themes and images, argue against a clearly developed plot. But in tension with our perception that the Song unfolds repetitively and not linearly is the powerful readerly tendency to read sequentially and to make sense of a literary work as a whole; in other words, to read for the plot.[18] When we read a biblical book like the Song, we typically start at the beginning and read through to the end. We are unlikely to say to ourselves, "I am reading fragments with no connections"; rather we naturalize events in such a way as to fit them into our understanding of the way the world works, either the real world or the fictional world of the text.[19] We create connections as we read, revising them, abandoning them and adopting others when necessary. When we imagine that the protagonists are the same two people throughout the Song and, consequently, relate the various experiences described therein to them, we have begun to create a "story" for them. We may discover a plot of sorts, revolving around their delight in each other and their efforts to overcome the obstacles that keep them apart. We can even let the Song's abrupt transitions and sudden shifts of scene, its inchoate stories and hints of drama, tease and tantalize us to find connections where they are lacking. What reader, for example, does not want to know more about the anger of the woman's brothers (1:6)? Yet we never learn anything about it. Black sees this, the Song's flirtation with a plot, as one of its amatory techniques by which it seeks to engage its readers (1999b; 2000a: 321).

The persistence of the dramatic theory of interpretation of the Song in various forms bears witness to readers' desire to find a plot, though dramatic theories falter on this very issue of plot, which they inevitably must provide from outside the textual world (see "The Dramatic Theory," pp. 78–79). Full-scale dramatic interpretations represent the extreme position of reading for a plot. Most readers make connections between the parts of the poem simply by reading for coherence and correlation and by naturalizing events in order to make them intelligible.

One can observe a tendency among recent commentators to find progression or a loose narrative development in the Song, while recognizing that the movement of the Song is not particularly progressive or linear. Bergant finds "a kind

18. See Peter Brooks, *Reading for the Plot: Design and Intention in Narrative* (New York: Random House, 1984).
19. See Jonathan Culler, *Structuralist Poetics: Structuralism, Linguistics, and the Study of Literature* (Ithaca, NY: Cornell University Press, 1975), 146 *et passim*.

of coherent plot of longing, searching, finding, losing, longing, etc." and "consistency in the characters' behavior" (xv) among poems in a collection. Longman, who views the Song as an anthology of twenty-three poems with no "overarching narrative or plot" (15), nevertheless finds "progression" in the Song (56) and remarks that consistency of character portrayal and repetition of scenes and refrains gives it a certain unity (15–17, 55–56). Weems also describes the Song as an anthology of love lyrics (366, 371) but maintains that it "chronicles one woman's journey to find fulfilling love" (371) and interprets the text in terms of a narrative dynamic:

> [T]he lyrics of Song of Songs record the personal predicament of a certain black-skinned maiden—her struggles to love and be loved by a man for whom she has been deemed, for reasons not exactly clear to modern readers, an unsuitable mate. Readers are asked to understand the innocence of their love, to recognize the purity of their longing, and to empathize with the absurdity of the obstacles and frustrations, both internal and external, they are forced to endure. (367)

Munro, who finds evidence of the Song's unity in its imagery and who well appreciates the circularity of the Song's "never-ceasing game of hide and seek," concludes that "even this circular movement tells a 'story,' for it is by means of this movement that the theme of longing and fulfillment, absence and presence, seeking and finding are explored and the depths of love laid bare" (146). More specifically, she finds a narrative or linear dynamic in some of the imagery of the Song, especially regal imagery:

> [T]he movement of this constellation of images tells the "story" of how the male lover, her "king," becomes captive to her beauty and how she rises to a position of quasi-queenship by virtue of his love. She, who in the opening verses of the Song is marginalized by the daughters of Jerusalem, is in 6.9 openly acclaimed by the entire female entourage of the king. . . . This remarkable shift in the use of the regal imagery is swiftly followed, however, by the rejection of the language of kingship; for if throughout the Song regal language is used to evoke the splendour of first one lover and then the other, in the closing verses it is asserted that love is not for sale, even to the most rich and powerful, that is, the king. If the wealth and splendour which accompany kingship are fitting metaphors for the lovers' splendour, they are also the foil against which love reveals its purity. (145)

On the basis of a detailed examination of correspondences between two episodes at the beginning of the Song (1:5–6 and 1:7–8) and two at the end (8:8–10 and 8:11–12), Landy, for whom the Song is bounded by an enormous symmetry (51), discerns a movement from absence of self to fullness of self, from the woman as unkept vineyard who keeps those of others to one whose vineyard is hers to give or withhold, from cast-out sister to cared-for sister (51, 142–76). Fox finds in these same sections, specifically in 1:5–6 and 8:6–12, a "loose narrative framework" within which the "basic love story repeats itself" (225–26). This framework "suggests a certain development in [the woman's] relations with her brothers," with the brothers in the end agreeing to give her in marriage in the face of her declaration of the power of love, though they still have doubts about her maturity (218).

Garrett, who argues that the Song is a collection of songs in "a single piece with a unified structure," "the work of a single poet" (26), speaks of a "quasi-story that stands behind the Song" (193). It tells of the marriage of the couple: she comes to the wedding in a marvelous palanquin (3:6–11) and the marriage is consummated in 4:16–5:1, the central point in the book according to Garrett's chiastic structure (32–35).

As these examples show, the readerly predilection to find development in the poem is strong. But tempting as it may be, we should be wary of looking for narrative progression in a lyric poem that meanders the way the Song does. It is true, for example, as Landy and Fox note, that the closing verses of the Song echo motifs from the opening verses. But, in my view, Landy reads too much into the connections, and Fox's interpretation is based on the assumption that Song 8:8–10 is a dialogue between the woman and her brothers, in which they challenge and she affirms her readiness for marriage. But nothing in the text indicates that the woman's brothers, mentioned only in 1:5–6, are the speakers in 8:8–9, and it is more likely that these verses belong to the woman, who tells an example story in 8:8–10 similar to the one the man tells in 8:11–12 (see, further, the Commentary under 8:8–12).

The only genuine narrative development in the Song takes place within the speeches of the woman, because only she tells stories about love (see "Different Ways of Speaking about Love," pp. 14–15). If, rather than making her a storyteller, the poet had given her only descriptive speeches like 5:10–16 and bits of dialogue such as we find in 1:2–7 and 7:10 [11 H]–8:14), would interpreters have looked so desperately for progression or plot development or read the Song as a drama?

There is, of course, poetic development. Meanings accumulate as themes, motifs, images, and key words are repeated across the space of the poem (see above, "Love Forever in Progress," pp. 11–13; cf. Munro 143–47). The disembodied voice with which the Song begins (1:2) is given a poetic, metaphorical body as the poem moves through time, the lovers materialize as individuals with distinctive ways of talking about love, and the climactic affirmation of love to which everything in the poem leads appears near the end,[20] followed by a kind

---

20. As Fox observes, "The statements of love's power and value are most appropriate to the end of the song, for they derive their force and credibility from the experiences of the speakers. At the start of the poem, they would sound grandiose, even somewhat hollow. Now they are a satisfying and convincing statement of truths the poem has demonstrated" (218).

of denouement culminating in the man's request to hear his lover's voice and her enigmatic reply ("Take flight, my love, and be like a gazelle or young deer upon the mountains of spices"). The last verse of the Song sends us back to the beginning, to the longing and seeking, the gratification and renewed desire that endlessly plays itself out. Perhaps readers simply cannot resist supplying the lovers with a "story," and the distinction between poetic development and plot development may be a fine one. But whatever narrative development we might perceive is secondary to the Song's principal dynamic, its circularity.

Fantasy, Reality, and Poetic Imagination

Desire is such stuff as dreams are made on. Lovers often indulge their fantasies in daydreams, and poets in flights of fancy. Fisch regards the whole Song as composed in the manner of a dream, with its free flow of images, though he also sees it as an "anti-dream" or "aborted dream poem . . . invaded by the sense of historical time" (1988: 98–100). Commentators typically speak of Song 3:1–5 and 5:2–7 as "dream sequences" (Fisch adds a third, 2:9–14 [88–89]), by which they apparently mean that the poet intends to represent a dream. Murphy observes that whether or not 3:1–5 and 5:2–7 are reports of dreams is not at all certain (146, 168), and of the latter says, "The woman is relating an episode, whatever the degree of the reality" (168). What is confusing here is the language of "dream" and "reality." Where in the text, one wonders, would the dream end and reality begin? (see, further, the Commentary under 5:2–7). Murphy here exemplifies a prevailing tendency among commentators to treat literary creations as if they were real people, and not personae created by the poet. The Song's lovers have no relationship, there is no episode, apart from what is on the page before us, or in the reader's consciousness.

Mariaselvam distinguishes between dreams (such as 5:2–7 and 3:1–4) and fantasies or extravagant imagination (as in the metaphoric bodily descriptions), on the one hand, and "down-to-earth realities" like 1:5–6, on the other (1988: 32–33). But he does not explain how one is to do this or why. The notion of reality when applied to a lyric poem like the Song is problematic. Reality is not the same thing as realism in literature, that is, fidelity to nature or real life. One could argue that the Song is too idealized to be realistic. The Song may be realistic in some ways: people live in houses, there are streets and squares and even watchmen who patrol them. But even here one could question the degree of realism, as Murphy, in fact, does when he criticizes what he calls historicizing the situation in 5:2–7 by those who ask practical questions like, would the man not have aroused the woman's family? How would they have responded to her opening the door? (170 n. 11). Even the idea that a woman would sleep in a room with a door to the street is unlikely (Krinetzki, Keel).

Often commentators seek to naturalize events in the Song, to make them seem less unusual, less fantastic, less imaginative. If they cannot explain a reference in terms of chronology, causality, coherence, and contiguity, or in terms of their knowledge of cultural and historical circumstances, then it must be the product of poetic imagination. Solomon's magnificent palanquin offers a good example of the search for some kind of reality behind the poetry. Krinetzki, who is sensitive to the poetic quality of the Song, says that the palanquin cannot in reality be as magnificently decorated as the text describes it (151). Similarly, Würthwein speaks of poetic exaggeration in the description of the palanquin and of its retinue. They are not heroes but only young men, who, through poetic exaggeration, are called "heroes" (49). But there is no palanquin apart from the one the text describes.

Even geography can pose a problem, as in the case of Song 4:6–8, where some commentators seem to have created a curious opposition: either there is a "reality" behind the text, and thus this verse refers to real mountains that need to be located, or we are in the unreal, make-believe world of love poetry. Rudolph, after striving to identify the precise locations of Amana, Senir, and Hermon, decides on the basis of geographical difficulties that 4:8 is figurative language (148). Similarly, Gerleman speaks of 4:6 as belonging to the realm of poetic unreality. Difficulty with the setting of parts of the Song also bothers Krinetzki, who cannot decide whether 7:12–13 refers to a real trip the lovers make to the countryside or is only an allegory for their entry into the paradise of love (227).

As noted above, literally minded commentators have difficulty with the unusual metaphoric descriptions of the body in the Song. The extent to which some commentators will go to naturalize poetic hyperbole can be seen in Rudolph's suggestion that the comparison of the woman's nose to the tower of Lebanon has too grotesque an effect if one thinks of it as an edifice on top of Mount Lebanon, and thus one should think of a rock formation or ridge overlooking Damascus that was called "Tower of Lebanon" (173).

The search for realism and clarity is a critical problem in the interpretation of the Song, one admittedly hard to avoid for commentators, whose job is to explicate. Rather than trying to tame the poem, why not take pleasure in its otherness, its imaginative flights of fancy, and its highly charged symbolism? In the Song, lovers praise, seek out, and enjoy each other, spending nights among the henna blossoms and endless hours in exotic pleasure gardens fit for a king. A luxurious palanquin armed against terrors of the night makes its way to a royal wedding. A lover is magically swept off his feet to find himself transported to remote, dangerous, and exotic mountaintops, while another lover recklessly runs through the streets at night in search of her beloved. Angry brothers take desperate, unusual measures, and city guards not only patrol the streets but go so far as to beat a woman simply for being out in the streets at night. How "real" are such things, and how much fueled by imagination? Lovers long to be in each other's company; they admire and desire each other's body, wishing for kisses, caresses, and sexual union. Lovers court. Lovers dally. Love makes them reckless, though they are aware of social expectations and social mores. The Song's is a magical world, but not unrealistic, and this makes it immanently accessible to readers who would identify with the lovers, since lovers know the world as real but magical as well (see "The Invitation to the Reader," pp. 7–8).

6. The Song of Songs and Its World

The Song of Songs tells us much about love, nothing about itself. How did it come into being? Who wrote it? Why? When was it composed, where, and under what circumstances? Is it belles lettres, composed for the pleasure of the elite, or is it the poetry of the common people, drawn from their folk songs, or something of both? We simply do not know, and anything that can be said about the prehistory of the book is only an educated guess. The considerable effort scholars have devoted to speculating on how and when the Song of Songs came into being has yielded some interesting hypotheses, but diminishing returns, often at the expense of appreciating the text we possess. Ironically, what frustrates scholarly reconstructions of the Song's compositional history—the poet's refusal to situate the poem in a particular time or place, or identify its sentiments with particular lovers of the past—is also what accounts considerably for the Song's timelessness and universal appeal. Nevertheless, although the data is sketchy, we know something about the Song's literary antecedents as a result of discoveries and decipherment, from the eighteenth century onwards, of literary texts belonging to Israel's ancient Near Eastern neighbors, and we can construct something of its wider cultural context from the rest of the Bible. Not only is the history of the Song before its inclusion in the Bible impossible to reconstruct, how a poem celebrating human love and desire came to be included in the Bible is also obscure.

Literary Context: Ancient Near Eastern Love Poetry

The vision of love in the Song of Songs may be original in a number of respects (for all poems have their own particular dynamic), but the poet clearly draws upon a rich cultural heritage of love poetry, as the Mesopotamian and Egyptian examples that have come down to us reveal. Of course the literary influences on the poet would not have been limited to love poetry. There are, for example, metaphoric descriptions of the body similar to those in the Song in both Egyptian and Mesopotamian hymns praising the bodies of gods, and descriptions of a person's beauty occur in a variety of literary contexts. Nor is influence limited to the fairly small amount of love poetry that happens to have been preserved.

Even the title of the Song, "the Best of Songs," tantalizingly implies that other Hebrew love songs may have existed. If so, some of them could also have influenced our poet.

To describe the Song properly in its ancient Near Eastern context would require a major study in itself. My aim here is to consider only some representative examples in order to illustrate how these ancient poets worked with common materials to celebrate love from different angles. Like the Song, the ancient Near Eastern love poems are difficult to translate and interpret, and their interpretation, like that of the Song, is debated. These poems come from diverse cultures, with different attitudes to love and to the relationship between the sexes, and even when they use similar themes and language, it may be to different ends. Comparisons with the Song, therefore, should not be drawn facilely. It is not a question of direct borrowing on the part of our poet, but of a cultural milieu in which such poetry flourished and by which the poet was nurtured.

The best way to appreciate the influence of this poetry on the poet of the Song of Songs is to read the principal published texts. Four major collections of love poems, as well as a few fragments, are preserved from ancient Egypt, all from the New Kingdom (thirteenth to eleventh centuries BCE), and they offer the closest parallels to the Song. Fox's 1985 study, in which he translates and annotates these texts, and compares them carefully and sensitively with the Song, is an invaluable resource. In this commentary I adopt Fox's numeration and organization of this corpus, and, as a rule, I use Fox's translations. Attractive translations of some of these poems can also be found in Lichtheim (1976: 181–93), and a lively free translation is available by Foster (1974).

Papyrus Harris 500 contains three groups of love poems and fragments of two love poems. The first two groups each contain eight poems, whose speakers are sometimes a young woman and sometimes a young man. These poems deal with various aspects of love and its effects on the speaker, its disappointments and minor aggravations, its joys and delights. The third group is a single poem of three stanzas, spoken by a young woman, in which each stanza begins with the name of a flower, leading to a pun that develops into a discourse about love. A mortuary text that advises seeking pleasure in this life appears between the second group and the third. The collection known as the Cairo Love Songs, which were written on vase fragments, is treated persuasively by Fox as two related poems. In one, "The Crossing," the lovers are on opposite sides of the river bank, separated by strong currents and a crocodile, but love emboldens the young man to cross the river in order to be with his beloved. Both lovers speak about their desire, and in their speeches they echo each other's sentiments, revealing the mutuality of their love, a technique the poet of the Song of Songs also exploits. In the other, "Seven Wishes," a young man speaks of his desire to be with a particular young woman, but she does not seem to be aware of him, and he never attains his goal. In Fox's view, these two poems have enough motifs in common to suggest that they were written by the same poet: the young man's gaze at his naked beloved, the seal ring on a finger as a sign of closeness; holding mandrakes ("mandragoras" in Fox's translation), being strengthened by love, and the assured union of the lovers. The poet of the Song works with similar motifs.

The Turin Love Song is unlike the others and unlike the Song of Songs in that, rather than allowing the lovers themselves to speak, the poet uses trees as spokespersons for love, as well as speaking in the authorial voice. Three different trees describe lovers' trysts and make bids for the lovers' attention. A fourth collection, Papyrus Chester Beatty I, contains three groups of love poems, two of which Fox identifies as unified poems. In the poem Fox calls "The Stroll," the poet uses the alternating speeches of two young lovers to explore their mutual infatuation from their different points of view. They have seen each other and fallen head over heels in love; each, as it happens, is both lovesick and awestruck (see, further, below). But, as Fox puts it, their "thoughts run in parallel tracks and never meet" (63), and the poem ends with the lovers apart. The poet of "Three Wishes" uses three elaborate metaphors to show a young woman's wish for her lover to come to her swiftly: like a royal messenger hastening to bring news to his master; like a royal horse, choice among all the steeds of the stables, whipped to a gallop ahead of an enemy; "like a gazelle bounding over the desert" to escape a hunter and his dog. An increasingly discordant note is struck by the imagery. The driven horse and, especially, the gazelle racing to escape death rather than to reach a desired goal, though they convey a sense of urgency and intensity, do not create a romantic mood. The group called the Nakhtsobek Songs, after the name of the scribe who wrote them down, is a loose collection of love poems. Two of them, in which a youth stands outside his beloved's door and complains of his exclusion, bear similarities to the classical Paraclausithyron, to which Song 5:2 is often compared (see the Commentary under 5:2).

The love poetry from Mesopotamia, written in Sumerian and in Akkadian, is scattered among a number of sources, dating from the third to the first millennium BCE. It is thus more difficult to classify and survey (for a brief overview, see Westenholz 2000: 2472–78; for detailed discussion and analysis, see Leick 1994). More Sumerian love poems have come to light than Akkadian ones. An Assyrian tablet from the end of the second millennium, a sort of library catalogue, lists the incipits of some 400 songs. Of the 275 titles preserved (two-fifths in Sumerian and the rest in Akkadian), many appear to have been love songs, but only one or two of these Sumerian poems and one Akkadian poem have so far been recovered. The principal texts, and the ones usually compared to the Song of Songs, are poems dealing with the courtship and marriage of the goddess Inanna and her consort Dumuzi (Jacobsen 1976: 27–47; Jacobsen 1987: 1–27, 85–98; Kramer 1969: 49–106; Sefati 1998: 120–364; Sefati, *COS*

1.169:540–43; Leick 1994: 64–110), and the royal love songs associated with the Sumerian King Shu-Suen (early third millennium BCE) (Jacobsen 1987: 85–98; Leick 1994: 111–29). Many of these poems emphasize sexuality, sexual intercourse, and fertility, which is viewed as a divine blessing and sign of divine benevolence toward the people and the land. In their present form, the texts are literary in nature, and not connected with specific rituals (Jacobsen 1976: 27; Kramer 1969: 78). For some of them a cultic ritual context can be assumed on the basis of related sources; however, the connection of the love poems with the so-called sacred marriage rite, championed in particular by Jacobsen and Kramer, is now disputed (see, e.g., Cooper 1993; Leick 1994: 64–138). An engaging and eminently readable collection of these poems can be found in Wolkstein and Kramer (1983), in which, however, the material, including royal love poems, has been arranged and combined to create a unified life story for the goddess.

Two other important texts for comparative purposes are the Sumerian Message of Lu-dingir-ra to His Mother (Civil 1964; Cooper 1971; Leick 1994: 153–56), and the Love Lyrics of Nabu and Tashmetu, in Akkadian (Leick 1994: 189–91; Nissinen 1998; Livingstone *COS* 1.128:445–46). In the former, Lu-dingir-ra sends a message of greetings to his mother, and gives the messenger five "signs" by which he might recognize her. In view of the erotic character of the descriptions, Cooper proposes that the "mother" may be Inanna in motherly guise; more likely she is a courtesan and devotee of Inanna, as Leick argues. The poem bears strong similarities to the metaphorical descriptions in the Song of Songs (see also, for another possible parallel, Sasson 1973a). The latter is a dialogue between the lovers, with a chorus (reminiscent of the women of Jerusalem in the Song) and is considered by Nissinen to be the closest Mesopotamian parallel to the Song. Its date, seventh century BCE, makes it closer in time to the Song of Songs than other parallels (Nissinen 1998: 624).

To date the Song of Songs is our only example of Northwest Semitic love poetry. Some features found in love poetry, however, appear in other texts as well; for example, from the Ugaritic Kirta epic, Kirta's description of the woman he wants for his wife bears comparison to the descriptions of the lovers in the Song of Songs:

> [Y]ou must give what my house lacks:
>> give me maid Ḥurraya,
>> the best girl of your firstborn offspring;
> Whose goodness is like that of ᶜAnatu,
>> whose beauty is like that of ᵓAṯiratu;
> The pupils (of whose eyes) are of pure lapis-lazuli,
>> whose eyes are like alabaster bowls,
>> who is girded with ruby;
> That I might repose in the gaze of her eyes.
>> (trans. Dennis Pardee, *COS* 1.102:335)

The Song shares many of the poetic features I discuss in this commentary with other ancient Near Eastern love poems. Its distinctiveness lies in the way it uses the tradition, selecting, refining, developing, and combining elements from a rich and varied poetic repertory to create a particular vision of love. Just how original the Song may be we cannot be sure, since so little ancient Near Eastern love poetry has survived. I would not wish to claim a position of superiority for the Song (though the title "the Best of Songs" makes such a claim), though, as this commentary makes clear, I regard it as a truly brilliant poetic achievement. All these poems are remarkable, each in its own way.

Prominent among the shared features is the dialogue format, which not only allows the poets to explore love from both a woman's and a man's point of view but also contributes to the impression of immediacy, making it seem as if we are overhearing the lovers as they speak. Dialogue in the Egyptian love lyrics, whose speakers are more introspective than the Song's lovers, takes a number of creative forms—interior monologue (soliloquy), exterior monologue (where the speaker addresses another), double monologue (where one lover's words are conjoined to the other's or the speakers alternate)—but we do not find dialogue in which the speakers address and interact with each other, as in the Song of Songs (Fox 259–65, 280–81). Interestingly, in the Egyptian love poems, females often address males as "you," but males never address females in the second person. Fox proposes that this may well be a convention (265–66). One is reminded of the different way the woman and the man in the Song describe each other's body, he addressing her directly as "you," whereas she speaks of him as "he" (see the Commentary under 5:10–16).

Most Mesopotamian love poems are dialogues in which the lovers are usually identified. Lovers address and interact with each other, as well as with a host of other characters. In the poems dealing with the courtship and marriage of Inanna and Dumuzi, for instance, Dumuzi's sister and Inanna's brother play prominent roles. Some poems, such as the love lyrics of the gods Nabu and Tashmetu, have a chorus that functions somewhat like the women of Jerusalem in the Song. Whereas in the Song the poet never speaks in the authorial voice, and in the Egyptian examples it is unusual for the poet to speak (e.g., the Turin Love Song), a number of the Mesopotamian love poems have a narrator. The presence of a narrator changes the dynamics of the poem, reminding us of its status as a poem (this is true even in the case of love poetry that might once have been performed as part of a ritual, where enacting it would have given it immediacy). On the whole, the Mesopotamian corpus could best be described as narrative, or dramatic, poetry rather than lyric poetry. The action, especially when accompanied by a narrator who reports events in sequence, progresses in a linear fashion. This is quite unlike the lyric poetry of the Song, where the movement is circular (see "Love Forever in Progress: Repetition and Resistance to Closure," pp. 11–13).

The dialogue format foregrounds the woman's role. The Song's picture of a woman as desirous and sexually active may be unusual in the Bible, but not in ancient Near Eastern love poetry, where women speak openly about their desire and the sexual pleasure they enjoy with their lovers. One amorous Egyptian woman clearly does not want her lover to leave her bed:

> Because you remember you are hungry
>> would you then leave?
> Are you a man
>> thinking only of his stomach?
> Would you [walk off from me
>> concerned with] your stylish clothes
> and leave me the sheet?
>
> Because of hunger
>> would you then leave me?
> [or because you are thirsty?]
> Take then my breast:
>> for you its gift overflows.
> Better indeed is one day in your arms . . .
>> than a hundred thousand [anywhere] on earth.
>>> (P. Harris 500, No. 1; Simpson 1973: 298)[21]

Another takes the initiative, while her beloved hesitates:

> While you (yet) argued with your heart—
>> "After her! Embrace her!"—
> as Amon lives, it was I who came to you,
>> my tunic on my shoulder.
>>> (P. Chester Beatty I, Group C,
>>>> No. 44, trans. Fox)

Others also actively seek out their lovers:

> I found my brother in his bedroom,
>> and my heart was exceedingly joyful.
>>> (P. Harris 500, Group B,
>>>> No. 14, trans. Fox)
>
> My heart thought of your love,
>> while (only) half my side-locks were done up.
> I have come hastily to seek you,
>> the back of my hairdo [loose].

21. In the translations, ellipsis . . . , when it appears within a poem, indicates lacuna or an illegible text; square brackets [ ] indicate restoration; round brackets ( ) contain words not in the text but added for clarity in English; a question mark in parentheses indicates an uncertain reading. An emendation is indicated by < >. In one case below, following the translator's practice, italics are used for a presumed reading.

My clothes and my tresses
   have been ready all the while.
      (P. Harris 500, Group B,
         No. 16, trans. Fox)

In the Mesopotamian love poems, the woman's voice dominates, expressing desire and demanding gratification, whereas the man's voice is often an imagined response to her petitions (Leick 1994: 56). In a love song to the Sumerian King Shu-Suen, the speaker, who is represented as unmarried and still living in her parents' house, appeals to her beloved:

O! that you would do
   all the sweet things to me,
my sweet dear one,
   you bring that which will be honey sweet!

In the bedroom's honey-sweet corner
let us enjoy over and over
   your charms and sweetnesses!
      (Jacobsen 1987: 88, punctuation corrected)

The thought that both she and he will enjoy his charms finds an echo in the Song, where the woman, whose kingly lover has brought her to his chambers, says "we will rejoice and delight in you, we will savor your caresses above wine" (see the Commentary under 1:4).

Mesopotamian love poetry tends to be more sexually explicit, less roundabout, than either the Song or the Egyptian love poems. For the woman of the Song of Songs, her partner's lovemaking is better than wine (1:2) and his fruit is sweet to her taste (2:3). In another royal love song from Sumer, a woman finds her partner's lovemaking honey-sweet (lettuce stands for pubic hair, and watering the lettuce for sexual intercourse):

Vigorously he sprouted,
   vigorously he sprouted and sprouted,
   watered it—it being lettuce!
In his black garden of the desert bearing much yield
   did my darling of his mother,
my barley stalk full of allure in its furrow,
   water it—it being lettuce,
did my one—a very apple tree bearing fruit at the top—
   water it—it being a garden!

The honey-sweet man, the honey-sweet man,
   was doing sweet (things) to me!
My lord, the honey-sweet man, the godly one,
   my darling of his mother,

> his hands honey sweet, his feet honeying,
>   was doing sweet (things) to me!
> His limbs being sweet, sweet honey,
>   he was doing sweet (things) to me!
>
> O my one who of a sudden was doing sweet (things)
>   to the whole (insides up) to the navel,
>   my darling of his mother,
> my desert-honey loins, darling of his mother,
>   you watered it—it being lettuce!
>   (Jacobsen 1987: 94)

To the image of the man as the darling of his mother, we might compare Song 6:9, where the woman is "unique to her mother, splendid to her who bore her." The first two stanzas above could refer to lovemaking that has just taken place, as Jacobsen's translation has it, or they could be translated as a commentary on the present (see "The Honey-man," trans. S. N. Kramer, *ANET* 645). In either case, the poem creates the impression of immediacy that we encounter frequently in the Song, especially in Jacobsen's translation with its direct address to the lover in the last stanza.

Since many of the Mesopotamian love poems, especially the ritual ones, deal with the marriage of the goddess and her consort (sometimes identified with the king), there is a good deal of emphasis on the preparation of the marriage bed. The woman is impatient for lovemaking:

> She has called for it! She has called for it!
>   She has called for the bed!
> She has called for the bed of heart's delight!
>   She has called for the bed!
> She has called for the bed for sweetening the loins,
>   she has called for the bed!
> She has called for the royal bed!
>   She has called for the bed!
> She has called for the queenly bed!
>   She has called for the bed!
>   (Jacobsen 1973: 40–41)

In this poem, Inanna does not speak for herself, but rather her emotional state is described by the poet, in Emesal, the dialect adopted for female voices in Sumerian literary works (Leick 1994: 100, 113; Jacobsen 1973: 40).

Metaphoric descriptions that conjure up the lovers are a shared feature of ancient Near Eastern love poetry. Nissinen draws attention to the function of such descriptions in Mesopotamian texts as magical or mystical in nature: "the reality is not only described, it is simultaneously created by comparing the deity with observable objects and, in this way, making the presence of the deity, or the beloved, real in a mystical sense" (1998: 612). The following Egyptian poem is similar to the descriptions in the Song, such as 4:1–5; 6:4–10; 7:1–6 [2–7 H], where the man praises his lover's body part by part:

> My love is one alone, without her equal,
>   beautiful above all women.
> See her, like the goddess of the morning star in splendor
>   at the beginning of a happy year.
> With dazzling presence and a fair complexion,
>   with lovely watching eyes,
> With lips that are sweet in speaking,
>   and not a word too much;
> Straight her neck and white her breast,
>   and her tresses gleam like lapis lazuli;
> Her arms are more precious than gold,
>   her fingers like lotus blossoms,
> With curving hips and a trim waist,
>   and thighs that only heighten her beauty.
> Her step is pleasing as she treads upon earth;
>   and she fastens my heart in her embrace.
> She makes the necks of the young men
>   swing round about to see her.
> Happy is he who can fully embrace her—
>   he is first of all the young lovers!
> Just look at her as she walks along,
>   like that goddess beyond, One alone!
>   (P. Chester Beatty I; Foster 1995: 163–64)

The Egyptian lover in this poem does something the male lover of the Song of Songs does not do: he imagines that other men feel the same way he does about the woman he adores. Though the woman in the Song imagines that all women are as infatuated with her lover as she is (1:4), the man never attributes his feelings to other men (rather, he too attributes his feelings to other women, 6:8–10).

In describing both the woman's body and the man's, the Song of Songs employs imagery similar to that used by Lu-dingir-ra to describe his mother:

> I shall give you a second sign about my mother:
> My mother is like a bright light on the horizon, a doe in the mountains,
> A morning star (shining even) at noon.
> A precious carnelian-stone, a topaz from Marḫaši.
> A treasure for the brother of the king, full of charm.
> A seal of nír-stone, an ornament like the sun,
> A tin bracelet, a ring of antasurra,
> Bright gold (and) silver—

(But) she is alive, a breathing thing.
(She is) an alabaster statuette, placed on a pedestal of lapis-lazuli—
A living figurine, (her) members are full of charm.
    I shall give you a third sign about my mother:
My mother is a heavenly rain, water for the best seeds,
A bountiful harvest, which grows a second crop:
A garden of delight, full of joy,
An irrigated fir-tree, covered with fir-cones:
An early fruit, the yield of the first month;
A canal which brings luxuriant waters to the irrigation ditches,
A sweet Dilmun date, sought in its *prime.*

    I shall give you a fifth sign about my mother:
My mother is a palm-tree, with a very sweet smell.
A chariot of pine-wood, a litter of box-wood.
A good . . . giving perfumed oil.
A bunch of fruits, *a garland growing luxuriantly.*
                              (The Message of Lu-dingir-ra to His Mother;
                                                          Civil 1964: 3, 5)

Among other things, this description calls to mind the woman's description of
her lover in terms of precious stones and other fine materials (see the Commentary under 5:11 and 5:14–15). Praise of the man similar to that in the Song
also appears in the Sumerian royal love songs:

    O my lapis lazuli beard!
        O my roped locks!
    My one with beard mottled
        like a slab of lapis lazuli,
    my one with locks arranged ropewise!
    You are my turban pin,
        my gold I wear,
    my trinket fashioned by
        a cunning craftsman,
    my trinket worked on
        by a cunning craftsman!
                        (Jacobsen 1987: 91)

The comparison of the man to a gold pin fashioned by a master craftsman finds
an echo in the comparison of the curves of the woman's thighs to ornaments
made by an artisan in Song 7:1 [2 H].
    The metaphoric descriptions of the body in the Song of Songs are bolder and
more elaborate than either the Egyptian or Mesopotamian examples (Fox
269–70, 277; Cooper 1971: 157–58). A distinctive feature of the Song is its use
of metaphoric descriptions as a poetic strategy for resisting closure, conjuring

up the lovers only to let them disappear so that it can conjure them up again (see "Conjuring," pp. 6–7).

Poems are addressed to their readers (or hearers, if we imagine nonliterate members of an ancient audience). The Song's use of an audience *within the poem* (the women of Jerusalem) as a way of inviting the audience *of the poem* into the lovers' intimate and seemingly private world is another of its important poetic strategies. There is nothing quite like this in the Egyptian love poems (see Fox 300–304). In the Mesopotamian corpus, the presence of a chorus or another speaker besides the lovers, with whom the lovers share their feelings and their joy, encourages audience participation. In the Love Lyrics of Nabu and Tashmetu, the chorus not only functions, like the women of Jerusalem, to invite the audience to participate in the lovers' experiences of love. Their speech "leads forward the action and links the parts of the texts together" (Nissinen 1998: 592), giving them a more important narrative role than the women of Jerusalem.

By presenting its lovers as types, typical lovers, the Song makes it easier for readers to identify with them—another of its vital poetic strategies. Readerly identification with the Egyptian lovers is similarly encouraged, for they, too, are not identified. Their feelings and actions are typical of lovers everywhere. In much of the Mesopotamian love poetry, the lovers are identified, usually with the gods, but they display typical human feelings and behavior. Of the poems dealing with the courtship of Inanna and Dumuzi, Jacobsen observes, "In these the names Dumuzi and Inanna seem in fact to stand merely for those of two young lovers without any suggestion that deities are involved" (1987:2; cf. Sefati *COS* 1.659:542). Inanna's unselfconscious joy at Dumuzi's proposal of marriage, for example, is a typical reaction. Like the woman of the Song of Songs, who intends to take her lover to her mother's house (3:4; 8:2), Inanna is sure of her mother's approval.

> He wants to stop at the gate of our mother,
> I am fairly running for joy.
> He wants to stop at the gate of Ningal,
> I am fairly running for joy!
> O that someone would tell my mother,
> and she sprinkle cedar perfume on the floor,
> O that someone would tell my mother Ningal,
> and she sprinkle cedar perfume on the floor!
> Her dwelling, its fragrance is sweet,
> her words will all be joyful ones.
>   (Jacobsen 1987: 11)

Similarly, upon hearing that the marriage arrangements have been made, her reaction could be that of any young woman upon learning she will marry the man of her dreams: "Is it true? —He is the man of my heart! He is the man of my heart!" (Jacobsen 1987: 15).

In a poem Jacobsen calls "The Wiles of Women," Dumuzi may be exhibiting the wiles of a typical male suitor when he seductively tries to persuade Inanna to stay with him and make love, and offer her mother the excuse that she was out with her girlfriend:

> Say my girl friend took me with her to the public square,
> There she entertained me with music and dancing,
> Her chant the sweet she sang for me,
> In sweet rejoicing I whiled away the time there.
> Thus deceitfully stand up to your mother,
> While we by the moonlight indulge our passion,
> I will prepare for you a bed pure, sweet, and noble,
> Will while away sweet time with you in plenty and joy.
>   (Kramer 1969: 78)

Ancient Near Eastern love poems share many other themes and motifs, such as wishing, desiring, praising the beloved, double entendre, and the appeal to the senses. Frequently the lovers address each other as "sister" and "brother" (though in the Song the woman does not call her beloved "brother"; see the Commentary under 4:9). Nature imagery abounds. The garden, in particular, provides a luscious setting for lovemaking.

> I am yours like the field
>   planted with flowers
>   and with all sorts of fragrant plants.
>   (P. Harris 500, Group C,
>   No. 18, trans. Fox)

> [He] brought joy into the garden.
> I am the [girl(?)], the lady, where are you, my man?
> [The shepherd (?)] brought joy into the garden.
> I am [the girl (?)], the lady, where are you, my man?
> Into the garden of apple trees he brought joy.
> For the shepherd (?) the apples in the garden are loaded (?) with attractiveness.
> Into the garden of grapes he brought joy.
>   (Alster 1992:18)

> A garden locked is my sister, bride,
>   a garden locked,
>   a spring sealed.
> Your watercourses, those of a pleasure garden
>   of pomegranates with choice fruits. . . .

> Let my lover come to his garden
> and eat its choice fruits!
>   (Song 4:12–13, 16)

In the Song and the Mesopotamian love poems, the garden is both the woman's body and the place where lovers meet to enjoy the fruits of love. In the Egyptian love poems, however, the garden does not seem to be a symbol for female sexuality (Fox 283–84). Nor is fertility a concern in either the Egyptian poems or the Song of Songs, as it is in some of the Mesopotamian poems. For further discussion of garden imagery, see the Commentary under 4:12–5:1.

I discussed above different ways the woman and man in the Song describe what it is like to be in love: she is lovesick, he is awestruck. In the Egyptian love poems, both lovers experience these feelings:

> I have departed [from my brother].
> [Now when I think of] your love,
>   my heart stands still within me.
> When I behold sw[eet] cakes,
>   [they seem like] salt.
> Pomegranate wine, (once) sweet in my mouth—
>   it is (now) like the gall of birds.
> The scent of your nose alone
>   is what revives my heart.
> I have obtained forever and ever
>   what Amon has granted me.
>   (P. Harris 500, Group B, No. 12, trans. Fox)

> Seven whole days I have not seen (my) sister.
>   Illness has invaded me,
> my limbs have grown heavy,
>   and I barely sense my own body.
> Should the master physicians come to me,
>   their medicines could not ease my heart.
> The lector-priests have no (good) method,
>   because my illness cannot be diagnosed.
> Telling me, "Here she is!"—that's what will revive me.
>   Her name—that's what will get me up.
> The coming and going of her messengers—
>   that's what will revive my heart.
>   (P. Chester Beatty I, Group A, No. 37, trans. Fox)

In another poem, a youth plans to feign illness so that his "sister" will come to visit him: "She'll put the doctors to shame (for she) will understand my illness" (P. Harris 500, No. 6, trans. Fox). And another lover agonizes, "If I spend a moment without seeing her, [I] get sick to my stomach" (Cairo Love Songs, No.21F, trans. Fox).

In the Song, only the man describes the way he feels in terms of being captured:

> You have captured my heart, my sister, bride,
> > you have captured my heart with one glance of your eyes,
> > with one pendant of your necklace.
> > > > > (Song 4:9)

> . . . the hair of your head is like purple;
> > a king is held captive by the tresses.
> > > (Song 7:5 [6 H])

Egyptian men feel similarly ensnared:

> How skilled is she—(my) sister—at casting the lasso,
> > yet she'll <draw in> no cattle!
> With her hair she lassos me,
> > with her eye she pulls (me) in,
> with her thighs she binds,
> > with her seal she sets the brand.
> > > > (P. Chester Beatty I, Group C,
> > > > > No. 43, trans. Fox)

> . . . her head is the trap of "love-wood,"
> > and I—the goose!
> The cord (?) is my . . . ,
> > [her ha]ir is the bait
> > > in the trap to ensnare (me) (?).
> > > > (P. Harris 500, Group A,
> > > > > No. 3, trans. Fox)

But so too does a woman, who should be trapping birds but finds herself ensnared:

> I'll take my nets,
> > but what shall I say to Mother,
> to whom I go every day
> > laden down with birds?
> I set no trap today—
> > your love captured <me>.
> > > (P. Harris 500, Group B,
> > > > No. 10, trans. Fox)

The male protagonist in "The Stroll" exclaims, "she has captured my heart in her embrace," while the female protagonist is not only captured but lovesick as well:

> My brother roils my heart with his voice,
>> making me ill.
> Though he is among the neighbors of my mother's house,
>> I cannot go to him.
> Mother is good in commanding me thus:
>> "Avoid seeing \<him\>!"
> (Yet) my heart is vexed when he comes to mind,
>> for love of him has captured me.
>>> (P. Chester Beatty I, Group A, No. 32, trans. Fox)

Their relationship, however, is different from that of the lovers in the Song: "He does not know my desires to embrace him, or he would send (word) to my mother." And she does not tell him. Unlike the woman of the Song, who happily admits to being lovesick (2:5; 5:8), she says, "Don't let people say about me: 'This woman has collapsed out of love'" (which is, of course, an open confession about her condition as far as the poem's audience is concerned; see, further, the Commentary under 5:8).

Inanna, too, experiences lovesickness and reveals it to Dumuzi's sister Geshtinanna, who, in turn, tells Dumuzi:

> As I was strolling, as I was strolling
> [as I was strolling] by the house,
>> as I was strolling by the house,
> [my dear] In[anna s]aw me—
> B[rother, what did she tell me,]
>> [and what] more did she speak of to me?
> Brother, it was [of love], allure,
>> and utter blissful things,
> and accordingly my sweet Holy Inanna
>> disclosed something to me:
> she had met you, my beloved man,
> when I was addressing myself
>> to some errand,
> and fell in love with you,
>> and delighted in you!
>
> Brother, she brought me into her house
> and had me lie down
>> on a honey of a bed
> and when my sweet darling
>> had lain down next to my heart,
> we, chatting with one another,
>> with one another
> she, my good-looking brother,
>> began moaning to me,

and there overcame her there
    like what overcomes
    one very weak,
and proneness to tremble
    from the ground up,
exceedingly much, befell her!
       (Jacobsen 1987: 8–9)

Is this not what the woman of the Song imagines her companions telling her lover? "If you find my lover, what will you tell him? That I am faint with love" (5:8).

A lover's fondest wish is to be with the object of her or his desire. In "Seven Wishes" (Cairo Love Songs, Group B, Nos. 21A–G), a young man dreams of the object of his affection. He wishes he were her maid so that he could gaze upon her naked body, her laundryman so that he could caress her clothes, her seal-ring so that he would always be with her, her mirror into which she gazes. He wishes that she were bound to him every day like a wreath of flowers, and that she would come to him and be with him forever. In "Three Wishes," a young woman wishes for her lover to come to her swiftly (see above). Lovers everywhere know the meaning of longing, and of finding their desire in tension with socially accepted conduct.

If only you were like a brother to me,
    who nursed at my mother's breasts!
I would find you in the street and kiss you,
    and no one would disdain me.
        (Song 8:1)

If only mother knew my heart—
    she would go inside for a while.
O Golden One, put that in her heart!
    Then I could hurry to (my) brother
and kiss him before his company,
    and not be ashamed because of anyone.
       (P. Chester Beatty I, Group A,
        No. 36, trans. Fox)

Determined lovers, however, will let nothing stand in the way of their being united. In the Song, only the woman undergoes suffering for the sake of love, when the city watchmen beat her and take her garment from her. An Egyptian woman declares herself willing to withstand blows for love's sake (P. Harris 500, Group A, No. 4), and in "The Crossing," mentioned above, a youth braves strong currents and a crocodile to join his beloved on the opposite side of the river bank (for discussion of these parallels, see the Commentary under 5:7).

Perhaps the most remarkable difference between our one example from ancient Israel and the other surviving love poems from the ancient Near East is that the Egyptian and Mesopotamian love poetry deals with a wider range of situations and emotions, and offers a more multifaceted vision of love, than the Song of Songs, as I hope even the brief discussion above reveals. One reason for this difference is that in the case of the Song we are dealing with a single poem with its own distinct vision of love, whereas a variety of love poems have survived from both Egypt and Mesopotamia. In the love lyrics of Egypt and Mesopotamia, in addition to desirous and besotted lovers, mutual delight, sexual pleasure, and devotion, one encounters, among other topics, jealous lovers (an Egyptian decides her neglectful lover's delay means he has found another), vindictive lovers (Dumuzi is not distraught at Inanna's imprisonment in the underworld, and his casual reaction seems to be what incites her to hand him over to take her place), unfaithfulness and its punishment (Dumuzi has sexual relations with one of Inanna's servants; Inanna has her killed but cannot forget Dumuzi's betrayal), petulant lovers (an Egyptian youth is peeved at the heartlessness of his beloved for barring the door to him), simple infatuation ("If only I were her Nubian maid . . ."), pining for the object of one's affections (the lovers in "The Stroll," who desire each other but do not appear to follow their hearts). Interestingly, in the cuneiform literature known to us, there are no poems about thwarted love and spurned affection (Leick 1994: 89).

Historical-Cultural Context

Although ancient cultures would not have distinguished sharply between sacred and secular literature, it is clear from their worldly content that the Egyptian love poems surveyed above are not overtly religious. They have nothing to do with worship and are not about gods. As far as we know, they were not associated with cultic activities. Rather they were probably composed for entertainment, for the pleasure, and possibly edification and uplifting, of an audience (see Fox 244–47). The headings of three groups of poems state their purpose as entertainment or diversion: "The Beginning of the Entertainment Song" (P. Harris 500, Group B, Nos. 9–16), "The Beginning of the Song of Entertainment" (P. Harris 500, Group C, Nos. 17–19), "The Beginning of the Sayings of the Great Entertainer" (P. Chester Beatty I, Group A, Nos. 31–37). The young lovers, in whose mouths the lyrics are placed, may seem natural and untutored, but the poems themselves are sophisticated literary creations (Lichtheim 1976: 181; Fox *passim*).

Such a background is plausible also for the Song of Songs. It is a very sophisticated artistic composition, with a rich vocabulary, and versed in the poetic tradition of the ancient Near East—all of which suggests that the poet moved in educated elite circles in ancient Israel. (This is not to say that the poet, and other ancient Near Eastern poets as well, could not have found inspiration in popular love songs, just as numerous composers have used popular melodies as themes for symphonies and other sophisticated musical compositions.) As entertainment, the Song of Songs may have been "a song to be enjoyed on any occasion—including religious holidays—when song, dance, or other ordinary diversions were in order" (Fox 247). Though we have no way of knowing whether or not it was performed, the Song, with its alternating male and female voices and chorus, lends itself to performance. The oldest evidence we have for the use of the Song—rabbinic arguments that the Song should not be recited in banquet halls and treated as an ordinary love song—shows that the Song was regarded as entertainment by some people in the first and second centuries CE (see "A Book of the Bible," pp. 70–73).

In time the Song achieved the status of religious literature. It is, however, highly unlikely that the Song originally had a cultic setting, as some have argued (see the discussions of Pope 145–53 and Fox 239–43). The present Song of Songs is a literary text, not a ritual text. Like the Egyptian love poems, it contains no instructions for ritual use, and God is not mentioned in it (if the *hapax legomenon šalhebetyâ* in 8:6 refers to the "flame of Yah"—*yah* being a shortened form of the divine name—that no more makes Israel's god the subject of the poem than "strong as death [*māwet*]" or "flames [*rešep*] of fire" makes the Canaanite gods Mot or Resheph its subjects; see the Commentary under 8:6 and 8:7). To establish an original cultic setting for the Song, one would need evidence of its ritual use from other sources, such as we have, for example, in the case of the Love Lyrics of Nabu and Tashmetu. The loose arrangement of the present text of the Love Lyrics "gives the impression of a literary composition rather than of a manual of a cult drama" (Nissinen 1998: 595), but the existence of a corresponding ritual is confirmed by other sources (Nissinen 1998: 592–97; Leick 1994: 133–36, 189–91). Although evidence of an original cultic setting for the Song is lacking, perhaps, as Nissinen urges, we should not rule it out. After all, the Bible is a collection of texts representing what became official normative religion. That ancient Israelite religion, as it was practiced, was more syncretistic than the Bible suggests is apparent from the Bible's polemic against what it regards as false worship. Indeed, according to 2 Kgs 23:4 there were vessels sacred to Baal and Asherah in the Jerusalem temple (cf. also 1 Kgs 15:13; 2 Kgs 21:7), and the practice of making cakes for the queen of heaven and burning incense and offering libations to her is attested in Jer 7:18 and 44:17–19. If there was a preexilic ritual of Yahweh and his Asherah, one could imagine a text like the Song of Songs having a role in it (Nissinen 1998: 625; cf. Pope 1988: 324).[22] It seems doubtful, however, that the Song would have been accepted into the canon were it known to have had such a background.

---

22. For a recent discussion of the evidence of a cult of Yahweh and a goddess identified with Asherah at Kuntillet Ajrud and Khirbet El-Qom, see Ziony Zevit, *The Religions of Ancient Israel: A Synthesis of Parallactic Approaches* (London: Continuum, 2001), 359–405.

What about authorship? Could the Song have been written by a woman? (Would the male editors and scribes, whose activity in producing the Bible was guided by social and religious agendas, have preserved intact an erotic poem written by a woman?) Some Mesopotamian women apparently composed or commissioned love poetry (Jacobsen 1987: 85–86; Leick 1994: 112–13),[23] and some Egyptian love poems may have been composed by women; for example, the "Great Entertainer," whose poetry is preserved in P. Chester Beatty I (Fox 55–56). How widespread literacy was in ancient Israel can only be surmised on the basis of biblical and epigraphic evidence (see A. R. Millard, "Literacy [Israel]," *ABD* IV, 337–40). There is no clear evidence of female literacy. The statement that Queen Jezebel wrote letters in Ahab's name, which she then sent to the elders and nobles of the city (1 Kgs 21:8), could mean simply that she had them written by a scribe (and had them delivered by a messenger). Since men would have had greater opportunity to have been educated (an education that included ancient Near Eastern erotica), the likelihood is greater that the Song was written by a man. But this does not rule out the possibility of an educated woman having composed the Song. Nor does it exclude the possibility that the poet drew on traditional materials, some of which were the products of women's culture. Indeed, love poetry, given its emphasis on a woman's point of view and its association with the domestic sphere, may have been a genre to which women made a special contribution (see Leick 1994: 112–13; Goitein 1988).

The sex of the author cannot be deduced from the poem. Shifting the question from authorship to "voice" as a means of identifying traces of women's traditions in texts written and edited by men—what Brenner and van Dijk-Hemmes refer to as "gendering texts" (1993)—is as conjectural as positing female authorship. The characteristics of a feminine or female voice, not surprisingly, appear difficult to distinguish. It seems to be any or all of the following: traces of a less androcentric intent, a (re)definition of "reality" from a women's point of view, striking differences between the views of male and female characters in a text (1993: 31). "Voice," as Brenner and van Dijk-Hemmes use it, turns out to be a rather slippery term, not least because in practice they do not maintain a rigid distinction between authorship and voice. Often they see the presence of female voices as pointing to female authorship, most probably at an oral stage. This slippage has some unfortunate effects, for whereas Brenner and van Dijk-Hemmes recognize that there is no way to prove that the Song of Songs is a product of women's culture, others have uncritically accepted their work as doing just that.

---

23. The earliest identifiable author in history was a woman, the royal priestess Enheduanna, daughter of King Sargon of Akkad, in the twenty-third century BCE; not all agree on the date, and most of her work is known only from later editions, dating from the Old Babylonian period (see Leick 1994: 56–62, 273).

Assuming that "voice" offers a clue to origins also fails to take adequately into account a good poet's ability to write successfully in different voices.

More important than the sex of its author is the fact that the voices in the Song are voices that readers perceive as authentic. Most readers of the Song find themselves in agreement with the poet and critic who hears "women speaking out of their own experiences and their own imaginations" and finds men's speech "authentically self-expressive" (Falk 1990: 117, 118). The poet of the Song has created believable female and male characters and explores what it is like to be in love from both their points of view with great sensitivity to subtle differences between men and women (see above "Gendered Love-Talk and the Relation of the Sexes," pp. 13–28).

As with authorship, decisive evidence is lacking for the date of the Song and its provenance. Scholarly opinions as to date vary widely; proposals range from the time of Solomon (see, e.g., Garrett 16–22) to the Hellenistic period (fourth to second centuries BCE; e.g., Fox 186–91). Date, like authorship, is connected with the question of unity. Those who view the Song as a collection would date the parts to different historical periods, but no one has carried through the dating of individual parts of the Song in any detail, and the date of the final edition remains a question.

Scholars who use evidence from the Song to establish its date disagree on how the evidence should be evaluated. From the fact that David is mentioned (4:4) and Solomon plays a small role (see the Commentary under 1:1), one can conclude no more than that the poem is no earlier than the time of Solomon. The appearance of Tirzah in parallelism with Jerusalem in Song 6:4 indicates that the Song (or at least this part of the Song) was not written during the United Monarchy, but it cannot be used to argue that the Song was written during the time that Tirzah was the capital of the Northern Kingdom (after the division of the monarchy until ca. 870 BCE) or that the Song has a northern provenance. At the time the poem was composed, Tirzah could have had simply a legendary status. The principal setting of the poem is Jerusalem—the women of Jerusalem are the audience—but a lover can be figuratively transported to the peaks of Lebanon (4:8). Jerusalem appears alongside many other place names: Damascus and the peaks of Lebanon in the north, En-gedi in the south, Heshbon in the east, Mount Carmel and the plain of Sharon in the West. None of these geographical references has anything to do with specific historical events. Apart from Lebanon, which has a special, quasi-magical status in the Song (see the Commentary under 4:8), almost all other references to geographical locations appear in metaphors. It does not therefore follow that these places were within the sphere of influence of the Israelite state at the time the Song was composed, as, for example, Garrett maintains (19). The places mentioned in the Song could have been chosen because they were famous—Lebanon for its cedars, En-gedi for its oasis, and so forth—or for their associations and ability to evoke a lyrical, magical time and place. Indeed, the Song's refusal to situate itself in a particular time and place is one of its important poetic strategies for immortalizing the love it celebrates (see "The Lovers as Representing All Lovers," pp. 8–9).

Most commentators tend to date the Song in or around the Hellenistic period, primarily on linguistic grounds. Not surprisingly, the linguistic evidence is also debated. The language appears to be late (see, especially, Fox 187–90, but see also the arguments for an early date by Garrett 16–18, Young 1993: 161–65). The Song has affinities with Mishnaic Hebrew, and the presence of foreign loan-words argues for a late date; for example, *pardēs* (4:13) from Persian, *ʾappiryôn* (3:9) from Greek, to mention two of the most frequently cited examples. Some maintain, however, that a new word could have been substituted at a later date for a word whose meaning was no longer understood.

Would knowing when it was written help us understand the poem? Probably not very much. If it were written in a time of crisis, one could say the Song is escapist literature, offering a respite from depressing circumstances. If it were written during a time of peace and prosperity, one could argue that it reflects a society that had the time for the pleasures of life and love and the leisure to compose and enjoy the literature that celebrates such pleasures. Love poetry, like love, knows no season.

Social World

Ways in which the Song reflects its patriarchal environment as well as some of the ways it challenges it are discussed above ("The Song and Conventional Gender Relations," pp. 25–28). Because its subject is the relationship between a man and a woman, the Song is immensely important for understanding sexuality in ancient Israel, but, at the same time, its value for this purpose is limited, for, like the fairy tale that ends with "and they lived happily ever after," it does not move beyond courtship and more intimate erotic encounters to describe other aspects of women's and men's day-to-day lives. Perhaps the unconventional behavior exhibited by the protagonists, especially the woman, is a feature of the genre, love poetry. In other ancient Near East love poems also, women play central roles and are allowed a freedom not normally accorded them in their society. It is also possible that the lovers' behavior is not so unconventional as one might think on the basis of the picture provided in the rest of the Bible. As Fox (315) observes,

> [I]t is surprising to find such a society [with strong religious and social strictures on unmarried sexual activity] producing a poem that accepts premarital sexuality so naturally that it does not even try to draw attention to its own liberality. But of vast areas of Israelite life, society, and attitudes we know nothing, for the overwhelming majority of the documents we have were preserved because they served religious and ideological purposes of various groups within that society. (In the

case of Canticles, it was not the book itself but an interpretation of it that served religious purposes.)

The Song is a lyric poem, the product of the poet's prodigious imagination (see "Fantasy, Reality, and Poetic Imagination," pp. 45–47). Love poetry need not correspond to social reality and, in fact, it may offer an escape from social constraints for women and men. The Bedouin poetry studied by Abu-Lughod offers a modern parallel. Abu-Lughod found that women could express in song and poetry passionate sentiments that their society, with its strict code of female modesty, would not tolerate in real life.

> Poems are vehicles for the expression of attachments to sweethearts or spouses that, if communicated in everyday social interaction, would damage reputations and jeopardize claims to respectability and, at the individual level, would ordinarily undermine self-image and self-presentation. (Abu-Lughod 1986: 232; see also Carr 2000: 242–44)

Perhaps one way the patriarchal society of ancient Israel controlled female eroticism was by allowing it a social outlet in love poetry.

Sex both animates and disrupts the social order. Love poetry provides insight into cultural aspirations and ideals regarding love and sex, even if it does not always conform to social custom. Behavior that conforms to social expectations is not the only social issue that the Song happily ignores. Anxieties associated with sexual activity elsewhere in the Bible are absent. There is no concern about body fluids and the possibility of pollution, and the unmarried lovers sing the praises of the pleasures of sexual intercourse without worrying about pregnancy as a possible consequence (cf., however, Brenner 1997: 87–89, who suggests that many of the plants in the Song are mentioned with an awareness of their contraceptive properties).

Like any literary text, the Song is not a window through which the reality of the past can be transparently read. One cannot use the Song of Songs as evidence of what ancient Israelites in love felt or how they acted. We do not know whether or not the situation—love, a one-to-one relationship—allowed a certain freedom from social constraints, or whether the genre, love poetry, or the social setting—private rather than public life—accounts for the Song's portrayal of gender relations as fairly egalitarian. What the Song reveals about the social world of ancient Israel is that its worldview included a vision of romance that attached importance to mutual desire. The Song not only testifies to the general availability of romantic ideas and ideals within the larger culture but also, by its very existence and popularity, may have played a role in perpetuating them. (It was surely popular; otherwise it is unlikely it would have been preserved.)

In the absence of historical data, another way of approaching the question of the Song's social world is to reason from the text back to its implied social matrix. This is what Clines does in asking "why is there a Song of Songs?" (1995). His answer is, because there were both a male public interested in erotica and a social context that approved the existence and distribution of erotic literature. He suggests, moreover, that the text served patriarchal interests "by representing the female and male lovers as more or less equal," thereby repressing the tensions between the sexes (1995: 101). Ironically patriarchy later had to repress the Song's egalitarianism by allegorization (117).

Taking Clines's line of argument in a somewhat different direction raises an interesting question. If the Song, by painting a rosy picture of gender relations, encouraged women to accept the status quo, who in particular needed to be convinced? The scenes of courting and the lovers' sense of wonder at the stirrings of love call up images of young love before marriage. The Song could therefore have proved useful in encouraging young women of marriageable age to accept happily the role society prescribed for them. Having observed how hard a wife and mother's lot was, how little control she had over her own life, would a young woman not see marriage and childbearing as daunting prospects? What might ease her mind and encourage her to be eager to marry? Sexual desire obviously plays a large role and is foregrounded in the Song. But the Song provides another answer as well. Suddenly the young woman, perhaps for the first and only time in her life, is the center of attention. She has power; her suitor had been conquered by her (4:9; 6:5; 7:5 [6 H]) and is at her beck and call. Love is something she decides if and when to give. The Song is reassuring: love is wonderful. Why resist? Leick makes similar observations about the Sumerian Bridal Poems when she proposes they may have functioned to alleviate feelings of ambivalence and anxiety on the part of a bride (1994: 68). Marriages may have been arranged, but that does not mean that the two young people involved would not have had feelings about the marriage and about each other. The love poems themselves bear witness to a young woman's feelings in such a situation ("Man who has become attracted to me, speak to my mother, she would let you! she has worn down my father," Jacobsen 1987: 89) and to the excitement she might feel about the arrangements made for her ("Is it true?—He is the man of my heart!" Jacobsen 1987: 15). The Song suggests that love, mutual desire, and mutual sexual gratification were important parts of male–female relationships. Thus not only would marriage appear desirable to a young woman, the future would look promising too. For love is strong as death.

One could imagine other scenarios and other social needs served by the Song. Ohler, for instance, proposes a wisdom school setting, in which young men were instructed in the art of love from a woman's point of view by fictive female speakers (1989: 196–97; Ovid's *Art of Love*, addressed to both men and women provides an interesting analogy). It would be naive to think the Song meant the same thing to all of its readers or functioned the same way for all segments of society at any one time. The poet sought to make the poem appeal to a broad audience, and succeeded. The Song never loses sight of its audience (see "The Invitation to the Reader," pp. 7–8). It encourages all readers to identify the lovers' experience of love with their own experiences or fantasies about love. Its success is witnessed by the way its readers, throughout the centuries, have done just that (see "The Song of Songs and Its Readers," pp. 73–86).

A Book of the Bible

How did a poem celebrating human love and desire, a text that contains no religious teaching and in which God is not mentioned, come to be included in a collection of sacred writings? To this fascinating question the simple answer is: we do not know. Current scholarship understands canonization, the process by which certain texts came to be considered "sacred" or authoritative for a particular religious community, as a long and complex process. As far as the Song of Songs is concerned, clearly it was not the case that, suddenly, Jewish communities everywhere agreed, at the same time, that the Song was a sacred text. Indeed, its status was called into question more than once. In the first and second centuries of the common era, different communities of readers and hearers understood the Song differently, as rabbinic statements on the use of the Song indicate. The Talmud records the following judgment from around the end of the first century: "Our rabbis have taught on Tannaite authority: He who recites a verse of the Song of Songs and turns it into a kind of love-song, and he who recites a verse in a banquet hall not at the proper time [but in a time of carousal] bring evil into the world" (*b. Sanh.* 101a).[24] To Rabbi Aqiba (ca. 50–135 CE) is ascribed a similar opinion: "Whoever warbles the Song of Songs in a banquet hall, treating it like an ordinary song, has no share in the world to come" (*t. Sanh.* 12:10). On the one hand, such statements show that some rabbinic authorities viewed the Song as a sacred text and considered its secular use to be a profanation. On the other hand, they reveal that, at the same time, people were enjoying the Song as entertainment. Fragments of the Song were found at Qumran, which indicates the acceptance of a religious interpretation among members of the Qumran community in the first century CE (though we do not know what kind of religious interpretation they gave it). References to Israel as a lily and dove in *4 Ezra* 5:23–27 (late first century CE) may bear witness to early stages of allegorical interpretation of the Song.

The earliest debate about the Song's authoritative status is recorded in the Mishnah (*m. Yad.* 3:5). On this occasion Rabbi Aqiba, responding to a minority view that the Song's status was disputed, uttered his famous and oft-cited words: "Heaven forbid!—No Israelite man ever disputed concerning Song of

24. Jacob Neusner, trans., *The Talmud of Babylonia: An American Translation*, vol. 23c: *Tractate Sanhedrin, Chapters 9–11*, Brown Judaic Studies 87 (Chico, CA: Scholars Press, 1985), 152.

Songs that it imparts uncleanness to hands. For the entire age is not so worthy as the day on which the Song of Songs was given to Israel. For all the scriptures are holy, but the Song of Songs is holiest of all. And if they disputed, they disputed only concerning Qohelet."[25] As this text shows, although the Song was already regarded by many as rendering the hands unclean (i.e., a sacred text), and by Aqiba as never in dispute, its status was still being disputed.[26] The text summarizes different views on the question, among them Aqiba's, and comes down in favor of canonicity. As it stands, it cannot have been edited before about 160 CE, and it may have been intended to resolve, once and for all, the issue of the canonicity of Ecclesiastes and Song of Songs. From about 160 onwards, there is little evidence of any dispute over the Song in the rabbinic tradition (Alexander 2003: 34–35). The Song's acceptance as canonical by Christians is witnessed, among other sources, in a Hebrew-Aramaic list of canonical books that may go back to the late first century CE[27] and in the canon list of Melito, bishop of Sardis, in the late second century (preserved in Eusebius's *Ecclesiastical History* 4.26.12–14).

Various factors may have contributed to the sacralization of the Song: its popularity, the attribution of the book to Solomon, and, conceivably, its widespread use on religious occasions, which would have eventually necessitated religious reinterpretation of the text in order to make this usage more acceptable. Undoubtedly religious acceptance of the book was facilitated by the traditional understanding of its title as indicating Solomonic authorship (see Sæbø 1996: 270–75). It was perhaps also the association with Solomon that helped the Song become national literature, if not national religious literature.

The question, which came first, the sacralization of the Song or its allegorization, has long been debated. Was it allegorization that made the Song acceptable for inclusion in the biblical canon? Or did inclusion in the canon lead to allegorization? Allegorization cannot have been the only reason the Song was canonized. For anyone to have taken the trouble to develop an allegorical interpretation of it,

25. Jacob Neusner, *The Mishnah: A New Translation* (New Haven: Yale University Press, 1988), 1127.

26. The meaning of the phrase "defile the hands" ("imparts uncleanness to hands" in the translation above) is usually taken to mean that a book was regarded as sacred, or canonical (and therefore touching it required ritual cleansing). A different interpretation is that it refers to books that contain the tetragrammaton (*yhwh*). These books should not be handled if one also handles food, lest they be nibbled by rodents or burned in a fire and the divine name desecrated (see Michael J. Broyde, "Defilement of the Hands, Canonization of the Bible, and the Special Status of Esther, Ecclesiastes, and Song of Songs," *Judaism* 44 [1995]: 65–79; Garrett 15). In this case, the issue in *m. Yad.* would not have been the Song's place in the canon, but only how the book should be treated, since it—like Qohelet (and also Esther)—does not contain the name.

27. See Jean-Paul Audet, "A Hebrew-Aramaic List of Books of the Old Testament in Greek Transcription," *JTS* N.S. 1 (1950): 135–54; idem, "Le sens de Cantique des Cantiques," *RB* 62 (1955): 202 n. 2.

the text must already have achieved a certain status (Alexander 2003: 35; Rudolph 83; Keel 7; Garrett 15), perhaps as national religious literature (Fox 250).

The sacralization of the Song may have been encouraged by its use at religious festivals, especially spring festivals, whence its later association with Passover (Benzen 1953: 45–47, followed by Fox 251). Feasts and festivals, many of which would have been celebrated on religious holidays, might be occasions for festivities and entertainment as well as prayer, sacrifice, and ritual. On such occasions, the Song, or parts of it, may have been sung, recited, or performed as entertainment. Spring festivals would have been ideal times for turning for inspiration to the Song, given its enthusiastic heralding of the wonders of spring and bounties of nature. According to a tradition placed in the mouth of Rabbi Simeon ben Gamaliel (ca. 140 CE), even on such a solemn religious holiday as the Day of Atonement, young women dressed up and danced in the vineyards to attract eligible suitors:

> There were no days better for Israelites than the fifteenth of Ab [in August] and the Day of Atonement [in October]. For on those days Jerusalemite girls go out in borrowed white dresses—so as not to shame those who owned none. All the dresses had to be immersed. And the Jerusalemite girls go out and dance in the vineyards. What did they say? "Fellow, look around and see—choose what you want! Don't look for beauty, look for family." And so it says, *"Go forth you daughters of Zion, and behold King Solomon with the crown with which his mother crowned him in the day of his espousals and in the day of the gladness of his heart."* (Cant. 3:11) (*m. Taʿan.* 4:8)[28]

The Mishnah here associates the Song with not one, but two religious festivals. Both were harvest festivals, which would have provided a good opportunity for young people to meet (Keel 6). They may have especially appreciated and enjoyed the amorous sentiments of the Song at such times.

It may have been fortuitous, it is certainly fortunate, that the Song of Songs was preserved when so much ancient Hebrew literature must have been lost. Most likely the Song would have been lost too, had it not become a book of the Bible. A question of equal, if not greater importance than how the Song came to be included in the canon is: what effect does its inclusion have on the canon? Among other things, the Song contributes to the Bible an unparalleled affirmation of the pleasures of the flesh, the strength of love, and the beauty of the created world. Its status as a biblical book serves as an obvious reminder that the Bible is not a univocal, unified text but a collection of widely diverse material, within which a plurality of voices speak, often in tension with other voices. On the allegorical level, the Song's portrayal of a loving relationship between God and Israel functions as a welcome alternative, and perhaps corrective, to the

28. Neusner, *The Mishnah: A New Translation*, 315–16.

prophetic marriage metaphor in which Israel is portrayed as God's wayward wife, whose chastisement by her righteous and long-suffering husband is viewed as both necessary and instructive (see Pardes 1992; Buss 1996).

7. The Song of Songs and Its Readers

Modern scholars are generally agreed that human love is the subject of the Song, and this is the view taken by the present commentary. But this has not always been the case. "There is no book of the Old Testament which has found greater variety of interpretation than the Song of Songs," writes H. H. Rowley in a now classic essay on the history of the Song's interpretation (1965: 197). Excellent surveys of the history of interpretation are available in the commentaries of Pope (89–229; see also Pope 1988), Murphy (11–41), and Garrett (59–91), making it unnecessary to go over the same ground here. Instead I offer only a sample of the great variety of interpretation by sketching what have been the major trends and considering some of the newer ones. The effects of theological presuppositions, cultural assumptions, intellectual currents, and social location on the interpreter are undeniable and should be recognized in assessing any interpreter's contributions (see, especially, Murphy 12). The history of the interpretation of this extraordinary ancient Hebrew poem about desire could be read as a history of its readers' desire—desire to find deeper meaning in it than its plain meaning alone, desire to find a story behind its lyrics or anchor it in a particular life setting (*Sitz im Leben*), desire not simply to read the Song but to participate in it. The Song may not tell us everything there is to know about love, but it is fair to say that there are few things its readers have not found in it.

Allegorical Interpretation

Allegory was the dominant mode of interpretation for centuries, until the rise of critical biblical scholarship in the nineteenth century, and was applied selectively to all biblical books. By and large, Jewish interpreters read the Song as an allegory of the relationship between God and Israel, while Christians saw it as an allegory of the love between Christ and the church, or Christ (or the divine logos) and the individual believer. There were occasional exceptions, but readers who held to the literal or plain meaning of the text did not fare well. Theodore of Mopsuestia (ca. 350–428 CE) saw the Song as love poetry composed by Solomon to justify his marriage to the daughter of Pharaoh (1 Kgs 11:1) and concluded that it should not be in the canon. He was posthumously condemned for his views on the Song, among other more serious charges, by the Second Council of Constantinople (553). His commentary did not survive and is known only from attacks on it. A similar fate befell the Protestant Reformer Sebastian Castellio, an associate of John Calvin. Like Theodore, he saw the Song as a profane work not worthy of its place in the canon. Calvin opposed his views, and Castellio was exiled from Geneva.

The more problematic a text, the more interpretation it requires to smooth over the difficulties. That early Jewish interpreters found the Song problematic is apparent from the amount of commentary it generated in proportion to its size: more than any other book of the Bible outside the Pentateuch (Alexander 2003: 34). Particularly influential among early Jewish expositions of the Song were the Targum, from the seventh or, more likely, eighth century CE, and Song of Songs Rabba (*Midrash Ḥazita*), from roughly the same period, possibly later (Alexander 2003: 55, 35–36). Both take a nationalistic historical-allegorical approach, connecting various elements in the Song with episodes from Israelite history, such as the giving of the Torah or the crossing of the Red Sea, and both identify the bride as Israel and the beloved as God. Whereas Song of Songs Rabba proceeds atomistically, in typical rabbinic fashion, interpreting words, phrases, or verses without much concern for their context, the Targum is unusual, possibly unique, in offering a sustained systematic interpretation with an overarching structure. The work of a single author, it reads the Song in terms of the relationship between God and Israel, starting with the exodus and concluding with the messianic age (Alexander 2003: xi, 13). The historical allegory of the Targum and Song of Songs Rabba was the dominant early Jewish approach to the Song, but there was also within Judaism, as within Christianity, a mystical tradition of reading the Song. This tradition may be represented in an esoteric text, the *Shi'ur Qomah*, a mystical reflection on the body of God, which some regard as inspired by the woman's catalogue of her lover's charms in Song 5:10–16 (cf., however, the criticisms of Alexander 2003: 37–38).

Among the great medieval Jewish allegorists of the tenth to twelfth centuries who followed the Targum's method of historical allegorization were Saadia, Rashi, and his grandson Rashbam. The illustrious twelfth-century scholar Ibn Ezra, in his commentary, dealt with the Song on three levels: the philological, the plain sense (an allegorical history of a man and woman, both shepherds), and the allegorical or midrashic sense (the relationship between God and Israel from the call of Abraham to the future messianic age) (see Ginsburg 44–46; Pope 101–5). Moses ibn Tibbon in the thirteenth century and Gersonides in the fourteenth expounded a proposal made earlier by Maimonides (1135–1204) that, in the Song, Solomon described the yearning of the individual soul (the receptive material intellect) for union with God (the active intellect that governs the created order). Don Isaac Abravanel (sixteenth century) identified the male lover of the Song with Solomon and the woman with his bride, personified Wisdom.

Of the Christian allegorists, perhaps the most influential was Origen, in the mid-third century, who wrote ten volumes of commentary and numerous homilies on the Song. Unfortunately nothing remains of Origen's original Greek corpus, apart from a few citations in later authors. The first four books are preserved in a Latin translation made by Rufinus, and two homilies were translated by Jerome, who had only praise for Origen's achievement: "While Origen surpassed all writers in his other books, in his *Song of Songs* he surpassed himself."[29] Origen was the first to identify the Song as an epithalamium, or wedding song, written by Solomon in the form of a drama, which, for Origen, had a deeper, spiritual meaning as a portrait of the nuptial relationship between Christ and the church (or, occasionally, the soul). Origen's influence on subsequent Christian interpretation of the Song was considerable; as one commentator puts it, "medieval Christian interpretation of the Song consists largely of variations on Origenist themes" (Murphy 21). Among the great patristic scholars who endorsed Origen's allegorical approach were Gregory of Nyssa, Jerome, Ambrose, Theodoret, and Cyril of Alexandria. Pope Gregory the Great (540–604), whose own homilies on the Song were extremely popular, was much indebted to Origen, as was the late medieval interpreter Bernard of Clairvaux (twelfth century), who wrote eighty-six sermons on the first two chapters of the Song alone. For Bernard, the union of the bride and groom represented the mystical union of the individual soul and God.

Another line of Christian allegorical interpretation, which flourished in the twelfth century in conjunction with the veneration of Mary, identified the woman of the Song with the Virgin Mary. Mystical interpretation also played an important role in the history of Christian exegesis of the Song (see Pope 183–88). Mention should be made of the mystical interpretation of Teresa of Avila in the sixteenth century, one of the few women to write about the Song. In its passionate lyrics Teresa discovered the mysteries of the spiritual marriage of the soul and Christ. Unfortunately, little of her work remains; she burned her manuscript on the orders of her confessor. Fortunately, another nun had copied the first seven chapters of the manuscript.

Allegorical and mystical interpretation continued during the Reformation, alongside newer, nontraditional forms of exposition (Murphy 33). For instance, the great German Reformer Martin Luther saw the Song as a kind of political allegory composed by Solomon to celebrate his kingdom's relationship with God. Luther identified God's spouse as Solomon's subjects, but also saw in her a prefiguration of the church, and sometimes the individual soul.

In the wake of the Enlightenment, the allegorical approach began to lose adherents and, as critical biblical scholarship became well established, was generally abandoned. A few twentieth-century Roman Catholic scholars continued to advocate some form of it (e.g., Robert, Tournay, and Feuillet 1963; Tournay 1982). Some writers preferred typological or parabolic or spiritual interpretation as a way of reading the Song in terms of the love between God and God's people, without having to account for every detail (for modern examples of spiritual

---

29. *Origen, The Song of Songs: Commentary and Homilies*, trans. and annotated by R. P. Lawson, Ancient Christian Writers 26 (London: Longmans, 1957), 265.

interpretation, see "Privileging the Reader," pp. 82–86). A modern political allegory is offered by Stadelmann: the man represents the monarchical state and the Davidic dynasty; the woman, the native population of Judah in the Persian period; and the Song expresses the hopes for restoration of the Davidic dynasty in Judah after the exile (1990: 1–2).

In allegorical interpretation, every detail of the text has a meaning. Thus Rashi saw Song 1:13 ("To me my lover is a sachet of myrrh, lying all night between my breasts") as a reference to the Shekinah, between the cherubim that stood over the ark, whereas Cyril of Alexandria believed it referred to the Old and New Testaments, between which stands Christ. Justus Urgellensis identified the breasts with the learned teachers of the church, and pseudo-Cassiodorus thought the verse referred to the crucifixion of Christ, which is kept in eternal remembrance between the believer's breasts. "Black am I, and lovely, women of Jerusalem" (Song 1:5) was taken by pseudo-Saadia to mean that Israel was black by reason of making the golden calf, but fair by reason of receiving the Ten Commandments, and by Moses ibn Tibbon to mean black in this world and fair in the world to come, whereas Origen took it to mean black with sin but fair through conversion (for these and other examples, see Rowley 1965).

The problem with allegorical interpretation, as well as its typological and parabolic variants, is apparent. It is not verifiable, and it is arbitrary. No agreement exists among allegorical interpreters. "If two allegorizers ever agree on the interpretation of a verse it is only because one has copied from the other" (Keel 8).

The Song is not an allegory; there is no indication that the poet ever intended it to be given an esoteric interpretation. When biblical writers used symbolic language to make a point, they were not usually subtle about it. Nathan's parable about the poor man and his ewe lamb required explication: "You are the man" (2 Sam 12:1–7). Jotham tells a fable in which, of all those invited, only the bramble was willing to become king over the trees. He then proceeds to apply it specifically to the kingship of Abimelech over the Shechemites (Judg 9:7–21). A love poem, or what looks like a love poem, can be an allegory—but how is one to know?

> Let me sing for my beloved
>   a love song concerning his vineyard:
> My beloved had a vineyard
>   on a very fertile hill.
> He dug it and cleared it of stones,
>   and planted it with choice vines;
> he built a watchtower in the midst of it,
>   and hewed out a wine vat in it;
> he expected it to yield grapes,
>   but it yielded wild grapes.
>   (Isa 5:1–2)

That this is not a love song might gradually be dawning on the prophet's audience, but, lest the audience miss the point, the allegorical meaning is spelled out:

> For the vineyard of the Lord of hosts
>   is the house of Israel,
> and the men of Judah
>   are his pleasant planting;
> he expected justice,
>   but, behold, bloodshed!
> righteousness,
>   but, behold, a cry!
>
> (Isa 5:7)

Although the Song is not an allegory, it may be admitted that it lends itself to allegorical interpretation. Ironically, some of the features that helped make the Song a great love poem—what I have identified above as the Song's controlling poetic strategies—were the very features that facilitated its allegorical interpretation. Because the lovers represent any and all lovers, their roles could be easily assigned to figures that suited the allegorist's predilections and goals. Moreover, the poem's invitation to its readers to identify their experience of love with that of the protagonists was readily accepted by allegorical interpreters, who proceeded to identify themselves (the individual soul) and the communities to which they belonged (Israel, the church) as the lover seeking the eternal, divine beloved. It is unlikely that allegorical interpretation of the Song would have been so necessary, or so popular, inventive, and influential, if the poem were about specific lovers of the past, for instance, Solomon and the queen of Sheba, or Solomon and a country maid, as in the dramatic theory (see below).

If some of its features appear to invite allegory, in other respects the Song poses serious challenges for allegorical interpretation. The equality of the lovers is difficult to reconcile with the obviously unequal relationship between God and Israel, or Christ and the church, or God and the individual believer. Whereas the woman in the Song is never subordinate to her partner, in allegorical readings the figures for whom she stands must take a subservient role. Further, the Song of Songs presents its readers with not one but two subject positions from which to read or with which to identify: the female's and the male's, either or both of which readers are free to adopt. In allegory, however, only one subject position is available to the reader: with few exceptions, that of the female. In the long history of allegorical interpretation of the Song, male readers have identified themselves with the woman who desires, seeks, suffers for, and rejoices in her beloved, who is identified with God. Not surprisingly, this gender confusion can lead to interesting, and sometimes bizarre, results (see Moore 2001).

The Dramatic Theory

The view that the Song is a drama was popular in the nineteenth and early twentieth centuries. Proponents of this theory, while not necessarily claiming that
the Song was a theatrical piece, assigned parts, provided scenes and stage directions, and supplied a plot. For some the drama had two main characters,
Solomon and the rustic maiden whom he saw on a visit to her village, fell in
love with, and took to Jerusalem to be his bride. So impressed was he by her
beauty, purity of soul, and virtuous conduct that he renounced his life of wan-
ton polygamy in favor of a pure and true love (see, e.g., Delitzsch). Other critics, who questioned the identification of Solomon with the male beloved and
found the two-character version lacking in progression, added a third main
character, the maiden's shepherd lover, to whom she remained faithful in spite
of the mighty King Solomon's attempts to win her affection. The Song thus
teaches a lesson about the virtue of fidelity in the face of temptation and about
the strength of true love (see, e.g., Ginsburg).

I mentioned above that the Song lends itself to allegory. It also lends
itself to interpretation as a drama. It consists entirely of speeches. Parts of it—
specifically the "stories" told by the woman—suggest something of a plot (see
"Different Ways of Speaking about Love," pp. 14–15, and "Lyric Poetry and
Reading for the Plot," pp. 42–45). Its open-endedness, the lack of background
information about the characters and their relationship, makes it easy to read
actions and motivations into it. Ironically, however, by identifying speakers and
making the Song into a story about specific lovers of the past, the dramatic theory undermines some of the Song's most important features, its universality and
timelessness (see "The Lovers as Representing All Lovers," pp. 8–9).

Apart from the fact that it consists entirely of speeches, the Song has no dramatic qualities; it could, as suggested above, be performed, but as a lyric poem,
not as a drama. To turn it into a drama, too much has to be read between the
lines. Moreover, interpreters can assume as many dramatis personae as they
desire and divide the speeches as they please (Budde 1894: 57). Even the meaning of a speech will vary according to who the interpreter thinks is speaking. A
speech in the mouth of the shepherd lover is pure and devoted. The same speech
placed by another interpreter in the mouth of Solomon is lustful and manipula-
tive (Garrett 77). The dramatic theory has few adherents today, but readers find
it surprisingly hard to resist looking for some kind of story "behind" the Song's
lyrics (see "Lyric Poetry and Reading for the Plot," pp. 42–45). A modern advocate of a dramatic approach to the Song is Goulder, who identifies two major
characters (Solomon and the Arabian princess who became his queen), divides
the Song into fourteen scenes, supplies stage directions, and invents an intricate plot that begins with the arrival of the princess at Solomon's court and finds
its resolution in her acknowledgment by the king as his favorite queen (1986:

2–4). Provan's three-character dramatic version (2001), in which an unhappy member of Solomon's harem remains steadfastly devoted to her first, true love, is even more arbitrary.

Wedding Songs

Viewing the Song as a collection of poems sung in connection with wedding ceremonies—a convenient life setting, especially for those uneasy with explicit sexuality in a biblical book—was given currency in the mid-nineteenth century by the studies of J. G. Wetzstein, who was then the German consul in Syria. Wetzstein observed that wedding celebrations tended to last seven days, during which the bride and groom were crowned and treated as queen and king, and descriptive poems (*waṣfs*) praising their beauty were sung in their honor. There were also war songs and a sword dance performed between rows of spectators (see, e.g., Wetzstein's "Remarks on the Song," which appears as an appendix to Delitzsch's commentary). It is easy to see how commentators of the time could have been carried away by the possible parallels with the Song, and some exegetes still appeal to Wetzstein's description of the dance in relation to the description of the woman in Song 6:13–7:6 [7 H] (see the Commentary). Critics challenged the relevance of Wetzstein's observations, which were based on modern Syrian peasant customs, for interpretation of the Song, and subsequent investigations questioned his findings (Rowley 220–21; Pope 141–44). There is no reason to restrict the use of love songs to weddings. Although the Song may occasionally allude to marriage (see the general discussion under 3:6–11 in the Commentary), the lovers are not a bride and groom, nor do they behave like a betrothed couple (see Fox 231–32).

Cultic Interpretation

Rowley's discussion of the cultic interpretation of the Song in his essay mentioned above shows how influential the cultic theory became in the first half of the twentieth century (1965: 223–42). The idea that the Song has its origins in myths and rites of divine marriage and the so-called "fertility cult" was spurred by ancient Near Eastern archaeology and the discoveries of ancient Near Eastern texts, especially the love lyrics of ancient Mesopotamia. The Song was connected with the liturgy of the Tammuz-Adonis cult, the cult of the dying and rising vegetation god (e.g., Meek), and with the Mesopotamian sacred-marriage rite, a view supported by so eminent a Sumeriologist as Kramer (1969). "Fertility cult"—an unfortunate term if ever there was one—is a misleading description of the intention of Mesopotamian religious practices. Evidence regarding the nature of "sacred marriage" (also not a very apt term), as well as worship of Tammuz in his various incarnations, is not clear-cut, and its assessment depends on how one interprets and connects a vast range of texts. The chief problem for cultic interpretation of the Song is that lovers, whether they are men and women or gods and goddesses, talk about love in the same way. The Song offers no reason to think of its lovers as gods. The bold metaphoric language that they use to describe each other and the flights of fancy that picture the loved one in exotic places like the peaks of Lebanon (4:8) are not uncommon features of love poetry in general. Although most scholars recognize ancient Near Eastern influence on the poetry of the Song, cultic interpretation is no longer in vogue. Now that its basis is being weakened by scholars of Mesopotamian religion who question the connection of the Mesopotamian love songs with the sacred-marriage rite, it is unlikely to win new adherents. The issue of a possible cultic background for the Song is discussed above under "Historical-Cultural Context" (pp. 63–67) and the Mesopotamian evidence under "Literary Context: Ancient Near Eastern Love Poetry" (pp. 47–63).

The argument that the cultic approach offers the best explanation of the erotic imagery of the Song finds perhaps its greatest proponent in Marvin Pope. In the copious notes to his commentary on the Song, Pope makes frequent reference to ancient Near Eastern parallels that, in his opinion, argue for an origin for the Song in cultic mortuary feasts. He does not, however, develop the implications of these parallels for the particular verses of the Song to which he relates them, nor does he apply them to the whole Song to develop a sustained cultic interpretation. The genuine parallels, rather than establishing a cultic *Sitz im Leben*, reveal no more, or less, than the shared cultural heritage of ancient Near Eastern love poetry.

Feminist Criticism

The influence of feminist biblical criticism on Song of Songs research has been considerable. Not surprisingly, feminist scholars were drawn to this book that seemed to offer a breath of fresh air in the patriarchal climate of the biblical world; see, for example, the articles in the collections edited by Brenner (1993) and Brenner and Fontaine (2000; many of the works discussed below are reprinted in, or originally appeared in, these volumes). Trible, writing in 1978, argued that in the Song there is no male dominance, no female subordination, and no stereotyping of either sex. Pope, while pointing out that Ginsburg had already read the Song as a treatise for the emancipation of women, agrees with Trible that the woman of the Song is equal and even dominant and that patriarchalism is absent (205–10). Meyers finds the Song remarkably free of androcentrism and proposes that a gynocentric mode predominates (1986: 218; see also 1988: 177–80). Praise for the Song's portrayal of sexual equality is expressed, among others, by Falk, who sees the Song as an "antidote to some of the themes of biblical patriarchy" (1988: 528), by Weems, who finds in it a call for "balance in male and female relations" and "mutuality, not dominance" (160), and by Bloch and Bloch, who regard the woman as the equal of the man and often his superior (4–5). Even Brenner, who acknowledges the inevitable influence of its patriarchal environment upon the Song, waxes enthusiastic: "There is no equality of the sexes in the Song, which is how Trible describes the situation. There is female superiority" (1993b: 273). Some, like Brenner and van Dijk-Hemmes, hail the Song as the product of women's culture, if not female authorship (Brenner 1993c; Bekkenkamp and van Dijk 1993: 79–83; Brenner and van Dijk-Hemmes 1993: 3–13, 71–83 *et passim*), possibilities discussed already above ("Historical-Cultural Context"). This view has gained considerable currency and, for some, serves as the starting point for their reading of the Song (see, e.g., the articles by Bekkenkamp, Arbel, and Butting in Brenner and Fontaine 2000, and the studies by LaCocque 1998 and Walsh 2000).

Not all critics have been so confident about the Song's gender equality and nonsexism. Pardes (1992) draws attention to the Song's simultaneous acceptance of and challenge to patriarchy and emphasizes the tension between female desire and patriarchal restraint, as seen, for example, in the way the city guards treat a woman roaming the streets at night (5:7), the woman's brothers' concern for her chastity (1:6; 8:8–10), and the woman's internalizing of patriarchal restrictions (5:3; 1:6; 8:10). Merkin, in a spirited and somewhat satirical essay, sees the Song as a cautionary tale advising women that passion is dangerous— a text that places the burden of sexuality, both its allure and its danger, on women (1994).

Whereas most earlier studies tended to praise the Song for its nonsexism, gender equality, and foregrounding of the woman, dissenting voices are growing. Both Clines and Polaski challenge the concept of an autonomous female protagonist whose point of view the Song represents, arguing that the woman and her supposedly authentic female subjectivity reflect a male consciousness. For Clines, she is a male fantasy in which a male author has created his ideal dream woman, one whose only pastime is dreaming about him (1995: 102–6). For Polaski, she has internalized the male gaze and can see, and judge, herself only through her patriarchal society's eyes (1997: 71–81). Black, using the concept of the grotesque as a heuristic tool, challenges the prevailing view that the Song's metaphorical descriptions of the body are complimentary and explores their grotesque nature as symptomatic of anxiety, dis-ease, and a darker side of desire (1999a, 1999b, 2000a, 2000b). Observing that the Song can be hazardous to a feminist's critical faculties, I discuss some of the difficulties facing the exegete expecting to find gender equality in this text (Exum 2000). To my knowledge, the present commentary is the first to examine systematically gender differences and the role they play in the presentation of the relationship between the lovers in the Song.

Privileging the Reader

Due in part to the contributions of feminist criticism, the Song has been the subject of considerable scholarly interest in recent years. Biblical scholars have also become increasingly interested in the Song as the body, sexuality, and the construction of gender have become fashionable subjects of study in the humanities in general. What more obvious text for investigating these topics than the Song of Songs? While a good deal of exegetical and traditional work continues to be produced on the Song of Songs, exciting new and provocative approaches have emerged in the postmodern era that, for all their variety, are informed by a critical recognition of the role of the reader in making meaning. Readers set the interpretive agenda by the kinds of questions they pose of a text—this set of questions rather than that set of questions. The questions thus determine, to a large extent, the answers that will emerge in any particular reading.

Attention to the role of the reader in making meaning is not strictly a postmodern development, but it has flourished in a postmodern climate, and postmodern theory has influenced, to varying degrees, the scholars mentioned below.[30] A focus on the reader leads one to ask different questions, not only of the text but also of the interpretation it has elicited, and sometimes of the interpreters themselves—their motivations, stated and unstated, conscious and unconscious. Ideological criticism is more text- than reader-oriented, but in asking such questions of a text as, whose interests are being served? and what rival discourses might the text be seeking to suppress? it makes the reader an equal, if not dominant, conversation partner in the dialogue with the text. Metacommentary asks similar questions of a text's interpretation.[31] For instance, shifting the emphasis from text to reader, a feminist interpretation might investigate how the Song makes different claims upon female and male readers. Are female readers asked to adopt a male point of view that requires reading against their interests? The subjectivity conferred upon the woman by the poet inevitably reflects a patriarchal worldview; how could it not? (see "The Song and Conventional Gender Relations," pp. 25–28). But once conferred, that subjectivity is no longer within the poet's control. In fact, we might ask why an ancient author's intention might matter at all. Even if it were the case that the poem subtly encourages women to adopt a male way of looking at themselves, it does

---

30. For a useful discussion of postmodernism in biblical studies, see David J. A. Clines, "The Pyramid and the Net: The Postmodern Adventure in Biblical Studies," in *On the Way to the Postmodern: Old Testament Essays, 1967–1998*, vol. 1, JSOTSup 292 (Sheffield: Sheffield Academic Press, 1998), 138–57.

31. Both these approaches are illustrated lucidly by David J. A. Clines, "The Ideology of Writers and Readers of the Hebrew Bible" and "Metacommentating Amos," in *Interested Parties: The Ideology of Writers and Readers of the Hebrew Bible*, JSOTSup 205, GCT 1 (Sheffield: Sheffield Academic Press, 1995), 9–25 and 76–93 respectively.

not follow that real readers have to read it that way. Moving into the realm of metacommentary, a reader could query—or queery, as Moore has done so brilliantly in the case of ancient and medieval allegorists—what happens when male readers adopt the woman's subject position? (Moore 2001; see also Burrus and Moore 2003: 45–48). It remains for future study to construct the history of gender ideology in Song of Songs interpretation by examining how and to what extent commentators reinscribe the gender ideology of the text or how they read sexual stereotypes of their times and their own culturally conditioned gender biases back into the biblical text.

The studies mentioned above by Clines, Polaski, and Black—all of whom are unwilling to accept at face value the Song's picture of what seems to be an ideal, loving relationship—could be described as resistant readings. Resistant readings seek to problematize the text or particular aspects of it; for Black, for example, the supposedly complimentary bodily descriptions. Black's work, in particular, offers an important, insistent reminder that all is not necessarily well in the garden of eroticism. By foregrounding recalcitrant details of the text that interpreters generally pass over with little comment, such as the beating of the woman by the watchmen (5:7), she seeks to unsettle coherent readings of the Song (2001; cf. Black and Exum 1998: 336–40, 342; see also Pardes 1992).

Black appeals to the psychoanalytic theory of Julia Kristeva, in particular her work on the abject, to explore the threat to order in the Song (1999a: 260–69; 2001). Boer's readings of the Song range from the psychoanalytic (2000) to the pornographic (1999), mixing arcane Lacanian analysis with what has been aptly described as X-rated X-egesis and "an orgiastic XXX-travaganza" by Burrus and Moore (see their critique of Boer in 2003: 34–39). At what would appear to be the opposite end of the spectrum from Boer's pornographic allegory (1999) are recent spiritual interpretations of the Song in terms of divine–human love. Ostriker, in a refined example of this kind of approach, proposes that the love celebrated in the Song may be understood as simultaneously natural and spiritual.

> It is no accident that every mystical tradition on earth speaks of God as the beloved, and that everyone in love sees the beloved's face and form as holy. If elsewhere we must divide the "sacred" from the "secular," that division is annihilated in the Song. Here, for once, it becomes meaningless. (2000: 37)

Taking her cue from the Song's vision of mutual desire, Ostriker speaks of a vision of nondivided reality and of the possibility of a nonhierarchal love relationship with God. David Carr recommends an approach to the Song that "redefine[s] and combine[s] sex and spirituality" (1998: 432). No text is an island; thus, for Carr, both the Song's origins as love poetry and its time-honored interpretation as symbolizing the love between God and God's people contribute to its meaning (1998, 2003). Two recent studies that find in the Song a spiritual meaning alongside its naturalistic meaning are LaCocque (1998), for whom the

love between the woman and the man "becomes paradigmatic for all authentic
love and, more particularly, for the love of God for his people" (209), and Walsh
(2000), who connects the unconsummated (in her view) desire that animates
the Song with a spiritual quest for the divine.

Whose desire *is* represented in the Song of Songs? That of any and all lovers,
I argue in this commentary (see, especially, "The Lovers as Representing All
Lovers," pp. 8–9), but, like other authors of commentaries, I treat love in the
Song as the poet represents it: as love between a woman and a man. In one of
the most avant-garde readings of the Song to date, Burrus and Moore critique
the "homiletics of heteronormativity in Song of Songs interpretation" that has
prevailed in virtually all scholarly writing on the Song since its widespread
recognition as love poetry and the demise of allegorical interpretation (2003:
25). "[T]he Song continues to be read unselfconsciously through the prism of
an unproblematized heterosexuality," they lament (28). What they desire, and
explore by staging an encounter between feminist and queer theories, is the possibility of "retrieving the eroticism of an ancient text, such as the Song of Songs,
that predates both (modern) 'sexuality' and (an equally modern) 'pornography,'
that is other than heterosexual, yet also not homosexual, thereby eluding the
hamfisted clutches of those dualistic categories altogether" (34). They end their
essay by proposing, as a way of countering heterosexist reading of the Song, a
theological reading that would recuperate the divine element missing in post-
allegorical readings; in their words, "a return of the divine repressed":

> Yet the God who returns to the Song cannot simply be identical to the God who
> long ago exited the Song, queer though the latter undoubtedly was. The God who
> returns will need to be queerer still, an infinitely malleable lover, embracing and
> exceeding all imaginable "positions" (gendered or otherwise), equally at home on
> the contemporary altars of sado-masochistic ritual as in the prayer closets of ancient
> and medieval monks. This God, who is now nowhere in the Song, would, once
> again, be everywhere in the Song, in command and under command by turns. (52)

One wonders what this god might have in common with the god Linafelt
envisions when he charts a somewhat similar course from the Song's lyrical
presentation of eros, via the tradition of allegorical interpretation, to a god who
risks erotic encounter with human beings. What if, he asks, "God were not 'by
definition' immune to risk? What if God were *not* above the fray of passion?
What if the divine were *not* understood to be perfection, but, rather, bound as
well to the vicissitudes of desire, with all the anguish and ecstasy that it
implies?" (2002: 325) Eroticizing theological discourse, he believes, could
have profound implications (336), though he tantalizingly leaves these implications for the reader to explore (341–42). Perhaps queer and spiritual readings
are not so far apart in what they desire. And why should they be? As Ostriker
observes, "Indeed, so much do the lovers mirror each other, and so little does

the poem seem to stress sexual difference as such, that it makes itself available to same-sex lovers in much the same metaphorical way as it makes itself available to lovers of God" (Ostriker 2000: 47).

Readerly desire seems to play a particularly important role in the interpretation of this book about desire, more so than for other biblical books. Taking her cue from Roland Barthes's erotics of reading, Black explores the relation between the Song and its readers as an amatory one, in which the Song as lover teases, beguiles, resists, and yields to its readers, and readers, for their part, are seduced by its romantic overtures and flirtatious techniques to overlook its faults (1999b). This relationship is explicitly addressed by autobiographical criticism, in which readers make themselves the subject of study alongside the Song and offer highly personal accounts of their relation to it (e.g., Brenner 2000, Fontaine 2000; cf. Landy 2002). The Song can be many things to many readers; for example, it can be a substitute for the real love object, it can instruct its reader how to be a better lover, it can raise false expectations about love or self-fulfilling ones.

Readers inspired by the Song over the centuries include numerous artists, musicians, and writers.[32] Only recently, however, have biblical scholars begun to consider ways in which biblical books or subjects have been interpreted in the arts.[33] Artistic interpretations of the Song can be studied in their own right and related to both artistic and cultural developments of their time, as part of the wider history of interpretation of the Song. Or one can stage a conversation between the arts and the text by relating artistic representations to interpretive issues in Song of Songs studies. This is what Black and I seek to do in an article that reads the Song in relation to a twelve-pane representation of it in stained glass by the Pre-Raphaelite artist Edward Burne-Jones. Among other things, we note that similar questions of unity and plot are raised by both works, thus posing similar questions for interpretation (Black and Exum 1998). Another study

32. For a brief survey of the Song in the arts, see *EncJud.* XV, 151–52. On the Song in English literature, see James Doelman, "Song of Songs," in *A Dictionary of Biblical Tradition in English Literature*, ed. David Lyle Jeffrey (Grand Rapids: Eerdmans, 1992), 727–30; "I Am a Rose of Sharon: The Song of Songs," in *The Bible and Literature: A Reader*, ed. David Jasper and Stephen Prickett, assisted by Andrew Hass (Oxford: Blackwell, 1999), 180–202; "The Song of Solomon," in *Chapters into Verse: Poetry in English Inspired by the Bible*, vol. I: *Genesis to Malachi*, ed. Robert Atwan and Laurance Wieder (Oxford: Oxford University Press, 1993), 368–85.

33. See, e.g., J. Cheryl Exum, ed., *Beyond the Biblical Horizon: The Bible and the Arts* (Leiden: Brill, 1999); J. Cheryl Exum and Stephen D. Moore, eds., *Biblical Studies/Cultural Studies: The Third Sheffield Colloquium*, JSOTSup 266, GCT 7 (Sheffield: Sheffield Academic Press, 1998); Martin O'Kane, ed., *Borders, Boundaries and the Bible*, JSOTSup 313 (Sheffield: Sheffield Academic Press, 2002); J. Cheryl Exum, *Plotted, Shot, and Painted: Cultural Representations of Biblical Women*, JSOTSup 215, GCT 3 (Sheffield: Sheffield Academic Press, 1996); Yvonne Sherwood, *A Biblical Text and Its Afterlives: The Survival of Jonah in Western Culture* (Cambridge: Cambridge University Press, 2000).

of the Song in art discusses how selected artists, in translating the Song into a visual medium, deal with questions of interpretation that also concern biblical scholars: what to make of the Song's unusual metaphoric descriptions of the body, its explicit and simultaneously delicate eroticism, and the inchoate narrative development in what is first and foremost a lyric poem (Exum forthcoming). In a study of the Song in music, Rogerson looks at how Bach's Cantatas 49 ("Ich geh und suche mit Verlangen") and 140 ("Wachet auf, ruft uns die Stimme") use the Song of Songs (1998).

Pope considers it "a blessing that Hollywood has not attempted a dramatic version of the Super Song with superstars" (1988: 317). Cinematic representation of the Song of Songs is made difficult by the Song's genre as lyric poetry, though, given what it has done with other biblical sources, it is hard to see why this should stop Hollywood. An amusing scene in the 1959 King Vidor film *Solomon and Sheba* has Solomon (Yul Brenner) recite to Sheba (Gina Lollobrigida) love lyrics she has inspired, as they drift along a river in a private barge, pushing aside the dense overhanging foliage that threatens to hit them in the face. He has composed his poem in the archaic language biblical films always use when they want to sound like the Bible: "Behold, thou art fair, my love, thine eyes are as doves, thy lips are as pomegranates. How much better is thy love than wine!" Another biblical epic, John Huston's ambitious *The Bible* (1996), has Abraham (George C. Scott) and Sarah (Ava Gardner) recite verses from the Song to each other before making love. In a dismal 1988 film, *The Wisdom of Crocodiles*, even a vampire (Jude Law), searching for the true love that will redeem him, resorts to the descriptive praise of the woman's body in the Song to affirm that his victim is all fair and there is no flaw in her. A story with a plot, along the lines of that suggested by the three-character dramatic theory, remains to be brought to the silver screen. A novel already exists upon which the screenplay could be based, *Solomon's Song*, by Roberta Kells Dorr: "She was his shepherdess, his bride, his only true love . . . and the one woman he was forbidden to have." "An aging king . . . a scheming queen . . . a young prince destined for the throne . . . the beautiful woman who captivated them all. . . . *Solomon's Song* brings the Bible's greatest love story vividly to life."[34] In the meantime, scholars can discuss the vision of love in the Song as compared with particular cinematic representations of love, as, for example, Keefer and Linafelt do for the Song and Lors Von Trier's 1996 film *Breaking the Waves* (1998; cf. Linafelt 2002).

To the making of many books there is no end says Qohelet (12:12), and surely there is no end to the making of many interpretations of the Song. As the long, varied, and ongoing history of interpretation of the Song reveals, its readers find what is true of scripture to be all the more true of the Song of Songs: "Turn it, and turn it again, for everything is in it" (*m. Avot* 5:22).

---

34. From the back cover of Roberta Kells Dorr, *Solomon's Song* (Nashville: Moorings, 1989).

COMMENTARY

Song of Songs 1:1
Superscription

1:1   The Song of Songs, which is Solomon's.

The title, or superscription, is later than the poem itself. It uses the relative pronoun *ʾăšer* ("which, who, that") whereas the rest of the poem uses *še-*, and it associates the book with Solomon, who plays a very small role in the poem, where the subject is the mutual desire of unidentified male and female speakers and the points of view represented are theirs. The translation "which is Solomon's" leaves open the question, in what sense is the Song Solomon's? for while *ʾăšer lišlōmōh* can indicate authorship, it can also mean that Solomon is the dedicatee, or that the Song is about him or connected with him in some way (cf. the use of *lĕdāwid* as an editorial superscription to many of the psalms). The title lends antiquity as well as authority to the poem. It is, as Fox observes, the first step in the religious appropriation of the book that would claim for Solomon the authorship of the Song, Proverbs, and Ecclesiastes.

The fact that Solomon is mentioned in the poem, together with his reputation as the composer of some 3000 proverbs and 1005 songs (1 Kgs 4:32 [5:12 H]) and his large harem, which suggests he must have been something of a lover (1 Kgs 11:3), no doubt facilitated the traditional assignation of the Song to him. Other features of the poem could have played a role as well. There is a general sense of leisure and luxury, which recalls some of the descriptions of Solomon's reign. We encounter a king, queens, and concubines, and a courtly ambiance is suggested in some verses (especially the first verses of the poem, 1:2–4). Jerusalem is foregrounded as a result of the role played by the women of Jerusalem (1:5; 2:7; 3:5, 10; 5:8, 16; 8:4; as opposed to only one mention of Jerusalem on its own, 6:4). References to northern and southern parts of the country (En-gedi, Sharon, Gilead, Tirzah, Heshbon, Carmel, Baal-hamon) give the impression of a unified Israel, and featured as well are Lebanon and its famed cedars, used by Solomon in his building projects. There is an impression of peace and well-being, for which Solomon's reign was renowned (1 Kgs 4:20, 24–25 [5:4–5 H]). The interest in flora and fauna is reminiscent of Solomon's (cf. 1 Kgs 4:33 [5:13 H]), and the many quotidian and unusual luxury items mentioned by name evoke an exotic atmosphere. The pervasive presence in the Song of perfumes, unguents, ornaments, jewels, gold and silver, scented garments, precious stones and metals, and rare aromatic woods and spices calls to mind the wealth of Solomon, as measured in cedar from Lebanon, gold, silver, ivory, apes, peacocks, garments, weapons, spices, horses, chariots, and so on (1 Kgs 10:22–29).

Solomon's name appears only six times in the poem: in a descriptive phrase "curtains of Solomon" (1:5); in a passage about his palanquin and his wedding day (3:7, 9, 11); and, in a somewhat dismissive vein, in connection with his vineyard (8:11 and 12). He is not the lover in the poem, nor one of the speakers. The Song is not "about" him, and yet he casts his shadow over it. The title represents an ancient tradition of reading the Song in relation to Solomon, and one that influenced the interpretation of the book for centuries, until the rise of critical biblical scholarship (and even beyond, for Solomon continued to play a role as a character in the dramatic theory popular in the late nineteenth and early twentieth centuries; see Introduction, "The Dramatic Theory," pp. 78–79).

The title has implications for the poem through its effect on modern readers as well. To the extent that we think of the Song at all in connection with a particular time and place in the past—for it is singularly unconcerned with locating itself in history—the title invites us to imagine a kind of vague Solomonic backdrop (regardless of the date we ultimately choose to assign to it). The association with Solomon at the very beginning encourages readers to think of Solomonic attributes or Solomonic splendor when a king is mentioned or regal imagery appears. And when city walls and squares and watchmen are mentioned, do readers not tend to think of Jerusalem? Indeed, by making the connection to Solomon for us, the title lends a Solomonic aura to the very features, mentioned above, that may have led an editor to associate the book with Solomon in the first place.

The title defines the composition as a *šîr*, a generic term for "song" or "poem." Sometimes, and especially in liturgical contexts, songs were accompanied by musical instruments, such as timbrel or tambourine (*tōp*), harp (*nēbel*), lyre (*kinnôr*), flute (*ḥālîl*), trumpets (*ḥăṣōṣĕrôt*), and cymbals (*mĕṣiltayim*); see, for example, Gen 31:27; Exod 15:20–21; 1 Sam 18:6; 1 Kgs 10:12; Isa 23:16; 30:29; Ezek 26:13; Amos 5:23; 6:5; Ps 144:9; Neh 12:27; 1 Chr 13:8; 15:16, 19; 16:42; 25:6; 2 Chr 5:12, 13; 9:11; 23:13. Though there is no mention of musical instruments in the Song, the format of alternating speeches lends itself to performance. Whether or not the Song was performed we do not know; what we possess is a literary text that calls itself a *šîr*, a poem of indisputable quality worthy of the sobriquet "the best," a "chef-d'œuvre de poésie pure" (Buzy 1940).

The use of the same noun in the singular and plural in the construction "the Song of Songs" is a way of expressing the superlative in Hebrew (GKC §133i). This is the song above all other songs, the best song (cf. "king of kings," Ezek 26:7, the king above all other kings; "holy of holies," Exod 26:33, the most holy place; "vanity of vanities," Eccl 1:2, the height of absurdity). The superscription presents the poem as the best, or perhaps most beautiful, there is (of its genre, one presumes, though Fox takes the superlative as referring to the poem's musical quality: the most musical, or harmonious, of songs). Such is a profound, and charmingly arrogant, assertion. It is certainly the best ancient Hebrew love poem, since no others are known to us.

We might also entertain the possibility that the Song of Songs is a single work composed of smaller songs, like the modern oratorio (Garrett), or the song wherein all songs can be found, in which all songs are included (Landy 16). This is not to say that the Song was understood as an anthology, for the word *šîr* in the title is in the singular. Whoever added the title seems to have viewed the book as a single song, not as a collection, in which case one might expect the title "Songs of Solomon," as in "Proverbs of Solomon" for the book of Proverbs (Fox). The Song of Songs contains no further superscriptions that might function, like those in the book of Psalms, to indicate composite status (see Introduction, "One Poem or Many?" pp. 33–37).

Song of Songs 1:2–4
The Voice of Desire

<She>

1:2   Let him kiss me with the kisses of his mouth,
        for your caresses[a] are better than wine!

3   The fragrance of your perfumes is good,[b]
        perfume poured out[c] is your name,
        for this women love you.

4   Draw me after you; let us run![d]
        The king has brought me to his chambers,[e]
    we will rejoice and delight in you,
        we will savor[f] your caresses above wine;
        rightly[g] they love you.

a. The translation "love" is too abstract for *ddym*. The meaning is better conveyed by "embraces" or "caresses." LXX and Vg. read "breasts," which has the same spelling.

b. Literally, "as for fragrance, your oils (perfumes) are good"; taking *l* as a dative of reference (GKC §143e; Joüon-Muraoka 133d).

c. The word *tûraq* looks like a *hophal* form of *ryq*, "pour out." The verbal form is feminine and *šemen* ("perfume") is masculine, but gender agreement is not always observed in Hebrew. Horst (BHS) suggests emending to *tamrûq*, which in Esth 2:3, 9, 12 refers to oil for purification. Numerous commentators have proposed that the word *tûraq* refers to a particular type of cosmetic oil or its place of origin. Pope, e.g., who sees it as a high grade of oil, translates, "Turaq oil is your name"; Fox, "'Oil of Turaq' is your name." Not only is this not very poetic but it also does not convey much to the English reader. I follow here the traditional translation, "poured out," based on the LXX and Vg. and perhaps also attested in 1QCant.

d. Following the Targum, and most commentators, against the MT punctuation, "after you we will run." LXX has a different reading: "They drew you. After you for the odor of your ointment we will run."

e. Reading as a precative perfect (expressing a wish), "Let the king bring me!" produces an attractive balance with "let him kiss me" in v. 2; so NIV, Ringgren, Munro 21, but balance seems an insufficient reason to abandon the usual sense of the perfect, especially in view of the Song's characteristic temporal shifts.

f. So JPS, Pope. Hebrew *zkr* in the *hiphil* has the sense of "recite, proclaim, celebrate, praise"; thus, "we will praise your caresses," continuing the idea expressed by the previous verbs, "rejoice" and "delight." In Lev 24:7; Isa 66:3; Hos 14:7 [8 H]; Ps 20:3 [4 H], the root is used in connection with incense and burnt offerings, suggesting their pleasing fragrance (Gordis, Pope). Since in English "savor" means not only to delight in something but also to taste or smell something with pleasure, it functions, like the suggestiveness of the Hebrew, to draw together the rejoicing of v. 4 and the sensations of taste and smell of vv. 2 and 3.

g. Taking *mêšārîm* as adverbial. 6QCant offers a variant reading, *myšrym ʾhwbym*, but it does not yield a meaningful translation.

[2–4] With the poem's first word, *yiššāqēnî*, "Let him kiss me!" desire bursts suddenly and dramatically onto the scene. A disembodied voice speaks, giving birth to a poetic Edenic world, as in those first moments of creation (imagine, for example, how startling Genesis would be if it began "Let there be light," without setting the stage in any way). Who is speaking? Our knowledge of the Song or our cultural assumptions about the context may lead us to conclude that the speaker is a woman, but this is not definitely established until v. 5, when the first clearly feminine form occurs. Verse 2 plunges us into a romantic relationship already in progress. The jussive here ("let him kiss") and the imperatives in v. 4, together with the direct address to another person ("you"), communicate a sense of urgency and create the impression that we are overhearing and observing as a love affair unfolds before us. That the Song begins in a woman's voice anticipates the important role she will play in the poem. Significantly the poem begins with a wish, a desire, for desire is what gives the poem its urgency and its raison d'être. Desire implies a lack. The lover is not there, and thus the woman speaks of him in the third person, "let him kiss me." But in the next part of v. 2, she addresses him directly as "you"; suddenly he is there, and in vv. 3 and 4, she continues to address him as "you." In v. 4 she speaks of "us" (meaning him and her), but then goes on to speak of "the king" and "we," as well as bringing in "they" at the end of the verse. Instances of enallage, the sudden shift of person, occur both in biblical poetry (GKC §144p) and in ancient Near Eastern love poetry, but the question still needs to be asked, what effect does the shift from "him" to "you" have on the meaning of the passage? It is as if, through speech, the woman is able to conjure up her lover in v. 2, as she will do elsewhere (e.g., 5:2–6:3). The kingly lover, with his intoxicating presence, materializes, brought into being by seductively beautiful poetry.

The poem begins *in medias res*. It ends without a sense of closure; the last verse brings us back to where we began, with the woman speaking of her desire. As a result, love in the Song of Songs is forever in progress (see Introduction, "Love Forever in Progress," pp. 11–13, and the discussion under 2:17 and 8:14).

[2] The woman wants to be the recipient of her lover's kisses. She does not say, "I am going to kiss him," or even "I want to kiss him," but rather desires him to take the initiative and kiss her. Of the thirty-one occurrences of *nšq*, meaning "to kiss" in the Bible, the majority are of men kissing other men, usually relatives; for example, Gen 27:26–27; 29:13; 33:4; 45:15; 48:10; 50:1; Exod 4:27; 18:7; 1 Sam 10:1; 20:41; 2 Sam 14:33. Laban speaks of kissing his daughters and grandchildren in Gen 31:28 and kisses them in v. 55 [32:1 H]), but the only instance of a man kissing a woman not of his immediate family occurs in Gen 29:11, when Jacob, upon meeting Rachel and recognizing her as a relative, kisses her. Women kiss other women in Ruth 1:9, 14. The only instance of a woman kissing a man is Prov 7:13, in a warning about the "loose woman" who seizes and kisses the unsuspecting youth. The two occurrences of *nšq* in the Song are both expressions of the desire for kissing rather than depictions of actual kissing: here in v. 2, the woman longs for her lover's kisses; in 8:1, she wishes he were a brother so that she could kiss him openly without reproach. Here she imagines kissing as something he will do to her; in 8:1, as something she will do to him.

Where does she want to be kissed? She does not say. Fox thinks mouth kisses are specified to distinguish them from nose kisses, but there is no mention of nose kisses in the Bible. This is, rather, the language of excess, and the excessiveness of love poetry. The poet could have said simply, "Let him kiss me." "Let him kiss me with kisses" is superfluous; with what else could he kiss her? "With the kisses of his mouth" is doubly superfluous. The translation, "let him kiss me with the kisses of his mouth," retains a sense of excess, as well as reproducing in translation the alliteration of the Hebrew, *yiššāqēnî minnĕšîqôt pîhû*.

He has not kissed her yet, but we might imagine he has already kissed her many times, for she knows that his lovemaking is better than wine. Here, as throughout the Song, the poet blurs the distinction between anticipation, or desire, and experience, or knowledge of lovemaking. Hebrew *dōdêkā* ("your caresses") is not love in the abstract but rather sexual activity, which can include kisses, caresses, and sexual intercourse (cf. 7:12 [13 H]; Prov 7:18; Ezek 16:8; 23:17). Verses 2–3 are difficult to translate into English in a way that suitably captures the repetition of the word *ṭôbîm* ("good") in reference first to caresses, as compared to wine, and then to perfumes. "For your caresses are superior to wine; the fragrance of your perfumes is superior" might serve the purpose, but is not very poetic. The translation of v. 3 offered here, "the fragrance of your perfumes is good," may sound banal, but actually we do tend to say things like "your perfume smells good" or "you smell good." Like its English equivalent "good," the Hebrew adjective *ṭôb* is a rather general term, and because it is not very specific, it invites the reader to consider in what ways caresses are better than wine and, if both caresses and perfumes are *ṭôbîm*, what they might have in common.

What do wine and love play, or lovemaking, have in common that makes the comparison between them so compelling? Love and wine are often associated in the Song; for example, 2:4; 4:10; 5:1; 7:9 [10 H]; 8:2. Surely it is the effect of love that is paramount here, which, like wine, is intoxicating, producing a sense of euphoria or giddiness (cf. Judg 9:13, "Shall I leave my wine which cheers gods and men, and go to sway over the trees?"). Kissing and drinking are connected through wordplay in Song 8:1–2, and such a pun suggests itself here: *yiššāqēnî*, "let him kiss me," if vocalized differently, would yield *yašqēnî*, "O that he would let me drink" (cf. Gordis, "Let me drink of the kisses of his mouth").

The Song routinely invokes the realm of the senses, and taste is also suggested by the comparison. Pope, following Albright (1963), translates "sweeter than wine," on the basis of the Ugaritic usage of *yn ṭb* as "sweet wine" as opposed to *yn lṭb*, "wine not good/sweet" (similarly, Fox, Murphy). In English, too, we speak not only of being besotted with a lover but also of love or kisses as sweeter than wine, which evokes both taste and intoxication. A tactile element is here as well, in the touching of the lips in kissing, and scent, introduced explicitly in the next verse, is hinted at in the bouquet of wine.

Both Pope and Murphy, following Albright, take the particle *kî* as asseverative or emphatic (truly your love is better than wine) rather than causal. This is unnecessary; the common causal meaning of *kî* as "for" or "because" makes better sense, as it gives a reason for the woman's desire to be kissed; namely, his kisses, as an instance of his love play, leave her feeling elated.

[3] Through the repetition of *ṭôbîm* (first in the comparative, "better," then in the positive, "good"), the inebriating effect on the woman of her lover's caresses seems to be carried over to his scent. Not only his caresses but also his scent—the fragrance given off by the perfumed oils and aromatic spices that men as well as women used—produce in her a feeling of euphoria. An Egyptian love song speaks of a young woman's fragrance as "an inundating aroma that intoxicates those who are present" (P. Chester Beatty I, Group C, No. 42, trans. Fox). Through synesthesia, fragrance is attributed to the man's name, probably the sound of his name when spoken (Budde). Just as his perfumes are intoxicating, so too is his name, which has the effect not simply of perfume, but of perfume poured out or wafted abroad; that is, the kind of overwhelming effect of heavily incensed or strongly scented air. It is no wonder then that not

his name is sweet?

only she but any woman in her right mind should find him irresistible (a theme present in the Egyptian example as well). The man's name may be fragrant and the woman may experience a sense of euphoria at the mention of it, but she never addresses him by name (nor he, her). The fact that the poet does not identify the lovers facilitates their identification with all lovers.

Hebrew *ʿălāmôt* refers to women who have reached sexual maturity. Precisely how young or old we are to imagine them is difficult to say, though the term is often understood as designating young women (LXX, *neanides*; Vg., *adulescentulae*). This is in keeping with the general impression the Song gives that the lovers themselves are young people. But the fact that the lovers are frequently pictured as young does not mean that the Song is about young love only. The speakers are not the same as the poet, who uses their voices to develop and explore a vision of love that is both fresh and mature (see Introduction, "The Lovers as Representing All Lovers," pp. 8–9).

[4] The woman addresses her lover with two imperatives, "Draw me after you; let us run!" a wish for him to take her away. And where should he take her? "The king has brought me to his chambers" suggests an answer. It also introduces a motif that appears four times in the Song, the bringing of the loved one to the house or chamber. The first two times this motif occurs, it is used of the man bringing the woman to the chamber or house (1:4; 2:4); the next two times, the woman brings or envisions bringing the man "to the house of my mother" (3:4; 8:2). In 3:4 house and chamber appear in synonymous parallelism, an indication that they are interchangeable members of the same image (Angénieux 1968: 136).

It makes no sense to assume that the king is a person other than the lover, for if he were, why would she and a king be rejoicing and delighting in the love of her absent lover? If, however, we take "the king" as another way of speaking about her lover (not that he is in fact a king, but that he is a king as far as she is concerned), then she has switched back to speaking of him in the third person, as she did at the beginning of v. 2, and in the next part of our verse she shifts back to second person "you," a shift she also made in v. 2.

But who, then, is the "we"? Possibly the woman is talking about herself and her lover, who is her king; that is, she and he together will delight in him and his love (in which case, "us" and "we" in this verse would refer to the same two people, and the delighting in him and his love could be something they are doing together; cf. the Sumerian poem cited on p. 53). More likely "we" refers to the speaker and the other women mentioned in v. 3, who are probably also the "they" of the end of v. 4. She is so besotted with him that she imagines other women will be similarly affected by him. They cannot help loving him (v. 3), and it is altogether fitting that they should (v. 4), and so she and they together will rejoice in him. These other women do not have to be present in the chamber with the lovers for the woman to claim that women everywhere will find him delightful. A third possibility—though it will not suggest itself until the next verse—is that "we" refers to the woman together with the women of Jerusalem, a subset of all the women in general who love him, and the only other speakers in the Song.

The meaning of the word translated "rightly" (*mêšārîm*) is debated. It frequently refers to ethical rightness (e.g., Isa 33:15; 45:19; Pss 9:8 [9 H]; 96:10; 98:9), which is reflected in the translations of LXX, "righteousness loves you," and Vg., "the upright love you." In two places it appears, as it does here, in connection with wine, Song 7:9 [10 H] and Prov 23:31, where it is best understood as describing wine that flows (*hlk*) "smoothly." These passages lead Fox to propose pointing *yayin* as *yên*, and translating *yên mêšārîm* "wine of smoothness," that is, "smooth wine." This leaves him with *ʾăhēbûkā* to account for, which he does by dividing the verse after *dōdêkā*: ". . . we will praise your caresses. / More than smooth wine do they love you." Besides involving minor changes in the Masoretic vocalization, this reading does away with the repetition of *dōdêkā miyyāyin* ("your caresses more than/above wine") in vv. 2 and 4, and, with it, the comparison that was twice drawn between caresses and wine to show the superiority of caresses. It also produces a less meaningful comparison: caresses may be praised as more intoxicating than wine, but what does "they love you more than smooth wine" mean? Since *mêšārîm* has the well-attested sense of "equity" or "rightness," it is preferable to take it as adverbial (as in Pss 58:1 [2 H]; 75:2 [3 H]), meaning "rightly" (so most translations and commentators). The third members of the two triplets, each ending in *ʾăhēbûkā*, thus balance each other: "for this women love you" (v. 3) // "rightly they love you" (v. 4), with *ʿal-kēn* ("for this, therefore") and *mêšārîm* ("rightly") functioning similarly to convey the logic and appropriateness of loving the man.

Might the other women, who, along with the speaker, are rejoicing and delighting in her lover, be present in the king's chambers? The fact that the lover is called a king suggests not only her attitude about his regal qualities. A king, particularly in his role as a lover (a Solomon?), has many women. What, then, if the speaker of vv. 2–4 is fantasizing herself as being singled out by the king (let him kiss *me*, not the others)? One might imagine her fantasy to be something like this: let him bring me to his harem, to the place where all the women praise and delight in his love, as his favorite one, the one all the queens and concubines will deem fortunate in his love (cf. 6:9). Song 1:2–4 fits very well the Solomonic atmosphere evoked by the title of the book. Taken by itself, it could be classified as a type of courtesan's song. In the light of what follows, it becomes one of the Song's many flights of fancy or "travesties," literary fictions in which the lovers assume various roles and identities in the poet's meandering romantic fantasy. There is both consistency and difference in the portrayal of the lovers as the poem develops, which leads some readers to see unity in the Song and others to view it as a collection. Like the fact that the lovers are anonymous, their various poses or "multiple conflicting stories," as Landy calls them (61), function to make the protagonists types of lovers rather than individuals (see Introduction, "The Lovers as Representing All Lovers," pp. 8–9).

Song of Songs 1:5–2:7
A Dialogue about Love

<She>

1:5   Black am I, and lovely,
       women of Jerusalem,
    like the tents of Qedar,
       like the curtains of Solomon.

6   Pay no heed[a] that I am black,   *Swarthy*
       that the sun has gazed upon me.[b]
    My mother's sons were angry with me;
       they made me keeper of the vineyards.
       My own vineyard I have not kept.

7   Tell me, my soul's beloved,
       where[c] do you graze,
       where do you lie[d] at midday?—
    lest[e] I be like a wanderer[f]
       by the flocks of your companions.

<Women of Jerusalem ?>

8   If you do not know,
       most beautiful of women,
    follow the tracks of the sheep,
       and graze your kids *goats*
       by the shepherds' tents.

<He>

9   To a mare[g] among Pharaoh's chariots
       I compare you, my friend.

10   Your cheeks are lovely with pendants,[h]
       your neck with beads.

11   Pendants of gold we will make for you,
       with spangles of silver.

<She>
12   While the king is on his couch,[i]
      my nard gives off its fragrance.[j]
13   To me my lover is a sachet of myrrh,
      lying[k] all night between my breasts.
14   To me my lover is a cluster of henna blossoms
      in the vineyards of En-gedi.

<He>
15   Look at you! You are beautiful, my friend!
      Look at you! You are beautiful.
      Your eyes are doves.

<She>
16   Look at you! You are beautiful, my love,
      what's more, delightful,
      and what's more, our bed is verdant.
17   The beams of our house[l] are cedars;
      our rafters are cypresses.

2:1   I am a rose of Sharon,[m]
      a lily of the valleys.

<He>
2   Like a lily among thistles,
      so is my friend among women.[n]

<She>
3   Like an apple tree among the trees of the forest,
      so is my lover among men—
   in whose shade I delight to sit,[o]
      and whose fruit is sweet to my taste.
4   He has brought me[p] to the house of wine,
      and his banner over me is love.[q]

5   Sustain me with raisin-cakes,
      refresh me with apples,[r]
      for I am faint with love.
6   His left hand is under my head,
      and his right hand caresses me.
7   I place you under oath, women of Jerusalem,
      by the gazelles or does of the open field,[s]
   not to rouse or awaken love
      until it wishes.

a. The verb is 2 masc. pl.; it is not unusual to find masculine forms used of the women of Jerusalem (e.g., 2:5, 7; 3:5; 5:8). For the syntax, cf. Prov 23:31.

b. Some ancient versions and some modern translations understand *šzp* as an Aramaic form of Hebrew *šdp*, "to burn"; *šzp*, "looked at, gazed," attested in Job 20:9 and 28:7 and supported by LXX, is to be preferred. It implicitly contains both meanings: the gaze of the sun burns.

c. The usual meaning of *ʾêkâ* is "how"; this could be a double entendre playing on both meanings.

d. Literally, "where do you cause to lie down"; on the absence of the object, see the Commentary. It is not possible in English to show the causative force of the verb without expressing an object, such as "flock"; "where you lie at midday" is also the way the line is translated by Vg., *ubi cubes in meridie*, and Luther, "*wo du ruhst am Mittag*."

e. So understood by LXX, Vg., cf. the similar use of *ʾăšer lāmmâ* in Dan 1:10 and the discussions of Ginsburg, Pope.

f. Reading *ṭʿyh* with the Syriac, Vg., and Symmachus (a reading the Targum also seems to assume). MT's *ʿṭyh*, "like one wrapped up, covered," is most likely the result of metathesis of *ʿayin* and *tet*; it is supported by LXX.

g. The *yod* is probably an old genitive case ending, perhaps used for euphony. LXX and Vg. read it as the suffix "my," followed by NJB ("to my mare") and some commentators (Bloch and Bloch note the similar construction in 2:14, "my dove in the clefts of the rock"), which has the advantage of envisioning the man as a charioteer.

h. Lexicographers generally separate *tôr* II, "turtledove" (LXX and Vg. read "like turtledoves") from *tôr* I, which in Esth 2:12, 15 means "turn, opportunity." Ginsburg proposed a meaning "something round, a circle" from the root *twr*, "to go round." It has been taken to refer to plaits (JPS, "plaited wreaths"; NEB, "between plaited tresses") or to circular ornaments or rows or strings. Given the parallelism with 10b (though *ḥărûzîm*, here translated "beads," is a *hapax*) and the description of *tôrîm* as made of gold in v. 11, "ornaments" (NRSV) or "pendants" (NAB, NJB) is more likely. The precise meaning of all of these terms for types of jewelry is uncertain.

i. The term refers to something that surrounds or is round, such as an enclosed couch. There may be a double entendre here, which Murphy's translation brings out: "While the king was in his enclosure, my nard gave forth its fragrance."

j. The verb in 12b is a perfect; I have translated it as present tense, since tenses in poetry are fluid, as is time in the Song.

k. The verb *lyn*, when used of people or animals, ordinarily means to spend the night; when used of abstract qualities and occasionally of persons (Pss 25:13; 49:12 [13 H]; cf. Job 17:2; Prov 15:31), it means to dwell or remain for a longer period of time (see *DCH* IV, 543a); the verb is an imperfect, but I have translated it as a participle to maintain the ambiguity of the Hebrew, in which either the lover or the sachet of myrrh can be the subject (see the Commentary).

l. Taking "our houses" as a plural of generalization; so most commentators and translations. Bloch and Bloch propose retaining the plural and see it as a reference to all the places the lovers meet. The proposal merits consideration, though the context suggests that the woman is talking about the specific place where they are (imaginatively) at the moment rather than speaking of their trysting places in general.

m. Or "I am a crocus of the plain"; see the Commentary.

n. Literally, "among the daughters." The next verse has "so is my love among the sons." The comparisons are to women and men in general; cf. Gen 30:13; Isa 32:9; Prov 31:29.

o. Verbal coordination (literally, "in his/its shade I desired and I sat"); see GKC §120d; cf. Gen 24:18; Deut 1:5; Hos 5:11. Though the syntax of my translation is somewhat awkward, I have used "whose shade" to bring out the ambiguity of the Hebrew, in which the shade can be either the lover's shade or the tree's. Since he is metaphorically an apple tree, it is both his and its shade at the same time.

p. So MT and Vg. LXX and the Syriac read a plural imperative, "bring me," and continue with a plural imperative in the next verse, which would make this verse part of her address to the women of Jerusalem in vv. 5–7. Whether the versions were influenced by the imperatives of the following verse (Pope) or simply had a different Vorlage is open to question.

q. LXX and Syriac continue with the imperative: "set love upon me." On the translation "banner," see the Commentary.

r. The meaning of these two lines is uncertain; see the Commentary.

s. Here and in 3:5, LXX renders, "by the powers and forces of the field." I use "open field" to distinguish the field from cultivated land.

I treat these verses together because they consist of short speeches in which alternating voices respond to each other in quick succession. Landy (50) describes 1:9–2:7 as the only sustained dialogue in the Song. I include vv. 5–8 with them, since they fit well with the antiphonal character of this part of the Song, with its shifting images and themes. Song 1:2–4 could also be included in this section.

Song 1:5–2:7 builds to a climax in 2:3–4 and is framed by addresses to the women of Jerusalem in 1:5–6 and 2:5–7. The mention of Jerusalem and of the curtains of Solomon in 1:5 connect these verses to the Solomonic ambiance of 1:2–4. The speaking voice in vv. 5–7 is still a woman's (here it is clear from the adjectival form *šĕḥôrâ*, "black," that the speaker is, indeed, female). Introducing the women of Jerusalem in v. 5 is both practical and significant, for it means that the poet has, within the space of four verses, presented the principal characters who provide the Song's only three identifiable speaking voices: the woman, whose speech began the Song and who continues to speak through 1:7; the man, addressed by the woman in 1:2–4 and 7 (he will speak in 1:9–11); and the women of Jerusalem (introduced in 1:5, they will speak shortly, if 1:8 belongs to them).

Since this is a love poem, and the principal voices are those of lovers, we might well ask, what is the function of the third voice, that of the women of Jerusalem, who speak in unison like a chorus? Munro recognizes their importance as "a kind of choir who call the Song forth," an audience who, by listening to the woman tell her love story, enable the lovers' dialogue to live again in the present (44–47). But it is more than this. The Jerusalem women are not "the chief target of [the Song's] message" (47), the Song's readers are. The women of Jerusalem are the audience within the poem whose presence—because it makes the relationship between the lovers less private, less closed—facilitates the reader's entry into the poem's world of erotic intimacy (or the audience's entry, if one wishes to imagine the Song as a performance). Song 1:5–2:7 begins and ends with the woman addressing the women of Jerusalem. In between, what begins as a three-part conversation modulates into a lovers' duet, full of mutual praise. The women of Jerusalem are forgotten or ignored as the exchange between the lovers reaches an intimate crescendo (2:3–4). At the moment when passion overwhelms her ("I am faint with love"), the woman calls on the women of Jerusalem, reminding us of their presence (2:5–7).

The poet does not offer a meditation on love but, rather, shows what love is like by reporting what lovers say. The exclusive use of dialogue, with no narrative explication, creates the impression that we are overhearing the lovers as they speak. What is love like? Love emboldens and makes one vulnerable (1:5–6). It is playful (there is badinage in vv. 7–8). It is mutual adoration (1:15 and 1:16, 2:2 and 2:3). It is stimulating and intoxicating (erotic feasting in the wine house, 2:3–4). It is overwhelming (2:5). Even when gratified, it cannot get enough (2:6). These verses are filled with wonderfully concrete images that convey the lovers'—especially the woman's—pleasure and delight in their sensuous surroundings and the trappings of love. Love transforms ordinary things into extraordinary ones. The tents of Qedar, the curtains of Solomon, the chariots of Pharaoh, the vineyards of En-gedi are not just any tents, curtains, chariots, and vineyards, but special ones associated with the richest and most illustrious of rulers both near and far, an exotically remote desert tribe, and a renowned luxurious oasis. Love delights in physical beauty and in accentuating it. The man compares his lover's eyes to doves (1:15), and praises her appearance as it is adorned and will be further adorned with pendants, beads, gold, and silver (1:9–11).

Love is springtime. Vineyards, especially metaphoric ones, need tending (1:6). Love awakens the senses to nature's beauty and bounty. In 1:12–17 the woman speaks of fragrant spices and aromatic woods: nard, myrrh, henna, cedar, cypress. In 2:1–5 she discourses on flowers and trees, singling out ones beautiful to look at and pleasing to smell (crocus [?], here translated "rose," lily, apple tree) and, stimulated by the last of these, the apple tree as metaphor for her lover, she fancies indulging in delicacies to eat (raisins, apples) to accompany the wine and fruit of love that is sweet to her taste. Animals traverse the landscape. Sheep and goats, which need tending, represent domesticity and responsibility (1:7–8), while gazelles and does of the open field are untamed and fleet of foot, symbols of freedom and spontaneity (2:7). Love is all these things, spontaneous and free, reliable and responsible. Love, says the poet, is intimate and private (the lovers' couch is verdant and their house, a bower sweet, 1:16–17), but it cannot be kept to itself. It spills over, bursting to announce itself to others: "Sustain me, refresh me," the woman calls to the women of Jerusalem. The lovers do not view the presence of these women as either intrusive or embarrassing. The invitation to the women of Jerusalem to participate in the lovers' pleasure is also an invitation to the reader.

[1:5–11] These verses form a chiasmus in which A and A′ describe the woman and praise her as "lovely" and B and B′ contain a question and answer involving "pasturing."[1]

    A   vv. 5–6   a description of the woman, black and lovely (*nā'wâ*)
                      (the woman, addressed to the women of Jerusalem)
    B   v. 7   a question, where do you pasture/graze (*tir'eh*)
                      (the woman, addressed to the man)
    B′ v. 8   an answer, pasture/graze (*rĕ'î*) your kids by the shepherds' tents
                      (the women of Jerusalem? the man?, addressed to the woman)
    A′ vv. 9–11 a description of the woman, whose cheeks are lovely (*nā'wû*)
                      (the man, addressed to the woman)

If v. 8 is spoken by the women of Jerusalem (see below), then the man responds to the speech addressed to the women of Jerusalem in vv. 5–6 and the women of Jerusalem answer the question asked of the man in v. 7. In A, the woman describes her appearance, "black and lovely," and in A′ the man praises her appearance: her bejeweled face is "lovely" and he will adorn her with jewelry of gold and silver. In B the woman asks her lover where he "grazes" (a double entendre; see below under v. 7), for she does not want to appear like someone who does not know, wandering about by the flocks of his companions (*'al 'edrê ḥăbērêkā*). In B′ the women of Jerusalem (or perhaps the man) reply teasingly that, if she really does not know where he is, she need only follow the trail, and "graze" her goats "by the shepherds' tents" (*'al miškĕnôt hārō'îm*). The distant tents of Qedar and the near king, Solomon, of A are replaced by the near tents of the shepherds in B′ and a distant king, Pharaoh, in A′ (Cook 1968: 136–37).

[1:5–6] As suddenly as the poem began *in medias res*, with a wish for kisses and the woman's urgent address to her lover ("Draw me after you, let us run!" v. 4), so suddenly the woman now speaks to a group of women about her appearance. The mention of work in the vineyards does not necessarily indicate that the setting has changed. It could still be the court, or at least the city, since it is addressed to the women of Jerusalem, literally "daughters of Jerusalem." "Daughters of Jerusalem" are the women inhabitants of Jerusalem, Jerusalemites (cf. "sons of Israel" for Israelites). There is no compelling reason to think

---

1. Chiasm (an abb′a′ or abcb′a′ pattern) is found in both Hebrew prose and poetry and occurs frequently in the Song (see Exum 1973 and the other structural studies mentioned under "Literary Arrangement and Its Significance," pp. 37–41; Landy 41–57). It occurs also in v. 6: "they made me *keeper* of the *vineyards* / my own *vineyard* I did not *keep*."

of them as a more select group, such as young, unmarried women; cf. "daughters of Zion" for married women in Isa 3:16–17 and 4:4. Some readers may, at this point, be tempted to identify the women of Jerusalem with the women mentioned earlier in v. 3 (cf. Murphy), though it makes perfect sense to see v. 3 as a generalization about all women. The setting here in vv. 5–6 could equally, and just as easily, be elsewhere than Jerusalem, in the vineyards perhaps, anticipating the pastoral milieu of vv. 7–8. In the sustained poetic dialogue of the lovers, indeterminate settings are typical. The events the lovers speak about are not restricted to a particular time and place but rather belong to the lyrical domain of desire and to the realm of the senses, where space and time are effortlessly traversed by lovers.

The woman describes herself (1:5; 2:1; 8:10), but the man does not describe himself. It appears that it is also only the woman who addresses and interacts with the women of Jerusalem (1:5; 2:7; 5:8, 16; 8:4; and probably also in 3:10–11, where the identity of the speaker is not specified). Perhaps both these features demonstrate the poet's concern to develop her point of view. Here she describes her appearance as black and as lovely and explains that her blackness is due to her exposure to the sun while working in the vineyards.

These verses are a source of controversy among interpreters: is the woman claiming to be "black and beautiful" or "black but beautiful" (see Pope's detailed discussion)? As Landy points out, in a daring poetic analysis, the difficulty of these verses is part of their meaning, and their beauty (142–52). Is the tone boastful or apologetic? Why should it be one or the other, and not both: a sign of pride and a token of vulnerability? Poetry, if it is worth anything—and all the world is not worth the day that the Song of Songs was given to Israel[2]—cannot be paraphrased as a straightforward prose narrative. Indeed, everything in these verses resists narrativization. Why are the brothers angry? What is the relationship of the vineyards they made her tend to her own vineyard, which she has not tended?

"Black" (*šĕḥôrâ*, v. 5) indicates color, not race; *šĕḥarḥōret* (v. 6) is a *hapax*, and is clearly related to it (some take it as a diminutive; thus NRSV, "dark"; JPS, "swarthy"). In 5:11 *šĕḥōrôt* is used to describe the man's hair as "black as a raven." Clearly the woman sees herself as both black and beautiful; the question is how beauty and blackness are related. Any answer a commentary provides can only be partial, for readers can and will tease out multiple meanings for poetry whenever it captures their imaginations. Verse 6 reads literally, "Do not look at me in that I am black."[3] How are the women of Jerusalem looking

---

2. This valuation of the Song is attributed to Rabbi Aqiba in *m.Yad.* 3:5.

3. An unambiguously positive statement on the part of the woman could be obtained by reading *ʾal* in v. 6 as asseverative, as in Ugaritic, "Look at me!" (Exum 1981), but there does not appear to be sufficient reason to give *ʾal* anything other than its normal negative meaning here.

at her? With disdain? With envy? With fear? All have been suggested by the commentators. The woman is not telling the women of Jerusalem not to look at her at all; the announcement "black am I and lovely" invites the gaze. She is saying not to take her skin color—caused by the sun's gaze—into account (cf. Bloch and Bloch, "Do not see me only as dark"). If everyone regarded skin darkened by the sun as a sign of beauty, there would be no reason for her to tell the women of Jerusalem to ignore it, or no need to explain it to them. Moreover, why does she tell them she is lovely? Can they not see it? The claim to beauty suggests that there may be some question about it. It also reveals something about the woman's view of herself. Her black skin, she explains, is the result of working outdoors, in the sun—something lower-class women would have done, whereas upper-class women would have led more pampered lives. Thus, by claiming to be black and lovely, the woman may be challenging what she takes to be the view of the city women: that skin darkened by labor in the sun, a sign of lower social status, and beauty are not compatible.

Is this their view? Because beauty is enviable, the woman may represent something more, or other, to the women of Jerusalem than an object of scorn. The beauty of the women of Jerusalem is a civilized beauty; the woman's, a natural one, which makes her "a wish-fulfilling image of freedom and sexual license, activity and open spaces, of all of which they are deprived, enclosed in the city" (Landy 144–45). Elsewhere they call her "most beautiful of women" (1:8?; 5:9; 6:1, where the word for "beautiful" is *yāpâ* rather than *nāʾwâ*, as here in v. 5).

[1:5] The woman qualifies her statement in v. 5a with two similes: "like the tents of Qedar" and "like the curtains of Solomon." Qedar, the name of a northern Arabian tribe (Gen 25:13; Isa 42:11; 60:7; Jer 49:28; Ezek 27:21, etc.), is derived from a root meaning "dark," and apparently the tents of Qedar were made of black goats' skins. Curtains could be made of various materials (see the description of the curtains of the tabernacle in Exod 26 and 36). Here "curtains" is a metonym for tent, as in Isa 54:2; Jer 4:20; Hab 3:7; 2 Sam 7:2 = 1 Chr 17:1 (Ginsburg, Pope, Fox). For MT "Solomon" some commentators and translations read "Salmah," the name of a south Arabian tribe, thus obtaining a better parallelism with Qedar. The opinion that the parallelism could be improved is not a sufficient reason to reject the MT vocalization "Solomon," supported by the ancient versions. Not only is "Solomon" poetically suggestive of royal splendor; it also links this verse to Solomon's name in the title and to the king and courtly setting in 1:2–4.

With these similes, is the woman comparing herself to (1) two objects known for their blackness (Fox, reading "Salmah"); or (2) two objects that are both black and beautiful, as she is (Pope, reading "Salmah"; Murphy, Loretz, Falk 168, all reading "Solomon"); or (3) one object that is black and one that is beautiful (Ginsburg, Budde, Meek, Krinetzki, Ringgren, Gordis, Garrett, all reading

"Solomon")? The indeterminacy of the similes is part of the indeterminacy of the overall picture. Since Solomon's tents, which would surely be beautiful, could also be imagined as made of black goats' skins, the third view seems unnecessarily restrictive. And since, as Pope points out, tents, even Bedouin ones, can be beautiful—beauty is, after all, in the eye of the beholder—so does the first. If the woman is claiming to be both black and lovely, it would make sense to use similes that combine both attributes in a single image. "The combination of the poor, exotic, and terrifying world of Kedar with the equally exotic and fascinating luxury of Solomon makes the blackness of the speaker at once frightening and fascinating; she is mysteriously different" (Keel 47).

[1:6] In 1:2–4 the woman desires love; here in v. 6 she is subjected to anger. In the verb *nihărû* (here translated "were angry"), we have a pun on *hrh*, "to burn, to be angry," and *hrr*, "to burn, scorch," and perhaps also *nhr*, "to rage, to snort" (Landy 321 n. 12; on *nhr*, see Driver 1933: 381 and 1934: 393). Anger, like the sun, burns. The anger of the woman's brothers is perplexing. It seems to have no role except to get the woman into the vineyards, and thus enable the poet to apply the vineyard image metaphorically to her ("my own vineyard I did not keep"). This is one of the Song's blind motifs, a loose thread that teases and tantalizes the reader to find connections where they are lacking (see Introduction, "Lyric Poetry and Reading for the Plot," pp. 42–45). Who does not want to know more about the brothers' anger? Yet we never hear more. We do not even hear of the brothers again. Though vineyards are mentioned again, there is no reason to read the brothers into the dialogue in 8:8–9, as many commentators do (see under 8:8–10). This does not mean, however, that their anger should be dismissed as insignificant. Who can forget it? Perhaps v. 6 is an allusion to the cost of loving (Ayo). Love, as the poet presents it, may be delight and exquisite pleasure, but it is not without complications.

The brothers are referred to by the poetic circumlocution, "sons of my mother." The possibility that they are half-brothers, the sons of her mother but not of her father (Delitzsch, Meek, Goulder) is hardly meaningful, unless, succumbing to the temptation to make a story out of this enigmatic verse, one imagines a kind of Cinderella background of wicked stepbrothers against whom the young woman struggles to assert herself. The mother is mentioned seven times in the Song (1:6; 3:4, 11; 6:9; 8:1, 2, 5), but there is no mention of the father. Since the word "brothers" is not used, but only "sons of my mother," no term for the woman's male relatives ever appears in the Song (the term "brother," however, appears in 8:1, applied to the male lover). The role of men as figures of authority thus seems to be downplayed or without interest.

The authority the brothers have over the woman in this verse suggests that she has not yet reached or is just reaching marriageable age. The Song's lovers, then, are pictured here as young. The woman asserts that she has not kept her own vineyard, a term symbolically used of her here and in 8:12. It is hardly likely that there is a suggestion of promiscuity in her claim (so Pope, in keeping with his cultic interpretation of the Song). Murphy rightly criticizes this view, though he seems overly concerned with defending the woman's reputation when he asserts that she has given herself to her lover not only freely but also "responsibly." As Murphy points out, there are at least two levels of meaning in the woman's claim: she has not kept herself (her vineyard) from her lover, and she has not cared for her beauty and protected herself from the sun. Another proposal, that the woman is asking a rhetorical question, "Have I not guarded my own vineyard?" (Sasson 1978–79: 191), has little to commend it. Although interrogative *he* is not always necessary to form a question, its absence is a stumbling block for such an interpretation here.

Fox takes the reference to not keeping her own vineyard more broadly to mean that she has not been able to tend to her own needs as a woman (presumably including sexual needs) but has been forced to stay within the confines of her family. This interpretation finds a "story" in v. 6 and makes the woman's statement, in effect, a comment on the brothers' authority. Does it extend, as male authority typically did in ancient Israelite society, to control over their sister's sexuality? No is her answer, if "my vineyard, which is mine, I have not kept" has a sexual meaning. With the Song, it is never one meaning or the other, for multiple levels of meaning and erotic double entendre are everywhere. She asserts her freedom to pursue love in the next verse.

[1:7–8] The lover, who was earlier a king (v. 4), is here envisioned as a shepherd (v. 7), and so, too, is the woman (v. 8). These verses picture them together in the countryside, pasturing flocks of sheep and goats. This motif (or "travesty"; see Murphy 47; Fox 292–94) is common in love poetry and especially well developed in the pastoral, in which, as here, the harmony and simplicity of life in tune with nature enjoyed by shepherds and other rural folk is idealized. The women of Jerusalem are also present in this setting, if v. 8 belongs to them. And they are always present implicitly as the audience of the lovers' dialogue.

Like vv. 5–6, these verses invite multiple readings. Are they playful? The sexual innuendos they contain suggest that they are. Is there a note of anxiety in the woman's question? It is possible to tease and be anxious at the same time. Who answers her, and what kind of answer does she receive—equally playful or distinctly unhelpful? A sense of urgency is conveyed by the imperative, "Tell me!" and the repetition of the question, "where? . . . where?" while the direct addresses, "my soul's beloved" and "most beautiful of women," create the impression of immediacy.

[1:7] The woman uses two forms of address for her lover, *šeʾāhăbâ napšî*, "you whom my soul loves" (here translated, following Fox, "my soul's beloved") and *dôdî*, "my lover," "my love." The former is used here. In general "soul" is a rather unsuitable translation for Hebrew *nepeš*, which is not soul as opposed to body, but the whole being. Here, however, it seems especially appropriate, since it has an English equivalent in such expressions of total devotion as to love someone with all one's soul, or with all one's heart.

Her question is a double entendre. Neither of the verbs has an object. The first, *r‘h*, when used intransitively, means "to feed, to graze"—thus, "Where (or how) do you graze?" From elsewhere in the Song, we know where the man grazes or feeds: among the lilies and in the gardens, figures for the woman herself (see under 2:16 and 6:2–3). The question, "Where do you cause to lie down at noon?" also contains a verb without an object, and so suggestively leaves open the question what or whom he causes to lie down. Nearly all translations make the question straightforward and chaste by supplying the flock that the woman neglected to mention. On this level, she is asking her lover where he pastures his flock and where he has his sheep lie down at noon, so that she can visit him in the heat of the day, the time of rest.

The meaning of the second part of this verse is debated. I have followed the Syriac, Vulgate, Symmachus, and a number of moderns in translating "one who wanders," a reading that involves changing only the order of two consonants in the MT. It is easy to see how a scribe might have reversed the two letters. "Lest I be like a wanderer" makes perfect sense and fits the context. The woman asks her lover to tell her where he spends his afternoons—as though she did not know—so she will not have to go looking for him and be taken, by anyone who might see her, as someone idly wandering around the shepherds' flocks.

MT's "like one wrapped," in contrast, does not make much sense. If she is referring to some form of covering she would need as a disguise to prevent her from being recognized by the man's companions (Murphy)—a veil, for example, as many translations have it (though nowhere else is the verb *‘ṭh* used of wearing a veil)—why does she say "lest I be *like* one veiled" and not "lest I be veiled"? "Like one veiled" is not an allusion to the possibility of being taken as a prostitute. There is insufficient evidence for the view that a veiled woman would be thought to be a prostitute, as a number of commentators suppose. In the only example cited to support this view, that of Tamar in Genesis 38, "he thought she was a harlot, for she had covered her face" (v. 15) does not mean that harlots wore veils but only that Judah thought a woman sitting by herself at the roadside was a harlot because he did not recognize his daughter-in-law, since she was veiled. Moreover, if wearing a veil *were* the mark of a prostitute, it would be odd for the woman to consider wearing one.

The possibility that we have here a word *‘ṭh* meaning "to pick lice" (so NEB, REB; see Driver 1974; Emerton 1993) has been recently advocated by Garrett, but this does not yield a very satisfactory meaning either, and Garrett's interpretation strains the sense of the text. Whereas Driver saw the phrase as referring to the custom of picking lice as "a way of whiling away time" (160), Garrett supposes that the woman is saying that if she goes in search of her lover among shepherds, she will catch their lice and start to pick at them. But if "'shepherds,' here representing the world of men, are a foul, dirty, lice-ridden lot" (138), what makes her shepherd lover an exception?

[1:8] The woman receives what sounds like a playful answer to her playful, sexually suggestive question. She is told that if she does not know where her lover spends his time at midday, then she will have to look for him, but the trail will be easy to follow. The implication is that she does know and does not need to seek him at all. Is this the lover's reply (e.g., Budde, Rudolph, Fox, Murphy, Munro 22)? Or are these the words of the women of Jerusalem (Ginsburg, Delitzsch, Loretz, Meek, Tournay, Exum 1973: 71–72, Keel, Goulder, Garrett)?[4] The man uses many terms of endearment for his lover (my friend, my fair one, my sister, my bride, my dove, my perfect one), but nowhere else does he call her "most beautiful of women." The women of Jerusalem, on the other hand, address her this way elsewhere (5:9; 6:1). The badinage here in vv. 7–8 bears some similarities to the verbal play between the woman and the women of Jerusalem in 5:2–6:3. There they ask her where her lover has gone, so that they can help her find him, and she reveals that she knows where he is and what he is doing there: in his garden, grazing. Here she asks where he is, and the answer she receives implies that she knows, which is, in fact, what her double entendre about grazing in v. 7 suggests.

The speech teases the reader with its ambiguities. If v. 8 is the man's speech, we have a guessing game: does she know where he is? does he tell her? (Landy 171). If "by the shepherds' tents" is the same place as "by the flocks of your companions," then he proposes she join him where she imagined having to look for him. If the phrases refer to two different places, then he may be arranging a rendezvous, a place they can meet while his companions are away elsewhere with their sheep (for further discussion of ambiguities, see Landy 169–76; Munro 94–96).

[1:9–11] Clearly the man is speaking here. He picks up on the reference to the woman's beauty (v. 5) and refines it by offering a specific example, that of her cheeks (synecdoche for the face, according to Ginsburg) and her neck adorned with jewelry (v. 10). So beautiful are they that he wants to give her even more costly ornaments to wear (v. 11). Comparing a woman to a fine horse, as the man does here, was a common trope in antiquity, indicating a male view of both as a coveted or prized possession (for examples, see, *inter alia*, Ginsburg, Pope). Another interpretation of the comparison, often entertained by commentators, is that of Pope (1970; see also his commentary). Since chariots would have been pulled by stallions and not by mares, he argues, v. 9 alludes

---

4. Some commentators have looked even further afield; e.g., Gordis, following Tur-Sinai, the shepherd's companions; Krinetzki, the man's friends; Gerleman, Snaith, the poet. There is no reason to look for speakers other than the three we know are represented, especially since all speeches can reasonably be assigned to them.

to the practice of setting loose an estrous mare among war horses to create a disturbance, as recorded of an Egyptian campaign under Thutmose III against Qadesh. The woman excites the man in a similar way. This view is not without its critics. Fox, for example, takes issue with it on the grounds that (1) chariots were used for "dignity and display" (citing BDB) and need not be war chariots and (2) a mare could be included in the term "Pharaoh's chariotry," as seen in another of Pope's examples, that of Amenhotep II's boyhood affection for a particular mare in Pharaoh's stables. One can distinguish between the meaning the simile itself provides and meaning that comes from an external referent, and appreciate the one without excluding the other. Verses 10 and 11 complete and explain the simile of v. 9: the woman's head and neck, with their jewels, call to mind the decorated harness and trappings on the finest horse imaginable, one belonging to the chariotry of the famed king of Egypt. Since Hebrew has only masculine and feminine forms for "horse," the speaker uses "mare," and not "stallion," because he is describing a woman, the woman he loves. If one looks for a further meaning in v. 9 beyond the explication provided in vv. 10–11, then Pope's proposal is worthy of consideration.

[1:9] One of the man's favorite forms of address for his beloved, *raʿyātî*, occurs only in the Song (1:9, 15; 2:2, 10, 13; 4:1, 7; 5:2; 6:4) and the *kethiv* of Judg 11:37. Related forms appear in Judg 11:37 [*qere*]–38 and Ps 45:14 [15 H] in reference to a woman's companions or attendants. The masculine form, *rēaʿ*, which the woman uses of the man in 5:16, is much more common, and has the basic meaning of "friend" or "companion." Clearly in the Song this is a term of endearment, and thus some translations render "my love" (KJV, NRSV, NJB), "my darling" (JPS), "my dearest" (NEB). I have used "friend" in the Translation, since it can have an intimate sense as well as a more general one.

[1:11] The speaker imagines having fine jewelry made for his lover. "We will make" can mean simply that he will have the work done, without specifying who will do it (Budde). If, however, we want to play the game of identifying the "we," it could be all-inclusive, like the "we" of 1:4: everyone will want to join in the game of adorning this beautiful woman. Or it could refer to the man and the women of Jerusalem, since they are the only other ever-present characters in the Song. The woman addressed them in v. 5, when she affirmed her beauty; perhaps here they will participate in enhancing it.

[1:12–2:6] In praising the beauty of his lover, the man evoked a busy world of chariotry, with horses adorned for show, and artisans who create ornaments to flatter beauty (1:11). Song 1:12–2:4 presents a contrasting picture, in which the lovers praise each other's beauty, enhanced only by fragrance, and enjoy lovemaking alfresco in a quiet bower. The sweet odors of costly unguents and perfumes blend with the natural scents of cedar and cypress to appeal to the sense of smell, while sight is foregrounded in their mutual invitation to see themselves through the eyes of the other: "Look at you! You are beautiful!"

Images and motifs from earlier in the Song take on new meaning through association and recombination. The poet merges the courtly imagery, with which the Song began, into imagery of the countryside. In 1:4 the setting is the king's chambers; the next time the king is mentioned, on his couch (v. 12), he seems perfectly at home in the vineyards of En-gedi (1:14). The king's couch becomes the lovers' verdant bed (1:16), and their house, a country bower under the trees (1:17), which, in turn, will become the house of wine (2:4). The couch and bed, as places that might be used for eating and drinking as well as for love-making (cf. Amos 6:4), combine the idea of banqueting and sex that becomes explicit in 2:3–6, where her lover's fruit is sweet to the woman's taste, the lovers tarry in the house of wine, and the besotted woman calls for raisin-cakes and apples to fortify her. A figurative location for the enjoyment of love, the wine house belongs as easily to the country setting of the immediately preceding verses as it does to a city setting, where, in the king's chambers, lovemaking is savored above wine (1:4). The imagery of unguents and spices that dominates these verses stands on the threshold of two worlds, the courtly and the natural world of the countryside (Munro 49–50). The cedars (v. 17) take us back to the king of v. 12 via their connection with Solomon, famously associated with the cedars of Lebanon, and the author or patron of the poem according to the title (see under 1:1).

The dialogue begun in 1:5 continues as a duet between the lovers: she speaks, 1:12–14; he speaks, 1:15; she speaks, 1:16–2:1; he speaks, 2:2; she speaks, 2:3–6. Desire in the Song is shared. The mutuality of the lovers is con-veyed by their antiphonal responses and mutual gazing and by the way they bor-row each other's words and images to declare their love. In these verses, they speak about each other, and they address each other directly. Even when speak-ing about each other, as one might in the absence of the other person, they are clearly engaged in conversation, for they answer and embellish each other's declarations. At the same time, the indirect forms of address remind us of the presence of an audience: the women of Jerusalem and, ultimately, the poem's readers. When the poet portrays the lovers as addressing each other as "you," as they do in 1:15–17 ("Look at you! You are beautiful!"), it is as if they are engaged in a private, intimate conversation. (This is, however, only an illusion, for "Look!" directs the reader's gaze as well as the lovers' gazes.) When the woman speaks about her lover instead of to him (1:12–14; 2:3–4), or even when the lovers seem to be addressing each other in the third person (2:2–3), the poem opens out to the reader.

[1:12–14] The male lover spoke earlier of the pharaoh, the king of Egypt, and of adorning the woman with jewelry (vv. 9–11). Now she speaks of "the king," her lover, whom she wears as an adornment of fragrance, a sachet of myrrh. She uses her favorite term for him, *dôdî,* "my love," which is related to *dôdîm* (love play) in 1:2 and 4. From the Hebrew of v. 13 it is impossible to tell whether it is the lover or the sachet of myrrh that lies between the woman's breasts; they are one and the same, poetically indistinguishable. The image resonates with Song 1:3, where she savored his fragrant perfumes and also spoke of him as a king, bringing her to his chambers, but here scent communicates the presence of both lovers. Her spikenard prepares a fragrant couch for her kingly lover, on which he becomes her fragrant intimate possession. "The Lover is brought from far away, from the exotic oasis, to become an attribute of the Beloved, to increase her attractions" (Landy 84). Just as v. 12 takes us back to the king of 1:4, the references to vineyards and En-gedi, which means "the spring of the kid," recall the vineyards of 1:6 and the pasturing of kids mentioned in 1:8. It seems rather forced to take "in the vineyards of En-gedi" as metaphorically equivalent to "between my breasts" (Fox, cf. Murphy). Like Sharon in 2:1 and the many other proper names in the Song, the place name En-gedi represents a desire on the part of the poet for concreteness, for transforming the ordinary into the specific, the unique, the exotic. If En-gedi, on the western shore of the Dead Sea, was well known in ancient times for the production of perfume (see Pope), then it is an ideal choice for specifying the idea of fragrance, just as the names of specific fragrances—nard, myrrh, henna blossoms—do.

Perfumes convey the appeal the lovers have for each other. Pleasing smells might function as an aphrodisiac (cf. the intoxicating scent of the man in 1:3). Many perfumes and spices mentioned in the Song had to be imported, often from great distances, and were thus luxury items. Genesis 37:25 mentions myrrh among perfumes carried by caravan. Like any precious commodity, the purer the quality, the more expensive.

[1:12] Hebrew *nērd*, or spikenard, occurs only in the Song (1:12; 4:13–14). Of Indian origin, it is an aromatic oil extracted from the *Nardostachys jatamansi*, whether the root or the entire plant is a matter on which ancient and modern authorities differ. There is evidence of nard being cultivated in Syria in Roman times (Pliny, *Natural History* XII.26.42). Its considerable value is witnessed in the New Testament by Mark 14:3–5 and John 12:3–5, where a flask or pound of pure nard is said to be worth three hundred denarii, almost a year's wages (Pliny gives the price of nard as 100 denarii a pound and says it holds a foremost place among perfumes). Some critics identify the spikenard with the lover (Ginsburg, Fox); however, "my nard" seems an odd designation for the male lover, and the absence of some such construction as the one in vv. 13 and 14, "to me my lover is . . . ," makes the identification dubious. As Murphy notes, nard stands implicitly for the woman, whereas the man (myrrh, henna blossoms) is a counterpoint to her.

[1:13] Myrrh is an aromatic gum that is naturally exuded from cracks in the bark of a tree (*Balsamodendron myrrha*) found in Arabia, Abyssinia, and India; it can also be obtained by tapping the tree. Myrrh was used in incense (Exod 30:23), as a perfume for garments (Ps 45:8 [9 H]) or a lovers' couch (Prov 7:17, where myrrh, aloes, and cinnamon are mixed to perfume the bed). In Esth 2:12 it is part of a cosmetic treatment to prepare young women for their first night with the king. Myrrh is mentioned often in the Song (1:13; 3:6; 4:6, 14; 5:1, 5, 13). To be worn around the neck in a bag, as in 1:13, it would have been pulverized into a powder. It could be mixed with oil by itself or with other spices to produce a fragrant unguent, such as the liquid myrrh mentioned in Song 5:5 and 13. Song 3:6 alludes to its use in incense.

[1:14] Henna, which also appears only in the Song (1:14; 4:13; 7:11 [12 H]), grows abundantly in Palestine and Egypt. The strongly scented flowers of this tall shrub (some report that it smells like roses) are delicate shades of white and yellow. Henna is well known for the red, yellow, or orange dye produced from its leaves and twigs, but in the Song it is chosen for its fragrant blossoms, which grow in dense clusters (see Moldenke and Moldenke 124–25).

[1:15–17] The particle *hinnēh* (KJV, "behold") invites its addressee to look, along with the speaker, and see what he sees from his point of view: the man is asking his lover to see herself through his eyes. She asks the same of him, praising him in terms that echo his praise of her. With *hinnēh*, the poet directs the reader's gaze as well, creating the illusion of immediacy by bringing what the lovers see immediately before our eyes.

> (He)   *Look at you! You are beautiful,* my friend!
>   *Look at you! You are beautiful.*
>   Your eyes are doves.
> (She)   *Look at you! You are beautiful,* my love,
>   what's more, delightful,
>   and what's more, our bed is verdant.

They speak as if they are not only delighted but amazed, as lovers always are, with the beauty of the other. As in 1:9–11, the man concentrates on the woman's face. It is not surprising that he singles out her eyes for comment, since lovers say so much with their eyes. The comparison of eyes to doves (v. 15) is repeated verbatim in 4:1, where it is followed by a description of other features of hers, and in 4:9 and 6:5 the man finds the look of her eyes almost too much to bear. Hebrew *ʿayin* is a homonym, meaning both "eye" and "spring," and the comparison to eyes may have been suggested by the woman's reference to En-gedi, "the spring of the kid," in the previous verse. The choice of doves for comparison suggests softness, gentleness, beauty, and perhaps shape (as Gerleman proposes on the basis of Egyptian art). The dove was used as a symbol of love in the ancient Near East (see Keel figs. 24–26, 39). For the range of romantic images it conveys by its aspect, movement, and behavior, as well as its association with the love goddess and with spring, the dove has attained a special status as a love bird in ancient and modern love poetry.

The adoration of the lovers is mutual, and so is the look. The woman repeats her lover's exclamation and shifts the reader's gaze from her to him: "Look at you! You are beautiful!"[5] She does not settle on any particular feature of her lover; instead she caps "beautiful" with a similar term, "delightful" (he describes her this way in 7:6 [7 H]), and, overcome by his beauty, turns her gaze from him to "our bed," where they can take further pleasure in each other. Each phrase begins with *ʾap* ("and, also"), as if she were gasping for breath in wonderment (here translated "what's more" to bring this out). Nature, in its fragrance and plentitude, reflects the fragrance and exuberance of the lovers.

[2:1] For the second time in the Song, the woman describes herself. In 1:5 she drew attention to her beauty, for which her lover then praised her (1:9–11). Here we have the reverse: her lover has praised her beauty, and she his; and now she responds to his praise by offering her view of herself. We can never be quite sure how to take her descriptions of herself. Most commentators think she is being modest here, saying she is just an ordinary flower among many in the fields—a description her lover takes up and turns into a compliment in v. 2. Earlier she compared her lover to henna blossoms (v. 14), a common flower, and this surely does not mean that he is ordinary. We might think of the qualities of a flower: its sweet scent; its color, whether subtle or dramatic; its shape, which can seem very erotic (as anyone who has seen Georgia O'Keeffe's paintings of flowers knows); its delicacy; its soft texture (cf. Ayo 99). Flowers coming into bloom are an exquisite wonder to behold. Perhaps the imagery points to the woman's proud awareness of her blossoming beauty (Bloch and Bloch).

We cannot identify the flowers to which the woman compares herself with any certainty, but we can assume that they were chosen for their beauty and fragrance, possibly also for their delicacy and sensuality. Hebrew *ḥăbaṣṣelet* is surely not a rose (which did not grow in Israel in biblical times) but perhaps a kind of crocus; the asphodel, the narcissus, the meadow saffron, and the hyacinth have all been suggested. Zohary thinks it is the *Lilium candidum* (176); Moldenke and Moldenke, a tulip (*Tulipa sharonensis*, 235). LXX and Vg. use *anthos* and *flos*, common terms for flowers. A rose by any other name would smell as sweet, so I have opted for the familiar, well-turned translation "rose of Sharon." The only other occurrence of *ḥăbaṣṣelet* in the Bible is in Isa 35:1–2, where it is described as blooming abundantly. It would seem, then, that the woman is comparing herself to a familiar flower, beautiful, fragrant, and in bloom.

The other flower, *šôšannâ*, has been variously identified as a lily (*Lilium candidum*, which has large white flowers, or *Lilium chalcedonicum*, with red flowers), the lotus (*Nymphaea lotus*), or the water lily (*Nymphaea caerulea*). The

---

5. Beauty is a quality valued in men in the Hebrew Bible; e.g., Joseph (Gen 39:6); Saul (1 Sam 9:2); David (1 Sam 16:12, 18; 17:42); Absalom (2 Sam 14:25); Adonijah (1 Kgs 1:6).

narcissus, chamomile, crowfoot, sea daffodil, sternbergia, yellow flag iris, and blue hyacinth are also candidates (see Moldenke and Moldenke 114–16; Zohary 176; Jacob and Jacob 813–14). The man's lips are described as lilies, but whether this refers to color (indicating that red lilies are meant) or shape or simply the pleasure his lips provide is debated (see under 5:13). Lilies adorned Solomon's temple (1 Kgs 7:19, 22), and the laver outside the temple is described as having a cuplike brim, like the flower of a lily (1 Kgs 7:26; 2 Chr 4:5). The lotus appears often in ancient Near Eastern art and love poetry and has a range of significant associations, as a symbol of creation, life, fecundity, rebirth, and love.

Sharon could be simply "the plain" (so LXX, Vg.), but a reference to the well-known fertile coastal plain between Jaffa and Mount Carmel would be in keeping with the poet's preference for specific place names to produce vivid, concrete images (see above on 1:12–14). Sharon is mentioned together with *ḥăbaṣṣelet* in Isa 35:1–2, where Sharon, Lebanon, and Carmel are richly forested areas.

[2:2–5] The man turns the woman's lily metaphor into a flattering comparison: she stands out from other women as a lily stands out among thistles (v. 2). The women (literally "daughters") of v. 2 certainly include the women ("daughters") of Jerusalem, and this verse thus serves as an indirect comment on 1:5–6. Once again the woman models her words on his, returning the compliment with a similarly phrased comparison: he stands apart from other men like an apple tree among the trees of the forest (v. 3). Their adulation is mutual; the lovers view each other as peerless, distinguished from all others (5:9–10; 6:8–9). I have rendered "apple tree" here, as do most translations. Although some believe a more likely candidate for *tappûaḥ* is the apricot (see Moldenke and Moldenke 187) and other fruit trees have also been suggested, it appears possible that the apple tree is meant (so Zohary, who identifies it as *Malus sylvestris* [70], and Keel, who mentions archaeological excavations in northeastern Sinai that have uncovered more than two hundred carbonized apples). In any event, the tree is here distinguished from others by its shelter and its sweet fruit (v. 3), and perhaps also its scent (the root etymology, *nph*, "to breath, to blow," suggests an aromatic scent, which could refer to the blossoms as well as the fruit). Among the trees of the garden, the apple tree figures prominently in ancient Near Eastern love poetry for its erotic associations, whatever its exact botanical identity (Westenholz 1995: 2482; see also below under 4:12–5:1).

In vv. 3–4, variations are played on the motif of bringing to the house or chamber (see under 1:4). In 1:2–4 the lover's embraces are compared to wine, and the king brings the woman to his chambers; here in 2:4 the man brings the woman to the house of wine. In an unmistakably erotic image, she tastes her lover's fruit and finds it sweet (2:3). The pleasing taste of wine, as well as its intoxicating effect, was evoked by kisses and caresses better than wine in 1:2, 4. Wine is a suggested metaphor for love, and the house is where the lovers dwell in their mutual intoxication (Cook 1968: 143–44). The house of wine fuses the two images.

[2:4] The meaning of *degel*, which I have rendered "banner," is disputed, and the appearance of the root three more times in the Song is of little help (5:10; 6:4, 10). On the basis of Akkadian *diglu*, "glance, wish, intent," from *dagālu*, "to look," some authorities render "intent" or "intention" (NRSV, Gordis, Pope, Fox). "Banner" (so KJV, NIV, NJB, JPS) continues the idea of covering or shelter expressed in v. 3: she is in his shade, and his banner over her is love. In Num 1:52; 2:2, 3, 10, 17, 18, 25, 31, 34; 10:14, 18, 22, 25, the Israelites are said to encamp and set out on the march by *děgālîm*, which could refer to the standard or banner by which tribal units were identified (see esp. Num 1:52; 2:2; cf. Ps 20:5 [6 H], where the verbal form seems to mean to raise a standard or lift banners; see *DCH* II, 414b), or, perhaps by extension, to the division of the tribe itself. The War Scroll from Qumran mentions banners bearing such mottos as "the truth of God," "the righteousness of God," the glory of God," "the justice of God" (1QM 4:6). Although the word the War Scroll uses for "banner" is *ʾôt*, this nonetheless indicates that a banner or standard could have an abstract concept written on it, under whose protection and guidance those bearing the standard go forth. In Num 2:2 *ʾôt* appears together with *degel*, where they seem to have a similar meaning. The woman in the Song may be announcing that she is under the cover, or refuge, of her lover. If so, the poet has taken a military image and subverted it to love's ends: on the male lover's banner is written "love." As reappropriated, the military metaphor is neither "virtually meaningless" (Gordis) nor "troublesome" (Pope), and it brings us back to the military imagery used by the man in praise of his lover in 1:9–11.

Perceiving a connection between vv. 3c and 4b, Ginsburg proposed a meaning of "cover, shade" for *degel*: "He led me into that bower of delight, / And overshaded me with love." Since the apple tree is a metaphor for the male lover, "his/its shade" and "his/its fruit" are thinly veiled erotic allusions to the delights of love. The erotically charged context makes "his banner" similarly sexually suggestive, as commentators generally recognize, regardless of how they translate *degel*.

[2:5] The first two lines in this triplet are difficult. Because the words used here, apart from "apples," occur so rarely, it is not possible to be sure about the meaning. The verb here translated "sustain," *smk* in the *piel*, occurs only here; comparable to the use here is Gen 27:37 in the *qal*, "with grain and wine I have sustained him" (cf. also Ps 51:12 [14 H]). The verb in the parallel line, *rpd*, occurs only here and in Job 17:13 in the *piel* and in Job 41:22 in the *qal*. In Job 17:13 it is used of spreading a bed. A nominal form, *rěpîdâ*, appears in Song 3:10, and appears to refer to some kind of covering or support (see the Textual Note to 3:10). Another related noun, *rěpîdîm*, refers to the resting places of the Israelites in the wilderness (Exod 17:1, 8; 19:2; Num 33:14, 15). Some therefore think that preparing a bed is what is meant here (Fox, Bloch and

Bloch, Garrett); thus Fox: "Put me to bed among fruit clusters, / spread me (my bed) among apricots." It should be noted, however, that, whereas Job 17:13 specifies a bed as the object of the verb *rpd*, no bed is mentioned in our verse. If *ʾăšîšôt* means "raisin-cakes," then one can hardly imagine a bed being made upon them, but here again the meaning of the word is not certain. They are mentioned in 2 Sam 6:19 and 1 Chr 16:3, along with date-cakes, among the food David distributes to the people. Hosea 3:1 speaks of *ʾăšîšê ʿănābîm*, apparently "raisin-cakes (made) of (dried) grapes." It seems more likely that the *ʾăšîšôt* here in our verse are some sort of prepared food, perhaps a delicacy, rather than simply fruits; see, further, the discussion of Pope.

Assuming the woman is calling for sustenance, it is not because she needs nourishment but because she is lovesick, faint from love and faint for love. Lovesickness is a well-known ancient and modern malady for which the cause, love, is also the cure (see Rudolph, Krinetzki, and the Egyptian parallels adduced by Loretz and Fox). The foods the woman calls for, raisin-cakes and apples, are delicacies, not staples; they imply eating for pleasure, not nourishment. Some commentators suggest they are aphrodisiacs, but things other than aphrodisiacs can enhance lovemaking (a contemporary analogy might be champagne or music). Sheer indulgence, experiencing the gratification of more than one sense or appetite, is a way of prolonging and heightening pleasure. Raisin-cakes, which may have some sexual or erotic symbolism as love cakes (see Pope's discussion), and apples, the fruit associated with her lover (2:3), continue the imagery of (sexual) feasting developed in 2:3–4.

To whom is she speaking? The imperatives in v. 5 ("sustain me," "refresh me") are second person masculine plural. The view that they are not addressed to any particular person (Delitzsch, Budde, Rudolph) or that they are addressed to everyone in general (Bloch and Bloch) misses an important feature of the Song's rhetoric. The plural imperatives reveal an awareness of the audience on the part of the poet, and on the part of the lovers as the poet presents them to us. Since the imperatives in v. 5 are plural and the woman addresses the women of Jerusalem by name in v. 7, it is reasonable to see vv. 5–7 as addressed to them, as the audience *in the poem*. Masculine verbal forms are used elsewhere of the women of Jerusalem (1:6; 3:5; 5:8), and the masculine form of the pronoun "you" is used to address them in v. 7. Ultimately the woman's words are addressed to the audience *of the poem*, its readers (see Introduction, "The Invitation to the Reader," pp. 7–8). By having the woman acknowledge the poem's audience, the poet invites the readers into the lovers' intimate relationship, while also keeping them out both through the indirection of language—as seen, for example, in the suggestive images of vv. 3–4 that are nearly explicit but roundabout at the same time—and through the related technique of blurring the distinctions between desire, anticipation of sexual fulfillment, and enjoyment of it. This slippage between anticipation and fulfillment is particularly evident in the next two verses.

(handwritten annotations in top margin: "Present tense! or anticipation" and "the reader can supply the answer!")

[2:6] The woman speaks of her lover's embrace, which is the typical position a right-handed man would take in caressing a woman. Bloch and Bloch call it "a stylized representation of lovemaking" and adduce a literary and a pictorial parallel from ancient Mesopotamia (see, e.g., Wolkstein and Kramer 1983: 43; Pope). Translating the imperfect verb in v. 6b as future tense yields "his left hand under my head, and his right hand will caress me," as the Septuagint understood it. But the action can also be understood as taking place in the present: "His left hand is under my head, and his right hand caresses me." This is how a number of commentators take it (e.g., Rudolph, Krinetzki, Ringgren, Pope, Fox, Keel, Murphy, Snaith, Longman). Indeed, it makes sense to take v. 6 as describing a present state of affairs, since it is preceded in v. 5 by imperatives ("sustain me . . . revive me") and a participle (*ḥôlat*, "sick," in the phrase "I am lovesick"). Verse 6 could also be understood as a wish: "O that his left hand were under my head, and that his right hand caressed me!" (NRSV, Ginsburg, Falk). The same declaration appears again in 8:3, where we encounter the same ambiguity (see under 8:1–4). The declaration need not have the same meaning both times it appears. Not only can it have a different meaning in different contexts, the slippage between anticipation and experience so characteristic of the Song guarantees that in each of the contexts in which it appears the meaning cannot be pinned down.

[2:7] The so-called refrain of adjuration here in v. 7 occurs again in 3:5 and, with variation, in 8:4. Here and in 8:4 it is preceded by the same declaration about the lover's embrace (2:6 = 8:3). The woman can scarcely mean not to arouse her desire or her lover's, since their desire is already aroused (and arousing their desire would not be something the women of Jerusalem had any control over). So is she speaking about the women's desire; is this a didactic statement, a "message"? The problem in this verse is how we should understand the key terms "love" (*ʾahăbâ*), ʿ*wr*, "arouse or awaken," and *ḥpṣ*, "desire/be willing."

It is hardly likely that *ʾahăbâ* refers to the woman (Vg. *dilectam*) or the man (KJV), who is not to be wakened from sleep. Nor is there any reason to think that the woman is prohibiting the use of artificial stimulants or aphrodisiacs, or calling for them (see Murphy, Pope).

The adjuration has generally been understood by commentators in two different ways. Some take v. 7 to mean something like this:

> I place you under oath . . .
> do not arouse or awaken love
> until it wishes [i.e., the time is right].

"Love," which appears with the definite article, is taken as an abstract (an emotion [Murphy], or erotic arousal [Bloch and Bloch]), and the verb ʿ*wr* has the sense of exciting to action (Pope, Murphy, Longman, Garrett). In the last clause, *ḥpṣ* is understood as eagerness in the sense of readiness, "until the time is right" (Pope, Murphy, Bloch and Bloch). In this interpretation, the speaker tells the women of Jerusalem that love is not the sort of thing to be rushed, that desire should not be aroused prematurely.

Others understand it as saying:

> I place you under oath . . .
> do not disturb lovemaking
> until it wishes [to be disturbed].

In this case, "love" is understood as the act of lovemaking (Rudolph, Loretz, Krinetzki, Fox, Snaith), and the verb *ʿwr*, "arouse, stir up," has the sense of disturbing or interfering with (Rudolph, Gordis, Fox). "Until it wishes" (*ḥpṣ*) is taken as elliptical for "until it wishes to be disturbed, woken up" (Gordis, Fox, Snaith, Rudolph, Loretz, Krinetzki, Falk). This produces an adjuration not to disturb the couple in their lovemaking before they are satisfied.

The evidence speaks in favor of the first option. For one thing, *ʿwr* only ever means "wake up" or "stir up," in the sense of "agitate, excite to action"; it does not mean "to disturb" (Fox's explanation that "the way one disturbs lovemaking is to wake the couple in the morning" strains the sense of the verse). For another, when it appears elsewhere in the Song, *ʾahăbâ* seems to be love in the abstract, not the act of lovemaking (2:4, 5; 3:10 [if "love" is the correct word here]; 5:8; 7:6 [7 H]; 8:6–7). Since the verb *ʿwr* means "to wake up," "to excite to action," the logical meaning of "until it wishes" or "until it desires" is "until it desires to be awakened/roused." Thus I agree with those who think that the woman is offering general advice about love to the women of Jerusalem (Murphy under 3:5, Bloch and Bloch, Munro 47–48, Weems, Longman). But I think she is saying something more important about love than that it should not be aroused prematurely.

Love, as the woman speaks of it here, is personified as something that has a will of its own. Apart from the adjuration refrain, there is only one other place in the Song where love is spoken of in the abstract and virtually personified: in the climactic affirmation of love in 8:6–7. It is reasonable to assume that these references are connected. The adjuration refrain, addressed to the women of Jerusalem (and thus indirectly to the reader), anticipates, and in a way prepares us for, 8:6–7, when the woman—addressing her lover and, ultimately, the poem's readers—will speak on behalf of the poet about love.

Love, says the poet in 8:6–7 (here, as in our verse, using the woman as spokesperson), is overpowering. When it makes its claim upon you, it is irresistible. If this is the case, why tell the Jerusalem women not to rouse love? How does one rouse love? One does not say, "Today I will fall head over heels in love." It happens. Maybe you think you are in love, but when it happens, when you are truly in love, there is no mistaking it. This seems to be what the woman is hinting at here in v. 7: do not seek to rouse love, because when it pleases love to be roused, you will know it. The point is really quite simple, but she makes it in a way that underscores its profundity, by placing her companions under oath. That she asks them to swear by gazelles and by does is a clue that the oath is lighthearted, not solemn.

The fact that here in v. 7 the woman does not say more, either to explain what she means or elaborate on this theme, is in keeping with the way the poet presents love, by showing what love is like through the lovers' speeches and actions, not by telling the audience about it. Until we reach the climax of the poem, the adjuration is rather like a riddle or puzzle. If love has a will of its own, how can one rouse love before it wishes to be roused? The question comes up again (3:5) and again (8:4), bringing us closer and closer to an answer.

"By gazelles and by does" is an unusual oath formula. The names of these animals sound like titles of God: *ṣĕbāʾôt* (gazelles) has the same form as *ṣĕbāʾôt* ("hosts," as in the divine name "Lord of Hosts") and *ʾaylôt haśśādeh* (does of the field) resembles the name *ʾēl šadday* (Gordis 28). Thus this inspired turn of phrase sounds like a more conventional way of swearing an oath in the name of God but lacks that kind of solemnity. Gazelles and does of the open field belong to the world of nature that participates in the love of the lovers. They also belong to the larger world of love and love poetry, of iconography and of ritual in the ancient Near East (see Rudolph, Loretz, Pope, Fox, Keel)—the cultural heritage upon which the poet draws. On their association with the love goddess, see Keel, figs. 45–48. The grace and beauty of these animals reflect the grace and beauty of the lovers (Ginsburg, Fox, Murphy; cf. Prov 5:19). Does are not domestic animals, so for the woman to call them "does of the field" is superfluous; it deliberately opens the poem outwards, beyond the habitation of the lovers to the open country, so that their love embraces all of nature. The choice of animals also establishes a link to the next verse, where the man is compared to a gazelle or young deer, the fawn of a deer, an image in which the swiftness and agility of these animals is foremost.

Song of Songs 2:8–3:5
The Woman's First Long Speech

<She>

2:8   Listen! My lover![a]
Look! He's coming,[b]
leaping over the mountains,
bounding[c] over the hills.

9   My lover is like a gazelle[d]
        or young deer.[e]
     Look! He's standing outside our wall,
        peering in through the windows,
        peeking through the lattice.

10   My lover answered and said to me,

     "Rise up, my friend, my fair one,[f]
        and come away,
11   for look, the winter is past,
        the rains are over and gone.[g]
12   Blossoms[h] are seen in the land;
        the time of singing[i] has arrived,
        and the voice of the turtledove is heard in our land.
13   The fig tree ripens[j] its first fruit,
        and the budding[k] vines give off fragrance.

     Rise up, my friend, my fair one,
        and come away,
14   my dove in the clefts of the rock,
        in the covert of the cliff.
     Let me see you,[l]
        let me hear your voice,
     for your voice is sweet,
        and you are lovely."[m]

15   Catch us foxes,
        little foxes,
     spoilers of vineyards,
        for our vineyards are in bloom.
16   My lover is mine and I am his
        who grazes among the lilies.
17   When the day breathes
        and the shadows flee,
     turn, my love, be like a gazelle
        or young deer
        upon the cleft mountains.[n]

3:1 On my bed nightly,[o]
        I have sought my soul's beloved.
        I sought him but I did not find him.[p]
     I will rise now and go about the city,
        in the streets and in the squares;

This song is not "romance just happens". It has to be cultivated.

> I will seek my soul's beloved.
> I sought him but I did not find him.
> 3 The watchmen found me,
> those who go the rounds of the city.
> My soul's beloved—have you seen him?[q]
> 4 Scarcely had I passed them,
> when I found my soul's beloved.
> I caught hold of him and would not let him go
> until I had brought him to my mother's house,
> to the chamber of her who conceived me.
> 5 I place you under oath, women of Jerusalem,
> by the gazelles or does of the open field,
> not to rouse or awaken love
> until it wishes.

nightly longing

draws out emotions in us.

Like the little love

longing for love-sickness ?

this is the secret place for women —

a. Literally, "the voice (or sound) of my lover"; for this usage of *qôl*, see Joüon-Muraoka §162e; Pope, Fox, Murphy.

b. Here and in the next verse, *zeh* reinforces *hinnēh* to emphasize the present action; see also 1 Kgs 19:5; Isa 21:9. Some give it an adverbial sense: "da kommt er!" (Loretz); "There he comes" (Pope); "he's coming now!" (Fox); "Here he comes" (NEB); cf. GKC §136d, Joüon-Muraoka §143a.

c. The verb *qpṣ* in the *piel* occurs only here; in the *qal*, the root means "to draw together, to shut," which suggests that the *piel* refers to making repeated contractions in taking leaps (BDB 891b); the meaning is confirmed by the parallelism with "leaping" in the previous line.

d. Deliberate (so Murphy) or not, there is a wordplay on *ṣĕbî*, which is a homonym; one word means "gazelle," the other "beauty."

e. The word *ʿōper*, "young deer," occurs only in the Song, and always in conjunction with "gazelle" (2:9, 17; 4:5; 7:3 [4 H]; 8:14).

f. LXX adds "my dove" after "my fair one" here and in v. 13, indicating that some Hebrew mss probably included the word; it is an epithet for the woman in 2:14; 5:2; and 6:9.

g. "Over and gone" is expressed by the alliteration of two asyndetic verbs, *ḥālap hā-lak*; the verbs are followed by the *dativus commodi* (GKC §119s; Joüon-Muraoka §133d). There is no warrant for deleting either verb: "the two verbs together emphasize the point that the rainy season is completely past, over, and gone" (Pope 394).

h. Hebrew *niṣṣānîm* is a *hapax*. The word appears in the phrase "blossoms of purple" in 4QBeat 2.iii.5; its cognate form *niṣṣâ* is used in Gen 40:10 and Isa 18:5 of grape blossoms and in Job 15:33 of olive blossoms. A related verbal form is used in Song 6:11 and 7:12 [13 H] of pomegranates and in Eccl 12:5 of the almond tree blossoming.

i. Hebrew *zāmîr* appears to be a homonym, meaning "pruning" (so LXX, Aquila, Symmachus, Vg., Targum) and "singing" (e.g., 2 Sam 23:1; Isa 24:16; 25:5; Pss 95:2; 119:54; Job 35:10).

dreamlike effect = timeless

j. The context indicates that the reference is to the ripening, that is, sweetening, of the first, unripe fruit. In Gen 50:2 and 26 the verb *ḥnṭ* refers to embalming, which was done by infusion of aromatic mixtures. The fig tree is pictured as sending its sweetening juices into its unripe figs (Ginsburg, Fox, following Ibn Ezra).

k. The Hebrew word here, *sĕmādar*, which appears elsewhere only in v. 15 and 7:12 [13 H], refers to the bud of the vine, as 7:12 makes clear.

l. Literally, "let me see your form." There is not a suitable poetic English equivalent for *marʾeh*, which is not simply the face, as many translations have it, but the appearance, the total visible form; it is used of the male lover in 5:15, "his form is like Lebanon."

m. Literally, "and your form is lovely." A woman "beautiful of form/appearance" (*yĕpat marʾeh*) is a beautiful woman (e.g., Gen 12:11; 29:17; 2 Sam 14:27); thus the translation "you are lovely."

n. Vg. reads a place name, Bether; similarly Aquila, Symmachus, who transcribe the Hebrew, *Ba(i)ther*; LXX has "mountains of the ravines"; Theodotion and Syriac read "spices." The root meaning of Hebrew *btr* is "to divide, cut in two"; thus the suggested meaning "cleft mountains."

o. Reading the plural, "in the nights," as indicating repeated action; i.e., nightly, night after night (cf. Pss 16:7; 92:2 [3 H]; 134:1). The same form appears in Song 3:8.

p. LXX adds, "I called him but he did not answer me"; some LXX mss also add the phrase at the end of v. 2. The addition may have been influenced by the appearance of this phrase in the parallel account in 5:6; see the Commentary under 5:6.

q. Literally, "my soul's beloved have you seen?" with the object first for emphasis. The Hebrew omits the interrogative particle; see GKC §150a.

Song 2:8–17 describes the man's visit to the woman's house and his invitation to her to join him outdoors, where spring's arrival is heralded by flowers coming into bloom, birdsong, budding vines, and fragrance in the air. The section ends as it begins, in an image of sexual energy, with the man leaping upon mountains like a gazelle or young deer. Song 3:1–5 describes the woman's nocturnal search for her lover and its resolution when she finds him, and concludes with her addressing the women of Jerusalem and placing them under oath, as she did in 2:7. Although a break occurs between 2:17 and 3:1 and the mood changes, I treat 2:8–17 and 3:1–5 together because they form one long, sustained speech by the woman (it could be called a speech in two parts or two movements). Also, taken together, they bear a remarkable similarity to 5:2–6:3, a tightly constructed and clearly articulated unit within the Song, where these two scenes—the lover's visit and the seeking and finding—are merged into one. Song 2:8–3:5 and 5:2–6:3 also share the refrain of mutual possession that in one case appears before the search and in the other at the conclusion of it (2:16; 6:3; for detailed discussion of the similarities between these parts of the Song, see under 5:2–6:3).

The woman's account of a visit by her lover in which he is outside and calls to her to join him (2:8–17) strongly resembles her account in 5:2–6 of another visit, on which occasion he is outside and calls to her to let him in. Song 3:1–5 introduces and develops the motif of seeking-and-finding, which 5:6–6:3 replays with variations, while including the same key features: the search that first fails but eventually ends successfully, an encounter with the city watchmen, and an oath placed upon the women of Jerusalem. The difference is that, in 5:2–6:3, the visit scene leads directly into the seeking-finding scene. In 2:8–3:5 the two scenes are merely juxtaposed instead of interwoven. If, however, the lover's coming and going in 2:8–17 is viewed as a variation of the seeking-and-finding motif of 3:1–5, the juxtaposition becomes less jarring than it first appears. As poetic acts of conjuring (see below), 2:8–17 and 3:1–5 are not so different after all.

Something new and, in terms of the unfolding of the poem, extraordinary happens in 2:8–3:5. The woman tells a story, or juxtaposes two stories, each with a narrative movement and a sense of closure, a tension and a resolution—in other words, with a plot. Indeed 2:8–3:5 and its counterpart 5:2–6:3 have more of a plot line than any other parts of the Song. For the first time, the Song of Songs acknowledges the presence of a narrator. This narrator is also a character, as distinguished from the poet as narrator, whose narrative presence throughout the Song is deftly effaced. The poet puts words into the woman's mouth, creating her speech (2:8–3:5) in which she puts words into her lover's mouth, creating his speech (2:10–14). Even when using a narrator whose presence is evident (to the point of such an obvious sign of narration as "my lover answered and said to me," v. 10), the poet maintains the illusion of immediacy so central to the Song's poetic effectiveness—the impression that, far from being simply reported, the action is taking place in the present, unfolding before the reader's very eyes. This is achieved in the woman's speech through a combination of poetic techniques: (1) the use of *hinnēh* ("look!") as a focalizer of present action, (2) the reliance on the erotic imperative that gives the impression of the lovers' presence at the moment of utterance ("Rise up, my friend, my fair one, and come away," "let me see," "let me hear," "turn, my love, be like a gazelle"), and (3) the prominence given to participles to capture action in process (the man is leaping, bounding, standing, and gazing, his activity arrested in time; see Introduction, "The Illusion of Immediacy," pp. 3–6). When the woman quotes her lover, it is as if we are overhearing him, so unobtrusive is the double narratorial voice, the poet telling us what the woman is telling us that the man is saying.

Another defining feature of the Song comes to the fore in the woman's speech: she excels at conjuring up her lover, letting him disappear, and conjuring him up again. First heard, then seen at a distance, he materializes through her poetic powers of representation (i.e., those of the poet who puts this speech in her mouth). She brings him to her house from afar (2:8–9) only to send him away in what is not really a sending away (2:17); then in 3:1–5 he is not there, and she seeks him, cannot find him, seeks, and finally finds him. Conjuring is what the woman does in both 2:8–17 and 3:1–5. It is a game of seeking and finding, of desiring and experiencing satisfaction, that mirrors the rhythms of love. Ultimately it is an attempt on the poet's part to capture in language what cannot be captured on the page, the presence of the loved one.

At key points in her story, the woman's narrative presence is as adeptly effaced as the poet's own. Her voice not only distinguishes itself as that of a narrator and a character in her own narration, it also merges with the poet's (as its creator) and her lover's (when she quotes him). The distinction between past and present is blurred; for example, the lover *spoke*, yet we hear him speaking (2:10–14); the watchmen *found* the woman, and we hear her questioning them (3:3). The artistry of the entire speech is complex, the result seems effortless—a mark of a great poet, as another great poet has put it so well: "A line will take us hours maybe; / Yet if it does not seem a moment's thought, / Our stitching and unstitching has been naught" (William Butler Yeats, "Adam's Curse").

The story the woman tells may have a plot of sorts, but it is no less lyric poetry than the rest of the Song. We should not therefore expect it to follow the conventions of prose narrative, which is what Murphy seems to do when he calls 2:8–17 a "reminiscence" on the part of the woman and speaks of the man as "present to her at least in the memory of the visit which she is evoking" (140) and "present at least in spirit" (142). To be sure, insofar as the woman is represented by the poet as recounting what her lover said to her, she is reminiscing. Interestingly, the reminiscence hangs entirely on only four words in the Hebrew: ʿānâ dôdî wĕʾāmar lî, "my-lover answered and-spoke to-me." Without this line, we would have a continuation of the pattern established in 1:5–2:7, in which alternating speeches are presented as direct discourse, and so appear to be taking place in the present. The effect of "my lover answered and spoke to me" on the status of the speech in 2:8–17 is remarkable, but for all the pressure they exert on its meaning, these words do not control the whole speech in the sense that they place the woman's entire narrative in the past. The immediacy effect works as a counter pressure against the reminiscence effect.

The beginning of the woman's speech (v. 8) is vividly situated in the present (the lover is approaching). The narrated story that follows (what the man *said*) is transformed, through the illusion of immediacy, into the present, as we overhear him *saying*, "Rise up, my love, and come away." By the time he says to her, "let me hear your voice" (v. 14), and she replies in vv. 15–17, the indicators of narration have faded away. In v. 17, she addresses him with a double imperative, "Turn, my love, be like a gazelle." Is v. 17 still part of her narration of the past, or has she conjured him up so vividly that she now speaks to him directly? The blurring of the boundaries between past and present is also a blurring of the distinction between the woman as narrator and the woman as a character in her own narrative. We cannot tell the storyteller from the story.[1]

Earlier, the antiphonal speeches of 1:15–2:3, in which the lovers played variations on each other's words, poetically represented the lovers' mutuality. Song 2:8–17 presents a somewhat conventional picture of gender relations. The man roams freely about the countryside and chooses when to come courting. The woman is inside the house, where one might expect a woman to be, when he comes to invite her to join him outdoors. Whereas he takes the initiative, the decision whether or not to go outside to join him is hers. When evening comes, either she sends him away or relies on the suggestiveness of poetic imagery to call him to her (the cleft mountains, v. 17). If we take v. 17 as double entendre, then both meanings are implied. In any event, she is sure of their mutual bond ("my lover is mine and I am his," v. 16). Whereas he seeks her out in 2:8–17, in 3:1–5 the situation is reversed and she seeks him openly in the city streets. When she finds him, she is determined to bring him inside, into her mother's house, the woman's domain (cf. 8:2, where she also speaks of bringing her lover to her mother's house and describes love in patently erotic terms as something she will give and he, by implication, will take).

[2:8–14] Her speech begins with his voice (*qôl dôdî*), a voice that signals his presence before he speaks. Hearing and seeing, the voice and the gaze, are central themes in the Song, and they play an important role in 2:8–3:5. "Listen!" and "Look!" in the translation reflect the immediacy of the Hebrew *qôl* and *hinnēh*. Who is supposed to listen and look? To whom is the speech as a whole directed? As elsewhere in the Song, we may think both of the women of Jerusalem (the audience in the poem, whose presence is acknowledged in 3:5) and, especially, of the poem's readers. The speculation that *qôl* more likely refers to the sound of the man's approach, apparently noisily clattering over the hills, than to his voice, which could probably not be heard at the distance envisioned in v. 8 (Pope, Snaith, Longman), is overly literalistic and unnecessary. This is a poem, not a literal description of how a man crossed a mountain. Anticipating the sound of his voice, the description in vv. 8–9 brings the man ever closer until we hear him speak. The woman creates a vivid picture of his approach: he is first observed at a distance, upon the mountains, and then seen from up close, outside her house, where we spy him spying, peeping in the windows to catch a glimpse of her.

The comparison of the man to a gazelle or young deer both begins and ends the woman's account in 2:8–17, a literary device known as inclusio. The

---

1. I allude here to Yeats, whom I quoted as a poetic authority above. The poet of the Song of Songs exemplifies Yeats's artistic ideal: "O chestnut-tree, great-rooted blossomer, / Are you the leaf, the blossom or the bole? / O body swayed to music, O brightening glance, / How can we know the dancer from the dance?" ("Among School Children").

comparison suggests speed and agility (2 Sam 2:18; 1 Chr 12:8 [9 H]) and freedom (Landy 72) and may also connote sexual desire or prowess (Fox; Pope
under 2:7). Meek sees the description of the man bounding over the hills as
hyperbole, unless the man is a god. Poets, and lovers, are not so literalistic; compare these lines from an Egyptian love poem:

> If only you would come to (your) sister swiftly,
> like a gazelle bounding over the desert.
> > (P. Chester Beatty I, Group B,
> > No. 40; trans. Fox)

Or, from a modern Palestinian love song:

> I crossed mountains, where there were no paths . . .
> > (Stephan 1922: 273)

Whereas she, and we (through her eyes), can see him coming closer (vv. 8–9)
until we can hear him (vv. 10–14), he, for his part, is trying to catch sight of her
through the windows (v. 9) so that he can tell her that he wants to see and hear
her (v. 14). As Murphy observes, in criticizing Pope's description of the man as
a "peeping Tom," he cannot very well speak to her if he does not know whether
or not she is within the range of his voice.

[2:10a] "My lover answered and said to me" simulates a narrative, and it
sounds as if the woman is going to report some event from the past. Robert
observes that, although the woman presents it in the form of a historical narrative, the scene is actually outside of time, but, because he reads the Song alle-
gorically, he proceeds to locate the scene in the future (as expressing hope for
restoration after the exile). Fox rightly perceives that the woman describes
events "as if they were happening in the present" (112), but he locates the events
in the past. Critics typically try to resolve the temporal fluidity as if it were a
problem, because they do not appreciate its poetic function in creating a sense
of immediacy and urgency.

Rendered in most translations of v. 10a as "said," ʿānâ normally means
"answered," and one has only to recall that the Song is a dialogue for "answered"
to make sense here. It is as if the man is replying to the woman's description of
his approach in vv. 8–9, transforming a reminiscence (to use Murphy's term)
into a conversation.

[2:10b–14] His speech is rhetorically effective in building up to the climax,
his request to see and hear her (v. 14). The direct address, "Rise up, my friend,
my fair one, and come away," repeated from v. 10 in v. 13, serves a dual function: it rounds off the first part of the man's speech, making it an inclusio, and
it introduces the second part. In the first part (10b–13b), he explains why *she*
should come outside; in the second (13c–14), he reveals why *he* wants her to

come out.[2] He first presents his case from her perspective, as it were: she should come outside so that she can enjoy the sights, sounds, and smells of early spring. With the beauty of nature he seeks to seduce her (Landy 72). Spring, when nature comes to life, is, after all, the season quintessentially associated with love (see under 1:5–2:7). Next he reveals why *he* wants her to come outside: so that he can see her and hear her voice.

[2:11–13b] With the particle *hinnēh*, "Look!," the man directs the woman's (and the reader's) attention to spring's unfolding. (The immediacy of "look" is even more pronounced in the fragment of this text found at Qumran, which reads *hinnēh* at the beginning of vv. 12 and 13 as well [4QCant[b], ll. 3, 5]). "Winter" refers to the rainy season, which usually ends around mid-April. The time described seems to be May or June, when figs and vines ripen and migratory birds, like the turtledove, appear. Hebrew *zāmîr* is associated with two different roots, one meaning "singing" and the other "pruning." Ginsburg argues that singing is meant, since, like all the other pleasures of spring depicted, it is a gift of nature to be enjoyed, whereas pruning involves engaging in labor. Verse 12b could be read as Janus parallelism, with the word *zāmîr* pointing in two directions, which allows it to convey both meanings at the same time. As "singing," it points forward to the song of the turtledove (12c), and as "pruning," it points backwards to the end of winter and the beginning of spring (vv. 11–12a) (Gordon 1978: 59). The Gezer Calendar speaks of the months of pruning (*zmr*) as the time between the month of harvesting and the month of summer fruit. Lemaire (1975: 22–24) argues that the term refers to the time of vintage, that is, the grape harvest in June–July. This is, however, later than the picture vv. 11–13 give of the arrival of spring.

The invitation to share the delights of spring derives its persuasive power from its appeal to the senses: blossoms are *seen*, the turtledove's cooing is *heard*, the budding vines fill the air with *fragrance*. There is even a hint of taste in the mention of ripening figs and grape vines. The repeated references to "the land," "our land," in v. 12 suggest a widening of perspective, with the entire countryside participating in the total sensory picture.

[2:13c–14] The sensuous blossoming of the season mirrors the awakening of love (Munro 117). The man wants to share the beauty of spring with the woman. He invites her outside again, this time calling her his "dove," hidden in clefts in the rocks. The imagery draws on the dove's reputation as gentle and affectionate (on the dove as lovebird and symbol of the love goddess, see Driver 1955:

---

2. The Masoretes placed a setuma at the end of v. 13, indicating a sense division. The alternative division of the speech I am proposing takes 13cd with the following, as introducing the second part of the speech. Each reason for her to come out—so that she can enjoy the springtime in the first part of the speech, so that he can see and hear her in the second—would then be preceded by the invitation to rise up and come away with him.

129–30, Pope, Keel). It also conveys the man's sense of the woman as inaccessible, beyond his reach in her house, and perhaps also as shy and hesitant, like a dove reticent to venture forth from its secure, secluded nest. At last he comes to the main reason for her to come outside: never mind the sights and sounds and smells of spring, he wants to see her and hear her (v. 14).

The sense of sight is understandably privileged in the Song; lovers love to gaze upon each other. In 1:15–16 the lovers invited each other to see themselves through the other's eyes. Detailed descriptions of the lovers play an important role in the Song (see under 4:1–5; 5:10–16; 6:4–7; 7:1–6 [2–7 H]). The voice also features prominently. The Song began with a disembodied voice asking for something other than speech from the beloved's mouth (Cook 1968: 115); it ends with the man asking to hear his lover's voice, as he does here in v. 14—to which he receives virtually the same reply that he gets in 2:17. The woman begins her account in vv. 8–17—in which the man's request to see and hear her is embedded—with the injunction to listen and look, and her first word is *qôl*, literally "voice." His request in 14 brings seeing and hearing together in one beautifully balanced chiastic couplet.

a   Let me see your *form*,
b   let me hear your **voice**,
b'   for your **voice** is sweet,
a'   and your *form* is lovely.

The repetition of "form," *mar'eh* (appearance, that which is *seen*, from the root *r'h*, "to see"), is not reflected in the Translation because there is no suitable English poetic equivalent (see Textual Note). Keel considers the translations "sweet" and "lovely" too colorless and maintains that they fail to do justice to the intensity of this verse. It is interesting to note, however, how often the poet uses commonplace words; for example, 1:3, "the fragrance of your perfumes is good (*ṭôb*)," and the epithets "my fair one" and "my friend" for the woman.

[2:15] This verse has long baffled commentators (see, especially, the discussions of Pope and Fox). To whom is it addressed; that is, who is supposed to catch foxes? What are foxes doing in this context, or do they represent something or someone other than foxes? What does catching them signify? Who is the speaker? Is this still part of the man's speech (as the placement of quotation marks in NRSV indicates)? Is it the woman's reply to the man's request to hear her voice in the previous verse (so most commentators)? Or, given the plural ("catch for us," "our vineyards"), have the women of Jerusalem suddenly interrupted to have their say (Exum 1973: 54–55, 58; Garrett)? Since the man has just asked to hear the woman's voice, and because the woman is clearly the speaker in vv. 16 and 17, I take vv. 15–17 as the woman's reply to her lover's request of v. 14—a reply intended for his ears (as well as the audience's) but only at the end (v. 17) addressed directly to him.

The suggestion that v. 15 expresses the wish of the lovers that nothing be allowed to spoil their blossoming love (so Delitzsch, followed by Munro 92, 99–100; similarly, Longman) is rather vague and puts all the emphasis on the vineyards *in bloom*. Surely the attention given in this verse to foxes implies that their role is an important one. How do foxes spoil vineyards? By burrowing in the ground and disturbing the roots, as some suggest? By eating grapes, as others aver? Just how much damage would foxes do to vineyards, especially since grapes are not a staple of a fox's diet?

As part of a love poem full of sexual symbolism and erotic allusion, v. 15 lends itself to a sexual interpretation, especially since "vineyard" has already been used in a sexually suggestive way in 1:6, where "my vineyard" refers to the woman. The vineyard image may be more or less sexually specific, depending on how explicitly one understands erotic innuendo. Fox gives examples of the jackal or wolf cub representing a lusty lover in Egyptian love songs, for example, "My heart is not yet done with your lovemaking, my (little) wolf [or jackal] cub!" (P. Harris 500, Group A, No. 4, trans. Fox). Others cite the evidence of Theocritus, Ode V, 112, where foxes symbolize amorous young men and women and the theft of grapes represents sexual intercourse. In Song 2:15, then, vineyards in bloom could represent young women who have reached sexual maturity, and foxes, lustful young men (Rudolph, Krinetzki, Würthwein, Loretz, Gordis, Fox, Keel, Falk).

Might the foxes be viewed as threatening and the verse as one of the "ominous undercurrents" in the Song (Falk 178)? Landy considers the threat minimized because the foxes are *little*; the peril of the foxes, he submits, is neutralized through displacement and wish fulfillment (240–41). Assuming "little foxes" refers to young ones, their romping in vineyards seems, at least, playful and innocent.

Murphy proposes that v. 15 was originally a song in which young women warn of the danger of damage to the vineyards (themselves), but, at the same time, practically invite it by announcing that the vineyards are in bloom (similarly, Rudolph, who points out that the phrase "little foxes" shows that the tone is playful). In his view, the woman uses it as a "saucy reply" to the man's request to hear her voice, v. 14. In v. 14 her lover has just described her as inaccessible, and, in quoting this song, she means to let him know, in a teasing way, that she is not so inaccessible after all (and here, again, one might compare her statement that she has not tended her own vineyard in 1:6).

Murphy's assumption that v. 15 was originally a popular song is shared by other commentators as well (e.g., Budde, Meek, Fox) and appears to rest on the fact that "the plurals 'foxes' and 'vineyards' do not exactly fit the situation in Canticles" (Fox 114). Other features of the verse, however, fit very well: the suggestive reference to vineyards recalls 1:6, and the vines in bud ("our vineyards are in bloom") relate to the man's description of the blossoming landscape in spring, specifically, the budding vines, v. 13, where the same word (*sĕmādar*, "in bud, in bloom") is used. Once the significance of *catching* the foxes, generally overlooked by critics, is taken into account, it becomes easier to imagine how the vineyards and foxes also fit the situation. We can understand the plural forms as indicating that the woman is speaking on behalf of women in general, expressing a view commonly held by women (a kind of proverbial wisdom), without having to assume that the two couplets existed previously as a song or part of a song. Verse 15 is only the first part of the woman's reply to her lover, and it means, in effect: young men can roam about freely in search of romance, like foxes romping through the vineyards. They want our favors, and we want theirs, but we are not so free as they are to dally. The important thing for us is not to enjoy the random fox but to catch a fox for our very own (each of us, her own fox). These free and easy young men need to be caught, seized hold of and brought home (here the imperative "catch" or "seize" [ʾḥz] is indefinite; who does the catching is not specified). This is the goal that the woman achieves in 3:4, when she seizes her lover—again the verb is ʾḥz—and refuses to let him go until she has brought him to her mother's house. (In the scenario of our verse, one assumes that, ideally, the man is caught and brought home for good.)

This interpretation fits with the general picture the Song of Songs gives of a society in which a man's freedom of movement is greater than a woman's, as well as its picture of love as something that women give and men take (see Introduction, "The Song and Conventional Gender Relations," pp. 25–28). It also fits the particular situation portrayed in the woman's account in 2:8–17, in which she is in the house and the man comes, when he chooses, to court her. Most important, it provides the context for understanding the next verse, for which it is only the prelude.

[2:16] Verse 15 is the general, and v. 16 the particular. The woman's caricature of the way women and men look at love differently, the former from the perspective of the vineyard and the latter from the perspective of the fox, does not apply to her and her lover. As a reply to her lover's request in v. 14 to hear her voice, v. 15 is only a teasing backdrop against which she makes a serious and profound claim in v. 16. Although she speaks about him in the third person as "my lover," her words, like her speeches in 1:12–2:6, are meant for him to hear. Their message is: lustful young men in general are rather like foxes, who by nature seek to take advantage of blossoming vineyards, but my lover, in contrast, is committed to me. Our relationship is exclusive and mutual: he is mine and I am his (see also 6:3; 7:10 [11 H]). He is not to be found in just any vineyard; he grazes among the lilies. In this context, grazing among or upon the lilies strongly hints of enjoying the delights of lovemaking, with the lilies serving as a symbol of the woman herself (cf. 2:1).

No compelling reason exists to look for a specific referent for the image of grazing or feeding on lilies; for example, as a reference to kissing, based on the comparison of lips to lilies in 5:13 (on the richness and suggestiveness of the imagery, see the discussions of Landy 73–92 *passim*, Munro 97–98). As in 1:7, the play on the verb *r‘h* ("pasture, graze") allows one also to imagine the lover as a shepherd, pasturing his flock (so NRSV, NJB, Rudolph). The so-called refrain of mutual possession occurs again in 6:3 with the order reversed, "I am my lover's and my lover is mine."

[2:17] She speaks in response to his request to hear her voice, but does she answer his plea to let him see her? Her account of her lover's visit does not mention her going outside to join him. Only if we want to maintain a strict narrative framework in vv. 10–17 will we need to imagine her speaking from inside the house. Rudolph resolves the issue by gap filling when he says that, without having to be told, we can reasonably assume she comes out. The point is moot. The fact that in this verse the woman now addresses her lover directly, as though he were there before her, is typical of the way the Song plays with presence and absence, conjuring up the lover only to let him disappear, so that the seeking and finding can begin again. Having replied to his request to hear her voice with an assertion about their love (vv. 15–16), here in v. 17 she urges him either to return home (at dusk? at dawn?) or to come to her—whichever she means depends upon how one understands this enigmatic verse.

There are three difficulties. (1) Commentators are divided as to whether v. 17 refers to the coming of the evening or the morning. When does the day "breathe" (*‘ad šeyyāpûaḥ hayyôm*)—in the morning, when it blows softly in, or in the evening, when it becomes cool (as in "the cool of the day," Gen 3:8)? Does the fleeing of the shadows refer to their lengthening until they disappear, as day draws to a close (cf. Jer 6:4), or to their disappearance when the sun rises? To complicate matters even further, *‘ad še-*, here translated "when" (so JPS) could be rendered "until" (NRSV, NAB, KJV, Pope, Murphy), or "while," as in 1:12 (so REB), or "before" (NJB, Fox). (2) There is also a question whether "turn" (*sōb*) indicates that the woman is calling her lover to her—in the sense of "turn to me" or "return" (Vg. *revertere*)—or sending him away (LXX *apostrepson*, "turn away"). (3) She exhorts him to be like a gazelle or young deer upon the mountains, using the same imagery she used to describe his approach in vv. 8–9. Here, however, the mountains are specified as *hārê bāter*, "cleft mountains," "mountains of separation," or "mountains of Bether." Do the mountains represent the woman (cf. the "mountains of spices" in 8:14), or are they the mountains beyond which the man came in 2:8, here specifically identified as the mountains of Bether, or are these some other mountains?

It is striking that v. 17 is ambiguous with regard to the lover's movements in so many respects. Fox proposes that we are perhaps not supposed to be sure whether the woman is urging her lover to go away or to come to her (in the end, Fox suspects she is probably telling the man to depart). Indeed, the poet seems to be playing with our expectations. When, according to the woman, should her lover "turn," and where? The second half of the verse offers a clue.

In the second half of v. 17 is the woman sending the man away and calling
him to her at the same time, in what seems to be a contradictory impulse? Such
appears to be the case in 8:14, where virtually the same exhortation appears. The
problem is resolved if one understands the woman's words as double entendre.
The previous verse ended with a double entendre—is the lover who grazes
among lilies engaging in love play or pasturing a flock? (see under v. 16 above
and under 1:7)—and double entendre is very much in evidence in 5:2–6, the other
story the woman tells of a visit by her lover. In the context of the woman's "story"
in 2:8–17, a story in which her lover comes to court her from afar (over the mountains), telling him to turn and be like a gazelle upon the mountains means that the
time has come for him to go home. "Turn," on the story level, would mean to
turn away from her, to return to the place beyond the mountains from where he
came (v. 8). But the woman does not say, "Turn, my love, be like a gazelle or
young deer leaping over the mountains, bounding over the hills." The change in
wording from v. 8 is significant. What are the cleft mountains (*hārê bāter*)?

Some authorities take *beter* as a place (e.g., KJV, NAB, NJB: "mountains of
Bether"; see Textual Note). I have translated "cleft mountains" rather than
"mountains of Bether" because, in spite of the Song's fondness for place names,
Bether does not have the connotations and associations that the Song's other,
better-known place names have, and also because the related passages 4:6 and
8:14 indicate that this expression is a double entendre for the woman's person.
Ginsburg explains *hārê bāter*, "mountains of separation," as the mountains that
separate the lovers. Others see *beter* as a type of spice (Peshitta reads "spices";
cf. JPS, "hills of spices," REB, "hills where aromatic spices grow"), and it is
tempting to emend *beter* to *běśāmîm* ("spices"), as in 8:14. Gerleman understands the Bether Mountains—as well as the Balsam Mountains of 8:14, and
the "Myrrh Mountain" and "Frankincense Hill" in 4:6—as beautifully scented
poetic fantasy lands, like the land of Punt in the Egyptian love lyrics. There does
not, however, appear to be any such topos in the Song, where the phrase "spice
mountains" or "cleft mountains" is most likely a double entendre suggestive of
the woman herself and the various pleasures her body has to offer. Perhaps,
more specifically, "cleft mountains" could bring to mind her breasts (Goulder,
Garrett), though it may be left to readers to find a specific referent, if they wish
(see, further, under 4:6).

On the erotic level (in contrast to the story level), the woman presents herself as the mountain on which her lover should now cavort (the "turning" would
thus be toward her). A similar double entendre appears in 4:6, when the man
says, "When the day breathes and the shadows flee, I will make my way to the
mountain of myrrh and to the hill of frankincense." These words strongly suggest that his movement is toward the woman.

Assuming that v. 17 is double entendre, the context suggests that she is inviting him to spend the night with her. So is she telling him to "turn" in the morn-

ing, after having been with her all night, or to "turn" in the evening, and stay with her all night? The latter seems preferable because it works better on the story level. He comes courting in the daytime, as indicated by the invitation to her to come outside and by his description of the sights and sounds to be enjoyed. She tells him that, when evening comes, it will be time for him to return home (his figurative absence will set the stage for her second "story," 3:1–5, in which she longs for him in bed at night and goes looking for him). On the erotic level, far from encouraging him to leave at evening time, she invites him to spend the night with her. He besought her to join him outside to enjoy the beauty of a spring day (vv. 10–14). Now she intimates, by means of sexual innuendo, that he should come to her for the night, where further pleasures will delight the senses.

The woman's words here in v. 17 are virtually identical to the last verse of the Song, where once again they are spoken by her in response to the man's request to hear her voice. The differences are (1) *běraḥ*, "flee," appears in place of *sōb*, "turn," which makes the movement away from the woman more apparent, and (2) "mountains of spices" replaces "cleft mountains," which more strongly suggests movement toward the woman. These differences pull in opposite directions, foregrounding the dual impulses already at work in 2:17. The similarity between 2:17 and 8:14 invites us to look more closely at how, in its poetic unfolding, Song 2:8–17 might offer a clue to the meaning of the Song as a whole. Song 2:8–17 ends as the Song ends, with the woman seemingly sending her lover away and calling him to her in the same breath. It is followed in 3:1–5 by a second "story" in which the woman seeks and finds her lover. This pattern indicates that the paradoxical sending away and calling for(th) is a prelude to the lovers' union, a union that throughout the Song is simultaneously assured, deferred, and, on a figurative level, enjoyed (see also under 8:14).

[3:1–5] The woman's long speech, begun in 2:8, continues with a second account of a lover's quest to be in the presence of the loved one. This time it is the woman who seeks out the man. The woman speaks in the present, telling the women of Jerusalem and us, the poem's ultimate audience, about something that happened in the past. Often at night, she says, she lay in bed longing for her lover. On this particular occasion she decided to go out looking for him in the city streets. At this point she reports what she said to herself, using cohortatives to signal her determination: either "I *will* rise now," "I *will* go about," "I *will* seek," or "Let me rise now," and so forth. She continues to relate (in a series of verbs in the perfect) that she *sought* him but did not *find* him; however, the watchmen of the city *found* her (vv. 2–3). About this encounter she reports only what she said to them, "Have you seen my soul's beloved?" (v. 3), for nothing else matters to the telling except the crucial detail that soon thereafter she *found* her lover (v. 4).

Within this brief account there are two places where the woman seems to be quoting words she said in the past, either to herself ("I will rise now and go about the city. . . . I will seek my soul's beloved," v. 2) or to the watchmen

("Have you seen my soul's beloved?" v. 3). NRSV indicates this by placing these words in quotation marks (similarly, JPS, Rudolph, Ringgren, Loretz, Gordis, Landy 114, Murphy, Munro 24–25, Goulder, Longman, Garrett), whereas others place only v. 3 in quotes (e.g., NJB, NIV, Ginsburg, Fox, Bloch and Bloch); REB inserts, "I said" in v. 2 (so also Munro 24; Goulder, "I thought") and "I asked" in v. 3 (where KJV adds, "to whom I said"). There are, however, no indicators of narration, as there was, for example, in 2:10 ("my lover answered and said to me"), and, as a result, these parts of the woman's account seem more immediate. Events that belong to the reported narrative are represented as taking place even as she speaks, as though she were getting up from her bed and standing before the watchmen, and not simply telling us about it. Here, as in 2:8–17, the telling merges with the action it describes.

In v. 4 the perfect, "I seized/caught hold of him," is followed by an imperfect (here translated "I would not let him go"). I follow Pope in taking this construction as durative, expressing the idea that she holds on to him until she has brought him to her mother's house. Fox, on the other hand, sees here a signal that the temporal perspective has changed: "she moves from narration to statement of the present situation" (118). He takes the verbal sequence as a way of expressing intention, and translates, "I seized him—now I won't let him go till I've brought him to my mother's house." With the finding of the lover, the present seems almost imperceptibly to have overtaken the narrated past, so that it is difficult to say where the one leaves off and the other takes over. Verse 5, which concludes the woman's speech, is situated in the present. The woman addresses directly the audience of her story, the women of Jerusalem: "Do not rouse or awaken love until it wishes."

The slippage between past and present contributes to the impression of immediacy that distinguishes the poem. By making it difficult to pinpoint the seeking and finding in time, the poet imbues these activities with a feeling of timelessness. Desire and fulfillment, seeking and finding, are not only repetitive, ongoing and never-ending, but also happening now, actualized in the act of reading.

The poetic preoccupation with conjuring—the drive to overcome absence with presence through language—becomes particularly intense in 3:1–4, where desire is channeled into one overriding concern, seeking and finding the loved one. This is conveyed through an ordered pattern of repetition in which a few key phrases take on particular weight with each repetition and variation (Exum 1973: 55–56; Krinetzki; Landy 46; Munro 134). Every extraneous detail is sacrificed to the intensely repetitive sequence as the narrative "strains relentlessly onward towards the resolution of the search" (Munro 134). The motif of seeking and finding dominates these verses until the lover is found (v. 4). Forms of the words "seek" (*bqš*) and "find" (*mṣ'*) appear four times, as does "my soul's beloved," the object of the quest.

> **I SOUGHT my soul's beloved.**
> *I SOUGHT him but I did not FIND him.*
> I will rise now and go about the city . . .
> **I will SEEK my soul's beloved.**
> *I SOUGHT him but I did not FIND him.*
> FOUND me, they did—the watchmen, those who go about the city.

The repetition retards the pace until suddenly a finding takes place, but not the one anticipated. Instead, the one doing the seeking is found—by the city's watchmen![3] The unexpected outcome is announced by a striking juxtaposition: *mĕṣāʾtîw* (in the phrase, "not did-I-find-him") and *mĕṣāʾûnî* ("they-found-me") (Krinetzki).

As the brief account reaches its climax, the pattern changes and references to the lover frame the woman's question and the resolution to her quest.

> **My soul's beloved**—have you seen?
> Scarcely had I passed them, when I FOUND **my soul's beloved.**

Once the goal is achieved, the intensely concentrated repetition yields to a greater poetic expansiveness in vv. 4c–5 (cf. Munro 134). The account that began with the woman in her bed ends with her bringing her lover to the bed-chamber in her mother's house. The locations are symbolically "the same and yet comprise a progression from restlessness to rest, from solitude to companionship" (Landy 46).

As compact as it is, within the account of seeking and finding in vv. 1–4 there appear echoes of 2:8–17 that establish connections with what has gone before. In 2:10 and 13, the man sought out the woman and called to her to "rise up" (*qûmî*) and come away with him. Here in v. 2, she does rise (*ʾāqûmâ*), and it is with the intention of seeking him. He wanted to see her (*harʾînî*, "let me see [you/your form]," v. 14), and now, in her desire to find him, she asks the watchmen if they have seen him (*rĕʾîtem*, v. 3). That the watchmen should have come upon the woman is not surprising, since they, like her, are roaming (*sbb*) about the city. Apparently her lover is roaming about the city streets, too, for not only does she soon find him but earlier (2:17) she had told him to "turn" (*sōb*, from the same root, *sbb*). When she finally finds him, she catches hold of him (*ʾăḥaztîw*, v. 4) and brings him to her mother's house, attaining the goal of catching her man, as in the enigmatic "catch (*ʾeḥĕzû*) us little foxes" in 2:15 (see under 2:15).

The setting at night, in bed, and the woman's apparently unconventional behavior in seeking her lover in the city streets at night lead many commentators

---

3. Perhaps vv. 2–3 are an example of antanaclasis, the repetition of the same word with a different meaning; see Anthony R. Ceresko ("The Function of *Antanaclasis* [*mṣʾ* 'to find' // *mṣʾ* 'to reach, overtake, grasp'] in Hebrew Poetry, Especially in the Book of Qoheleth"), *CBQ* 44 (1982), 564, who translates: "I sought but did not find him. They met me, the watchmen who patrol the city."

to ask whether 3:1–5 and its companion piece in 5:2–8 are dreams, and to raise questions about the mixture of "reality" and "fantasy" in these accounts (see, further, under 5:2–7). To be sure, 3:1–5 does have a dreamlike quality, particularly in the way in which, as in a dream, the woman tries over and over to find her lover but is repeatedly unable to do so. Its timelessness also contributes a dreamlike effect. But if this is a dream, where does it end? The way the present overtakes the past at the end of the woman's account makes this question moot. Indeed, whether something represents "reality" or "fantasy" is a curious kind of distinction to press when it comes to a lyric poem whose artistic hallmark is the blurring of boundaries between wishing for, desiring, anticipating, and experiencing sexual gratification (see Introduction, "Fantasy, Reality, and Poetic Imagination," pp. 45–47).

[3:1] When the woman says that she seeks her lover upon her bed at night, she may mean simply that she longs for him (Murphy; seeking him in her heart, as Fox puts it; cf. P. Harris 500, Group B, No. 13). Since erotic suggestiveness permeates the poem, the statement may also imply that she expects him to be there (so Budde, in a dream; Ginsburg supposes he did not come in the evening as she requested and, unable to wait any longer, she went to bed). Her seeking takes place "nightly" (see Textual Note), which suggests that she has often lain in bed at night longing for him. One can imagine that the setting here is the same as that in 2:8–17 and that the woman's house is inside the city walls. Since the countryside was just outside the city walls and not some distance away, the man could have been inviting her to come outside her house in the city to the country in 2:8–17. However, the scene need not necessarily be the same. Scenes change abruptly in the Song, and one of the reasons may be that changes of scene function, like the various guises the lovers assume, to represent the lovers as types rather than individuals.

[3:2] By quoting her thoughts rather than simply reporting that she got up and sought her lover in the city streets, the woman draws attention to her decision as a pivotal moment in her narrative. The cohortative verbal forms underscore her determination.

[3:3] The woman, who is roaming the city looking for her lover, is found (in the sense of "come upon") by the watchmen, who patrol the city. Two forms of the same root, *sbb*, are used, a simple *qal* for the watchmen's routine activity of making their rounds and a *poel*, indicating intensity, for the woman's search (Krinetzki 1981: 256 n. 225). The juxtaposition of the straightforward statement that the watchmen found her and the direct speech, "Have you seen my soul's beloved?" is abrupt, almost as if, in her surprise at running into them, all she can think of to say is the thing that is uppermost in her mind. Are they to know who her soul's beloved is? That is irrelevant for the story she is telling (cf. the similar situation in 5:9–16, where her description of her lover would not help anyone identify him). Fox posits that the absence of a response on the part of the watchmen suggests "steely indifference" (118). It seems to me, rather, to be the poet's way of conveying the woman's lack of interest in reporting any accessory details ("in her hurry to find her beloved, [she] does not tell us the answer which she received," Ginsburg 149). She and the watchmen pass in the night without incident; the watchmen neither help her nor interfere. The encounter with the watchmen seems to be a blind motif here, like the brothers' anger in 1:6—a potential story, inviting the reader to fill in the gaps. Like the brothers, the watchmen strike a discordant note; unlike the brothers, they appear again later, where they do interfere, and the potential threat they represent here becomes a real one (see under 5:7).

[3:4] The woman's search ends successfully. In contrast to the version in 5:2–6:3, which is more elaborately developed, there are no complications. The "mother's house" appears elsewhere in 8:2 and in Gen 24:28 and Ruth 1:8. Meyers argues that the mother's household is a counterpart to the more frequently mentioned social grouping, the "father's house," and that the four passages in which it appears suggest the involvement of the mother in love and marriage arrangements (Meyers 1991, 1993). A young woman in an Egyptian love poem also speaks of "my mother's house" and of her mother (who in this case has advised that the young people not see each other again; P. Chester Beatty I, Group A, No. 32). In the Sumerian account of the goddess Inanna's marriage to Dumuzi, Inanna's mother counsels her before her wedding (Jacobsen 1987: 19–21; Sefati 1998: 291–94).

Once she has found her lover, the woman's account moves in progressively narrowing concentric circles from the city streets, to the mother's house, to the bedchamber (Munro 134–35). "The chamber of her who conceived me" reminds us that the mother has also known the passion that the woman experiences (Keel).

Based on 8:1–2, where the woman wishes she could bring her lover to her mother's house, but social convention seems to preclude it, Fox speculates that, here in v. 4, she has not yet realized her intention to bring him home but only expresses her determination to do so in the future. Bringing her lover to her mother's house would be a way of making their love public, and, based on 8:1–2, Fox concludes this is "something she cannot do quite yet" (118), even though he does assume that the lovers are together and engaged in lovemaking. But bringing her lover to her mother's house is not the same thing as making their love public, even in 8:1–2. Moreover, the Song is not a narrative poem in which a continuous story line develops from 3:4 to 8:2. Here, as elsewhere, the poem blurs the distinction between anticipation of sexual fulfillment and enjoyment of it.

[3:5] See under 2:7. Unlike its appearance in 2:7 and 8:4, the adjuration refrain here is not preceded by the description of the man's embrace with his

danger for lovesickness!
not mature enough to handle this?

left hand under his lover's head and his right hand caressing her. Nevertheless, it seems clear that the time for lovemaking has come. In both 3:5 and 8:4 the adjuration follows references to finding the beloved and bringing him to the mother's house, as the setting for making love. Here, as in 2:7, the adjuration addressed to the women of Jerusalem raises the question: if love has a will of its own, how can it be roused before it wishes to be? When it wishes to be aroused, it will be. The lovers, whose desire is aroused, know this. The silence with regard to what takes place inside the house excludes the reader from the lovers' pleasure, while the appeal to the audience here in v. 5 affirms the reader's presence.

Song of Songs 3:6–11
The Woman's First Long Speech,
A Continuation

<She>

3:6   What is this coming up from the wilderness
      like columns[a] of smoke,
  redolent[b] with myrrh and frankincense,
      from the merchant's many powders?[c]

7   Look! It is Solomon's litter!
      Sixty warriors surround it
      from the warriors of Israel,

8   all of them skilled[d] with the sword,
      trained in warfare,
  each with his sword at his side
      against terrors of the night.[e]

9   King Solomon made himself a palanquin[f]
      from the wood of Lebanon.

10   Its posts he made of silver,[g]
      its upholstery[h] of gold,
  its seat[i] of purple cloth,
      its interior inlaid[j] with precious stones.[k]
  Women of Jerusalem, 11 come forth,[l]
      look, women of Zion,
  at King Solomon
      in the crown with which his mother crowned him
  on the day of his wedding,
      on the day of his heart's joy.

a. Some mss and Vg. read singular, and some critics (e.g., Pope, Murphy) take the plural as a plural of generalization and render it as singular; cf. Joüon-Muraoka §136j. The plural does not pose a problem; what is seen from a distance could resemble columns of smoke, and not just one column. Some emend *k* to *b* and read "in columns of smoke."

b. The *pual* participle of *qṭr*, which in the *piel* means to make incense or animal sacrifices go up in smoke (i.e., to offer them by burning), is attested only here; cf. LXX *tethumiamene*, "perfumed."

c. Literally, "from all kinds of powder of a merchant" (cf. GKC §127b; Joüon-Muraoka §133e, §139h). Although the feminine noun, here in the construct *ʾabqat,* is not attested elsewhere, the meaning "powder" is supported by the masculine form, *ʾābāq*, which means "dust" (Exod 9:9; Deut 28:24; Isa 5:24; 29:5; Ezek 26:10; Nah 1:3); the context indicates that aromatic powders are meant.

d. On the basis of the parallelism with "trained (*melummĕdê*) in warfare," the passive participle *ʾăḥūzê* is best understood as "skilled" or "trained" with the sword (Perles 1922: 52–53, with reference to Akkadian *aḫāzu*, "learn").

e. The same plural form, *ballêlôt*, "nightly," appears in 3:1; the singular *paḥad lāyĕlâ*, "dread of night" or "terror of night" appears in Ps 91:5 among a list of dangers that those who trust in God need not fear.

f. The word translated "palanquin," *ʾappiryôn*, is a *hapax*. It appears to be a loanword from the Greek *phoreion* ("sedan chair"), which is how LXX renders it; cf. Vg. *ferculum* ("litter").

g. "Posts" or "pillars" or "columns" not made out of silver but overlaid with it (cf. the pillars of the tabernacle in Exod 27 and 38).

h. "Upholstery" (*rĕpîdâ*) is a *hapax* related to the verb *rpd* in 2:5; see the Commentary under 2:5. The root, meaning "spread out" (Job 17:13; 41:22 [30 H]), suggests some type of covering or support for reclining on, which Pope captures well with the translation "bolster"; I have used the fairly unspecific term, "upholstery." The gold would refer to gold thread woven into the material. A related noun, *rĕpîdîm*, refers to the resting places of the Israelites in the wilderness (Exod 17:1, 8; 19:2; Num 33:14, 15). LXX renders *anakliton*, "couch"; Vg. *reclinatorium*, "pillow"; Syriac *tšwyth*, "its carpets, blankets."

i. A *merkāb* is a seat of some sort (cf. Lev 15:9–10), perhaps here a cushion covered with cloth dyed purple. LXX has *epibasis*, "means of access," perhaps "rungs, steps"; Vg. *adscensum*, "ascent."

j. Another *hapax*; a related noun *riṣpâ* means "pavement" in Ezek 40:17–18; 42:3; 2 Chr 7:3; Esth 1:6. The Akkadian and Arabic cognates mean "to join together" and in Esth 1:6 the word seems to refer to a mosaic pavement (cf. LXX, "within a tesselated pavement, a love [gift] from the daughters of Jerusalem"), so the verb may mean "to fit out (with)" or "to inlay (with)." It appears that the verb can take one or two objects, "to fit out (something, e.g., a palanquin) with (something, e.g., love, leather); cf. *lābaš*, "to clothe someone (with) clothes, to put clothes (on) someone"; Gen 41:42, "he clothed him (in) garments of linen"; Exod 28:41, "you shall put them (on) Aaron your brother"; Exod 29:5, 8; 40:13, 14; etc.

k. Reading *ʾăbānîm*, "precious stones," for MT's *ʾahăbâ*, "love."

l. Reading with the parallelism between "women of Jerusalem" and "women of Zion," against the Masoretic division, and taking the *m* of *mibbĕnôt* with the preceding line, as the final consonant of *ʾăbānîm*.

In these verses the Song takes what many critics regard as a new and unexpected turn. In a poem devoted to lovers' declarations of desire and praise of each other, what is the relevance of a description of Solomon's bed or litter (v. 7), also called his palanquin (v. 9), on what turns out to be his wedding day? The attention to Solomon is not a problem if one understands these verses as presenting a travesty (Murphy) or royal disguise (Fox), in which the male lover is figuratively identified with Solomon. It should be noted, however, that Solomon's appearance here is different from other appearances of Solomon or "the king" in the poem. Apart from the title of the book (1:1) and the descriptive phrase "curtains of Solomon" (1:5), Solomon or "the king" is mentioned elsewhere in relation to one of the lovers: "the king has brought *me* to his chambers," 1:4; "while the king is on his couch, *my nard* gives forth its fragrance," 1:12; "*my own vineyard is before me*; the thousand is yours, Solomon," 8:12. In vv. 6–11 no such connection is made, which would clarify Solomon's relation to the lovers. This, in turn, raises doubts as to who the speaker is in vv. 6–11 and whether or not the speaker remains the same throughout these verses.

If these verses are about Solomon, and not about the lovers, what is their connection, if any, to the rest of the poem? Gordis proposes that this pericope was originally composed for Solomon's wedding, but the fact is we have no way of knowing. Most critics consider it unlikely that these verses have anything to do with the historical Solomon, and understand Solomon in these verses as a literary fiction (as Budde points out, if one is going to play the role of a king, then it would be as Solomon). Some think that these verses reflect the practice of referring to a groom and bride as king and queen and carrying them in a wedding procession (often considering the name of Solomon as a later addition), but no evidence exists for such a custom in ancient Israel. If these verses once existed as an independent unit, why would the poet, or a later editor, include an epithalamion at this point in the Song? Would not a more logical place for it be at the end (Brenner 1993b: 267)? That is where some rearrangements of the text place it; for example, Haupt 1902a: 206; Angénieux 1968: 107.[1] Given the many signs of structural organization in the Song, it seems highly unlikely that the placement of this pericope is the result of haphazard redaction.

Indeed, too many aspects of these verses resonate with the rest of the poem too well for us to dismiss these verses as unrelated to their context. Solomon is certainly not out of place, given the Solomonic aura that hovers over the poem, and a wedding day, complete with a procession, is easily at home in a love poem. Here, as elsewhere in the Song, the women of Jerusalem provide an audience within the poem; they are called to gaze upon King Solomon on his wed-

---

1. It is also where the pre-Raphaelite artist Edward Burne-Jones moved it in his representation of the Song in stained glass; for discussion of similar issues of unity and structure in the Song and Burne-Jones's twelve-panel window, see Black and Exum 1998.

ding day. The introduction of Solomon's mother, which some commentators find rather curious, is very much in keeping with the focus on the mother elsewhere in the Song, where a part is played by both the woman's mother (1:6; 3:4; 6:9; 8:1, 2) and the man's (8:5).

In the context of the whole poem, if vv. 6–11 are about Solomon and not the lovers, then the poem at this point opens out to look beyond the world of the lovers, wrapped up as they are in each other, to a famous public occasion of celebration and joy—perhaps in anticipation of their own wedding day. The poet leaves the lovers temporarily at a moment of finding (3:5), to present, as an interlude, a wedding day on a grand, national scale. The speaker of these verses could be either the woman or the man—but probably not the women of Jerusalem, since they are addressed in vv. 10–11. Some exegetes think that, in this instance, the poet addresses the reader directly, but this would be quite unusual, since throughout the rest of the poem three speakers (the woman, the man, and the Jerusalem women) serve as the poet's mouthpiece.

If, on the other hand, these verses are about the lovers, and only about Solomon for what he represents, a lover-king par excellence, then vv. 6–11 belong to the realm of poetic fancy in which lovers take on various identities (sometimes as shepherds in a bucolic setting, sometimes as royalty in an opulent one). That Solomon here is a guise or role in which the woman casts her lover seems to be the most likely sense of these verses, especially since elsewhere the male lover is figuratively identified as a king. Moreover, it is difficult to believe that at one point in this composition the poet would introduce a different, albeit thematically related, topic or that the poet would interrupt what is otherwise a sustained lovers' dialogue to offer an anecdote about Solomon.

In addition to the Solomonic aura, the presence of the women of Jerusalem, and the focus on the mother, these verses share some of the distinguishing poetic features of the Song as a whole. The illusion of immediacy is sustained throughout, from the introductory question (v. 6) and the interjection "look" (v. 7) to the direct address to the women of Jerusalem and call for them (and us) to "look" at the end (vv. 10–11). With the question "What is this coming up from the wilderness?" (v. 6), the poet draws the reader into the poem; by not as yet specifying the addressee, the speaker seems to be addressing the reader directly. "Coming up" (*'ōlâ*), a participle, is action in progress. The illusion is that we are watching along with the speaker, our eyes riveted upon something just entering our field of vision, poised between the wilderness and the unspecified location of the speaker, and moving ever closer. There is also the appeal to the senses, the sight of something gradually drawing nearer, accompanied by the smell of incense that announces its approach ("redolent with myrrh and frankincense, from the merchant's many powders"). Another feature these verses share with other parts of the Song is the conjuring up of the loved one (see below). Also, here as elsewhere in the Song, temporal boundaries are blurred; is the day in question the present or the past, the day Solomon's mother *crowned* him?

Song 3:6–11 is constructed in such a way as to bring a luxurious conveyance bearing Solomon (the lover in his royal guise) from the furthest imaginable horizon, the wilderness, closer and closer to the speaker who describes the procession, and through whose eyes we perceive the sight in greater and greater detail. To whom is the question, "What is this coming up from the wilderness?" (v. 6), addressed? As elsewhere, the audience is the women of Jerusalem (they are addressed directly at the end in vv. 10–11) and the poem's readers. By means of a question, the speaker calls our attention to what looks like columns of smoke on the horizon. The question that immediately arises is, who or what is the cause?

The question receives its answer in the next verse: Solomon's litter. The speaker identifies the litter as Solomon's, but on what basis we do not know. Something about it is regal, perhaps the nature of the conveyance, perhaps the size, and consequently importance, of the entourage. Once we know that a litter is approaching, we will want to know who is riding in it. We might expect it to be Solomon, since this is Solomon's litter, but this information is withheld until the climax of the unit in v. 11, where we learn not only the identity of the palanquin's occupant but also the occasion for all this commotion. In the meantime, first we see something moving, throwing up dust that looks like columns of smoke. Then comes an appeal to the sense of smell as the air grows denser, perfumed from unseen censers, as though incense were being burned. Is this perhaps a caravan laden with aromatic powders (v. 6)? One might expect a caravan, since the question, "What is this coming up from the wilderness?" anticipates as an answer something that is feminine in gender, and the Hebrew word for caravan, *ʾōrĕḥâ*, is feminine. But, no, this is not a caravan. Suddenly the speaker recognizes the litter: "Look!" and we see it too. Although we now see what is responsible for the columns of smoke and the heavy scent, we cannot yet see who it is—apart, that is, from the impressive armed escort that accompanies the litter. Such an entourage could occasion a good deal of dust that rises like columns of smoke and that mingles with the smoke of incense. Soon these warriors are close enough for us to distinguish the swords at their sides.

This is not a description of any "real" procession but rather the product of a fruitful poetic imagination capable of delighting the reader with relatively unessential but well-chosen details, such as a retinue of warriors armed against unnamed, and thus provocatively mysterious, alarms in the night. It is unnecessary to take the description literally and to try to identify the wilderness with a specific place (e.g., Gordis, Goulder). The wilderness represents the furthest horizon the eye can see. The reader occupies the unspecified location from which the speaker perceives the procession in the distance and watches it approach through the speaker's eyes.

An imaginative transformation takes place in v. 9: the litter, as it draws closer, becomes a magnificent palanquin, whose trappings progressively come into view (cf. Barbiero 1995: 101). We see that it is made of wood and that it has silver posts. As it comes even nearer, we catch a glimpse of its upholstery, with the gold thread woven into it perhaps catching the light, and its cushioned seat covered in expensive purple cloth. Finally we look into its very interior (*tôkô*, v. 10) and view the inlaid work that decorates it. And who is inside? Why Solomon, of course, as we might have expected! The palanquin has brought him before us, and we (as the audience of whom the poem is ever mindful), along with the women of Jerusalem, are invited to gaze upon him, wearing his crown, on what we now discover to be his wedding day.

There is considerable disagreement as to who the speaker of these verses might be. Ginsburg and Delitzsch, for example, assign these verses to four onlookers; Meek and Garrett, to the daughters of Jerusalem; Krinetzki, vv. 6–8 and 9–10d (as a later addition) to the chorus of women and vv. 10e–11 to a soloist; Munro, v. 6 to the daughters of Jerusalem and vv. 7–11 to the narrator. Fox observes that vv. 7–8 could be spoken by the man, with the woman expanding on the description in vv. 9–11, or vv. 7–10d could be spoken by the women of Jerusalem, in which case vv. 10e–11 is the woman's reply. He concludes on grounds other than literary that vv. 7–11 belong to the woman. Murphy marks these verses with a question mark, indicating uncertainty about the identity of the speaker.

In cases where the identity of a speaker is uncertain, a useful procedure for guarding against arbitrary assigning of dialogue is to posit the same speaker throughout a poetic unit, unless there is strong evidence to the contrary. If the poetic analysis offered above has any merit, then it is fairly obvious who the speaker of these verses is: the woman. It cannot be the women of Jerusalem, since they are addressed directly by the speaker. And it cannot be the man since, in his Solomonic guise, he is the subject of the speech. Only the woman is not mentioned in these verses, and this is because she is the one describing the scene. Always when the man is "the king," the woman appears as herself; that is to say, she participates in a royal fantasy or guise—as, for example, in 1:2–4, where she is imaginably a member of the court, if not of the royal harem—but she does not have a designated role, such as queen or courtesan (in contrast, for example, to the bucolic guise, where she and he appear as shepherds, 1:7–8). Here in vv. 6–11 she conjures up her lover from afar, from the *midbār*, the unsettled, uncultivated steppe beyond the place from which she is watching the procession. She conjured him up earlier, bounding over hills like a gazelle or young deer (2:8–9); now in a sedan chair, a portable couch, a magnificent palanquin coming toward her, he materializes as a kingly Solomon. He is not contrasted to Solomon, as in 8:11–12, but rather appears in Solomonic guise.

Fox assumes that the description of Solomon's bed and wedding day in these verses is triggered by the lovers' experience: the lovers are in their country

bower, imagining their leafy bed as a majestic couch in a splendid regal pavilion and thinking of their own wedding day, which is a royal one in their fantasy. The woman then boasts of the magnificence of their bower to the women
of Jerusalem. It is unnecessary, however, to posit a particular setting in the lives
of the (fictional) lovers to account for the scene depicted in these verses. Gerleman thinks the poet was inspired by a familiarity with processions in Egyptian festivals, and there are Mesopotamian analogues as well (see Pope). There
seems to be an Israelite backdrop too, an allusion, through the choice of
imagery, to the Israelites' entry into the land of Canaan from the wilderness,
where they were led by a column of cloud.

What is achieved in this act of conjury? In addition to the aesthetic pleasure
they offer, how might these verses function in the context of the poem? We
might view vv. 6–11 as the third of the woman's "stories" begun in 2:8, and read
these verses in the light of the relations between the sexes reflected in 2:8–3:5
(see esp. under 2:15). The first story, 2:8–17, is a poetic evocation of courtship.
The man, whose freedom of movement is underscored by the comparison to a
gazelle bounding over the mountains, comes calling on the woman, who is
inside the house, secluded, as he suggests in 2:14, in a domestic setting, which
is the sphere typically associated with women. He asks to hear her voice, and
she replies with a rather cryptic ditty, "Catch us foxes, little foxes, spoilers of
vineyards, for our vineyards are in bloom," that seems to oppose the freedom
of movement and sexual freedom a man enjoys to a woman's more socially
restricted position and desire to "catch" a man. In 2:16, "my lover is mine and
I am his," the woman makes clear that she and her lover are already resolutely
committed to each other.

In her second story, 3:1–5, she takes the initiative and does, in fact, "catch"
(ʾḥz, 2:15; 3:4) her man and bring him home, to the mother's house, the domestic setting in which she will possess him. In terms of the social context of the
poem—though not of the poem itself, whose subject is desire, not social reality—the desired outcome for a woman in this situation is marriage (as 8:1–2
indicates, she is not, as things are in this society, in a position to kiss him
openly). Thus, in her third story, 3:6–11, the woman envisages a wedding, and
a royal one at that, a wedding day on which her kingly lover comes to her in all

Whatever the cultural influences and literary precursors—and surely there
were influences—the poet has put an Israelite stamp on this exotic depiction
(the litter is Solomon's and the warriors are warriors of *Israel*, v. 7) and used it
in the service of an artistic feat of conjury (we read nowhere else of kings being
carried in litters in Israel). Here the woman engages in her favorite pastime,
evoking the presence of the loved one through the power of poetic representation. Conjuring up the loved one and letting the loved one disappear, seeking
and finding, enjoying and deferring love's delights are all ways of rendering the
rhythms of love through the medium of poetry.

his splendor and in joy. Then the fact that they belong to each other will be publicly celebrated. This is not to say that 3:6–11 represents the lovers' marriage in anything more than an indirect way, however, for marriage is never mentioned in the text apart from this reference to Solomon's wedding.

[6] The question here, *mî zō't*, can mean "who is this?" or "what is this?" The interrogative pronoun *mî* is sometimes used of things, especially when persons are understood or implied (*DCH* V, 242b; Joüon-Muraoka §144b; BDB 566a; Ginsburg). This is the sense here, where the answer is not simply that it is a litter but that it is *Solomon's* litter. Presumably Solomon is riding in it (Ringgren), but it will not be close enough for us to see him until v. 11. The feminine pronoun *zō't*, "this," can be used in the sense of the neuter as an abstract of generalization (cf. Isa 5:25; 43:9; Mic 1:5; GKC §136b; Joüon-Muraoka §152a). The feminine participles in the question ("coming up" and "redolent") anticipate as an answer something that is feminine in gender, and this is what we get in *miṭṭâ*, "litter" (v. 7).

On the basis of 8:5, where the question "Who is this coming up from the wilderness?" also appears and where the answer is clearly the woman, some commentators conclude that here too the question refers to the woman as the occupant of the litter (Delitzsch, Gordis, Keel, Pope, Garrett; Müller sees vv. 6–8 referring to the bride and vv. 9–11 as the reciprocal scene of the groom brought to meet the bride in his sedan chair, she as a divine apparition, he as King Solomon). Others propose that the litter stands for the woman as a surrogate (Pope) or metaphor (Holman 1995) for her. Some imagine that the bridegroom and his friends are journeying to the bride's house in order to fetch her and bring her back to the groom's home, or that the groom's friends are bringing the bride to meet the bridegroom (e.g., Rudolph, Krinetzki, Würthwein, Loretz). This, however, is speculation based on the questionable evidence of Psalm 45, 1 Macc 9:37–39, and later wedding customs among Jews and Arabs. Fox and Bloch and Bloch, who sever this verse from the following description of the litter, see the question as referring to the woman, and point to 6:10, "Who is this looking forth like the dawn?" as further evidence. Although the question "who is this?" in 6:10 refers to the woman, the context, as Murphy observes, is quite different from that of 3:6.

Just because *mî zō't* refers to the woman on two other occasions does not mean that it must refer to her every time it occurs. In 8:5 the woman comes up from the wilderness, and the man is with her. Here a palanquin comes up from the wilderness and the man, in his Solomonic guise, is in it. The text gives no indication that the woman is the palanquin's occupant, whereas, if the analysis of the poetic development of vv. 6–11 offered above is adopted, v. 11, as the climax to the description, identifies the occupant as Solomon. Moreover, if the woman were the occupant, one would have to divide vv. 6–11 among different speakers (e.g., vv. 6–10d to the women of Jerusalem and vv. 10e–11 to the woman), for the woman would hardly be describing herself as approaching herself in a palanquin. Since these verses make sense as a whole with the woman as the speaker, there is no reason to complicate interpretation by dividing the speech into parts.

What looks like columns of smoke appears on the horizon. The dust stirred up by the sizable retinue could create this impression (Budde, Meek, Gordis). Dust could be mingled with smoke as well, as suggested by the second part of the verse, "redolent with myrrh and frankincense, from the merchant's many powders." An important procession might be accompanied by incense profusely burned, which would produce a fragrant, enveloping cloud of smoke.

On myrrh, see above under 1:13. Frankincense is the resin of a tree that grows in Arabia and Somalia (genus *Boswellia*, regarding which there is a variety of opinion as to the number of species; see W. W. Müller, "Frankincense," *ABD* II, 854; Moldenke and Moldenke 56–59; Zohary 197). Jeremiah 6:20 mentions Sheba as the source of frankincense, and Isa 60:6 describes it as carried, along with gold, by camel caravan. Frankincense is harvested by making cuts into the bark of the tree. The first cut opens the "pores" of the tree; subsequent cuts in the same spots allow the gum to exude, and the third cut is said to produce the most gum. The sap, milky white in color (the root meaning of its Hebrew name *lĕbônâ* is "white, to be white"), hardens into a semitranslucent, light yellow or green resin that can be scraped off the tree. The gum resin is said to have a pleasant smell even before it is burned (Mackintosh-Smith 2000: 17–23). Apart from Isa 60:6 and Song 3:6; 4:6, 14, which testify to its wider usage, the seventeen other occurrences of *lĕbônâ* are in cultic contexts, as incense and as an ingredient for offerings to produce a pleasing odor (often added to flour or grain and oil; Lev 2:1–2, 14–16; etc.). Like myrrh, frankincense was a luxury item. Whereas v. 6 mentions these two aromatics in particular, the phrase "from the merchant's many powders" conveys the impression of many perfumes. The term *rôkēl* denotes a merchant involved in trade between one place and another; here we might think of a caravaneer, since most spices, including myrrh and frankincense, were imported, often from great distances (cf. the description of trade in Ezek 27).

Commentators are virtually unanimous in connecting v. 6 to the following description of the palanquin in vv. 7–11. Fox and Bloch and Bloch (who appear to be following Fox on this point) are exceptions; they connect this verse to the preceding verses (vv. 1–5). Fox bases his reading on (1) the combination of the refrain of adjuration and the question "who is this coming up from the wilderness?" in 8:4–5, which, in his opinion, shows that the question does not begin a unit but rather responds to the adjuration (in this case, to 3:5), and (2) the assumption that "who is this?" here in v. 6 refers to the woman. It is, however, by no means evident that 8:5 belongs with 8:4, and, as indicated above, the question in 3:6 does not require that the answer be the woman. Joining this verse to the preceding vv. 1–5 leaves Fox somewhat uncertain as to the identity of the speaker. He thinks it is probably the women of Jerusalem, but that they should speak now, having just been told in the previous verse not to disturb the lovers (Fox's understanding of the adjuration refrain), is odd. Indeed, Fox is hard-pressed to explain why the woman would charge the women of Jerusalem not to disturb her and her lover in 3:5 and 8:4 and then suddenly appear coming up from the wilderness both here in 3:6 and in 8:5.

Perhaps the strongest argument against reading this verse with the preceding vv. 1–5 is that it spoils the closure achieved in these verses. Like the section that precedes it (1:5–2:7), 2:8–3:5 ends with the appeal to the women of Jerusalem not to arouse love until it wishes. The lovers are together, enjoying the delights of love, and it is hard to imagine a more suitable form of closure. There follows in each case something new. In 2:8 "Listen! My lover! Look! He's coming" invites the reader to watch the man's approach from afar through the woman's eyes. Similarly, here in 3:6, "What is this coming up from the wilderness?" invites the reader to watch the man's approach in his palanquin through the woman's eyes. It is thus a fitting introduction to her description of the palanquin gradually drawing closer until it is possible to see its occupant, the lover in his Solomonic guise.

[7–8] "Look!" (*hinnēh*), like the question "what is this coming up?" in the previous verse, conveys an impression of immediacy and draws the reader into events that seem to be unfolding in the present. A *miṭṭâ* is a bed or couch or litter and can be either stationary (Amos 6:4; Esth 1:6) or portable (2 Sam 3:31). Severing these verses from v. 6 is crucial to Fox's argument that nothing in vv. 7–11 suggests that the bed is moving and so a stationary bed, and not a litter, is meant here. With most commentators, I take *miṭṭâ* as portable because I see the question "what is this coming up from the wilderness?" as referring to it. Moreover, I do not agree with Fox that nothing in vv. 7–11 suggests motion. If *ʾappiryôn* in v. 9 is a sedan chair or palanquin (Fox thinks not), then it is moving. Furthermore, motion is implied in the way the magnificent conveyance, first called a litter, then described as a palanquin, is pictured as coming closer and closer to the speaker.

An honor guard of the most highly trained warriors surrounds the litter, whose journey is represented as a long one, since preparations for the night are necessary (v. 8). There is something excessive in the size and degree of military skill of this bodyguard. They are armed against the dread, or perhaps even terror, of the night. Fear (*paḥad*) can refer both to the emotion and to the object of fear. The eeriness of the night, the fear of what might lurk in the dark, is acknowledged and prepared for, but not specified. Are the terrors of the night ones that a large company of warriors can easily dispel, for example, animals[2]

2. Mitchell Dahood, *Psalms I, 1–50* (AB 16; Garden City, NY: Doubleday, 1965), 81–82; *Psalms II, 51–100* (AB 17; Garden City, NY: Doubleday, 1968), 331.

or marauders (Ginsburg, Delitzsch)? Or are they intangible and thus more sinister (demons? death?; cf. Ps 91:5–6)? Landy is one of the few commentators to appreciate the seriousness of the discordant note sounded here (208–9); such a degree of preparedness betrays a deep sense of unease. Why are so many warriors necessary? Perhaps the honor guard is only for show. Fear of nocturnal demons who threaten the bridal pair on their wedding night may lie behind the image (cf. Tob 3:7–8; 6:13–15; Pirqe di-Rabbi Eliezer 12; see the discussions of Kraus 1936 and Pope), although this theme is not developed here. Night does, of course, present real dangers, and it would be normal for a king to have his guards (Robert, Fox). The procession seems to move through time as well as space; night and its attendant fears yield to day—a wedding day and its attendant joy in v. 11.

The picture the woman creates of her lover as a king in his litter surrounded by a well-equipped bodyguard expresses both her pride in his strength and nobility (Krinetzki) and the sense of security she feels in his presence. Even so, to feel protected against something feared does not remove the fear. Anxiety for the safety of the loved one is a staple of love and love poetry.

[9–10d] What was described in the distance as a litter is now envisioned as a magnificent carriage, or palanquin, whose accoutrements are now visible. Exactly what kind of construction is meant by *ʾappiryôn* is open to question; see the discussions of Pope and Fox. The word is a *hapax*, whose meaning and origin are debated. Most likely it is a loan word derived from the Greek *phoreion* (Rundgren), and this is how LXX renders it. A *phoreion* is something that is carried, a sedan chair. What seems to be envisioned in these verses is an enclosed litter, since it is said to have an interior (*tôkô*, v. 10). Some critics, however, think that the *ʾappiryôn* is a fixed structure, with pillars and an inner area. Gerleman, who sees these verses as separate from vv. 6–8, proposes that a palace room or throne room is meant. Goulder maintains that the description is of the throne itself (cf. Budde, who sees the description of the litter as recalling that of Solomon's throne in 1 Kgs 10:18–20). On the basis of its Aramaic cognates, Fox argues that *ʾappiryôn* has a wider range of meaning than Greek *phoreion*, and that Solomon's *ʾappiryôn*, with its columns, interior, and "(probably) a paved floor" resembles the court of the garden of the king's pavilion in Esth 1:6. He proposes that *ʾappiryôn* is used here as a metonym for the chamber or pavilion-like structure in which Solomon's couch is set. That *ʾappiryôn* refers to a pavilion is also accepted by Bloch and Bloch.

The description of the *ʾappiryôn* in these verses contains a number of words whose meaning is uncertain, and thus it is of little help in deciding the exact nature of the *ʾappiryôn*. Conversely, because we do not know exactly what an *ʾappiryôn* is, we cannot be sure about the details of the description. A litter or palanquin could have pillars or posts and an interior. Delitzsch draws attention to the similarity between the *ʾappiryôn* here, with its silver pillars and purple seat, and descriptions of *phoreia* provided by Athenaeus. On one occasion, Athenaeus mentions a silver-legged *phoreion* with purple coverlet (*The Deipnosophists*, v.212c5), and on another, he describes a festal procession by Antiochus Epiphanes in which two hundred women, sprinkling perfumes from gold pitchers, were followed by eighty magnificently clad women carried on golden-legged *phoreia* and five hundred on silver-legged *phoreia* (v.195c2). Whatever the precise meaning of the various terms used to describe it, it is clear that the palanquin is lavish in craft and ornamentation. It is made from not just any wood but wood imported from Lebanon (cedar would be fitting for Solomon) and adorned with silver and gold and coveted purple cloth. Purple dye from the murex shellfish was expensive and thus a symbol of royalty. Nothing in the description suggests that Solomon's wealth and grandeur are being parodied (so Whedbee 1998: 267–68); rather they are being appropriated to picture the woman's sense of the luxury that love bestows on her and her lover (Fox).

What serves to decorate the palanquin's inner recesses is debated. Is the interior "inlaid with love" (*rāṣûp ʾahăbâ*), as MT has it? If so, what would that mean? Pope's suggestion that the reference is to inlays depicting love scenes is appealing (see his Plates I and II), but it is difficult to believe that, if this were the meaning, it would be expressed in such an odd way. Ginsburg translates, "Its interior tesselated most lovely by the daughters of Jerusalem" which reflects the reading of LXX ("within a tesselated pavement, a love [gift/work] from the daughters of Jerusalem"), and points out that palanquins were often painted inside with flowers and mottos expressing the power of love. Similarly, Landy reads "its midst is paved with love of the daughters of Jerusalem" and contrasts the expensive "outer framework" of the palanquin with its true fashioning with love (91), that is, "true perfection" (209; cf. Munro 59). Garrett, although he admits the difficulty of MT's "love," goes to extreme lengths to retain it. He proposes that "its interior is fitted together" ends the description of the palanquin, which is then followed by a one-word exclamation, *ʾahăbâ*, "this is love!" Not only is such a use of *ʾahăbâ* grammatically improbable, but for the poet to describe the palanquin's interior as fitted together would be rather strange, leaving one to wonder what kind of palanquin would have an interior not fitted together.

As much as one might like to have the word "love" in this description, or love scenes adorning the interior of the palanquin, the Hebrew text does not yield a meaningful translation. Moreover, because everything else in this list is made from some specific material, the abstract "love" seems out of place.[3] Emendation thus appears to be in order here. The most widely adopted proposals are

3. Mitchell Dahood (*Proverbs and Northwest Semitic Philology*, Scripta Pontificii Instituti Biblici 113 [Rome: Pontifical Biblical Institute, 1963]: 54) proposes taking the final consonant of *rāṣûp* as the particle *pa*, meaning "and," as in Ugaritic, and reading *tôkô rāṣô pěʾahăbâ*, "within it there is pleasure and love," but this, too, does not fit the context, where the fittings of the palanquin are described.

those of (1) Driver (1936: 111), that *ʾahăbâ* means "leather," in accordance with an Arabic cognate, which has the advantage of not requiring textual emendation, (2) Gerleman, taking the *m* from the following word and reading *ʾăbānîm*, "precious stones," and (3) Graetz, emending to *hobnîm*, "ebony." Some propose that both "leather" and "love" are meant here, as one of many instances of double entendre in the Song (Grossberg 1981: 76; Goulder; Elliott 1989: 88). Any of these proposals—leather, precious stones, ebony—suits the context well. Since the related noun *rișpâ* refers to pavement (Ezek 40:17–18; 42:3; 2 Chr 7:3) and in Esth 1:6 seems to refer to a mosaic pavement, I have opted for "precious stones." Hebrew *ʾeben* can refer to a precious stone with or without the adjective "precious" (*DCH* I, 112b), and if the text is speaking of a mosaic inlay in a lavish palanquin, clearly precious stones would be used (cf., e.g., 1 Chr 29:8, where the stones brought to the treasury in the temple must be precious ones), perhaps carnelian, chrysolite, emerald, onyx, antimony, marble, and other colored stones (cf. Exod 28:17; 1 Chr 29:2).

[10e–11] At the end of the description, the participation of the audience is enthusiastically invited. With a number of commentators and translations (e.g., Krinetzki, Pope, Fox, Keel, Murphy, Garrett, REB, NRSV) I read "daughters [women] of Jerusalem" in parallelism with "daughters [women] of Zion" (see Textual Note). The phrase "daughters of Zion" appears elsewhere in Isa 3:16–17; 4:4 in reference to married women, but here, where it is used synonymously with "daughters of Jerusalem," it appears simply to designate the female inhabitants of the city. The women of Jerusalem (and the readers of the poem) are invited to gaze upon Solomon and to notice the crown with which his mother crowned him. Is this a king's crown or a garland worn by a bridegroom? Does his mother crown him prior to his wedding day or on his wedding day? Nothing is known of mothers crowning their sons, either as kings or as bridegrooms, in ancient Israel, just as nothing is known of kings or bridegrooms riding in litters. The mother is here associated with the public celebration of the couple's union, a union that tacitly has the mother's approval in 3:4 and 8:2, where the woman brings her lover to her mother's house for lovemaking.

With regard to the king's crowning on his wedding day, Murphy observes that one cannot "eliminate the possibility that this detail may be *only* a poetic flourish" (152, italics added). One often finds among commentators a tendency to ascribe to poetic imagination what they cannot "explain" in the text in any other way, as though poetic imagination did not shape everything in the poem (see Introduction, "Fantasy, Reality, and Poetic Imagination," pp. 45–47). The description of the bridegroom's arrival in his palanquin, like so many images in the Song, exhibits verisimilitude while complementing it with unusual and exotic features: a wedding procession that originates in the wilderness, a king who travels to his wedding in an ornate litter, an especially large escort of warriors armed against fear in the night, a king crowned by his mother.

Our looking, the crowning, and the wedding all seem to be happening at once, yet the coronation belongs to some unspecified time in the past. Past and present, coronation and wedding are merged in a royal wedding day that symbolically anticipates that of the lovers. If the male lover likened to Solomon becomes a king on his wedding day, it is because love makes him a king. The woman conjures up her lover as a bridegroom in all his Solomonic splendor, but she does not describe the wedding itself. She appears in this royal fantasy not in a royal guise but only as herself, the speaker whom the palanquin approaches, bearing her kingly lover on his wedding day. The wedding day thus embraces the present (we watch the groom arrive) and the future (it seems that the wedding is about to take place) as well as the past (when the groom was crowned). What begins as a display of grandeur concludes in a display of joy.

Song of Songs 4:1–5:1
The Man's First Long Speech

<He>

4:1 Look at you! You are beautiful, my friend!
     Look at you! You are beautiful.
  Your eyes are doves
     behind your veil.[a]
  Your hair, like a flock of goats
     winding down[b] Mount Gilead.[c]

2 Your teeth, like a flock of shorn ewes[d]
     that have come up from the wash,
  all of them have twins,
     none has lost a lamb.[e]

3 Like a scarlet thread, your lips,
     and your mouth[f] is lovely.
  Like a slice of pomegranate, your cheek[g]
     behind your veil.

4 Your neck, like David's tower,
     built in courses,[h]
  a thousand shields hung on it,
     all sorts of warriors' bucklers.[i]

5 Your two breasts, like two fawns,
     twins of a gazelle,
     grazing among the lilies.

6 When the day breathes
     and the shadows flee,

I will make my way[j] to the mountain of myrrh,
  and to the hill of frankincense.
7 You are wholly beautiful, my friend,
  and flawless.
8 With me[k] from Lebanon, bride,
  come with me from Lebanon.
Come forth[l] from the peak of Amana,
  from the peak of Senir and Hermon,
from the dens of lions,
  from the lairs[m] of leopards.
9 You have captured my heart,[n] my sister, bride,
  you have captured my heart with one glance of your eyes,[o]
with one pendant[p] of your necklace.[q]
10 How pleasing[r] are your caresses, my sister, bride,
  how much better are your caresses than wine,
  and the fragrance of your perfumes than any spices!
11 Your lips drip flowing honey, bride,
  honey and milk are under your tongue,
and the fragrance of your garments
  is like the fragrance of Lebanon.
12 A garden locked is my sister, bride,
  a garden[s] locked,
  a spring sealed.
13 Your watercourses,[t] those of a pleasure garden[u]
  of pomegranates with choice fruits,
henna with nard,
14   nard and saffron,
sweet cane and cinnamon,
  with all trees of frankincense,
myrrh and aloes,
  with all the finest spices.
15 Garden spring,[v]
  well of fresh water,[w]
  flowing streams[x] from Lebanon.

<She>
16 Awake, north wind,
  and come, south wind,
blow upon my garden
  that its fragrance may pour forth.[y]
Let my lover come to his garden
  and eat its choice fruits!

<He>

5:1 I come to my garden, my sister, bride,
     I pluck[z] my myrrh with my spice,
     I eat my honeycomb with my honey,
     I drink my wine with my milk.

<Women of Jerusalem>
     Eat, friends,
        drink yourselves drunk on caresses![aa]

---

a. I.e., as seen through her veil. The word translated "veil," *ṣammâ*, which occurs only in the Song (4:1, 3; 6:7) and Isa 47:2, posed difficulties for early translators and commentators; see the discussion in Pope. The opinion that the term refers to the hair is defended by Bloch and Bloch.

b. The root *glš* appears only here and in 6:5. Vg. has the goats ascending rather than descending; LXX reads "that have appeared from Gilead." On the basis of Ugaritic *glṯ*, Tuell (1993: 99–104) suggests a meaning "flowing in waves." I have translated "winding down" to suggest the wavy movement, since the image refers to the flock of goats in the first instance, and goats do not "flow," though they could seem to move in waves. They may "stream" down a mountainside, as some translate (e.g., Pope, Fox, Murphy), but "stream" suggests a rapid movement not indicated here. For detailed discussion of the term, see Pope.

c. Some Hebrew mss and LXX read "from the Gilead" as in the parallel 6:5. MT is supported by 4QCant[a].

d. The text here has "shorn ones (feminine)"; Song 6:6, where the same description appears, has a variant reading, "ewes," without the word "shorn." The translation "shorn" reflects the Hebrew, which has a passive participle; some translations and commentators, on the basis of the view that sheep were washed before shearing, understand it in the sense of "ready to be shorn" (Joüon-Muraoka §121i; e.g., NAB, NJB, Meek, Robert, Loretz, Gordis, Keel, Murphy).

e. The Hebrew words for "teeth" and "shorn ones" are both feminine, and the pronominal suffixes on *šĕkullām*, "all of *them*," and *bāhem*, "among *them*," are masculine; this type of disagreement in gender is not uncommon in the Song.

f. The word *midbār*, meaning "mouth," is a *hapax* related to *dbr* I, "to speak." Some take it to mean "speech" (cf. LXX *lalia*, Vg. *eloquium*), but the context, where body parts are described, indicates that the mouth, as the organ of speech, is meant.

g. The precise meaning of *raqqâ*, "cheek," is debated (is it the cheek, the temple, or the brow?). It occurs in the parallel 6:7 and elsewhere only in Judg 4:21–22 and 5:26 (references to Jael driving a tent peg through Sisera's temple, if indeed that is the meaning of the word there). The term may refer to a more extensive area of the face around the eyes. I have translated "cheek" because it makes more sense to imagine the cheeks as showing through a veil. 4QCant[a] reads *mzqntk*, which is not found elsewhere; Tov connects it with *zkn*, a different area of the face, perhaps "chin" (*DJD*, XVI, 202). 4QCant[b] has the same reading as MT.

h. A *hapax*, from the root *lpʾ*, "to arrange in courses" (Honeyman 1949: 51–52).

i. As the parallelism indicates, *šelet* is another word for shield; in 2 Sam 8:7 = 1 Chr 18:7, for example, they are made of gold; 2 Chr 23:9 mentions them together with spears. There is some question whether the word might refer to "quivers" in Jer 51:11 and Ezek 27:11 or, indeed, to some other type of weapon. LXX reads *bolides* (darts, javelins, spears) here in v. 4 but elsewhere translates the word variously; Vg. renders *armatura*, "armor." On *kōl* as "all sorts of" cf. GKC §127b, Joüon-Muraoka §139h.

j. Following Fox, whose translation admirably captures the sense of the ethical dative *lî*, giving emphasis to the verb *ʾēlek* (GKC §119s).

k. Some commentators read *ʾětî*, "come," with LXX, Syriac, and Vg., in place of MT *ʾittî*, "with me" (e.g., Würthwein, Pope, Fox, Garrett), but there are already enough verbs of motion in the verse, and the man can as easily be inviting the woman to come with him as to come to him. I have retained the Hebrew word order in the first half of the colon to reflect the emphasis; the phrase "with me" is further emphasized through repetition in the second half of the colon (where it again comes first, "with me from Lebanon come," though here I have changed the word order for the sake of a smoother English translation).

l. Hebrew has two words *šwr* (homonyms), one meaning "look, look down," the other "travel, journey, descend, climb down" (BDB 1003b; *HALOT* 1449b); a verb of motion is preferable here, since, as the first part of the verse shows, the man is asking the woman to come with him, and nothing in the context indicates that he wants her to look at the scenery. None of the ancient versions understands the verb as "look"; LXX reads *eleuse kai dieleuse apo arches pisteos* ("you shall come and pass from the top [or "beginning"] of faith"); Vg. translates *veni coronaberis de capite Amana*, "come, you will be crowned [or "surrounded"] from the peak of Amana."

m. The parallelism argues for emending MT *harěrê* ("mountains") to *ḥōrê* ("lairs"); so Fox, Garrett; cf. Nah 2:12 [13 H].

n. The verb *lbb*, from the noun *lēb, lēbāb*, meaning "heart, mind," occurs only in this verse (in the *piel*) and in Job 11:12 (in the *niphal*); its precise meaning, not surprisingly, is debated. LXX renders *ekardiosas hemas*, "you have heartened us" or "encouraged us," and Vg. *vulnerasti cor meum*, "you have wounded my heart," the latter clearly privative.

o. Hebrew "with one of your eyes" (similarly LXX, Vg.); see the Commentary.

p. The word translated "pendant" (*ʿănāq*) in the plural refers to some type of jewelry for the neck (necklaces or pendants in Prov 1:9, and neck ornamentation for camels in Judg 8:26); since it is singular here, it is probably either a strand of a necklace or some sort of ornament on it, such as a gem or bead or pendant. I have opted for "pendant" rather than "strand" because of the suggested similarity to the eye.

q. A *hapax* related to the word for neck, whose meaning "necklace" is supported by the context.

r. Literally "how beautiful," translated "pleasing" because "beautiful," as applied to lovemaking (*ddyk*, "your caresses"; see Textual Note a under 1:2), refers to the pleasure perceived by the speaker.

s. Reading *gan*, "garden," for MT *gal* with a number of Hebrew mss, LXX, Syriac, and Vg. This kind of repetition is well established in the Song (e.g., peak and peak in v. 8cd; "you have captured my heart" repeated in v. 9ab, "with one" repeated in 9bc; fragrance and fragrance in 11cd, etc.). But variation is also typical of our poet. Some (e.g.,

JPS, Gordis, Meek, Ringgren) retain MT's *gal*, and understand it to mean "fountain" or "spring," thus relating 12b to 12c rather than 12a. Good (1970: 94 n. 44) proposes "pool," on the basis of Ugaritic *gl*, "cup," a translation accepted by Pope; cf. Brown (1969: 158–60), who relates Ugaritic *gl* and Hebrew *gullâ* to various vessels or receptacles for wine, milk, or honey.

   t. Most likely either shoots or branches (NJB; cf. JPS "limbs") or channels or watercourses (NRSV); see the Commentary.

   u. The Hebrew reads literally, "your watercourses (?), a pleasure garden of pomegranates." I take this as elliptical for "your watercourses are (like) the watercourses of a pleasure garden"; cf. Budde: *Deine Schüsse sind die Schüsse eines Lustgartens* [your shoots are the shoots of a pleasure garden]. There are two kinds of analogy: (1) in some cases where a noun is predicate in a noun clause; e.g., Ezra 10:13, "the time is (the time of) rains"; Ps 45:8 [9 H]; GKC §141d; and (2) in some cases where the preposition *k* ("like") is used in a pregnant way with a substantive (Joüon-Muraoka §133h); e.g., Ps 18:33 [34 H], "who made my feet like the (feet of) deer"; Isa 63:2, "Why are your robes red, and your garments like (those of) one who treads the wine press?"; Jer 50:9, "his arrows are like (the arrows of) a warrior." The difference is that here we have a metaphor rather than a simile.

   v. Literally, "spring of gardens," i.e., a spring that irrigates gardens.

   w. Literally, "living water," the expression used for fresh or running water (Lev 14:5–6, 50–52; 15:13; Num 19:17).

   x. Taking the participle *nōzĕlîm* ("flowing") as a substantive, used synonymously for water, as in Exod 15:8; Isa 44:3; Ps 78:16, 44; Prov 5:15; it could also be read as modifying "water" in the previous colon: "a well of fresh water flowing from Lebanon" (Murphy, similarly REB, NAB, NIV).

   y. The same verb (*nzl*) as in v. 15, literally "that its spices may flow," i.e., be dispersed and waft on the breeze; cf. Deut 32:2, where *nzl* is used figuratively of words distilled like dew. "Spices" (*bĕśāmîm*) appears also in v. 14, and it is tempting to retain it in translation to show the connection, but since it is the odor of the spices that is meant, I have opted for "fragrance."

   z. The verb ʾrh ("pluck, gather") occurs only here and in Ps 80:12 [13 H]; the meaning "eat" is also possible (see Pope), but "pluck" seems more appropriate to the sequence and also because one does not eat myrrh. On this last point I would not wish to be too literal, however, since, on the one hand, myrrh is used figuratively of the woman's charms, and, on the other, apparently it was mixed with wine (Pope). Spiced wine is mentioned in 8:2, though without specifying the ingredients.

   aa. Taking the plural *dwdym* as referring to acts of love, as elsewhere (Song 1:2, 4; 4:10; 7:12 [13 H]; Ezek 16:8; 23:17; Prov 7:18). LXX, Syriac, and Vg. and some moderns (e.g., RSV, NJB, NIV) take *dwdym* as "lovers" in parallelism with *rᶜym*, "friends." "Drink yourselves drunk" is Fox's apt rendering of "drink and be drunk," i.e., "drink until you are drunk."

The Song began with short, alternating speeches expressing the lovers' desire for, delight in, and praise of each other (1:2–2:7). Then the woman had a long, uninterrupted speech from 2:8 to 3:11. Now it is the man's turn to offer a long speech. The dialogue format enables the poet to explore the nature of love and longing from both a woman's and a man's point of view. Their voices are in harmony and their desire is mutual, but they do not look at love or at each other in quite the same way (see Introduction, "Gendered Love-Talk and the Relation of the Sexes," pp. 13–28). Whereas she expresses her desire and explores her feelings for him, and his for her, by telling stories in which they are characters (2:8–17; 3:1–5; 5:2–6:3), he looks at her, tells her what he sees, and how it affects him. In two places in his speech here (4:6 and 10–11) he responds to her urgent desire by picking up words she addressed to him earlier and playing variations on them to show how completely his desire matches hers. But whereas she quotes him speaking to her (2:10–14; 5:2), he never quotes her. His first long speech lacks the complexity of hers because there is no double narratorial voice (see under 2:8–3:5), but what it lacks in narrative complexity it makes up for in range.

He begins by inviting her to see herself through his eyes ("Look at you, you are beautiful, my friend! Look at you, you are beautiful!" v. 1), and he describes, in densely metaphoric language, her eyes, hair, teeth, lips, mouth, cheeks, neck, and breasts (vv. 1–5). These verses are about the pleasure he takes in looking at her, a pleasure he wants her to appreciate and share in. If they verge on objectification, the mood changes in v. 6, where he puts himself in the picture. In reply to her ambiguous behest in 2:17, "When the day breathes and the shadows flee, turn, my love, and be like a gazelle or a young deer upon the cleft mountains," he now declares, "When the day breathes and the shadows flee, I will hasten to the mountain of myrrh and to the hill of frankincense." His response indicates that he has understood her as calling him to her.

After telling her again that she is beautiful (v. 7), he seeks her out. In v. 8, he calls to her to join him, as she had pictured him doing in her narrative ("Rise up, my friend, my fair one, and come away, my dove in the clefts of the rock, in the covert of the cliff. Let me see you, let me hear your voice," 2:13–14), but in his version he depicts her not as a shy dove, hidden safely away in crevices among the rocks, but on remote mountaintops and in wild places, where lions and leopards make their dens. He does not associate her with the domestic security of the house, as she had presented him doing in 2:8–17, but rather with powerful, untamed animals whose abode in open spaces she shares. By means of this striking imagery, he expresses his awe of her.

In the next verse he discloses the devastating effect she has on him. She has captured his heart (v. 9). He who gazed upon her and very deliberately catalogued her charms in vv. 1–5 is thunderstruck when she looks at him. In vv. 10–11 he responds to her praise of his lovemaking at the beginning of the Song (1:2–4) by praising her lovemaking in similar terms. He develops her imagery further by adding spices to the perfumes of which she spoke, and milk and honey to the wine. Verses 11–15 further describe her as sweet tasting and

develops her image

sweetly scented, a garden of choice fruits and spices, and a spring of fresh, flowing water. This description is different from the one vividly picturing selected parts of her body, one by one, in startling metaphors, with which he began. Not only is it more intimate and erotically charged but also the man is less interested now in an inventory of his lover's features than in what she represents for him: voluptuous bounty and life. Here, for example, her lips are not compared to something sweet but are themselves the source of nectar (v. 11). And in place of an inventory in which only one simile or metaphor represents each body part (vv. 1–5), the man now relies on a cluster of metaphors to create an overall picture of the woman as a fragrant and fecund garden, where a bountiful meal of erotic delights awaits him.

She is a garden locked (v. 12). Her body holds the key to pleasure, as the entire speech proclaims. Natural and human-made scenes superimposed on it suggest that the woman's body contains within it the meaning of the world, starting with the eyes that neither her face nor even the world can contain. Compare these lines from a modern poet:

> Beauty,
> your face cannot contain your eyes,
> the earth cannot contain your eyes.
> There are countries, there are rivers
> in your eyes,
> my homeland is in your eyes,
> I walk through them,
> they give light to the world
> through which I walk,
> my beauty.[1]

Suddenly, in v. 16, the woman speaks, and with her words, the speech, which had been wholly the man's, becomes antiphonal. It is as if, her lover's speech having reached an erotic crescendo, she cannot keep quiet any longer. She interrupts, taking up his image of her as a fragrant garden of choice fruits, and invites him to come to his garden and there to taste all love's pleasures. The seamlessness of the imagery communicates the lovers' complete concord. He ardently accepts the invitation and underscores both his claim to all the pleasures the garden offers and his savoring of them by repeating the possessive pronoun "my": my garden, my sister bride, my myrrh, my spice, my honeycomb, my honey, my wine, my milk (5:1). Here, as at sundry other points in the Song, love is seen as something the woman offers or gives and the man receives or claims (7:8, 12 [9, 13 H]; 8:2).

---

1. Pablo Neruda, "Bella" ["Beauty"], *The Captain's Verses*, trans. Brian Cole (London: Anvil Press Poetry, 1994), 53, 55.

The final word (5:1ef) is left to the women of Jerusalem, who encourage the lovers in their mutual intoxication ("be drunk with love"). We are thus made aware of their presence, as is so often the case when a section of the Song seems to reach a certain closure in the uniting of the lovers (2:7; 3:5; 6:1; 8:4). The presence of these women is always a reminder that what seems to be a closed dialogue between lovers is addressed to us. The lovers, though they take on distinct personalities as we get to know them, are types rather than individuals, and they play various roles throughout the course of the poem. They represent all lovers, and show us how glorious it is to be lovers too. And so the poem speaks to its readers through the lovers and, as here, through the women of Jerusalem, inviting us to become lovers as well: "Eat, friends, drink yourselves drunk on embraces!"

[1–5] These verses, describing the woman's eyes, hair, teeth, lips, mouth, cheeks, neck, and breasts, are one of four places in the Song where parts of the lovers' bodies are described sequentially by means of a simile or metaphor for each body part (4:1–5; 5:10–16; 6:4–7; 7: 1–5 [2–6 H]). Interpretive issues raised by the bodily descriptions in these passages are discussed under "Speaking Metaphorically about the Female and Male Body" in the Introduction (pp. 17–22). Modern readers may be struck by the bold and unusual imagery used in the comparisons. How are teeth like newly washed ewes, coming up from the wash, each having twins (v. 2)? How are breasts like fawns feeding among lilies (v. 5)? No scholarly consensus exists concerning what principles should be followed in interpreting the images. Are they to be taken literally as a description of the woman's appearance? Are they connotative and associative images whose purpose is to communicate the speaker's feelings? Are they designed to convey a particular quality of each body part? Do they reveal conflicted emotions the poet is unaware of? The range of scholarly interpretations of the imagery well illustrates the reader's role in making meaning. Readers of this commentary, too, will no doubt draw their own conclusions about such matters as whether the body as it is presented here is the object of the voyeuristic gaze (looking that intrudes upon that which is seen) or the erotic look (looking that participates in that which is seen), and whether the imagery is complimentary or ambivalent.

Although I discuss below some of the more common proposals for understanding the imagery in these verses, I do not mean thereby to suggest that the meaning of poetic images can be isolated and pinned down. Beyond the question of the meaning of the specific comparisons is the larger question of how a fundamental poetic quality like metaphor works in relation to the Song's overarching poetic strategies: the illusion of immediacy, the conjuring up of the loved one, the way the poem invites readers into the lovers' private world and also keeps them out, the creation of echoes across the space of the poem, double entendre, and so forth. While the man's speech draws on all these techniques, metaphor as it is used in the anatomical descriptions is particularly allied with the drive to include but also, at certain intimate moments, hold off the reader. Through metaphoric descriptions of the body, the poet invites the reader into the private world of the lovers—the inventory is intimate, the images are sometimes erotic, the overall picture is sexually suggestive. At the same time, metaphor functions as a way of keeping the reader out: the lovers seem to have their own private code, and the metaphors conceal more than they display.

[handwritten margin note: dual role of the metaphor]

Clearly the description here in vv. 1–5 is not meant to inform the reader what the woman looks like, for it does a very poor job of that. It is, moreover, addressed to the woman herself; that is, within the context of the poem the man is telling his lover how he perceives her (though of course everything in the poem is ultimately addressed to the reader). Typically the image receives more attention than the referent. Her hair (the referent) is not like a flock of goats, but like a flock of goats moving down a mountainside, and not just any mountainside, but Mount Gilead. The point of the comparison lies in the whole image. Her neck is not like a tower, but like the tower of David, a tower that is built in courses, and on those courses there hang shields, a thousand of them, and they represent all kinds of shields that a warrior might wield. Sometimes, as in the case of the tower, it seems almost as if the poet has forgotten the referent (her neck) in the interest of developing the image. The images seem to be striving for completion, as if to compensate for the dividing up of the body into parts by creating a total picture. Here one finds the kind of specificity and attention to detail, the interest in particulars, that makes the poetry discrete, unique (see under 1:5–2:7). The comparisons are rendered more dynamic through parataxis (the juxtaposition of referent and image without connecting verbs).

The use of vibrant imagery to describe the lovers is nothing new; it pervades the entire poem, which is richly metaphorical. The man offered his first description of his lover in 1:9–11, where he compared her to a mare among Pharaoh's chariots, mentioning specifically her cheeks and neck, which he describes again here in vv. 3–4. She has compared him to a sachet of myrrh between her breasts and a cluster of henna blossoms (1:13–14), to an apple tree with sweet fruit (2:3), to a gazelle or young deer (2:9), and herself to a lily of the valleys (2:1), a comparison he extended by calling her a lily among thistles (2:2). "Look at you, you are beautiful, my friend, look at you, you are beautiful; your eyes are doves" here in v. 1 is identical to 1:15, where the man first asked the woman to see herself through his eyes.

The desire to know is most often imaged as the desire to see (Brooks 1993: 9). All the images here are strong visual ones (v. 5 is also tactile, in Falk's opinion). Most of them are panoramic. They need to be seen from a distance in order to take in the entire picture: goats moving down a mountainside, v. 1; ewes coming up from the wash, v. 2; a tower decorated with weapons, v. 4; fawns grazing, v. 5. The body is seen in parts, each part invested with meaning by means of a striking simile or metaphor. In this way the reader is offered poetic access to the pleasure of looking at and knowing the body. Clothing the body in metaphors, however, while it impels the poetry forward, never quite gives access to the object of desire (cf. Brooks 1993: 123).

The injunction "look" (*hinnēh*) and the man's description of the woman as though she stands before him create the impression of immediacy. He speaks to her; we overhear. He describes her, beginning with her eyes and moving progressively downward to her breasts. We follow his gaze. Describing the body aims to make the loved one present through language. Through a series of venturous metaphors, the man conjures up his lover, just as she had caused him to materialize in her speech just prior to this one (3:6–11). Their techniques are similar in that both speakers apprehend details that progressively build up a fuller picture. She describes his approach in a litter whose accoutrements become visible as it comes closer and closer. He builds up a picture of her part by part, starting with her eyes and moving down as far as her breasts. The difference is that she described the litter in detail but offered no description of its occupant (apart from mentioning his crown), whereas he describes her person and does it metaphorically.

The introduction, "Look at you, you are beautiful, my friend, look at you, you are beautiful!" (4:1), indicates that the series of comparisons that follow illustrate the woman's beauty. This intention is underscored by the similar exclamation, "You are wholly beautiful, my friend, and flawless" (v. 7), which concludes the inventory and sums it up, making this part of the man's speech an inclusio. Beauty, like love, arouses a range of feelings, and some critics have asked if the descriptions that follow betray signs of ambivalence on the man's part (see Introduction, "Speaking Metaphorically about the Female and Male Body," pp. 17–22; on the ambivalence of beauty in the Song, see Landy, esp. 137–79; Black 2000a and 2000b). Beauty in the Song is communicated primarily by metaphor, and in these verses the metaphors obscure the reality of the person by clothing her in images. So it is that metaphor contributes to the aesthetic process that distances the object of desire (Landy 176).

Lingering over the details of her body, part by part, provides the man with a way of dealing with the powerful feelings the woman arouses in him, which he admits to in v. 9. She stirs up within him a depth of passion that alarms him (cf. 6:5), a disturbance in his psyche, a delicious threat to his equanimity that is both exhilarating and scary. The totality of her overwhelms him. In order to keep at bay the overpowering feelings she arouses, he distances himself from the whole person through the breakdown of the body into parts—eyes, hair, teeth, lips, mouth, cheeks, neck, and breasts—each inchoately anticipating a successful assemblage. Then, as if to make the parts less threatening, he compares them to familiar things. Each part is *like* something in the everyday world he knows, things that do not arouse such strong and disturbing emotions in him, such as a flock of goats moving down the mountainside. The closest he comes to describing something potentially awe-inspiring is the fanciful tower of David, which, while it may be imposing with layers of shields hanging on it, is not a particularly frightening image. As an image of defense, it is well suited to serve as a kind of defense mechanism against the anxiety the woman arouses. The tower image used of her neck yields to the tranquil, nonthreatening image of fawns feeding among lilies for her breasts.

The looking in these verses does not seem overtly intrusive and, therefore, less voyeuristic than erotic in intention (see Introduction, "Erotic Look or Voyeuristic Gaze?" pp. 22–24). The man has a purpose in looking beyond displaying his lover's body for his and her visual pleasure—that is, her appreciation of her beauty in his eyes (cf. 8:10). From her eyes down to her breasts, her body is organized in an effort to know and to possess it. The man focuses especially on the woman's facial features. "The articulate face," says Landy, "is a displacement of the body" (90).

[1] On the delight in her beauty and comparison of the eyes to doves, see under 1:15–17 and 5:12. Similes dominate the description in vv. 1–5, but here in v. 1 the eyes are described by means of metaphor ("your eyes are doves") rather than simile, which would have made the point of the comparison more explicit ("your eyes are like doves," presumably in shape or appearance, or, as some take it, "your eyes are like doves' eyes" [e.g., like the dove's bright pearl-eyes, according to Würthwein]). The only difference in this verse and 1:15 is that here the eyes are glimpsed behind a veil, assuming "veil" is the meaning of the rare Hebrew word ṣammâ.

In the context of an inventory of body parts that both discloses the body and veils it at the same time, the specific reference to a veil not once but two times— here, and again in v. 3—is a curious feature. Is it a sign of modesty? Is it a reflection of custom? Did women wear veils on special occasions? Nothing in the Bible indicates that women in ancient Israel wore veils as a matter of course, and there is insufficient evidence to indicate on what occasions women would have worn veils. The word used here appears only in the Song (4:1, 3; 6:7) and in Isa 47:2, as an item of clothing worn by personified Babylon. Another word for veil or shawl (ṣāʿîp) appears in Gen 24:65 and 38:14, 19. Rebekah covers herself with a veil in Gen 24:65, so it seems she was not wearing it as a matter of course. This text hardly supports the claim often made that brides wore veils, for it gives no indication how much time passed between Rebekah's arrival at Isaac's tents and the marriage. Some appeal to the Song as evidence that brides wore veils, but the Song is not about marriage as such, and "bride" when used in the Song is a term of endearment (see under 4:9). Neither Song 1:7 nor Genesis 38 supports the claim that prostitutes wore veils; see under 1:7.

This veil must be diaphanous, if the eyes and cheeks (v. 3) can be glimpsed through it. If the poet wanted to suggest the woman's modesty, then why allow

us to view her breasts at the end of this catalogue of body parts (v. 5)? Not only
are her breasts on view in v. 5, but later (vv. 13–15) the references to her body,
though indirect, are even more intimate. It is therefore reasonable to assume
that the poet makes use of the veil not to conceal but rather to draw attention to
the mystery that lies behind the veil, to what is not quite or not yet seen. A veil
arouses the viewer's desire to see what lies behind it. The veil will be gradually
lifted. When the woman's eyes are mentioned again in 6:4–7, verses that repeat
verbatim part of the description in 4:1–3, they are not behind her veil, though
her cheeks (seen through her veil here in v. 3) still are, and no veil appears in
the very intimate description of the woman in ch. 7.

The hair of goats in ancient Israel was commonly black or dark colored,
whereas that of sheep, used for comparison in the next verse, was commonly
white. Perhaps the place name Gilead suggested itself to the poet because of its
mountainous terrain and its rich pastureland (cf. Num 32:1; Jer 50:19; Mic
7:14), perhaps for its wider associations if the place name derives from a root
meaning "difficult (of terrain)" or "curly (of hair)" (M. Ottosson, "Gilead,"
ABD II, 1020–22). Many critics comment on the way black-haired goats seen
from a distance winding down a mountainside may be said to resemble the flowing tresses of wavy black hair. Hair can contribute greatly to a person's sexual
appeal, and lovers are often captivated by the hair of their beloved, as the man
is enthralled by his lover's flowing, dark, and shining hair in 7:5 [6 H]. His wavy
black hair is one of his arresting features (5:11).

[2] The man continues with a second rural image, which balances the descent
of the flock of goats in the previous verse with the ascent of a flock of ewes
from the wash. Commentators agree that the point is that the woman's teeth are
white and evenly paired, with none missing. The praise the man has for the perfection of his lover's teeth would relate to the effect on her smile, since a smile
reveals the teeth. This is an extended simile of two couplets. In the first, the
whiteness of the woman's teeth is suggested by ewes that have been washed.
In the second, the fact that none of her teeth is missing is conveyed by the
imagery of pairs, or twins, and underscored in a word play on *šĕkullām* ("all of
them") and *šakkūlâ* ("bereaved").

The *hiphil* of *tʾm* ("be double") appears only here and in the parallel 6:6.
Some take it in the sense of "to appear double" (Ginsburg) or "all in twins"
(Gordis), since, as Ginsburg argues, the image demands it (similarly, Garrett).
Others take it to mean "bearing twins" (e.g., NRSV, JPS; see also BDB 1060b,
HALOT 1675a). As appealing as it may be to translate the second couplet as "all
of them in pairs, none bereft of its twin," and take the phrase in reference to the
ewes, this does not seem to be the picture that lies behind the metaphor. More
likely the poet has in mind two baby lambs, "twins," tagging behind their
mother, for grown sheep do not run around, or come out of the wash, in perfectly matched pairs. In many of the man's metaphoric descriptions of his lover,

the image tends to overshadow its referent in an effort to create a total picture (cf., e.g., v. 4) and that is what appears to happen here. In the second couplet, the image of twinning takes over, while the referent ("your teeth") lags behind. First the teeth are identified with ewes, but once the ewes are said to have twins, then the teeth come to be identified with the twins and not the ewes with their twins (in which case the woman would have too many teeth).

Some critics perceive a reference to fecundity in the image of ewes that bear twins and do not miscarry (e.g., Meek, Krinetzki, Landy 94, Fox, Keel; surprisingly, given his emphasis on the Song's connections to fertility rites, Pope disagrees). Since the possibility of miscarriage is raised, Black finds here a hint of loss, of life's uncertainty, and of death (2000a: 312).

[3] A simile in the first half of the couplet describes the woman's lips as red. Rudolph draws attention to the vivid color contrasts: black hair, white teeth, red lips (a contrast that he sees continued in the next couplet in the dark red of the outside of the pomegranate and its more delicately colored inside). The second half of the first couplet is a straightforward statement that the woman's mouth is lovely, which makes her mouth the only part of her body not described metaphorically in this inventory of parts. Pope and Fox point out that Egyptian women painted their lips red but do not say whether they take the use of red here to indicate the lips' natural color or painted lips. Some see the lips as too thin or out of proportion to the rest of the woman's body; others insist that the comparison does not mean that the woman's lips are thin. Rudolph (followed by Krinetzki) thinks that the fact that they are thin rather than thick makes them beautiful. Beauty is, of course, culturally constructed. One need only think of fifteenth-century paintings of women with their long limbs and rounded bellies to recognize that standards of female beauty not only vary from culture to culture but also change over time within the same culture.

The comparison of the woman's cheek or temple or brow to a slice of pomegranate has also occasioned some difficulty for interpreters. Is the reference to the exterior—the color and shape of half a pomegranate—or the interior of the pomegranate, with its red seeds and white membrane? Ginsburg thinks of the vermilion outside of the pomegranate, showing through the veil; Delitzsch of the mixing of dark red and pale red berries (seeds) inside. Like the eyes in v. 1, the cheeks are seen through a veil. Falk visualizes ruddy skin glimpsed through a white mesh veil which seems to resemble the red seeds of the pomegranate showing through a net of white membrane (131). On the basis of the representation of sliced pomegranates in Egyptian art, in which the two contrasting parts are depicted, Gerleman understands the veil as dividing the woman's temples into a visible light-colored half and a dark half, faintly visible through the semitransparent veil. Ginsburg and Pope say that Near Eastern poets frequently compare the color of cheeks with pomegranates or apples, but they do not support this claim with adequate evidence. Pomegranates are love fruits (see under

4:13). They appear also in the decorations on the capitals of Solomon's temple (1 Kgs 7:18, 20, 42; 2 Kgs 25:17; Jer 52:22–23) and the hems of the high priest's robes (Exod 28:33–34; 39:24–26). On the veil, see under v. 1.

[4] Nothing is known of a tower of David in ancient Israel. There is no reason to assume it must have been a well-known structure, probably in Jerusalem (Rudolph, Ringgren). This seems to be one of many cases where the poet creates a sense of particularity and authenticity by providing concrete details, like the curtains of Solomon and tents of Qedar in 1:5 and Solomon's litter in 3:6–11. A wordplay occurs here as well: a transposition of two letters transforms David (*dwyd*) into Dodi (*dwdy*), the affectionate name the woman uses for her lover. The interesting similarity of this verse to Ezek 27:11 suggests that shields hung on the walls of towers may have been a familiar image and, in any event, a sight considered beautiful: "Men of Arvad and Helech were on your walls all around; those of Gamad were at your towers. They hung their shields all around your walls; they made your beauty complete" (cf. 1 Macc 4:57).

The poet's virtuosity lies in applying the image to the woman's neck. A common view is that the comparison of the neck to a tower refers to a long, perhaps graceful neck. An Egyptian love song praises a lover as "long of neck, white of breast" (P. Chester Beatty I, Group A, No. 31, trans. Fox; this poem has striking similarities to the descriptions of the lovers in the Song; for the complete text, see the Introduction, "Literary Context: Ancient Near Eastern Love Poetry," p. 55). In the opinion of most critics, the courses of stone hung with shields indicate that the neck is adorned with a necklace made up of several rows of beads (see Pope, Keel, for illustrations; Isserlin 1958, for an attempt to match the description to a type of ancient Near Eastern necklace; and Dales 1963, for a survey of ancient Near Eastern examples). In 7:4 [5 H], the woman's neck is compared to an ivory tower, stressing its whiteness and smoothness, whereas here it seems to be its adornment with necklaces that catches her lover's eye.

The description of the neck blends royal, military, and architectural imagery. Apart from the comparison of lips to a crimson thread in the previous verse, this is the only image in the series not from the world of nature (and fibers spun or twisted together to make thread have a connection to the natural world). Her neck is compared not simply to an impressively adorned tower but to the tower of David, the warrior-king par excellence. Delitzsch finds here an allusion to her regal quality. A number of commentators see in the comparison a reference to her self-assurance and proud bearing. Keel, for example, argues that, because the neck in Hebrew thought is associated with pride (Ps 75:5 [6 H]; Job 15:26; cf. Isa 3:16), the simile pictures the woman as a proud, unconquered city, symbolizing her inviolability. Some think the comparison implies her inaccessibility, but is she remote if she is so accessible to the man's gaze? Landy (74–78, 87–89) and Meyers (1986) find it significant that conventional male imagery of warfare and architecture is applied to the woman and see it as a sign of the woman's power.

The question is, what kind of power? This poetic metaphor cannot be used to support Meyers's claim that women exercised power in rural, domestic settings in ancient Israel. The power the woman has here is erotic (so Landy; see Introduction, "The Song and Conventional Gender Relations," pp. 25–28).

The man reveals in v. 9 that the woman has vanquished him; it is not surprising therefore that here in v. 4, and also in v. 8, he connects awe-inspiring images with her. The warriors' shields hung around the stone courses of the tower to which her neck is likened recall the battle-ready warriors armed with swords surrounding the Solomonic lover's litter in 3:7–8. Weapons hung upon walls are not in use, and not so threatening as brandished weapons; they give an impression of peace and security. The woman wears symbols of military might like trappings, intimating perhaps that the power of love is superior to that of armies.

Not a few commentators have remarked on the size of the neck in proportion to the rest of the woman's body. Gordis, for example, proposes that a large neck, like a prominent nose (7:4 [5 H]), was a mark of beauty; Pope sees here evidence that the woman is a goddess (1988: 322–25); Black finds in the simile support for interpreting the body as grotesque (2000a: 311–12). One wonders if a poet's main concern in composing a metaphoric description of a lover's body would be proportion rather than the way each image captured an idea the poet wanted to express. One might ask if a particular perspective is implied in the image; it could be that of a man reclining beside a woman, who leans her head back so that he is looking up at her neck, in which case the neck would look longer and more imposing than usual. Significantly, however, the poet does not place the lovers in any kind of setting—for example, reclining together in a regal bed or a grassy bower—to suggest where the man is vis-à-vis the woman when he describes her features the way he does. Thus, while it is possible that the poet is thinking about a woman's body from a particular perspective when describing the female lover in vv. 1–5, it is left to the reader to decide whether a particular perspective is implied and what perspective to adopt (see also under 7:1–5 [2–6 H]).

[5] The man's description of his lover's breasts as *like* fawns (ʿŏpārîm), twins of a gazelle (ṣĕbiyyâ [fem.]), grazing among or on the lilies, resonates remarkably with her image of him as *like* a gazelle (ṣĕbî [masc.]) or young deer (literally "fawn [ʿōper] of a deer") in 2:9, 17 and 8:14 and, especially, as the one who grazes among or feeds on the lilies, a double entendre for erotic play in which the lily or lilies signify the woman (1:7; 2:2, 16; 6:2–3). This description perplexes some commentators for two reasons. The meaning of the image is not entirely clear, and the woman's breasts are described as doing what the male lover otherwise does, feeding upon lilies. If the woman is symbolically identified with the lilies upon which her lover feeds, how can her breasts be feeding upon the lilies? In view of some of the outlandish proposals one encounters in

the commentaries, Murphy's concise confession of bafflement is refreshing: "Still, the point of the comparison is not obvious (color or form?), nor is it clear why the fawns are described as 'browsing'" (155).

In the comparison of breasts to fawns, Landy sees the combining of color, warmth, liveliness, and delicate beauty (76). Keel finds sprightliness, softness, life, and renewal, while Pope thinks that youthfulness and small size are indicated. Longman wonders if they are pictured from behind, their rounded rumps with small tails resembling breasts with their protruding nipples, a view espoused by Rudolph and Würthwein, and dismissed by Murphy as "insensitive literalness" (159). The twin fawns recall the twinned sheep to which the woman's teeth are compared in v. 2 (the root is the same, *tʾm*). Many items in the description of the woman are doubled or halved; that is, they refer to parts of the body that appear in pairs: eyes, teeth, lips, cheeks, breasts.

The same description of the woman's breasts appears again in 7:3 [4 H], but without the concluding phrase "grazing among the lilies." Some delete the phrase "grazing among the lilies" here, and thereby eliminate what they see as the main impediment to interpretation. Pope seems to favor this proposal, though he does not emend the text accordingly. Fox opposes the deletion of the clause and lists a number of expressive dimensions the phrase contributes to the image (some more convincing than others); for example, it creates a delicate pastoral picture, the fawns are pampered to the point of being pastured among lilies rather than simply on grass, and the breasts take on the fragrance of lilies. The fawns feed either "among the lilies" or "on the lilies"; *baššôšannîm* can mean either. The ambiguity allows the lilies to be both nourishment for the fawns and the pasture-ground where they feed.

Since breasts come in pairs, why does the poet say "your two breasts" and not simply "your breasts"? Perhaps for alliteration (*šĕnê šādayik kišnê ʿŏpārîm*) or balance with "two fawns." Or perhaps, in describing body parts, the poet wants to show that the man is attracted to each breast on its own, as well as in relation to the other (as its twin). When the man is grazing, he can feed on only one breast at a time. Here, in a paradoxical appropriation of the image, he pictures the breasts doing the grazing. Later his lips are described as lilies (5:13). The simile of the man's lips as lilies plays off the image of the breasts grazing among the lilies here in v. 5. Landy describes the exchange of imagery as an instance of projection: the man sees himself in the woman's breasts; she sees herself in his lips. "If the breasts/fawns are paradoxically imagined as feeding, the lilies/lips are analogously imagined as giving, both in our verse (4.5), and in its sister verse (5.13), where they 'drop flowing myrrh'" (Landy 78). The stress on "two"—two breasts like two fawns, twins—may be anticipatory. If the next verse, where the man says he will go to the mountain of myrrh and the hill of frankincense, continues the thought of this one, then the two breasts are symbolically represented as a mountain of myrrh and a hill of frankincense.

[4:6–5:1] With v. 6 the man's speech becomes more erotically explicit. Similes focusing on the woman's facial features and comparing them to the sorts of things one might imagine seeing in the world of nature or architecture (vv. 1–5) now yield to one long, extended metaphor for the woman that is more explicitly sexual and erotically charged, but less specific with regard to the body part or parts in question (no doubt due to the intimate nature of the description). The similes in vv. 1–5 tended to distance the object of desire; the body was looked at but not approached. Now in v. 6, the distance is eliminated, as the man puts himself in the picture: "I will make my way to the mountain of myrrh and to the hill of frankincense" (cf. a similar statement at the end of a description of the woman's body in 7:8 [9 H]: "I say I will climb the palm tree, I will take hold of its branches"). In vv. 1–5 the woman was a landscape upon which goats and sheep gamboled, gazelles fed, and a decorated tower stood erect. Here in v. 6 she becomes the landscape her lover will frolic upon and feed on. He continues to describe her body metaphorically, but in the rest of his speech he approaches it as source of comestibles and unguents that he will savor with delight (and by the end relish with abandon, 5:1). The point of transition could be the breasts of v. 5, insofar as they suggest the mountains of myrrh and frankincense in v. 6. He visualizes them in a relatively innocuous pastoral image of fawns grazing, but he savors them as parts of his lover's body that is itself as sweet and intoxicating as expensive, exotic unguents or is perfumed by them, or both.

[6] In this verse, the man responds to the woman's exhortation of 2:17:

> When the day breathes
> and the shadows flee,
> turn, my love, be like a gazelle
> or a young deer
> upon the cleft [spice?] mountains.

He begins with words identical to hers, and then states his intention in terms of the image she used in urging him to action:

> When the day breathes
> and the shadows flee,
> I will make my way to the mountain of myrrh
> and to the hill of frankincense.

Where she spoke of cleft mountains or spice mountains (see under 2:17), he speaks specifically of mountains of myrrh and frankincense, spices whose heady fragrance announced the approach of the loved one in 3:6. His figurative language here confirms the impression given in 2:17 that the mountains represent the woman herself and offers support for emending *hārê bāter* ("cleft mountains") in 2:17 to *hārê bōśem* ("mountains of spice") or *hārê běśāmîm* ("mountains of spices"), as in 8:14. Where earlier she likened him to a sachet of precious myrrh lying between her breasts (1:13), now her breasts, with which the woman herself is metonymous, are spiced mountains of myrrh and frankincense upon which he will cavort, no doubt like a gazelle or young deer. At the end of the Song, when she repeats a version of her exhortation in 2:17, she will draw upon these associations, symbolically calling him to herself by sending him to the "mountains of spices" (8:14).

Gerleman thinks that the mountains of myrrh and frankincense have no connection to the woman's breasts but rather, together with the previous image of gazelle twins grazing among lilies, evoke a distant wonderland, like the Egyptian land of Punt. Whereas it is true that the image is paradisiacal, the immediate poetic context cannot be ignored. Our verse is transitional: following on the reference to the breasts, it suggests their connection with the mountains of myrrh and frankincense; preceding a reference to her perfect beauty in the next verse, it alludes to the pleasures of her body in general rather than to any specific part. "Mountain of myrrh" and "hill of frankincense" are parallel metaphors and may apply to one and the same referent, the woman's person (the "and" joining cola of couplets is often pleonastic, and a number of manuscripts, including 4QCant[a], omit the conjunction in this couplet). The mountains of spices are the woman's breasts, the woman herself, and the place the lovers create for themselves, where they will enjoy love's pleasures. In this respect the mountains are like the garden of 4:12–5:1, which is both the woman as a source of erotic pleasure—quite generally but also with innuendo that could be taken as describing parts of her anatomy—and a luxurious, private paradise for lovemaking.

[7] The woman is totally beautiful (JPS: "every part of you is fair") and flawless (literally, "there is no blemish in you"). As blanket praise of his lover's beauty, this verse rounds off the previous part of the man's speech begun in v. 1, making it an inclusio, and leads into the following part.

[8] The mountains of myrrh and frankincense, which were the man's destination in v. 6, give way in this verse to the far-away mountains of Lebanon (creating a word play with *lĕbônâ*, "frankincense"), where lions and leopards make their dens. The majestic, awe-inspiring setting in which the man imaginatively locates his lover anticipates the feelings she arouses in him, feelings he will describe in the next verse. Thus this verse is hardly an isolated triplet unrelated to the context (Budde, Rudolph, Gerleman, Würthwein, Loretz, Müller). As in 2:13–14, where the man came to the woman's house and invited her to "rise up . . . and come away," he again comes to her (v. 6) and, here in v. 8, invites her to come away with him. He does not say, nor does he need to say, where they will go; soon enough it becomes clear that their destination is a special place known to lovers, in the realm of the senses, for the garden of love opens up to them.

Commentators who are troubled by what they perceive as the geographical difficulties posed by this verse fail to appreciate both the poetic symbolism and lyric development in the man's speech. This is a poem, not a travel itinerary. The man has, in effect, poetically transported himself to the mountains of spices, with which the woman is metonymous, with the intention of gratifying his desire, and found himself faced with remote mountains and wild animals, representing what he now perceives as her inaccessibility and awesomeness. In this verse, the man associates his lover not with goats, ewes, and fawns (cf. vv. 1–5) but rather with menacing lions and leopards, and not with the tower of David in their native land (v. 4), impressive though it may be, but with the awe-inspiring peaks of far-off Amana, Senir, and Hermon. Keel suggests that he pictures her with the attributes of a goddess (see esp. his fig. 97, where a goddess stands on a mountain peak, flanked by two lions; cf. also Pope).

Amana, Senir, and Hermon perhaps designate the middle, northern, and southern parts of the Anti-Lebanon mountain range (Keel). According to Deut 3:9, Senir and Hermon are different names for the same peak, but in 1 Chr 5:23 Senir and Hermon also appear together and may therefore refer to different parts of the Anti-Lebanon (Rudolph). We are dealing here with the geography of the imagination, which attempts to be exhaustive (Rudolph, Würthwein) as well as specific; compare the interest in the specific names of spices in vv. 13–14, for the same reasons. Mountain peaks in the far north, at the remote boundary of the land, are named for their evocative power (e.g., Deut 11:24; Josh 1:4; 11:17; 13:5). Lions and leopards are beautiful and threatening. This is no chance conjunction, for so is the woman. Landy is one of the few critics to take this conjunction seriously (see esp. 137–79). It is, however, a frequent theme of poets. Lions and leopards were associated with Ishtar, whose icons were popular for centuries; her dominion over predatory animals signified her wild and unapproachable aspect (see Keel, who also notes the continuation of this association into modern times, where advertisers pose women with lions and leopards).

Not only are lions and leopards not approachable, they are predators. There is thus a hint of danger here. The man wants to be the woman's captive (cf. the next verse and 7:5 [6 H]). The danger he senses is exciting, the thrill of attraction to another person so intense that one both passionately wants to lose oneself (itself an exceedingly revealing metaphor) and is in danger of doing so.

The awe the woman inspires is part of her attraction, and so her presence in this fantastic setting transforms it into a place of terrible beauty and enchantment (cf. Fox). If love is something she gives and he takes (e.g., 4:16 and 5:1), taking involves a risk, a threat to his equanimity and his autonomy. He takes only by invitation, when her desire matches his. Thus he wants her to come with him, to make herself accessible, and this is what happens when the mountains are left behind for the garden of erotic delights in the following verses.

Here in v. 8 the man uses the affectionate epithet "bride" for the first time in addressing his lover. The Song is not about marriage nor does it ever describe the couple's wedding or even assume their betrothal, though in subtle ways it could be said to anticipate it (see above under 2:15; 3:6–11). The epithet "bride" may be such an anticipation; it is certainly a term of endearment and intimacy. All its occurrences are in the man's speech in 4:8–5:1, at the point where his speech becomes most erotically provocative. Twice it appears on its own (here and in v. 11), where it never has a possessive pronoun, and four times in the intimate dual epithet, "my sister bride" (4:9, 10, 12; 5:1), where "sister" is used with the possessive pronoun "my."

Lebanon is a far-off, almost magical place, legendarily associated with Solomon and sweetened by its own wondrous cedars (cf. the "scent of Lebanon," v. 11). Its glory is venerated and coveted (Isa 35:2; 60:13), and its lofty cedars are a byword for might, majesty, and pride in story and fable (Isa 2:13; 10:34; 14:8; 2 Kgs 19:23 = Isa 37:24; Ps 92:12 [13 H]; Judg 9:15; 2 Kgs 14:9 = 2 Chr 25:18; Ezek 17:3). The man's form is like Lebanon and distinguished like its cedars (5:15), and the woman has the fragrance of Lebanon (4:11). According to Ps 104:16, the cedars of Lebanon were planted by God and watered abundantly, and Ezekiel offers an allegory in which even the trees in the garden of Eden could not rival a mighty cedar in Lebanon (Ezek 31). Like Eden, Lebanon is an exotic place of origins in the Song, a source of fragrance in v. 11, and of fresh, flowing streams in v. 15. Lebanon suggests, through paronomasia, both the redolence and worth of frankincense, *lĕbônâ*, and the excitement the man experiences in the woman's presence (*libbabtinî*, "you have captured [or stirred] my heart," v. 9). Fox draws attention to a number of puns in 4:8–5:1 that suggest that the names of places and animals were chosen to call to mind the names of spices and sweet things. Possibly, through its association with the Adonis myth (which may be older than the second-century-BCE sources of information we have about it), Lebanon represents a romantic setting for love (see the discussions of Pope, Müller).

[9] The verb *libbabtinî*, from the noun meaning "heart, mind," has traditionally been understood in different senses as "to hearten, to encourage" or as "to dishearten, to steal the heart." The *piel* verb form could indicate that the heart does something intensively, such as racing (for example, with excitement): "you have stirred my heart." Or it could be the privative *piel* (GKC §52h), as most translators and commentators render it: "you have captured (or stolen) my heart." The difference is not so great as it is sometimes presented by the commentators, for a stolen heart is an enflamed, aroused one.

Clearly the verb refers to the powerful feelings the woman kindles in the man. Although in the scholarly literature one often finds stress placed on the connection of Hebrew "heart" (*lb*, *lbb*) to intention and thought, the term is by no means so limited, and emotions plainly fall within its semantic range, especially feelings of joy, grief, fear, and courage (see *DCH* IV, 498b; cf., e.g., "the day of his heart's joy" in 3:11). Similar expressions appear in Egyptian love poems: "she has captured my heart in her embrace" (P. Chester Beatty I, Group

A, No. 31, trans. Fox); "Indeed it is she who captures my heart, when she looks at me, (I) am refreshed" (O. Gardiner 304, no. 54, trans. Fox). Pope draws attention to the Sumero-Akkadian use of "heart" in reference to male sexual arousal and potency (cf. also Waldman 1970: 215–17). No doubt the man in the Song is sexually aroused by the woman, but it is hardly necessary to limit the verb in the present verse to this sense.

When we say in English "you have stolen my heart," we are expressing a feeling of not being in possession of our senses (we have "lost" our heart, a part of ourselves, to use another image so commonplace that it has become a dead metaphor). If someone steals your money, you may feel wronged, but to say your heart has been stolen is a far cry from a complaint. Having your heart stolen does not deprive you of anything; on the contrary, it enriches you with a feeling of euphoria. No one can steal your heart if you are not willing. The man is more than willing; he is enflamed with desire and his feelings overwhelm him. It takes only a glance from his beloved, only a fleeting glimpse of the sparkle of a pendant on her necklace to excite him. In this verse he speaks again of her eyes, the first thing he singled out to praise about her when he began his speech (4:1; see also 1:15). Not only do lovers speak volumes with their eyes, but "the look of love alarms, because 'tis fill'd with fire" (William Blake), or, as our poet has the man exclaim later, "Turn your eyes away from me, for they overwhelm me!" (6:5). The Hebrew here in v. 9 says simply "with one of your eyes." Many translations and commentators insert "glance," as I have done, on the assumption that it is not the sight of one of the woman's eyes that so affects the man but what the eye does. The mention of one eye suggests a quick look, a glance.

One pendant or strand or jewel of her necklace has the same effect. The juxtaposition suggests the sparkle of the eye, and the likeness of the eye to a beautiful jewel. Stephan (1922: 212) gives this example from a modern Palestinian love song: "For your eyes are black and sparkle, and have slain (me) indeed." With regard to our verse, Fox thinks of strands, as on an Egyptian collar (see his figs. 1–5, 9). Earlier her necklace with jewels or beads was likened to shields, weapons of war, hanging on a defensive tower. Now with just one bauble she has conquered.

Here the man uses the composite epithet, "my sister, bride," as a pet name (cf. the previous verse, where he called her "bride," and 5:2, where he calls her "my sister"). He will address her in this intimate way three more times before his speech comes to an end (4:10, 12; 5:1). Just as the woman is not literally a "bride" in the Song, the epithet "sister" does not imply that the couple is related (as, e.g., when Abraham claims that Sarah is his half-sister in Gen 20). Lovers call each other "brother" and "sister" in Egyptian and Mesopotamian love poetry. It should not be surprising therefore to find these stock terms of endearment used in the Song (cf. also Add Esth 15:9; Tob 5:20; 7:16). As it happens, only "sister" is used; the woman never refers to her lover as "brother" in the Song, though in 8:1 she wishes that he were like a brother, so that she could be openly intimate with him. A few critics speak of a latent incest fantasy here (Cook 1968: 119, and esp. Landy 97–101), the desire for one's mirror-image. Imaged as a sister, the woman is more "self" than "other"; in other words, she is more like the man than different from him. As a term of endearment, "sister" may represent a striving toward completeness or wholeness, whose realization the man can only imagine in his mirror-image from the opposite sex. The combination of sibling and marriage imagery in the epithet "my sister, bride" epitomizes the desire to achieve oneness with the other.

Here in v. 9, we find another difference in the way the lovers speak about love. The difference is subtle, for both feel overwhelmed by the other, but whereas she describes it in terms of the feelings she experiences ("I am faint with love," 2:5; 5:8), he speaks in terms of conquest, of power relations (see Introduction, "Lovesick and Awestruck," pp. 15–17). He does not talk about his emotions but rather describes the way *he* feels as something *she* has done to him: "you have captured my heart." As a man, he is used to feeling in control. Now it seems to him as though he has surrendered control, and his autonomy is thereby challenged. The feelings he is experiencing are wonderful and welcome but also unfamiliar and thus disconcerting. And so he is in awe of her.

[10–11] Across the space of the poem, the man answers the woman's declaration of intense longing with which the Song began. He uses the same cluster of images to praise her lovemaking that she used of his in 1:2–4, and develops them through variation. She declared "your caresses are better than wine." He intensifies it, "How much better are your caresses than wine!" (Cook 1968: 143). Again the reader is invited to ponder in what ways love is better than wine (see under 1:2 above). The man increments the woman's olfactory and gustatory images of 1:2–4 by adding spices to perfumes and honey and milk to wine. "Lips" and the more precise term "tongue" are substituted for the mouth of 1:2, and kisses, rather than being mentioned, are described metonymically as flowing honey, honey, and milk. Two words for "honey" occur here: *nōpet* refers specifically to honey from the honeycomb, flowing honey, whereas *dĕbaš* is a common word for honey. These verses develop the thought of 1:2–4 and complete it by establishing a correspondence between what his caresses represent for her and hers for him. They are antiphonal across the space of the poem, building on the harmony of the lovers' voices to reinforce the mutuality of their desire.

Spices, referred to here in v. 10, permeate the speech with their fragrance (myrrh and frankincense in v. 6, and the many spices mentioned by name in v. 14). Her perfumes are more fragrant than these, though paradoxically they may well contain one or more of them. The Hebrew word *bōśem*, which occurs also in 4:14, 16; 5:1, 13; 6:2; 8:14, refers to spices and perfumes in general (Moldenke and Moldenke 52), as well as to balsam specifically. Balsam is usually identified as *Commiphora gileadensis*, a shrub native to southwest Arabia and Somaliland, whose small clusters of white flowers produce fruits containing a fragrant yellow seed. Its fragrant resin was highly prized in antiquity. Legend has it that balsam was among the gifts brought to Solomon by the queen of Sheba (Josephus, *Ant.* 8.6.6), and Pliny reports that every other scent ranks below balsam and that it came from Judea, where it grew in only two gardens, both belonging to the king (*Natural History* XII.44.115). Zohary suggests that a species of balsam may have grown wild in En-gedi and was subsequently cultivated (198–99). Balsam was raised in En-gedi and Jericho, and excavations in En-gedi indicate that balsam was being planted there in the seventh or sixth century BCE (Keel).

The man described his lover's lips and mouth in v. 3; now he enjoys them. He does not use a simile here, as he did for her lips in v. 3, but a dense metaphorical image. Her lips are not "like" something sweet; they drip, like the honeycomb, with succulent flowing honey, whose sweetness and thick, smooth consistency is savored as it glides over the tongue, and whose flow is captured in the assonance of *nōpet tiṭṭōpĕnâ śiptôtayik*. The attraction of lips dripping with honey is also attested in Prov 5:3 (where, however, the lips are those of a woman who should be avoided) and in Song 5:13, where the woman describes the man's lips as dripping with flowing myrrh. In our verse the sense of abundance and sensual indulgence conveyed by the image of lips exuding honey complements the taste and fragrance and intoxicating effect of the wine alluded to in the comparison of the woman's caresses to wine. Honey and milk provide the crowning touch to the sumptuous erotic meal. "Honey and milk" is an inversion of the familiar "milk and honey," encountered in the biblical text only in the phrase "a land flowing with milk and honey." The woman is a landscape (see under 4:6–5:1), a promised land, and, particularly, an Edenic garden flowing with honey and milk. This may be an allusion to Israel as the promised land, the land of dreams, or, for all we know, "milk and honey" or "honey and milk" may have been a common expression for satisfaction and plenty in biblical Hebrew (cf., e.g., Isa 7:22; Job 20:17; Deut 32:14).

The man describes the fragrance of his lover's garments as "like the fragrance of Lebanon," the only simile in the dense metaphoric language used to describe the woman in 4:11–5:1. The legendary scent of Lebanon (Hos 14:6 [7 H]), from where she has figuratively come (v. 8), still clings to her. Besides being a symbol for all that is fragrant (Murphy), Lebanon romantically partakes of the refreshing scent of its celebrated cedars and its abundant fruit (Ps 72:16; on Lebanon and its further associations, see above under v. 8).

[4:12–5:1] The Song reaches its most sensual pitch in these verses. Through an extended metaphor, the man describes his lover as a luscious pleasure garden with sinuous rills, where blossoms many an incense-bearing tree, and where he will feed on honeycomb and drink the milk of paradise.[2] Her body is mellifluous, dripping with fragrant unguents and tasty comestibles. Verse 12 identifies the woman as the metaphor's referent; from then on, we are in the garden (see Good 1970: 93–97). As a garden of edible delights, the woman is a garden of eros, and eating and drinking are symbols of sexual intimacy. The man's speech appeals to the senses of sight, smell, and taste, as well as to hearing, by suggesting the sound of fresh water cascading from Lebanon. So seductive are his words that his lover interrupts him in v. 16 to invite him to come to his garden and savor its pleasures, an invitation he readily accepts (5:1).

A feeling of excessiveness is conveyed by the compounding of lush nature imagery (she is a garden and a spring and a pleasure garden in vv. 12–13, a garden spring, well of fresh water, and streams from Lebanon in v. 15), the piling up of exotic fragrances (henna with nard, nard and saffron, cane and cinnamon, frankincense, myrrh, aloes—and "all the finest spices" for any he may have neglected to mention by name) and, by the end of the speech, the gluttony implied in eating not only the honey but also the honeycomb, and drinking wine as well as milk. The poet is borrowing here from a common ancient Near Eastern stock of images of woman as a garden to be tended or enjoyed; compare, for example, the description of the woman in these verses and that of the mother in the Sumerian text known as The Message of Lu-dingir-ra to His Mother, probably not a mother at all but a courtesan and devotee of Inanna (Leick 1994: 155–56):

> My mother is rain from heaven, water for the finest seed,
> A harvest of plenty . . . ,
> A garden of delight, full of joy,
> A watered pine, adorned with pine cones,
> A spring flower, a first fruit,
> An irrigation ditch carrying luxuriant waters to the garden plots,
> A sweet date from Dilmun, a date chosen for the best.
>
> (Cooper 1971: 161)

Another Sumerian text, dealing with the courtship of Inanna and Dumuzi, presents a striking parallel to the Song, not least because of its dialogue format:

> Dumuzi spoke:
>   "My sister, I would go with you to my garden.
>   Inanna, I would go with you to my garden.
>   I would go with you to my orchard.
>   I would go with you to my apple tree.
>   There I would plant the sweet, honey-covered seed."

2. I have slightly adapted here Samuel Taylor Coleridge's description of Kubla Khan's stately pleasure dome, which recalls the Song and shares its melodiousness and ability to evoke a sensuous setting.

Inanna spoke:
> "He brought me into his garden.
> My brother, Dumuzi, brought me into his garden.
> I strolled with him among the standing trees,
> I stood with him among the fallen trees,
> By an apple tree I knelt as is proper.
> Before my brother coming in song,
> Who rose to me out of the poplar leaves,
> Who came to me in the midday heat,
> Before my lord Dumuzi,
> I poured out plants from my womb.
> I placed plants before him,
> I poured out plants before him.
> I placed grain before him,
> I poured out grain before him.
> I poured out grain from my womb."
> (Wolkstein and Kramer 1983:40)

Here the lovers call each other "sister" and "brother," there is sexually suggestive garden imagery, and the garden is "his garden." The attention to trees is also reminiscent of Song 2:3 and 8:5. At the same time, there is a noticeable difference: the Song does not share the emphasis on conception and fertility. In the Sumerian text, the man, in effect, invites himself into the garden, and the woman speaks of being brought there by him (cf. Song 2:4, "he brought me to the house of wine"). In both texts the garden is symbolically the woman and the place where the lovers enjoy each other.

Similar motifs appear in an Egyptian love poem:

> I am your favorite sister.
> I am yours like the field
>> planted with flowers
>>> and with all sorts of fragrant plants.
> Pleasant is the canal within it,
>> which your hand scooped out,
>>> while we cooled ourselves in the north wind.
> (P. Harris 500, Group C,
> No. 18, trans. Fox)

[12] In the dry climate of the ancient Near East, a lush garden was a highly prized luxury. Paradise is a garden filled with every tree pleasant to look at and good for food (Gen 2:9), and other biblical texts speak longingly of the garden of God (Gen 13:10; Isa 51:3; Ezek 28:13; 31:8–9; 36:35). Here the garden is a sexual image for the woman herself and her sexuality in particular. The man sees his lover as his private, locked garden for his exclusive pleasure. Elsewhere in the Bible *n⁽l* refers to bolting or locking a door (Judg 3:23–24; 2 Sam

13:17–18). While a "locked garden" might refer to a woman's chastity (Ginsburg, Würthwein, Gordis, Pope), the issue here is the man's exclusive access and not his lover's chastity, for it is in the garden that the lovers will enjoy sexual pleasure, expressed through double entendre in images of eating and drinking the delicacies the garden yields.

A locked garden is a secluded garden, an enclosed garden hedged or walled in to protect it from intruders. A garden depends upon water, and the figure of the sealed spring complements and completes the garden image. "Springs" is used in connection with female sexuality in Prov 5:15–19. Do "spring" and "garden" suggest not only sensuality but also potential fertility (so Fox)? To be sure, images carry with them a range of associations; however, I am inclined to see the man, as the poet portrays him here, as thinking only of erotic enjoyment, not reproductive capacity. The verb *ḥtm* is used of sealing a letter or a document (e.g., 1 Kgs 21:8; Isa 8:16; 29:11; Jer 32:10; Dan 12:4), of preventing access (Deut 32:34), and of hiding from view (Job 9:7; 14:17). Ginsburg proposes that a spring might be sealed by cords to which a seal was affixed, as in Dan 6:17 [18 H]. The spring is closed off, perhaps hedged in, so that others do not have access to its waters, or it is secluded from view, or both.

[13] The abundantly watered garden of the previous verse becomes even more luxurious and exotic in this one. The private garden becomes a private pleasure garden (*pardēs*) and the spring flows into watercourses. The meaning of the obscure term *šĕlāḥayik*, here translated "your watercourses," has long baffled interpreters. LXX renders *apostolai sou*, "your shoots"; Vg. *emissiones tuae*, "your emissions." On the basis of the verbal root *šlḥ* ("to send forth"), the word seems to refer either to shoots or branches (cf. the noun *šĕlūḥôt* in Isa 16:8, and the use of the verb for trees sending forth roots in Jer 17:8 and branches in Ezek 17:6–7 and Ps 80:11 [12 H]) or to channels or watercourses (as in mishnaic Hebrew; cf. *šelaḥ* meaning "water-channel" in Neh 3:15; Shiloah in Isa 8:6; Haupt 1902a: 238; Good 1970: 94). In Ezek 31:4 the verb refers to sending forth streams, and in the next verse the form *bĕšallĕḥô* seems to mean "in its shoots," but could also mean "in its watercourses."

Either shoots or watercourses is sexually suggestive of the woman and particularly her body as a place of pleasure (suggesting body parts? bodily fluids?), but, for modern readers at least, there is a delicate lack of specificity. Of course, readers attuned to sexual innuendo in the Song can always come up with a specific referent for obscure terms. Ancient readers may well have had an erotic code of their own, as we do today. Keel, for example, draws attention to Canaanite pendants depicting a stylized plant growing from the navel of a goddess or from the pubic area, which sometimes takes the shape of a canal (figs. 104–7). Our verse, he maintains, makes sense only when "canals" is understood euphemistically. This is not to say that suggestive language here is a code that needs to be cracked in order to be appreciated, for unlike the comparisons in

vv. 1–5, the referent of the metaphor is virtually lost in the development of the metaphoric image. The erotic atmosphere seems equally or more important than the metaphor (Müller), and, as any poet knows, allusion and innuendo stimulate the imagination more than graphic images.

I take the term *šĕlāḥayik* to refer to the watercourses of the sealed spring, which spill over into this verse from the previous one, in which the woman was metaphorically identified as a spring. The focus continues on the metaphor of the garden and not its referent, the woman. A pleasure garden like this one needs irrigation, even more than an ordinary garden does, for it is particularly lush and full of exotic plants. The word *pardēs*, from which we derive the word "paradise," is a loanword from the Persian *pairidaeza*, where it refers to an enclosed park. Such luxury gardens were the gardens of the aristocracy in the ancient Near East. Elsewhere in the Bible *pardēs* is used of Qoheleth/Solomon's royal gardens and parks planted with all kinds of fruit trees (Eccl 2:5), and of the park belonging to the Persian king (Neh 2:8).

Only the finest fruits grow in this pleasure garden. The term used here for "choice" or "best" (*meged*) appears only in the Song (here and in v. 16 and in 7:13 [14 H]) and in Deut 33:13–16, where Moses blesses the tribe of Joseph with heaven's bounty and the finest produce of the land. Here in v. 13, among all choice fruits, pomegranates are singled out. In ancient Near Eastern love poetry, pomegranates, like apples, are love fruits associated with sexuality, fertility, and the love goddess (see Westenholz 1998: 33–37). They appear in depictions of lush, refreshing gardens in ancient Near Eastern iconography (see Keel, figs. 80–82, for illustrations).

This is a utopian fantasy garden (Gerleman). No garden in the ancient Near East would have contained such a wide variety of spice-bearing plants and trees from such far-away places as Arabia, Africa, and India, growing side by side. On henna and nard, see under 1:12–14. Henna and nard, and the spice-producing plants mentioned in the next verse, are not cultivated for nourishment but for the beauty of their blossoms and their pleasing fragrance. The poet seems more interested in the exotic aromas than in the plants themselves (Würthwein). All the plants of the garden are for pleasure; staples like wheat, barley, leeks, onions, and cucumbers do not grow in such a garden (cf. the lists of the valuable produce of the promised land in Deut 8:7–8 and of Egypt in Num 11:5). Fruit is a luxury food, pleasing to taste and sensual in its appearance, and very often needing to be peeled or burst open to reveal its exquisiteness. With pomegranates, for example, one thinks of the clusters of bright red berries inside, which the man's strenuous tongue will burst against his palate fine.

[14] Fox sees the profusion of exotic plant names in this verse as indicating the intensity and fullness of the man's feelings. Harper views the itemized list in relation to the woman, as hints that her charms are similarly rare. Murphy is more to the point when he suggests that the terms are chosen for their sound

and their exotic qualities (cf. similar evaluations by Gerleman, Müller). The entire poem bears witness to the poet's love of concrete images and pleasure in using a rich and varied vocabulary (e.g., three words for "honey" in 4:11 and 5:1, *nōpet*, *dĕbaš*, *yaʿar*), all in the interest of making the lovers' experience vivid and conveying with precision their preoccupations. The man lingers over the details of his lover's extraordinary attributes (How do I love thee? Let me count the ways). In their striving for completeness, such lists in antiquity seem to be trying to produce an inventory of the world (Gerleman, Keel), the world whose meaning the lover's body contains (see under 4:1–5:1).

Names of exotic plants piled up in a kind of sensory overload suggest something of the woman's sexual ampleness and ripeness and, along with it, the glutting of sexual desire. One might say to a lover, "You are everything nice," but lovers like to hear more. "You are sugar and spice and everything nice" both conveys the desire to nibble and gives the loved one the pleasure of hearing particulars, sweet nothings (and, of course, the accumulation of exotic sweet nothings here is for the pleasure of the reader, whom the poet never takes for granted).

It is possible that each of the spices named in this verse had an erotic significance known to the original audience (Delitzsch, Würthwein, Pope). As a fairly recent parallel, we might think of the language of flowers, popular in earlier times but almost forgotten today; for example, rosemary for remembrance, pansies for thoughts (Shakespeare, *Hamlet*, Act 4, Scene 5); white-flower'd Jasmin and the broad-leav'd Myrtle as emblems of innocence and love (Coleridge, "The Eolian Harp").[3] As in v. 13, where the comprehensive term "choice fruits" points to the variety and abundance of fine fruit in the garden, the man adds "all the finest spices" at the end of the list to assure that it is all-inclusive.

Like flowers, spices mentioned in the Bible are difficult to identify with certainty. Hebrew *karkōm*, a *hapax*, may be saffron (*Crocus sativus*), best known for its yellow color. According to Jacob and Jacob, an Egyptian papyrus dated as early as 2000 BCE mentions this plant. A local variety grows in Syria-Palestine. The plant is bulbous and has grassy leaves and a stemless lilac or purple flower. Its stigma is used to produce a dye, flavoring, and incense. It takes the stigmas of 4,300 flowers for one ounce of saffron, and thus saffron is considered one of the world's most expensive spices. Another possible candidate is safflower (*Carthamus tinctorius*), also known as "Bastard Saffron" or "False Saffron," which has orange-yellow flowers (Jacob and Jacob 815; Moldenke

---

3. *The Language of Flowers* and *Say It with Flowers* are familiar book titles; e.g., *The Language of Flowers, Being a Lexicon of the Sentiments Assigned to Flowers, Plants, Fruits, and Roots* (Edinburgh: Paton and Ritchie, 1849); Lucy Hooper, ed., *The Ladies' Hand-Book of the Language of Flowers* (London: H. G. Clarke & Co., 1844); Marina Heilmeyer, *The Language of Flowers: Symbols and Myths* (Munich: Prestel, 2001); Marthe Séguin-Fontes, *The Language of Flowers* (New York: Sterling Publishing Co., n.d.).

and Moldenke 87). Zohary (207) relates it to turmeric (*Curcuma longa*), a plant native to southeast Asia, as does Keel, on the grounds that it is more exotic, and the plants of the garden are meant to be as exotic as possible.

Hebrew *qāneh* may be sweet cane, or sweet flag (*Acorus calamus*; the full name *qāneh-bōśem* appears in Exod 30:23). It flourishes near water, and the root was used for perfume. According to Pliny, the best aromatic cane grew in Syria, had a pleasant odor that could be smelled from a long way off, and was soft to the touch (*Natural History* XII.48.104). Other candidates include sugar cane, giant grass, ginger grass, lemon grass (Jacob and Jacob 813, Moldenke and Moldenke 40), and palmarosa (Keel). Frankincense from Sheba and sweet cane imported "from a distant land" are mentioned in Jer 6:20, and Ezek 27:19–22 lists cassia, sweet cane, and the finest of spices among the luxury items that Tyre imported from Arabia. Aromatic cane, liquid myrrh, cinnamon, and cassia were the "finest spices" mixed with olive oil by a perfumer to produce sacred anointing oil (Exod 30:23–26), and Isa 43:24 refers to buying cane, presumably at some expense, for sacrificial use.

Hebrew *qinnāmôn* is, of course, cinnamon (*Cinnamonum zeylanicum*), a fragrant bark used as oil, incense, perfume, and food flavoring. Obtained from the inner bark of a tree native to Sri Lanka, it was a rare and expensive import. The other two occurrences of the Hebrew term are in Exod 30:23, mentioned above, and Prov 7:17. In Prov 7:17, whose amorous context most closely resembles the Song of Songs, myrrh, aloes, and cinnamon—three of the spices mentioned in our verse—are used to perfume a love bed.

On frankincense and myrrh, see under 3:6 and 1:13. Aloes (here fem. pl., *ăhālôt*) have been identified with eaglewood (*Aquilaria agallocha*), a tree native to northern India (Jacob and Jacob 812; Moldenke and Moldenke 47). Hansen (2000) mentions different species of Aquilaria, for which the common English names are aloeswood and agarswood. In response to fungal infection, the tree produces an aromatic resin that infuses its own tissues. Known in Arabic as *ᶜud* ("wood"), the resinous wood has a 3000-year history in the Middle East, China, and Japan and is today the world's most expensive incense (as a perfume it sells for about $500 an ounce; oil distilled from it can cost up to $850 an ounce, and Hansen reports that in Singapore the best aloeswood sells for $5,000 to $10,000 per kilogram). Aloeswood, collected by cutting down well-infected older trees, comes in various grades. To date, no one has successfully cultivated it, though attempts are being made to infect the trees artificially. The darker the wood, the more resin it contains, so the best aloeswood is heavy (the Chinese name for it is *ch'en hsiang*, "the incense that sinks in water"). Hansen describes its fragrance as like cedar and sandalwood with a subtle hint of roses and balsam. It is used as incense, to perfume the hair and skin, and to scent clothes. Its fragrance lingers in rooms, clings to persons and clothing, and, according to Hansen, survives several washings.

Psalm 45, celebrating a royal wedding, describes garments fragrant with myrrh, aloes, and cassia, which is reminiscent not only of the spices mentioned in our verse (and in Prov 7:17) but also the reference to the woman's garments as scented like Lebanon in v. 11.

[15] The woman is metaphorically an inexhaustible source of water to make the garden an inexhaustible source of pleasure. In the lavish liquid imagery—the spring (v. 12), watercourses (v. 13), and now the garden spring, well of fresh water, and waters cascading from Lebanon—there seems to be a veiled allusion to bodily secretions and the exchange of body fluids, in kissing, fondling, and sexual intercourse. Word play on Lebanon (vv. 8, 11, 15), *lĕbônâ* (frankincense, vv. 6, 14), and *libbabtinî* ("you have captured my heart," v. 9) connects a range of images associated with the woman, culminating here in v. 15 with the woman imaged as water from Lebanon, fresh and bountiful, cool and refreshing, and sustaining herself as the garden and her lover as its resident. It is not clear why Fox believes "from Lebanon" describes the quality of the water in a well, clear and cool, rather than its source; is he thinking of a "real" garden? If the garden of metaphorical delights contains trees that grow in India, Africa, and other distant lands, there is no reason it cannot have water from Lebanon, for Lebanon has in the Song a significant and quasi-mythical status (see under v. 8 above).

[16] The speaker in this verse calls upon the winds to come into "my garden" to stir up its fragrances and waft them abroad upon the air. The north wind is enjoined to "awake" (*'wr*), a verb that calls to mind the woman's injunction addressed to the women of Jerusalem not to awaken, or rouse, love until it wishes (2:7; 3:5; 8:4), and the south wind is invited to "come" (*bw'*), the verb used to invite the man to "his garden" at the end of the verse. Clearly the woman is the speaker in the second half of this verse, where she calls the garden "his garden." But it is debatable whether the speaker who refers to "my garden" in the first half is the man or the woman. Ordinarily the garden, as a metaphor for the woman, belongs to the man; she calls it "his garden" here in this verse (and in 6:2), and he calls it "my garden" in the next. In the present context, however, the woman could be using "my garden" to refer to herself and her physical charms, which are hers alone to give and which, in her next breath, she offers to her lover by calling herself "his garden." Such is the case with the vineyard, also a symbol of the woman, which she calls "my vineyard" in 1:6 and he calls "my vineyard" in 8:12.

If the speech is the man's, one might ask why he would need the winds to waft his lover's fragrances to him (and he surely would not want them wafted abroad for anyone else to enjoy). Keel proposes that he wants the winds to awaken a garden that is slumbering, but this interpretation depends on taking 4:12–5:1 as a separate poem, for the woman is not a "Sleeping Beauty" in vv. 10–11 ("Sleeping Beauty" [*Dornröschen*] is Keel's term), and one might question whether streams cascading from Lebanon (v. 15) are particularly somnolent.

The description of the garden gives way to a series of behests. The verbs here in v. 16 are all imperatives or expressions of wishes—an invocation of the winds, an invitation to the man. Although it could be argued that this apostrophe to the winds is a fervent culmination to the man's speech, it seems more likely that the woman is speaking here, first inviting the winds into the garden, and then her lover. It is an effective way for her to move gradually into an invitation to lovemaking by being initially indirect about it. The apostrophe is a rhetorical technique for whetting her lover's appetite—using the pretext of invoking the winds to appeal first to his sense of smell with her sweet odors—before offering him an amorous carnal banquet.

The man has been speaking for some time. As his long speech draws to a close, the poet has the woman break in with what seems to be a spontaneous burst of enthusiasm on the part of a desirous partner. In terms of the Song's poetic development, the woman's interjection is the poet's way of reestablishing the dialogue format, which is essential to the Song's distinctive version of love, in which eroticism is shared. It is clear from the woman's response that eating the garden's fruit is mutual sexual indulgence and delectation. As in the dialogue at the beginning of the Song, which consisted of relatively short, alternating speeches, the lovers borrow each other's words to express their rapport (cf. 1:15–2:3). To him, she is a garden laden with choice fruits (vv. 12–13); here she invites him to come to his garden and dine on its (or his, the Hebrew can mean either) choice fruits. To him, she is the finest spices (v. 14) and flowing streams from Lebanon (v. 15); here she invites the winds to blow upon her garden "that its spices may flow" (i.e., that its fragrance may be carried upon the breeze; see Textual Note). In 4:8 he called for her to come (*tābô'î*) with him from distant Lebanon; now, as his speech comes to a close, she invites him to come (*yābō'*) to her, a garden of choice fruits watered by streams from Lebanon and ripe for the picking.

"Let my lover come to his garden!" is like "Let him kiss me!" (1:2), an impatient outburst of desire. It has the same urgency as the beginning of the Song and, like the beginning of the Song, creates the impression that we, the readers, are watching and overhearing the lovers. The difference is that here, in contrast to the Song's opening verses, the man replies immediately.

[5:1] In terms of metaphors used earlier (spices, wine, honey, milk, 4:10–11), he claims possession of the lover who has just invited him to an erotic feast. Their speeches are bound together by catchwords, the intertwining of their voices representing the bonds of love. Myrrh is added to spices, honeycomb to honey, and wine to milk in an attempt to be exhaustive, a sort of "you're so wonderful I could eat you up, every last bit." The man emphasizes his claim to the garden both by the sequence "I come . . . I pluck . . . I eat . . . I drink" (ending up both satiated and besotted) and by the eightfold repetition of "my": "I come to *my* garden, *my* sister bride, I gather *my* myrrh with *my* spice, I eat *my* honeycomb with *my* honey, I drink *my* wine with *my* milk."

The four verbs in the perfect tense—come, pluck, eat, drink—have been variously rendered by translators and commentators as past, present, or future, and the decision usually depends on whether or not they think the woman and man consummate their love at this point. Since in the Song the distinction between the anticipation and enjoyment of sexual union is constantly blurred, there is no point in arguing over whether the couple has enjoyed, is enjoying, or will enjoy a sexual banquet. Through both the blurring of temporal distinctions and the indirection of language, sexual union is simultaneously anticipated, deferred, and enjoyed (see Introduction, "Blurring Distinctions between Anticipation and Enjoyment of Love," pp. 9–11).

The woman's invitation in the previous verse ("Let my lover come to his garden!") and the man's reply here in this verse ("I come to my garden," etc.) are complementary expressions of desire gendered in terms of a cultural version of love as something a woman gives and a man takes. The garden, its plenteous water supply, and its lush plants suggest female sexuality; entering the garden, gathering, eating, and drinking its produce describe male sexual activity (as does pasturing elsewhere; 1:7; 2:16; 6:2, 3).

The lovers are encouraged in their mutual intoxication and satiation: "Eat, friends, drink yourselves drunk on caresses!" This is another place in the poem where the identity of the speaker is debated. Keel, for example, thinks the man says these words to his companions. But why, suddenly, should the poet introduce additional characters into the poem, and who are these companions? Rudolph reads all of 5:1 as the man's speech to his friends and emends the beginning of the verse accordingly. Because he sees no reason why the man should tell the woman what she already knows, he proposes that the man, on the basis of his experience of marriage (another assumption), advises his friends to go and do likewise. Bloch and Bloch see the injunction to eat and drink as a self-contained epigram, which may have been taken from a popular drinking song, spoken by the man. Gordis proposes that it could possibly be the words of the woman addressed to the man, using the plural for the singular, which is hardly likely. Gerleman and Würthwein see these words as an aside addressed by the poet to the lovers, but the poet never intrudes on the poem to address the characters. Müller proposes that the poet addresses the audience, but this is only indirectly the case, insofar as the speaker's encouragement of the lovers becomes the poem's invitation to its readers.

There are only three clearly distinguishable speaking voices in the poem, and thus only three "characters," and all the parts can be assigned to them without difficulty: the woman, the man, and the women of Jerusalem. Assuming that the lovers are the ones addressed as "friends," these words must be those of the women of Jerusalem. The women's presence is ubiquitous, and they are often referred to when the poem seems to reach a climax in the uniting of the lovers (2:7; 3:5; 8:4). Having them as witness to the lovers' intimacy is the poet's way of welcoming readers into this private pleasure garden. They address the lovers as "friends," the plural form of the tender form of endearment "my friend" that the lovers use for each other (he for her in 1:9, 15; 2:2, 10, 13; 4:1, 7; 5:2; 6:4, and she for him, 5:16). "Eat," "drink," and "be drunk," plural forms addressed to both lovers, leave no doubt that eating and drinking in the garden is mutual sexual indulgence and satisfaction. Proverbs 5:19 and 7:18 speak similarly of drinking one's fill of love. Taking up the theme of lovemaking as intoxicating (4:10–11 and 5:1)—the theme with which the Song began—the women encourage the lovers to abandon themselves to sensual delight in their mutual besottedness.

Song of Songs 5:2–6:3
The Woman's Second Long Speech

<She>

5:2   I was sleeping but my heart was awake.
      Listen![a] My lover is knocking![b]

     "Open to me, my sister, my friend,
       my dove, my perfect one,
     for my head is drenched with dew,
       my locks with mist of the night."

3   I have taken off my robe.
       Am I to put it on again?[c]
     I have washed my feet.
       Am I to get them dirty?

4   My lover reached his hand into[d] the opening,[e]
       at which my body thrilled.[f]
5   I rose to open to my lover,
       and my hands dripped myrrh,
     my fingers, flowing myrrh,
       on the handles of the bolt.
6   I opened to my lover,
       but my lover had turned[g] and gone.
       I swooned because of him.[h]
     I sought him but I did not find him,
       I called him but he did not answer me.

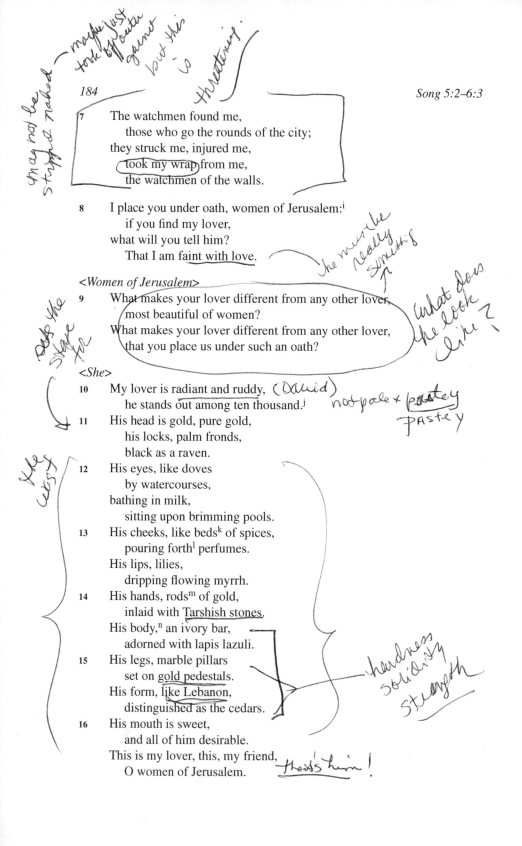

7   The watchmen found me,
        those who go the rounds of the city;
     they struck me, injured me,
        took my wrap from me,
        the watchmen of the walls.

8   I place you under oath, women of Jerusalem:[i]
        if you find my lover,
     what will you tell him?
        That I am faint with love.

<Women of Jerusalem>

9   What makes your lover different from any other lover,
        most beautiful of women?
     What makes your lover different from any other lover,
        that you place us under such an oath?

<She>

10   My lover is radiant and ruddy,
        he stands out among ten thousand.[j]

11   His head is gold, pure gold,
        his locks, palm fronds,
        black as a raven.

12   His eyes, like doves
        by watercourses,
     bathing in milk,
        sitting upon brimming pools.

13   His cheeks, like beds[k] of spices,
        pouring forth[l] perfumes.
     His lips, lilies,
        dripping flowing myrrh.

14   His hands, rods[m] of gold,
        inlaid with Tarshish stones.
     His body,[n] an ivory bar,
        adorned with lapis lazuli.

15   His legs, marble pillars
        set on gold pedestals.
     His form, like Lebanon,
        distinguished as the cedars.

16   His mouth is sweet,
        and all of him desirable.
     This is my lover, this, my friend,
        O women of Jerusalem.

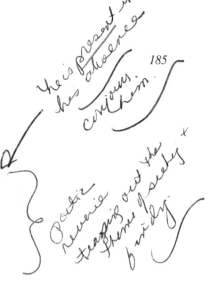

<Women of Jerusalem>

6:1   Where has your lover gone,
       most beautiful of women?
    Where has your lover turned,
       that we may seek him with you?

<She>

6:2   My lover has gone down to his garden,
    to the beds of spices,
    to graze in the gardens
    and to gather lilies.

3   I am my lover's and my lover is mine,
    he who grazes among the lilies.

a. Hebrew *qôl*, "voice, sound," as in 2:8 (see Textual Note above).

b. There are only two other occurrences of the root *dpq* in the Bible: in Gen 33:13 it means to drive [cattle] excessively, to press them on, and in Judg 19:22 (*hithpael*) it refers to men hurling themselves against, pushing on, or beating upon the door. LXX, Vg., and Syriac understand the verbal form here to mean "knock," which is how most translators render it; LXX and the Old Latin supply a door as the object.

c. Literally, "How should I put it on?" Hebrew *ʾêkākâ*, here and in the next couplet, introduces a rhetorical question; cf. also Esth 8:6.

d. The preposition *min* has the sense of "in through"; as in 2:9, it represents the perspective of one who is inside, i.e., "in from outside" (Delitzsch).

e. Literally "hole"; see the Commentary.

f. More literally, "my insides were stirred because of him." Some mss and editions read ʿ*ālay*, "within me," in place of ʿ*ālāyw*, "because of him" or "for him," which fits well with the sexual innuendo. The versions support MT. Vg. understands "at his touch" (*ad tactum eius*), which is also sexually suggestive.

g. The verb *ḥmq* (lacking in LXX) occurs here in the *qal* and in Jer 31:22 in the *hithpael*, where it means to turn this way and that. The passive participle is used in 7:1 [2 H] to refer to the curves of the woman's hips.

h. Vocalizing *bidbārô* for MT *bĕdabbĕrô* (so Fox; cf. NJPS footnote). Some (e.g., Pope, Murphy, Keel) take the verb as *dbr*, "to turn" (see *HALOT* 209b, *dbr* I, "turn aside"; *DCH* II, 396b, *dbr* III, "turn the back"; Driver [1934: 55–56; 1930/31: 250]); see also the bibliography in *DCH* II, 624a.

i. LXX adds "by the powers and forces of the field"; cf. 2:7; 3:5.

j. Literally, "eminent (*dāgûl*) among ten thousand"; *dāgûl* is related to *degel* in 2:4 (see the Commentary under 2:4) and *nidgālôt* in 6:4, 10 (see the Commentary there).

k. Reading as plural, with some Hebrew mss, LXX, Vg., Syriac, as in MT in 6:2, and in agreement with "cheeks," instead of MT's singular pointing.

l. Vocalizing consonantal *mgdlwt* as the piel participle of *gdl*, as witnessed by LXX (*phyousai*, "pouring forth").

m. The meaning of the term is uncertain; the root *gll*, "roll," suggests it refers to something round, such as "rods" or "rings" or "cylinders," but perhaps "pivots." LXX reads *toreutai*, "turned, worked in relief," which it uses to describe the woman's navel (or vulva?) in 7:2 [3 H] and elsewhere of silver or gold that is hammered out (Exod 25:18, 31, 36; Jer 10:9); Vg. *tornatiles*, "turned in a lathe."

n. I.e., body as distinguished from limbs and head; see the Commentary.

The woman had a long speech or, if one prefers to divide it, three consecutive speeches in 2:8–3:11. Then the man had a long speech in 4:1–5:1, which became a dialogue with her at the end. Now in 5:2–6:3 the woman again speaks at length, and, again, she tells a story in which she and he are characters. It is a variation of the same story she told in 2:8–3:5—an account of a visit by her lover followed by her seeking him in the city streets. Whereas the man's speech in 4:1–5:1 became a brief dialogue at the end, here at the climactic turning point in 5:2–6:3—the point at which the search seems to end disastrously with the woman being beaten by the watchmen of the city (v. 7)—the woman's narrative turns into a dialogue with the women of Jerusalem that enables her story to reach the desired outcome, the union with her lover. The woman intervened in the man's speech (4:16), the women of Jerusalem join in now in hers, giving her the opportunity to launch into descriptive praise of her lover (5:9–16), through which his presence is poetically evoked. Thus it transpires that the woman knows where he is—in his garden (6:2); that is, with her, as he was at the end of the previous unit (5:1). What were two episodes in her earlier story (her account of his visit in 2:8–17 and her seeking and finding him in 3:1–5) are thus seamlessly combined to create a single, finely crafted unit, whose integrity is recognized by virtually all critics.

The chief parallels between her two "stories" may be seen from the following schema (Exum 1973: 56–61).

The First Story (2:8–3:5)

    I.   The call to the woman (2:8–17)
          "Listen! my lover" (*qôl dôdî*, "the voice of my lover," v. 8)
          the man is outside: coming, standing, peering in the windows
          he calls to the woman: "rise up" (*qûmî*, vv. 10, 13)
          epithets: my friend, my fair one, my dove (vv. 10, 13–14)
          reason for call: it is springtime
                he wants her to come outside
          refrain of mutual possession, "my lover is mine and I am his" (2:16)
   II.   The seeking and finding (3:1–5)
          takes place nightly (*ballêlôt*, v. 1)
          "I will rise" (*ʾāqûmâ*, v. 2)
          "I sought him but I did not find him"
          "the watchmen found me, those who go the rounds of the city" (v. 3)
          finding of the lover leading to oath placed upon the women
             of Jerusalem (3:4–5)

The Second Story (5:2–6:3)

I. The call to the woman (5:2–5)
    "Listen! my lover" (*qôl dôdî*, "the voice of my lover," v. 2)
    the man is outside: knocking
    he calls to the woman: "open"
    epithets: my sister, my friend, my dove, my perfect one
    reason for call: it is wet and night (*lāyĕlâ*)
                he wants to come inside
    her response: "I rose" (*qamtî*, v. 5)

II. The seeking and finding (5:6–6:3)
    "I sought him but I did not find him" (5:6)
    "the watchmen found me, those who go the rounds of the city" (5:7)
    oath placed upon the women of Jerusalem leading to finding
      of the lover (5:8–6:2)
    refrain of mutual possession, "I am my lover's and my lover
      is mine" (6:3)

Both units begin with the voice (*qôl*, "voice" or "sound"), which functions to arrest attention, thus the translation, "Listen!" The voice ("listen"), along with the look, or gaze (often indicated by *hinnēh*, "look, behold," as in 2:8 and 4:1), is a central theme in the Song. In the previous unit (4:1–5:1) the man constructed his lover through the gaze, inviting her (and the poem's readers) to see herself through his eyes. The woman owns the gaze too (e.g., 1:16; 3:6–11), but she relies more heavily on the voice to construct her lover, controlling the way we view him by telling stories about him in which she puts words in his mouth (2:10–14). Now in 5:2–6:3 she uses both equally effectively. Here the poet combines narration (storytelling), the report of sequenced actions, which distinguished the woman's earlier speech in 2:8–3:5, and figuration, static description of the loved one cast in densely metaphoric language, which dominated the man's speech in 4:1–5:1. Instead of finding her lover at the end of a search through the city streets (cf. 3:4), she "finds" him through describing him, conjuring him up by depicting him from head to foot in simile and metaphor, as he had conjured her up in his speech (cf. esp. 4:1–5), until he is there, in his garden, with her, in an image of sexual intimacy.

The lover whose voice/sound is heard is outside. In 2:9 he is looking through the windows, and in 5:2 he is knocking at the door. Participles ("looking," "knocking") indicate action in progress and contribute to the illusion of immediacy that characterizes both of the woman's "stories." In 2:10–14 the woman reports the words her lover says to her. Likewise, in 5:2 she recounts his words, but here there are no indicators of narration, like her prosaic "my lover answered and said to me" in 2:10. Thus the impression of immediacy—the sense one gets that one is overhearing a dialogue between the lovers—is especially strong. In 2:10 and 13 he invites her to join him outside, "rise up (*qûmî*)

... come," and in 3:2 she says, "I will rise" (ʾāqûmâ). According to 5:2 he wants to join her inside, and she reports that she rose to admit him (qamtî, "I rose," 5:5). He calls her "my friend, my fair one, my dove" in 2:10, 13–14, and "my sister, my friend, my dove, my perfect one" in 5:2. Two of the epithets remain the same. In both "stories" he offers a rather transparent pretense for her to grant his request to be with her: in 2:11–14 it is springtime and therefore she should join him outside; in 5:2 it is wet outside and nighttime, therefore she should let him in. At least part of the action of both accounts takes place at night: "upon my bed nightly" (3:1); "my locks with the dew of the night" (5:2).

In each of the woman's narratives, her report of her lover's speech is followed by an account of seeking and finding. She seeks him in the city streets, and in both accounts she reports, "I sought him but I did not find him." In the process, she encounters the city watchmen, an event she describes each time in the same way: "they found me, the watchmen, those who go the rounds of the city." The seeking–finding motif finds its resolution in 2:8–3:5 when the woman finds her lover. She holds him and refuses to release him (3:4). In 5:2–6:3 she enlists the aid of the women of Jerusalem to find her lover, and together they engage in the process of what Cook has aptly described as "finding-by-praise" (1968: 134). The two "stories" share the refrain of mutual possession. "I am my lover's and my lover is mine, the one grazing among the lilies" (6:3) is the chiastic repetition of "my lover is mine and I am his, the one grazing among the lilies" (2:16). This refrain appears before the search in 2:8–3:5, where it provides a note of assurance at the conclusion of the first of the two episodes the woman narrates. In 5:2–6:3 it comes at the end of the search, bringing the entire unit to closure now that the lovers are reunited. The refrain of adjuration (3:5) appears in a variant form in 5:8, and provides the transition from the woman's narration to her dialogue with the women of Jerusalem. Whereas in 3:4–5 the finding of the lover gave rise to an oath placed upon the women not to rouse love, here the oath, with a message for the woman's lover ("I am faint with love") gives rise to the finding.

Though the stories the woman tells are similar, there are important differences. On the poetic level the most striking differences are the interweaving of narration and figuration in 5:2–6:3 and the dialogue with the women of Jerusalem, the only time they engage in a purposeful conversation with a character in the poem. On the story level, the woman's encounter with the watchmen of the city takes a different, disturbing turn. Whereas earlier they ignored her (3:3–4), here they abuse her (5:7).

In a dazzling feat of conjury the woman describes her lover so that he materializes before our eyes (5:10–16). Perhaps he has been there all along, for her "story" unfolds on two levels and offers the most sophisticated, well-developed example of double entendre in the poem. Double entendre occurs throughout the Song and was last employed in the man's speech just before this one ("I come to my garden . . . I pluck my myrrh with my spice," etc., 5:1), but here it is creatively interwoven with the dramatic action to produce a "story" whose two levels seem to move in different directions (cf. the dual impulses in 2:17 and 8:14). On one level, 5:2–7 appears to be an account of the lover outside the woman's chamber at night, seeking admittance (a topos of love poetry). He departs before she can get up to let him in, and she goes in search of him. On the erotic level, these verses may be viewed as an account of coition veiled by the indirection of language (cf. Cook 1968: 123–24), not a stage-by-stage description to be deciphered by matching body parts and fluids to oblique references, but an overall suggestion of sexual intimacy created by the pace, the imagery, and the choice of terminology (e.g., the repeated use of "open" without a direct object, such as "door," draws attention to its sexual sense). On this level, the search for the lover that follows his withdrawal may express the woman's desire for further gratification—the literary equivalent of "I can't get enough of you!" In 6:1–3 she reveals that she knows where he is—in his garden; that is, with her, indulging in sexual divertissements. The revelation at the end of the unit that she did not need to look for him at all has some bearing on the interpretation of 5:2–7. It cautions us against an overly literalistic reading of these verses as if they needed to be explained as an event in the life of the lovers or a dream or a fantasy. While it begins by exploiting the lyric potential of dream and fantasy, 5:2–6:3 is first and foremost another instance of the Song's blurring of the distinctions between longing and gratification, desire and its satisfaction. The woman is always conjuring up her lover and letting him disappear in an endless deferral of presence that impels the poem forward.

As in 2:8–3:5, the poet casts the woman in the role of narrator: "I was sleeping but my heart was awake." To whom is she relating these events? By now the women of Jerusalem are well established as the audience within the poem (contra Murphy). The woman addresses them directly in v. 8, and in response they enter into a dialogue with her. Their presence at the end of the unit as interlocutors (5:9; 6:1) who enable the "seeking" of the lover to end successfully in a "finding-by-praise" is the most vivid instance of audience participation in the poem, and their participation, as elsewhere, functions to draw the reader into the world of the poem (cf. 2:7; 3:5; 3:11; 5:1; 8:4–5). They and we are the audience of the woman's narrative in 5:2–7, and we are the audience of their dialogue with the woman, which seems to be taking place before us, in 5:8–6:3.

The unit ends, as did the previous one, with the man in his garden, feeding upon its foliage. By now the sexual symbolism of the garden is also well established. Entering the garden and enjoying its produce signify male sexual activity, while the garden symbolically represents female sexuality (see under 5:1). The sought-after lover has gone down to his garden (6:2), which waits expectantly for his visit. Similarly, at the beginning of the unit (5:2–7), the man visits the woman, seeking admittance to her chamber, while she bides her time attentively ("I was sleeping but my heart was awake"). As in the parallel "story" (2:8–3:5), he does the courting and she, for her part, decides whether or not to respond to his overtures. Against this rather conventional portrayal of relations between the sexes is the story of the woman going out in the streets to seek her lover in 5:6–7 (cf. 3:1–3). (Such behavior is not, however, unusual in love poetry; see, e.g., Introduction, "Literary Context: Ancient Near Eastern Love Poetry," pp. 47–63.) In addition, in vv. 10–16 the woman takes on a role more often associated with men, that of owner of the gaze. The male lover assumes this role three times, describing the woman from her head downward in 4:1–5 and 6:4–7, and from her feet to her head in 7:1–5 [2–6 H]. If the Song contained descriptions of only the woman's body and not the man's, its picture of gender relations would be significantly asymmetrical. The fact that here in 5:10–16 the woman is the subject rather than the object of the look, describing the man's body (even if the description is different in kind from his descriptions of her), means that looking in the Song is constructed as mutual, not one-sided. This makes it easier to interpret the gaze as erotic rather than voyeuristic (see under 5:14 and Introduction, "Erotic Look or Voyeuristic Gaze?" pp. 22–24).

[5:2–7] One of the first issues commentators often raise about these verses (and the companion episode in 3:1–5) is whether or not the woman is relating a dream. It is frequently assumed that she is because of the reference to sleeping, the lack of temporal and spatial continuity (Müller, Munro 120), and the unusual or improbable features of the account (e.g., Ginsburg, Delitzsch, Budde, Meek, Rudolph, Würthwein, Gordis, Falk, Müller). Others (Gerleman, Keel, Longman) see no need for recourse to dream interpretation in order to explain the flights of imagination characteristic of lyric poetry. "Earlier interpreters, who could not imagine this scene to be real, saw v. 2a as an unambiguous reference to dreaming (the notion that the piece was poetic fiction lay beyond them)" (Keel 188; see also Introduction, "Fantasy, Reality, and Poetic Imagination," pp. 45–47).

Discussion of the degree of reality and fantasy in these verses becomes even less meaningful in view of the double entendre here. Double entendre, which gives the impression of gratification taking place even as it is longed for, makes it possible to read the woman's account on two different levels. This slippage from one mode to another, the blurring of distinctions between the more literal level of wishing, dreaming, desiring and the figurative level of consummation is one of the poetic techniques that makes the Song so sensual. The woman begins her speech with a story that also blurs distinctions, the nebulous boundary between sleep and wakefulness ("I was sleeping but my heart was awake"). On a literal reading, she recounts a nighttime visit by her lover, who seeks entry to her chamber. It seems that he is outside the door in the damp night air, calling to her. She makes some rather weak excuses for not letting him in, at which point he tries to open the door by putting his hand through the keyhole or latch.

She then gets up to let him in (smearing myrrh, with which she has prepared her bed in anticipation of his visit, on the handles of the bolt), but when she opens the door he is gone (5:2–6).

It takes from v. 2 (the lover's invitation) to v. 6 for the woman to open to her lover, compared to the compression of time in the events described in vv. 6–7 (Landy 47). The discovery of the lover's departure is the point at which the mood changes. The rest of the woman's account resolves around the theme of seeking and finding. Before the lover is "found" (6:1–3) there are complications. She reports that she goes out looking for him but is unsuccessful; instead of finding him, she is found by the watchmen and beaten (5:6–7). With v. 8 she stops narrating and turns to the women of Jerusalem with a petition, a behest so urgent that she puts them under oath to tell her lover about her lovesickness, if *they* find him.

On an erotic reading, these verses seem to offer a veiled account of coition. Müller, who never loses sight of the way double entendre permits a completely "innocent" reading, shows how sexual allusions can be found in most of the details. A notoriously graphic reading is that of Pope, though Eslinger outdoes him in anatomical detail (1981: 275–76) and Garrett finds an even greater number of anatomical double entendres (e.g., "my head is full of dew" refers to seminal fluid on the man's penis). Pope sees "feet" (v. 3) as a possible euphemism for the genitals ("I have washed my feet, how could I soil them?"). But the key is v. 4, which reads literally, "my lover reached his hand in through the hole." Pope concludes:

> Given the attested use of "hand" as a surrogate for phallus, there can be no question that, whatever the context, the statement "my love thrust his 'hand' into the hole" would be suggestive of coital intromission, even without the succeeding line descriptive of the emotional reaction of the female. (519; cf. also Müller)

(Presumably by "the emotional reaction of the female" Pope means orgasm, though, surprisingly, he never explicitly says so.)

Fox disagrees, claiming that a double entendre for coition in v. 4 interferes with the course of the narrative, since it is not until v. 5 that the woman gets up to open to her lover (cf. Gordis 90; Sasson 1978–79: 196). Verse 6, he argues, makes it clear that the man has not entered the woman's house, and, if this were a veiled description of coition, it would produce an "ugly picture" of a man who has sex with a woman and then leaves (145). But that rather depends on whether one takes his withdrawal literally or figuratively (as, for example, orgasm having been reached and desire beginning anew [Haller]). Readers who are looking for explicitly sexual allusions in 5:2–7 can find them easily enough; what is more difficult (and here Fox is right) is matching the dramatic action sequentially to stages of sexual intercourse. The specifically erotic and delicately suggestive are superimposed in such a way that what the poet has so elegantly constructed cannot be taken apart and retold in terms of the kind of one-to-one correspondence between images and sexual references some interpreters seek.

The poem works on two levels at once, one of which seems to suggest that the couple would have had intercourse if the woman had opened the door sooner and the man had not left so suddenly (so Fox). The other represents sexual passion poetically, not only through allusion and double entendre, but also by means of the poetic configuration of the account. While the woman's narrative ostensibly moves in one direction (a missed encounter), the poetic composition moves in another (coition)—through its choice of vocabulary and imagery and, particularly, in its artistic design.

Sexual intercourse is not to be found here in vv. 2–6 by matching verbal clues to body parts or sexual functions, but it can be perceived in the progression and emphases of the woman's account. Three actions by the woman, underscored by the use of the personal pronoun "I" (*ʾănî*), mark the division of her narrative into three parts: "I was sleeping" (v. 2), "I arose" (v. 5), "I opened" (v. 6). Each of these parts contains a reference to opening (*pātaḥ*), its erotic suggestiveness heightened by the absence of a direct object: first, the request by the man to "open to me," v. 2; second, the woman's intention "to open to my lover," v. 5; and third, the act itself, "I opened to my lover," v. 6. The pace becomes faster and the parts of the poem grow shorter as the woman's narrative, and the sexual union it symbolically represents, reaches its climax in v. 6, which combines the man's turning and withdrawal and the woman's swooning (Exum 1973: 50–53). Here too, as in vv. 4–5, the sequence of events does not need to correspond to stages of intercourse. The poet has only to be suggestive and leave the rest to the reader's imagination. Verses 2–6 offer an impressionistic picture of sexual intimacy created by allusion, innuendo, and patterning that conveys sexual excitement poetically, in the way, for example, that music can convey sexual excitement even in cases where the lyrics seem to move in a different direction (Exum 1999b: 78–84). In the denouement the mood of the poem modulates, and intense longing gives rise to dramas of seeking and (initially) not finding the loved one (v. 6) and encountering adversity for the sake of love (v. 7).

[5:2] In a move typical of the Song, two kinds of distinctions are blurred here: that between past and present and that between sleep and wakefulness. The verse could be translated either "I was sleeping but my heart was awake," as here, or "I sleep but my heart is awake" (NEB, NJB). Only the anomaly of a person who is sleeping reporting that she is sleeping might suggest that this is an account of something that happened in the past rather than of something the speaker reports as it happens. We are not unprepared for this sort of temporal ambiguity; the distinction between past and present was blurred in the parallel "story" the woman told in 2:8–14. If she is speaking here of the past, it sounds like the immediate past, for the injunction "listen!" the participle "knocking," and the man's erotic imperative, "open to me," create the Song's by-now familiar illusion of immediacy (see Introduction, "The Illusion of Immediacy," pp. 3–6).

"I was sleeping but my heart was awake" suggests a light sleep, in which the woman, desiring or anticipating her lover's visit, was half listening for his voice. It captures poetically the transitional moment between sleep and wakefulness that we experience when we are asleep and hear something, and then, in a state of partial wakefulness, are initially unsure whether we actually heard something or dreamed it. And so we do what she does: we listen. A heart that is awake is attentive (on "heart," see under 4:9). There is an allusion here to the woman's injunction in 2:7 and 3:5 that the women of Jerusalem not rouse, or waken, love, where the same root, ʿwr, is used. Her desire for her lover is already aroused, even before she hears his fervent "open to me."

First she hears his knock (see Textual Note). Fox's suggestion, following Ibn Ezra, that the root meaning of the verb *dpq* (here translated "knocking") is probably "push" and here means "urge" or "entreat" is appealing, especially because what follows is the text of the man's entreaty. Fox, however, is too literalistic when he says knocking "might wake up the whole family!" (144). Because in Judg 19:22 the object of the verb is a door, I take the verb here to refer to knocking or perhaps pushing (with "door" implied but probably not expressed because of the double entendre). We might understand the ideas of knocking and entreating to be combined in the one term, a combination supported by the context: the man is both outside, knocking on the door (on a literal reading as opposed to a figurative erotic one) and entreating the woman to let him in at the same time. One can almost hear the knocking in the onomatopoeic Hebrew, *dôdî dôpēq*.

He speaks to her. She does not tell us that she is reporting his words (cf. 2:10), though this is indicated by her narrative introduction ("I was sleeping but my heart was awake") and confirmed by vv. 4–7, which locate the events she relates in the recent past. He appeals to her to "open to me" with a string of endearments. Three of them he has used before (see under 4:9; 1:9–11; 2:10–14), and now he adds a fourth, "my perfect one," which he will use again and elaborate upon in 6:9. The reason he gives for wanting to enter is only a pretense: he asks for shelter from the damp night air, but he has really come to be with her (cf. 2:10–14, where he takes some time to get to his real reason for inviting her to join him outside). The lover's entreaty at the door of his beloved is a topos of love poetry, and this verse of the Song is often compared to the classical Paraclausithyron—the complaint or lament of the lover who stands outside his beloved's door and pleads to be allowed in—though in the Song the man does not complain. The excluded-lover topos appears in Egyptian love songs (see Fox 282–83; Gerleman). For example, in P. Chester Beatty I, Group C, No. 46, a suitor stands at his beloved's door and complains of his exclusion on a night he expected would belong to him:

As for what she—(my) sister—did to me,
   should I keep silent to her?
She left me standing at the door of her house
   while she went inside,
and did not say to me "Welcome!"
   but blocked her ears in *my* night.
                                        (trans. Fox)

[5:3] It appears that the woman has already undressed and gone to bed. She has removed her robe or tunic, and washing one's feet is something one would do before retiring. The bed at night sets the scene for erotic play. That the woman has undressed is sexually suggestive and has given rise to various speculations on the part of readers. Is she naked? Delitzsch and Rudolph think so; so does Keel, who provides comparative examples from Egyptian art. Pope speculates whether "feet" might be a euphemism for the genitals here, a level of insinuation that seems somewhat unlikely at this point.

Again distinctions are blurred between what appears to be happening in the present (if we connect this verse directly with the preceding one) and what has taken place already (if we take it with the following verses). Either the woman is answering the man or explaining to her audience, the women of Jerusalem, why she did not let him in at once. I have translated this verse as a reply addressed to the man, which highlights the sense of immediacy. To his request, the man receives a playful answer in kind. Some translations (e.g., NRSV, JPS) understand the verse as narration rather than quoted speech; thus v. 3 would belong with vv. 4–7 as part of the story the woman narrates in the past tense. If she is addressing her audience rather than her lover, one could imagine that she did not reply to him at all but simply hesitated, at which point he tried to enter (v. 4) and she got up to let him in (v. 5).

It seems fitting, however, that the woman would answer the man, and her riposte seems well suited to his request. He did not say, "Open to me, I want to be with you," but rather, "Open to me, it's wet outside." She responds in effect, "You want me to get up, get dressed, and get my feet dirty again so you can come in and dry off?" Some commentators find this a weak excuse and see it as a coy retort, or the sort of thing one finds in a dream (Budde), or part of a literary convention, the love test (Krinetzki) or the lament of the lover at the door (Gerleman). The effect of her hesitation is to heighten the dramatic, and erotic, tension. "Implied refusals are only delays, and delays intensifications" (Cook 1968: 144). Her reply is no more or less teasing or playful than the reason the man gives for wanting to enter. This is verbal foreplay, corresponding to sexual foreplay on the erotic level, and abetted by the suggestiveness of the request to "open," the readiness of the bed, the woman's state of undress, and, especially, the double entendre in the next verse.

In contrast to most commentators, Garrett assigns this verse to the man. In his view, the man is trying to persuade his reluctant bride, hesitant to lose her virginity and fearful of the pain, to have sexual intercourse with him. Not only is this not a very convincing interpretation of the erotic level but, in spite of Garrett's efforts to argue otherwise, it rules out the possibility of interpreting the woman's account of her lover's nighttime visit on the dramatic or "story" level, where it would make no sense for the man to be out in the streets naked or to claim that he does not want to get his feet dirty.

[5:4] This verse situates the events of the woman's narrative in the past. She relates that the man tried to open the door, an action that implies that he understood her reply as banter. His gesture, she says, aroused strong emotions in her. That this verse is a double entendre for coition seems likely, as numerous commentators have observed. Hebrew *yād* ("hand") is a euphemism for penis (e.g., Isa 57:8, 10; 1QIsa^a 65:3; 1QS 7:13 = 4QD^a 10.2.11; *DCH* IV, 82a, 94a) and *ḥōr*, here translated "opening," literally means "hole."

The word translated "insides," *mēʿîm*, refers to the internal organs in general and often specifically to the organs of procreation; e.g., Gen 15:4; 2 Sam 7:12; 16:11; Isa 48:19; 2 Chr 32:21, of men; Gen 25:23; Num 5:22; Isa 49:1; Ps 71:6; Ruth 1:11, of women (it is unusual to find the term referring to part of the body as seen externally; see under 5:14). The verb *hmh*, here translated "stirred," denotes tumult or stirring; when used of the emotions it can mean to murmur, moan, or stir; for example, Isa 16:11; Jer 4:19; 31:20; 48:36; Pss 42:5 [6 H], 11 [12 H]; 43:5; *DCH* II, 565b). The image of internal arousal conveys anticipation and excitement and is suggestive of orgasm. A double entendre in this verse, however, does not mean that every verse has a sexual referent that, when deciphered, provides a sequential description of sexual intercourse (see under 5:2–7).

[5:5] In v. 2 the man implored "open to me," and in v. 3 the woman demurred, protesting that admitting her lover to her chamber would require her to get dressed again and to dirty her feet. Now she reports that she got up to admit ("to open to") her lover. It appears that she had recently perfumed herself and some of the myrrh still clung to her hands. In opening the door she got some of it on the handles of the bolt. Liquid or "flowing" myrrh is myrrh mixed with oil (cf. "oil of myrrh," Esth 2:12; and see under 1:13). Some think that the man anointed the bolt with myrrh, and the woman got it on her hands when she tried to open the door. In a frequently cited parallel, Lucretius's *De rerum natura* IV.1171, the excluded lover who laments not being able to gain entrance to his beloved's house weeps, leaves flowers, and anoints the doorposts, but the man in the Song does none of these things. More likely the woman had been awaiting her lover's visit, and the myrrh on her hands is that with which she had either anointed herself or, like the woman in Prov 7:17, perfumed her bed, or both.

The lovers are aroused by each other's perfumes (1:2–3; 4:10), and, in keeping with the sexual innuendo of these verses, hands dripping with flowing myrrh suggest the intimacy of touches, caresses, and bodily fluids that feature in love-making (cf. Müller). Dripping myrrh is an image of "gratuitous abundance" befitting "a love which can no longer be contained" (Munro 49).

[5:6] The poem moves in two directions. On the erotic level, here in v. 6 as in v. 4, it hints at sexual union ("I opened," "I swooned"), while in terms of the dramatic action it tells of a missed encounter. When the woman opens the door, she finds that her lover has gone. In contrast to his response of seeking entry in v. 4, his departure suggests that he did take her demurral (v. 3) seriously or that she delayed too long in opening the door. Alternatively, if v. 3 does not represent words spoken to him but rather her explanation of her delay to the women of Jerusalem (an explanation he is unaware of), then he called to her (v. 2) and, when it seemed to him that she either did not hear him or for some other reason did not respond, he went away.

Her reaction, literally, "my soul (*nepeš*, i.e., consciousness, life force) went forth," has been understood variously by exegetes as a sign of her bewilderment, disappointment, or longing. The expression is used elsewhere of dying (Gen 35:18; similarly, Ps 146:4, where *rûaḥ*, "spirit, breath," is used instead of *nepeš*). Lovers in the throes of sexual ecstasy often speak of expiring (cf. French *la petite mort* for orgasm). Because it conveys the ideas of both bewilderment and ecstasy, "I swooned" in the translation provides a double entendre in English well suited to the sexually suggestive Hebrew context.

According to the Masoretic vocalization, she swooned "when he spoke" (so NRSV). Inasmuch as she has described other events since quoting his words in v. 2, it seems somewhat odd for her to relate this now, unless it is a sort of flashback in which she expresses her regret at her delay (thus Bloch and Bloch translate, "How I wanted him when he spoke!"). Alternatively the verb may be *dbr* "to turn" rather than *dbr* "to speak" (see Textual Note). This would suggest that she was dismayed at his departure (thus Pope: "My soul sank at his flight"; Murphy: "I swooned when he left"). A change in vocalization yields "because of him," a reading that suits both the sexual double entendre (she is sexually excited because of her lover) and also the dramatic action (she swooned because she discovered that he had gone, or her "soul went forth" in longing after him [so Fox]). His withdrawal kindles her desire, her impetuous, restless seeking after him.

"I sought him but I did not find him" appears in the parallel "story" in 3:2, where it is followed immediately by "the watchmen found me, those who go the rounds of the city" (3:3). In the present passage these two statements are separated by another, "I called him but he did not answer me." LXX has this clause in the earlier story as well (see Textual Note on 3:1), but it is more suited to the context here. Here she calls to him because he has just left and may still be within the range of her voice; in 3:1–3 there was less reason to call, since she sought him on her own initiative and there was no indication that he was close by.

[5:7] In the previous verse the woman said that she sought her lover but did not find him; here she relates that the watchmen found *her*. The transition is somewhat abrupt, since she does not say that she went out in the city streets looking for her lover, as she did in the parallel account in 3:1–5. In her earlier account, she related what she said to the guards ("My soul's beloved—have you seen him?"), but of their reaction she had nothing to say. Here she does not speak to them, and they behave surprisingly. The verb *nkh* can mean either to strike or to beat (cf., e.g., Num 22:23, 25; Job 16:10; Prov 19:25; Exod 5:14, 16; Jer 20:2; 37:15), and *pṣ‘* can mean to bruise, wound, or injure. Does she say that they struck her, perhaps only once, which resulted in bruising, or that they beat her, seriously wounding her? Striking someone can result in serious injury, and often death (Exod 21:12, 18–20; 22:2 [1 H]; Deut 25:2–3, 11; cf. Prov 23:13). The combination of striking and wounding appears also in 1 Kgs 20:37, where a prophet has a man strike him so that he can use a bandage to disguise himself as a wounded soldier in order to prevent the king from recognizing him, but here, too, it is not clear whether he was struck with a single blow or repeatedly. Our verse is ambiguous regarding the severity of the watchmen's attack, but not regarding their aggressive behavior, which includes taking the woman's wrap from her. The term used here, *rĕdîd*, occurs elsewhere only in Isa 3:23, in a list of finery worn by Jerusalem women, but exactly what type of garment it is is not clear. Perhaps it designates a veil or light cloak. LXX renders *theristron*, a light summer garment or veil, here and in the Isaiah passage, a term it also uses for *ṣā‘îp*, "veil," in Gen 24:65 and 38:14, 19. For men to strip off part of a woman's clothing, even if it is not an essential piece of clothing, is a contemptuous act of exposure.

Are we to imagine the woman as naked or half-naked (Fox) except for this garment, since in v. 3 she indicates she has undressed for bed? It depends, of course, on how we understand v. 3. There she used her concern about her state of undress as a pretense not to open to her lover; here in v. 7 she is stripped of her wrap. If there is an element of voyeurism here, then there is in v. 3 as well, though here there is the added element of unwanted exposure.

The argument that the watchmen abuse the woman because they take her to be a harlot is an explanation often put forward, but not demonstrated, by commentators. Keel, in fact, thinks this scene "proceeds much more realistically" than the parallel in 3:1–5, and cites in support the following Middle Assyrian law (twelfth century BCE): "A prostitute dare not veil herself; her head remains uncovered. Anyone seeing a veiled prostitute should arrest her, gather witnesses, and bring her to the entrance of the palace. Her jewelry may not be taken, but the one who arrests her receives her clothing. She should be given 50 blows with a club and have asphalt poured over her head" (195; see also

"The Middle Assyrian Laws," trans. Theophile J. Meek, *ANET*, 183, No. 40). Surely the sudden and violent behavior of the watchmen here in v. 7 is less realistic than in 3:1–5, where no response is reported. In any case it is equally the product of poetic license. Like other details in the woman's account in vv. 2–7 (e.g., the woman sleeps in a room facing the street, a woman goes out in the streets at night seeking her lover), the watchmen's behavior serves as a reminder that we are in the world of a poem and not the everyday social world of ancient Israel. There is no biblical evidence to indicate that a woman on the street at night would be treated so ruthlessly. The Middle Assyrian laws, in any event, are particularly harsh in their treatment of women. Moreover, even the law cited by Keel calls for witnesses to confirm the woman's behavior or identity as a prostitute before punishment is meted out.

Some favor a psychological interpretation of the event. Krinetzki, who develops an elaborate theory of how the lovers are testing each other (she by not letting him in, and he by leaving the scene), finds the abusive encounter "psychologically necessary" (183). Müller proposes that it is the result of a bad conscience regarding the hidden desires expressed in the woman's dream. Both Pardes (1992: 136–39) and Polaski (1997: 78–79) compare what happens to the woman to an anxiety dream, in which the dreamer's forbidden wishes are punished. The woman, they suggest, has so thoroughly internalized patriarchal standards and judgments that she disciplines herself for her fantasies. The storyteller or dreamer is thus responsible for her abuse. Among the more bizarre readings is the symbolic interpretation offered by Garrett, which includes a psychological dimension. He takes our verse, along with the preceding vv. 2–6, as "a symbolic representation of the woman's loss of virginity"—an event he curiously assumes is necessarily traumatic.

The woman's harsh treatment at the hands of the watchmen is a disturbing event in the poem for which the text offers no justification, and, however one explains it, it intimates that all is not well in the garden of erotic delights (cf. Black 2001). Like the previous encounter with the watchmen and the anger of the brothers in 1:6, it is a blind motif. The woman ends the "story" she is relating to her audience at this point and continues speaking without further attention to it. But like these other discordant notes, it is memorable, and it is much more serious, for it describes physical abuse (in the case of the brothers' anger, their mistreatment of their sister is not so explicitly represented).

Even if the woman seems unaffected by this setback, it is not so easy for modern readers to dismiss it. Moreover, one cannot ignore the fact that it is a woman whom the poet represents as abused by men in a role of authority. Her lover does not undergo suffering for her sake, and this disparity may well reflect the different expectations ancient Israelite society had for men's and women's behavior (see Introduction, "The Song and Conventional Gender Relations," pp. 25–28).

If behaving boldly risks punishment, is the poet here implicitly cautioning women not to conduct themselves so freely? It seems unlikely, since, even if there is a price to pay, the woman is not deterred by the experience and her quest for her lover ends successfully (6:1–3). Desire leads her to throw caution to the winds. Is this a bad thing? Lovers do it all the time. Because in the end it is rewarded, the woman's behavior represents a successful defiance of and a challenge to social restrictions.

Whatever else it may be, the woman's treatment at the hands of the watchmen is certainly a forceful reminder of the perils of love, if not the willingness of love to suffer—or, as Burrus and Moore ask us to consider, its desire to suffer (2003: 41–49). Perhaps demonstrating one's love by undergoing hardship was a culturally recognized experience that the Song represents here poetically. A modern example is the ritual beating of women at a young man's coming-of-age ceremony among the Hamar people of southwest Ethiopia. In a BBC documentary, "The Hamar Trilogy," women were interviewed about this custom, and one explained, quite matter-of-factly, that it shows you love him enough to suffer for him.

The poet may be alluding to literary antecedents or drawing on a familiarity with other ancient Near Eastern cultural traditions, though none of the parallels mentioned by commentators throws much light on the significance of our passage. In a Sumerian poem, an amorous young woman unlocks the door for her betrothed ("our son-in-law") and urges him to come to her, stressing the importance of avoiding the watchmen of the walls:

> There is the (watch on its) round of the wall!
>   When the patrol has passed,
> O our son-in-law, when the patrol has gone to rest,
> seize the twilight by the hand, whatever such
>   there (still) be,
> they have unleashed daylight!
>   Come to our house quickly!
>   (Jacobsen 1987: 90)

The theme of love willing to undergo trials appears in some of the Egyptian love songs. A young woman is willing to brave a beating, with a whole range of rods, for the sake of her love:

> My heart is not yet done with your lovemaking,
>   my (little) wolf cub!
>   Your liquor is (your) lovemaking.
> I <will not> abandon it
>   until blows drive (me) away
>   to spend my days in the marshes,
> (until blows banish me)

> to the land of Syria with sticks and rods,
>> to the land of Nubia with palms,
>>> to the highlands with switches,
> to the lowlands with cudgels.
> I will not listen to their advice
>> to abandon the one I desire.
>>>> (P. Harris 500, Group A,
>>>> No. 4, trans. Fox)

From Egypt a comparable text describes a young man willing to brave danger for love's sake. He throws caution to the wind and crosses a river in spite of the strong currents, not to mention a crocodile, in order to be with his beloved who is on the other side of the river bank.

> (My) sister's love
>> is over there, on the other side.
> The river is about my body.
>> The flood waters are powerful in (their) season,
>>> and a crocodile waits on the sandbank.
> (Yet) I have gone down to the water
>> that I may wade across the flood waters,
>>> my heart brave in the channel.
>>>> (Cairo Love Songs, Group A,
>>>> No. 20D, trans. Fox)

Although the theme is similar, in both these poems the tone is lighter than in our verse, and the ordeals, as they are described, do not seem quite so disquieting.

Some scholars compare the woman's treatment by the watchmen to the ordeals suffered by the goddess in the accounts of the descent of Inanna or Ishtar to the netherworld, for which we have both Sumerian and Akkadian versions. In this epic, seven items of the goddess's dress and ornamentation are removed one by one at each of the seven gates to the underworld. This is a dubious parallel at best. Rather than undergoing tribulation for love's sake, Inanna offers her lover Dumuzi as a substitute in order to save herself (for the text, see Jacobsen 1987: 205–32).

[5:8] Having reached a grim point in her story with the watchmen's abuse, the woman turns suddenly to address her audience. The sudden transition gives the impression that the events the woman has been narrating have just happened. Now her search continues in another mode, as she, with the help of the women of Jerusalem, engages in the process of conjuring up her lover by praising his attributes.

The woman addressed the women in a similar manner in 2:7 and 3:5, placing them under oath not to awaken love before it wishes. Here she seems to be asking for their help, "if *you* find him," though soon enough we discover she does not need it (cf. 3:3–4, where she appealed to the city guards for help but also did not need it). What is so urgent about her request that she places them under oath? They are to tell her lover that she is lovesick, an exquisite malady of which he is the cause and he alone is the cure (cf. 2:5). The urgency is both real, from a lover's perspective, and part of the game she is playing with her audience. After all, they can give him the message only if they find him, and, as it turns out, she has already found him (6:1–3), or, as double entendre in both 5:2–7 and 6:1–3 suggests, she has never really "lost" him. The implication that many people might be roaming the city streets (the man, the woman, the watchmen, the women of Jerusalem) is another fanciful (nonrealistic) feature of this unit. The streets are soon enough left behind, and the finding takes place in the metaphorical garden that represents both the woman and the place where lovemaking brings mutual pleasure.

Appealing to the occasional negative use of *mâ* (whose usual meaning is "what?"), Fox understands this verse differently from most commentators as the woman's request that her friends not tell her lover how she has behaved, about which she is embarrassed. He compares her embarrassment to that of a young woman in an Egyptian love poem who is concerned about her lack of poise and tells her heart, "Don't let people say about me: 'This woman has collapsed out of love'" (P. Chester Beatty I, Group A, No. 34, trans. Fox). If this were the meaning of our verse, we might have more reason to perceive in vv. 2–8 a caution to women not to behave so unconventionally as our protagonist. There is, however, nothing specific in her account to indicate that the woman in the Song is embarrassed about her behavior and not, for instance, proud of it as showing how strong her love is. Nor is this the first time she has acted unpredictably (cf. 3:1–5). Moreover, if she did not want her lover to know about her behavior, she might have said so more directly, rather than speaking simply of being lovesick, which is, after all, a nice state for a lover to be in. In 2:5 she also told the women of Jerusalem of her lovesickness. There the indirection of language left open the possibilities that lovemaking was anticipated and also being enjoyed. This is also the case here, where double entendre in 5:2–7 and 6:1–3 evokes the sexual intimacy that cures but also feeds lovesickness, while the dramatic action in 5:2–7 makes it seem that the lover's absence triggers an attack of overpowering desire.

[5:9–6:3] This dialogue between the woman and the women of Jerusalem seems to take place in the present, creating the impression that we are overhearing it. Their questions and her answers reveal that the characters are not taking the search too seriously. First they ask her what is so special about her lover, and she responds with a metaphoric description of him hardly helpful to anyone trying to pick him out in a crowd. Next they ask her where he is, which suggests that they know that she knows, and her answer reveals that she does indeed know: he has gone down to his garden, where spices abound, to graze and pluck lilies (6:1–3). Repetition lends the women's questions a kind of singsong quality. Each time they ask their question, they address the woman as "most beautiful of women," and then repeat the question with a kind of explanatory embellishment that harks back to her "story" and specifically to her adjuration in v. 8 ("that you place us under oath so," v. 9, picks up her "I place you under oath"; and "that we may seek with you," 6:1, responds to her "if you find my lover"). They help her find her lover by asking a question that prompts her to invoke his presence through praising his physical charms (vv. 9–16). Having conjured him up, she needs no further help in order to find him.

[5:9] On this, the third occasion that the woman places the women of Jerusalem under oath, they answer her (cf. 2:7; 3:5). They play the game of seeking and finding with her; compare the similar use of a messenger as the provocation for a hymn of praise in the Sumerian poem, The Message of Lu-dingir-ra to His Mother, where the densely metaphorical language Lu-dingir-ra uses to describe his mother is supposedly offered to help the messenger recognize her (see Introduction, "Literary Context: Ancient Near Eastern Love Poetry," pp. 55–56, and below, under 5:14–15). The women of Jerusalem ask, in effect, "What is so special about your lover—what does he have that other lovers don't?—that you place us under oath to tell him of your infatuation?" On their epithet for her, "most beautiful of women," see under 1:8.

[5:10–16] Their question is all the provocation she needs for her paean. One could imagine any number of things that make her lover special in her eyes; for example, being an amorous suitor (2:8–14; 5:2) or belonging to her exclusively as she does to him (2:16; 6:3). What she singles out as setting him apart from other men is his body, every bit of which is desirable (v. 16). This is the answer of a lover fascinated by her partner's physical attributes, which she describes metaphorically not so much in terms of things he resembles but rather in terms of what he means to her. Her description moves from the head downward, with thirteen cola devoted to his head and face (cf. his concentration on her face in 4:1–5; 6:4–7) and six to his torso, and two couplets devoted to comprehensive praise (vv. 10, 15cd). The head of gold (v. 11) anticipates the description of his hands and legs as gold (vv. 14–15), and the reference to his mouth at the end of her description (v. 16) looks back to her earlier praise of his lips (v. 13).

The woman's figurative depiction of the various parts of her lover's body is intimate and erotically suggestive, just as his descriptions of her are. If, on the whole, his imagery is more vivid and animated than hers, hers is more relational than his. His statuesque body of precious materials is less an engrossing visual image than a comment on his value to her. His head, hands, and legs do not look like gold in the way that, for instance, wavy hair resembles goats winding down a mountainside (4:1); rather he shares qualities with gold. Like gold he is rare and precious, and dazzling. She describes some of the same features he did in 4:1–7 (eyes, hair, lips, cheeks, mouth), but some of her comparisons are clearly different in emphasis from his. Whereas he says, "your mouth is lovely" (4:3), she says, "his mouth is sweet" (5:16). He exclaims, "all of you (*kullāk*) is beautiful" (4:7); while she proclaims, "all of him (*kullô*) is desirable" (5:16). He concentrates on the outward appearance (lovely, beautiful), she on what he is to her. His mouth is not sweet in itself, and to say that he is desirable means that *she* desires him.

An important difference between the woman's description of the man and his descriptions of her is that she speaks of him as "he," whereas he addresses her as "you." She describes him to the women of Jerusalem, the audience within the poem, rather than addressing him directly (see Introduction, "Speaking Metaphorically about the Female and Male Body," pp. 17–22). Her inventory of parts of his body is not offered in response to the sight of him (as his descriptions of her are) but is motivated by the women's question, "What distinguishes your lover from other lovers?" Its purpose is to construct him and, by describing him part by part, to conjure him up through the evocative power of language. All the bodily descriptions in the Song are poetic acts of conjuring that bring the lovers' bodies into view, for their mutual pleasure within the world of the poem, but ultimately for the pleasure of the poem's audience, our pleasure in the text and in the poetic representation of the body. Here in vv. 10–16 the woman describes her lover's body to her companions, thereby inviting them to look—not directly but through her eyes. Later—if he is the speaker of 6:13 [7:1 H])—he will invite others to look, along with him, at her.

[**5:10**] The adjective *ṣaḥ* is used in Isa 18:4 and Jer 4:11 to describe hot, shimmering air, and in Isa 32:4 of clear (lucid or distinct) speech. The woman describes her lover as *ṣaḥ* and ruddy, a combination found also in Lam 4:7, where healthy bodies are described as whiter (*ṣaḥû*), or brighter, than milk and ruddier than coral. As the combination shows, applied to skin, *ṣaḥ* indicates a radiant or glowing complexion rather than the color white. A glowing, ruddy complexion was a sign of health, youthfulness, and beauty (Ps 104:15; 1 Sam 16:12; 17:42).

The women of Jerusalem asked what distinguishes this man from any other lover, perhaps from any other lover they might encounter in the city streets at night. She replies that he stands out in a crowd. We might say, "he's one in a million"; she says, "he stands out among thousands" (literally, "eminent among ten thousand"). The participle translated here as "he stands out" (*dāgûl*) is related to *degel*, "banner," in 2:4 (see also under 6:4, 10), and is variously rendered as *eklelochismenos* [standing out] (LXX), *electus* (Vg.), "distinguished" (NRSV), "preeminent" (JPS), "outstanding" (NIV). Gordis proposes a connection with Akkadian *dagālu*, "see, look upon," which leads Pope to prefer "conspicuous." "He stands out" captures both the sense of distinguishable from others and visually distinctive or conspicuous. "Ten thousand" or "myriad" designates an exceedingly large number (e.g., Deut 33:2, 17; 1 Sam 18:7; Mic 6:7; Pss 3:6 [7 H]; 91:7).

[5:11] In 5:2 the man spoke of his head and his locks as dew-drenched; perhaps this leads the woman to begin her description with his head and his locks. Two terms for gold, *ketem* and *paz*, are used to describe his head. Since they appear in apposition, some translate "his head is finest gold" (cf. JPS, NRSV, Pope, Fox), but I have retained the apposition as more poetic. The woman uses a third term for gold, *zāhāb*, to describe his hands in v. 14, so clearly she thinks of him in terms of this most precious of metals. Like gold, the man is rare, precious, and desired for his worth and beauty. Perhaps the woman is continuing the image of his glowing complexion in the previous verse by declaring that, like gold, he is dazzling. Gerleman finds the entire description of the man's body more applicable to the plastic arts (69; cf. also Müller). Pope compares the description here with the image Nebuchadnezzar saw in his dream, with its head of gold, in Dan 2:32, but Dan 2:31–45 describes an image made only of various metals and has a different purpose altogether, to show decreasing value down to feet of clay.

The woman describes the man's hair as *taltallîm*, a *hapax legomenon* whose meaning is uncertain (cf. *HALOT* 1741b). Most interpreters follow LXX and Vg. in understanding it as a part of the palm, either the palm spathe or the date panicles. The word has the same pattern as three other *hapax legomena* that designate plant shoots or branches, *sansinnîm* in 7:8 [9 H], *zalzallîm* (Isa 18:5), and *salsillôt* (Jer 6:9) (Pope). The image may suggest wavy (NRSV) or luxuriant (Pope) locks, or both. Keel thinks that if date panicles are meant, the image points to wild and unruly hair (cf. Krinetzki); if the palm spathe, which is black on the outside, then the point of the comparison is color (Gerleman). His hair is "black as a raven"; he described her hair as black and wavy in 4:1 (cf. also 7:5 [6 H]). A man's hair is praised in similar terms in this Sumerian poem (Jacobsen 1987: 91):

> O my one fair of locks!
>   Oh my one fair of locks!
> Sweet one, tree well grown!
>   Oh my one fair of locks!
> O my one fair of locks
>   —like a date palm!
> O my one fair of shaggy neck
>   —like the date fibers!

[5:12] In 1:15 and 4:1 the man described the woman's eyes as doves. Here she likens his eyes to doves, using a simile rather than a metaphor. As in most of the metaphoric descriptions of body parts in the Song, the image receives more attention than its referent: the eyes are not by watercourses (though some exegetes think of the tear ducts) but are "like doves by watercourses," "bathing" and "sitting." Doves in pellucid pools, as though bathing in milk, suggest the pupil and iris surrounded by the wet milky whiteness of the eye. Ginsburg thinks specifically of "[t]he deep blue or grey dove, reflecting the lustrous dark hue about its neck when bathing in the limpid brook," and cites an arresting parallel from the Gita-Govinda: "The glances of her eyes played like a pair of water birds of azure plumage that sport near a full-blown lotus pool in the season of dew" (169; also cited in Pope). Goulder imagines eyelids "like a pair of fantails going up and down, and so 'bathing' in the milk of the iris" (45). The clarity and brightness of the eye seems to be implied, perhaps also a liveliness or sparkle in the eyes, continuing the imagery of brightness suggested by the man's glowing complexion in v. 10 and his dazzling appearance in v. 11.

The translation here, which envisions the doves sitting by or upon brimming pools, reflects the understanding of LXX and Vg. (cf. NEB, NJB, JPS, Pope, Fox). KJV and NRSV translate "fitly set" and NIV "mounted like jewels," based on the use of *ml'* with reference to the setting or inlay of precious stones (Exod 25:7; 28:17; 35:9, 27; 39:13; 1 Chr 29:2). "Sitting by brimming pools" applies to doves, whereas "fitly set" would refer to the eyes. Doves bathing in milk as a metaphor for the man's eyes forms a contrast to the raven and its blackness used to describe his hair. Some authorities insert teeth as the referent of "bathed in milk, fitly set" (NAB, Rudolph, Würthwein, Loretz, Murphy, Müller), for which there is no textual support.

[5:13] To the visual images of vv. 10–12, the woman now adds scent. Taste, which becomes explicit in v. 16, is intimated in her description of his lips, which suggests kisses. In 1:13 she likened him to a sachet of myrrh between her breasts. Here she also thinks of him in terms of fragrance; his cheeks are garden beds of spices (on *bōśem*, "spice," see under 4:10–11), and his lips are lilies dripping with flowing myrrh. Earlier it was the woman's hands and fingers that dripped with flowing myrrh (5:5), and in 6:1–3 beds of spices and lilies represent the woman's charms. The shared imagery accentuates the mutuality of the lovers.

The form *mgdlwt*, here translated as a participle, "pouring forth," is read by MT as a noun, "towers." Vocalizing the consonantal text as a participle, whose subject is the spice beds to which the man's cheeks are compared, produces a better parallel between the two couplets in this verse: his cheeks are like spice beds pouring forth perfumes and his lips like lilies dripping flowing myrrh. This reading is preferred by a number of translations and commentators; for example, NRSV ("yielding fragrance"), NIV ("yielding perfume"), Murphy ("putt[ing] forth aromatic blossoms"), Gordis ("exuding perfumes"), Pope ("burgeoning aromatics"). The image is one of abundant and palpable fragrance. If, however, one accepts MT's "towers," the result is a hyperbole that outdoes the previous comparison ("a bed of spices . . . no, towers of perfumes!"), with the intensification expressed in the shift from singular to plural and from the smaller to the larger (Bloch and Bloch). Tower imagery is used of the woman's neck in 4:4 and 7:4 [5 H] and of her breasts in 8:10. As in the previous verse, the point of the comparison in our verse seems to lie in the total impression: his face is as sweet as a tower filled with spices (Fox).

Whichever translation is preferred, the meaning of the verse is not greatly affected. Some take the fragrant cheeks as referring to the man's perfumed beard (Rudolph, Ringgren, Würthwein, Pope, Murphy). Ginsburg suggests that his round cheeks with the pullulating beard resemble beds growing aromatic plants (similarly Delitzsch, Krinetzki). Since a beard is not mentioned, it seems more likely that the poet portrays the woman as thinking of his perfumes in general, as in 1:3, and she mentions his cheeks specifically because it is his face she would smell in kissing him.

Kissing is suggested in the description of his lips as lilies dripping liquid myrrh. The sensuous image of flowing myrrh dripping from a lover's body was applied to her hands in v. 5. Elsewhere in the Song lilies are associated with the woman (2:1–2; 2:16; 4:5; 6:2–3; 7:2 [3 H]). The man grazes among or on the lilies, feasting on the pleasures the woman's body offers. Here, in a striking transposition of images, the lips with which he grazes on the lilies are compared to lilies, on which, when she kisses him, she will be grazing. On the identification of the flower, see under 2:1. Here, too, commentators try to mine the image for qualities of the referent, proposing, for example, that because the image is applied to the lips, a red flower is meant (Ginsburg, Rudolph, Gerleman, Ringgren, Würthwein) or that the flower metaphor refers to the form of the lips (Krinetzki 1980) or that both color and shape may be indicated (Murphy). The main point of the comparison is the pleasure his lips provide, for they drip myrrh just as her lips drip honey (Keel, Murphy).

[5:14–15] Having described her lover's face in some metaphoric detail, the woman now moves on to consider his torso and limbs, which she describes in terms of gold, precious stones, and other exotic materials (anticipated in the head of gold, v. 11). This extraordinarily valuable figure is sometimes described as a static or artificial construction, as if she were describing a statue (Gerleman, Ringgren, Loretz, Keel, Murphy, Müller). There are numerous ancient Near Eastern literary precedents that could have influenced our poet; compare, for example, the description of the mother in the Sumerian Message of Ludingir-ra to His Mother:

> Precious carnelian, a topaz from Marḫaši.
> A prize for the king's daughter, full of charm,
> A *nir*-stone seal, an ornament like the sun,
> A bracelet of tin, a ring of *antasura*,
> A shining piece of gold and silver,
> . . . .
> An alabaster statuette set on a lapis pedestal,
> A living rod of ivory, whose limbs are filled with charm.
>   (Cooper 1971:160)

An Egyptian love poem describes a woman in similar terms:

> Long of neck, white of breast,
>   her hair true lapis lazuli.
> Her arms surpass gold,
>   her fingers are like lotuses.
>   (P. Chester Beatty I, Group A,
>   No. 31, trans. Fox)

Further examples are offered by Keel.

As in the previous verses, here in vv. 14–15 the woman is describing her lover's body as she experiences it. Not only is its value inestimable, his body is also hard, solid: his hands are rods of gold, his torso an ivory bar, his legs marble pillars on gold pedestals. There is something sexually suggestive in all these images of hardness—not simply that one or more of these images might be a veiled reference to the man's penis but also the sturdiness of his legs and musculature of his abdomen would be especially evident and appreciated during sexual intercourse.

[5:14] His head was golden (v. 11), his hands are golden (*zāhāb*, the third term for gold in her description). Because the meaning of the metaphoric image is uncertain, it is difficult to know whether this verse describes the man's fingers, his hands, or his arms. They are compared to something seemingly round in shape; the term *gĕlîlîm*, from the root *gll*, "roll," is used of some feature of the doors in Solomon's temple (pivots? folding doors? twice in 1 Kgs 6:34), and it seems to refer to rings or rods on which curtains are fastened in Esth 1:6. Since Hebrew *yād*, which usually means "hand," can include the forearm (Gen 24:30, 47; Ezek 16:11; 23:42; Jer 38:12), some see the referent as the arms, described as rods or cylinders of gold ("rods of gold," NAB; "golden rods," NEB; "rounded gold," NRSV). I take *yād* in its usual sense, "hand," and see the metaphor as applying to the whole hand, with the fingers as rods (so Ginsburg, Delitzsch, Budde, Gerleman).

The rods of gold are "inlaid with Tarshish stones," perhaps a reference to the fingernails (Ginsburg, Delitzsch, Budde; Ginsburg, who identifies the stone as chrysolite, "golden stone," considers its glass luster well chosen to represent the nails). One could imagine a fixation with the hands and fingers, precious for their tender caresses. Some see the image as referring to the jewelry the man wears on his arms (e.g., Keel, Murphy). Rudolph's proposal (following Haupt 1902a: 230) that the reference is to tattoos on the man's arms has little to recommend it. Tarshish is a gemstone named for its place of origin; it is variously identified as beryl, jasper, topaz, chrysolite, and garnet. The identity of ancient Tarshish is debated; the city, mentioned a number of times in the Bible, is best known for its ships and as the place to which Jonah sought to sail in order to escape his prophetic mission.

The word translated "body" (*mēʿîm*) usually designates internal organs (cf. v. 4, where it is used of the woman). Here, as in the description of the molten image in Dan 2:32, it refers to the abdominal region, which is described as a bar of ivory. Used only here in the Bible, the word translated "bar" appears in a similar phrase ʿšt zhb, "bar of gold" in the Copper Scroll from Qumran (3QTr 1:5; 2:4); it also means "bar" in Mishnaic Hebrew. The metaphor of an ivory bar for a part of the torso is thought by commentators to refer to the color of the skin, or smoothness, or worth, but the next part of the verse, which describes the midsection of the man's body as "covered" or "draped" (cf. Gen 38:14), "overlaid," or "adorned" with lapis lazuli, presents a challenge to interpretation. Hebrew *sappîrîm* is not "sapphires," but lapis lazuli, a blue semiprecious stone. Fox maintains that "adorned with lapis lazuli" does not refer directly to the man's body, but it is hard to believe that it has no other function than "to extend the description" of the ivory bar (149). Nor is the assumption that "adorned with lapis lazuli" refers to a statue but not to the man (Gerleman) a satisfactory explanation of the phrase. Delitzsch thinks of the branching blue veins under the skin, and Rudolph of veins or tattoos, but both these proposals are farfetched.

Some see the description of the torso as alluding to the man's genitals (Goulder 6; Murphy 72 n. 305; Weems, Garrett). Gold and lapis lazuli are the stuff of the bodies of gods in numerous ancient Near Eastern texts (Gerleman, Keel). As Keel observes, "These costly, divine materials are used in a discreet way to describe the area of the hips, the belly, and perhaps indirectly the genitals of the beloved" (205). A Sumerian love song offers an interesting parallel:

> My fruiting garden of the apple tree,
>   sweet are your charms!
> Dumuzi-Apsû himself,
>   sweet are your charms!
> O my pure pillar, my pure pillar
>   sweet are your charms!
> Pillar of alabaster set in lapis lazuli
>   sweet are your charms!
>   (Jacobsen 1987: 98)

Some take "adorned with lapis lazuli" in our verse as a reference to clothing (e.g., Ginsburg). In a variant version of the Eden story, Ezek 28:13 lists precious stones that provided a covering for the primordial human. Perhaps a similar tradition lies behind the picture here in the Song. Is the man pictured as naked or clothed? For Delitzsch, the description hovers between the two. This question applies to the portraits of the woman as well (esp. in ch. 7) and raises the question, to what extent are the descriptions of the lovers voyeuristic? Because the woman describes the man's body to others, looking in this instance may seem objectifying. I understand the look here, as elsewhere, as erotic rather than voyeuristic or objectifying. The woman is not represented in the act of looking at the man but rather, in an act of memory and conjury, she describes metaphorically what his body signifies to her (see Introduction, "Erotic Look or Voyeuristic Gaze?" pp. 22–24).

[5:15] His head was golden (v. 11), his hands golden (v. 14), and here one of the terms for gold (*paz*) that described his head is applied to his legs—he is most precious, gold from top to bottom. Hebrew *šôq* is "leg" or "thigh." "Marble [or alabaster] pillars set on gold pedestals" is an image of solidity and exceptional worth. Ben Sira compares the beautiful legs and feet of a woman to gold pillars on silver pedestals (26:18). Here in v. 15, as in the previous verse, commentators have found the language erotically suggestive. Krinetzki, for example, sees "thighs" as a phallic symbol, with the pillars suggesting the erect penis (1981).

The man described his lover's form as lovely (2:14) and her scent like that of Lebanon (4:11). In vv. 10–14 she has been using metaphoric language to describe his appearance, including his fragrance (v. 13), and now in this verse she compares his form to Lebanon. The shared imagery reflects the mutuality of the lovers, and the mention of Lebanon again, in reference to the man, calls to mind all the associations it had for the woman (see under 4:8). As the lofty scented cedars of Lebanon are unrivaled by other trees, so he is distinguished among men, a metaphor that takes us back to the theme with which she began, "he stands out among thousands" (v. 10; cf. also 2:3, where she describes him as standing out from other men like an apple tree among the trees of the forest).

[5:16] Again the woman picks up an image she used earlier in describing her lover. Kissing was alluded to and taste intimated in her description of his lips in v. 13. Here she describes his mouth as sweet. Although this could be a reference to both kisses and speech, kisses come to mind first, since she is describing his physical attributes. Kissing is a diversion of fascination for lovers, so it is not surprising that she would return to his mouth, having completed her survey of his charms from head to foot. In 7:9 [10 H] the man expresses his wish for the woman's mouth (i.e., her kisses) to be like the best wine. Her first words (1:2) were a wish for kisses, not speech, from the mouth of her lover, kisses whose taste and intoxicating effect were likened to wine.

This verse and v. 10, neither of which uses metaphoric language, frame the woman's part-by-part depiction of her lover's body with more general, comprehensive praise. Everything about him is desirable, she affirms, and she sums up her conjuration (cf. his summary statements in 4:1 and 7; 6:9; 7:6 [7 H]) and rounds it off by declaring, "This is my lover," which harks back to her introductory, "My lover is . . ." in v. 10. She also calls him "my friend," her only use of a term of endearment he uses frequently of her (1:9, 15; 2:2, 10, 13; 4:1, 7; 5:2; 6:4). She concludes by turning to her audience, the women of Jerusalem, saying, in effect, "Now I've told you what is so special about my lover," a riposte that invites them back into the dialogue.

[6:1] It sounds as if they are volunteering to help her search for him, responding to "if you find . . ." (v. 8) by offering to seek him with her. But like their

6:4–10 less sensual? emphases on personal authority!

confident woman

does mirror?

on the other hand

7:1–10 very sensual

question in 5:9, the question here is rhetorical. They have, in fact, helped her seek her lover, first by asking a question (5:9) that gave her the opportunity to find him by praise, and now by asking a question that gives her the opportunity to reveal her success.

[6:2–3] Her lover is in his garden, symbolic of the woman herself (cf. 5:1). The woman is both a lily (2:1) and lilies, a garden and gardens. Her lover grazes among the gardens, gathering and grazing upon lilies, double entendres for erotic play. Fox finds the woman's reply "puzzling, because if she knows where her beloved is, whether in a literal or a figurative garden, why does she ask her friends to help her find him?" (143). He concludes that we are meant to infer that she has found him in the meantime, but this is to impose prose narrative conventions upon the poem. (Moreover, she does not exactly ask the women to help her find him, but only to tell him of her lovesickness *if* they find him, a message Pope thinks is forgotten in the course of the description.) As finding-by-praise and as part of a poetic unit (5:2–6:3) that works on two levels at once through the artful use of double entendre, her reply is not puzzling at all. Fox, in fact, senses the force of the conjury: "It is as if the girl's praise brings about his presence: he is absent, she describes him, and he is immediately at her side" (143). "The point of vv. 2–3 is that the lover was never really lost to her, even though he was absent according to the story she related in 5:2–7" (Murphy 173).

At the end of the previous unit (4:1–5:1) the man came to his garden of exotic spices to glut himself on its delicacies. A similar double entendre here in 6:2–3 brings the unit begun in 5:2 to closure. The double entendre here in these verses encourages us to go back to the woman's account in 5:2–7 and read it in terms of double entendre as well.

The women of Jerusalem participate in the woman's act of conjury at her invitation (v. 8), and along with them, the reader is drawn into the search and the finding-by-praise. Now that the "search" is over, the woman excludes her companions and the poem's readers from the garden of intimacy. "I am my lover's and my lover is mine," the refrain of mutual possession (cf. 2:16; 7: 10 [11 H]), expresses the lovers' total absorption in each other and leaves no room for company.

Song of Songs 6:4–7:9 [10 H]
The Man's Second Long Speech

<He>

6:4   You are beautiful, my friend, like Tirzah,
      lovely as Jerusalem,
      as awesome in splendor as they.[a]

5   Turn your eyes away from me,
           for they overwhelm me.
      Your hair is like a flock of goats
           winding down from Gilead.[b]
6   Your teeth, like a flock of ewes[c]
           that have come up from the washing,
      all of them have twins,
           none has lost a lamb.
7   <Like a scarlet thread, your lips,
           and your mouth is lovely.[d]>
      Like a slice of pomegranate, your cheeks
           behind your veil.
8   Sixty queens there are,
           and eighty concubines,
           and countless women—
9   unique is she, my dove, my perfect one,
           unique is she to her mother,
           splendid[e] is she to her who bore her.
      Women saw her and called her fortunate,
           queens and concubines praised her.
10   Who is this that looks down like the dawn,
           beautiful as the moon,
      splendid as the sun,
           as awesome in splendor as they?[f]

<She?>
11   I went down to the nut garden
           to see the blossoms[g] of the valley,
      to see if the vine had budded,
           if the pomegranates had bloomed.
12   I did not know myself,
           carried off amid[h] chariots with a prince.[i]

<He?>
13 [7:1 H]   Come back, come back, O Shulammite!
           Come back, come back, that we may gaze upon you.

<She?>
           How you gaze upon the Shulammite
                as upon[j] the dance of two camps!

<He>
7:1 [2 H]   How lovely are your sandaled feet,
           O noble woman!

The curves[k] of your thighs are like ornaments,[l]
   handwork of an artisan.

2 [3 H]   Your navel[m] is a rounded[n] bowl—
            may it not lack[o] mixed wine![p]
         Your belly, a heap of wheat
            encircled by lilies.

3 [4 H]   Your two breasts, like two fawns,
            twins of a gazelle.

4 [5 H]   Your neck, like an ivory tower.[q]
         Your eyes, pools in Heshbon
            by the gate of Bath-rabbim.[r]
         Your nose, like the tower of Lebanon,
            looking toward Damascus.

also Lebanon for frankincense to lie but this seems to be geography

5 [6 H]   Your head crowns you like Carmel,[s]
            and the hair[t] of your head is like purple;
         a king is held captive by the tresses.[u]

6 [7 H]   How beautiful you are, and how pleasing—
            love with delights!

7 [8 H]   You are tall like a palm tree,
            and your breasts are like clusters.

8 [9 H]   I say,[v] I will climb the palm tree,
            I will take hold of its branches.
         May your breasts be like vine clusters,
            and the scent of your breath[w] like apples!

9 [10 H] And your mouth[x] like the best wine,
            flowing smoothly[y] to lovers,[z]
            gliding over my lips and teeth.[aa]

---

   a. Literally, "awesome as the(se) distinguished sights," i.e., the beautiful cities of Tirzah and Jerusalem. The niphal participle of *dgl*, *nidgālôt*, appears only here and in the identical phrase in v. 10. It is related to *degel* "banner" (2:4) and *dāgûl* "distinguished" (5:10); see the Commentary on 2:4 and 5:10. The connection to *degel* "banner" is reflected in LXX *tetagmenai*, "drawn up in order"; Vg. *castrorum acies ordinata*, "ordered battle line of camps." Syriac "chosen, select thing" seems to reflect the sense in 5:10. Both *dgl* I, "to raise a banner," and *dgl* II, "to look," in the passive could connote being conspicuous or prominent (see *DCH* II, 414b), a combination I have tried to indicate in the word "splendor."

   b. The parallel couplet in 4:1 has "Mount Gilead."

   c. The parallel 4:2 has a variation, "shorn ones," rather than "ewes"; see Textual Note on 4:2.

   d. Reading with LXX, Syriac, Symmachus, Aquila, OL, the Syro-Hexaplar, and the parallel passage (4:3). The omission of this couplet here in 6:7 appears to be a copyist's error.

e. Hebrew *bar*, usually translated "clean" or "pure," is associated with luminosity in v. 10; cf. also Ps 19: 8 [9 H]. I have translated "splendid" here and in v. 10 to show the connection. LXX, Syriac, and Vg. render "chosen, select" here and in v. 10.

f. See Note a.

g. The word here, *ʾēb*, refers to fresh growth or green shoots; it occurs also in Job 8:12 and 4Q251 3:14.

h. Some Hebrew mss supply the preposition *b* or the comparative particle *k*, though this is not necessary with verbs of motion to support the translations "in," "on," "among," or "like" (cf. Ginsburg, Pope).

i. The Hebrew text is too corrupt for any simple suggestion for emendation to solve the problems in this verse. The ancient versions, too, seem to have been struggling to translate a corrupt Vorlage; cf. LXX "my soul did not know; it made me chariots of Aminadab"; Vg. "I did not know; my soul disturbed me because of the chariots of Aminadab." The conjectural translation above is based on what little sense can be made of the various phrases; see the Commentary.

j. Leningradensis, supported by LXX, Syriac, has *k*, "like, as"; some Hebrew mss have *b* ("*in* the dance"). The comparative is preferable, since nothing in the following description suggests that the woman is dancing.

k. Hebrew *ḥammûqê* is a *hapax legomenon* from a root meaning "to turn" (see Textual Note to 5:6).

l. Another *hapax*. It appears to be some item of jewelry: the singular construct appears in Prov 25:12, "a wise reprover is an ornament of gold," and a variant form in Hos 2:13 [15 H], both times in conjunction with *nezem*, "ring."

m. Possibly "vulva"; some commentators connect *šōr* to Arabic *sirr*, meaning "secret, pudenda"; for discussion, see Pope.

n. Hebrew *sahar* (here with the definite article), another *hapax*, may be a genitive of specification or a noun referring to one who fashions objects on a lathe, a "turner", in which case the phrase would mean "the turner's bowl," a well-turned bowl (see Pope, Fox). "Turned" is how LXX (*toreutos*) and Vg. (*tornatilis*) understood it, using the same word they use in 5:14 to describe the man's hands as "turned [wrought, crafted] gold." With most translations and commentators, I take the reference to be to the shape of the bowl; cf. NRSV "rounded bowl"; NAB "round bowl"; NEB "rounded goblet"; NAB "round bowl"; JPS "round goblet"; NJB "a bowl well rounded."

o. The particle *ʾal* is used to express desire that an action will not occur (*DCH* I, 249b); some translations (e.g., NRSV) read "that does not lack."

p. The word here, *mezeg*, is a *hapax*; cf. *mesek*, "mixed wine" in Ps 75:8 [9 H] and the use of the verb *msk*, "mix," applied to wine in Prov 9:2, 5.

q. A line seems to be missing here; the other descriptions are either couplets or triplets.

r. Since the comparisons here and in the next couplet, as well as at the beginning of the next verse, all use place names, this would seem to be a place name as well; cf. LXX *en pylais thygatros pollōn* ("by the gates of the daughter of many"); Vg. *in porta filiae multitudinis* ("in the gate of the daughter of a multitude").

s. The Hebrew reads literally, "Your head, upon you like Carmel."

t. "Locks" would be a more precise translation of *dallâ*, which appears elsewhere only in Isa 38:12, where it refers to threads of warp hanging in a loom. I have used the more general "hair" because "the locks of your head" or "the thrums of your head" (Fox) is not very poetic.

u. A meaning something like "flowing tresses" or "ringlets" (Ginsburg) is indicated by the context. Elsewhere (Gen 30:38, 41; Exod 2:16) the word refers to runnels or troughs through or into which the water runs for watering flocks. LXX has *en paradromais*, "in courses"; Vg. *canalibus*, "in canals." Possibly the flowing tresses resemble rivulets.

v. I.e., "I say to myself" or "I think," in the sense of "I intend to climb."

w. Literally, "nose." The proposed readings "nipple" (Dahood 1976: 109–10) and "vulva" (Pope), based on evidence from Ugaritic, have nothing to commend them. Ugaritic *ap* also means "nose."

x. Literally, "palate." From the context it is obvious that kisses are meant; cf. 1:2.

y. The phrase *lĕmêšārîm* here and *bĕmêšārîm* in Prov 23:31 apparently describe wine that flows (*hlk*) smoothly. On the meaning of *mêšārîm*, see the Commentary under 1:4.

z. Following Gordis in taking *lĕdôdî* as an apocopated plural for *lĕdôdîm*.

aa. Reading with LXX, Aquila, Symmachus, and Syriac (cf. Vg. "his lips and teeth") for MT's "lips of sleepers" (*śpty yšnym*); similarly, NRSV, NAB, NIV. This reading can be obtained by reading the *yod* of *yšnym* as a *waw* (*šnym* is thus a dual, referring to rows of teeth; see *HALOT* 1594a; see Pope for this suggestion of David Noel Freedman). An attractive alternative, "scarlet lips" (Keith N. Schoville, "The Impact of the Ras Shamra Texts on the Study of the Song of Songs" [Ph.D. dissertation, University of Wisconsin–Madison 1969], 99, adopted by Fox) assumes dittography of only one letter, the *yod* of *yšnym*.

The woman has just finished a long speech in which she first tells a story about seeking her lover and then "finds" him by praising his physical charms, one by one, until she has successfully conjured him up. In response, the man now launches into a long speech in which he conjures her up by praising her physical charms in detail, not once but twice. As in his first long speech (4:1–5:1), he is concerned primarily with looking at her, describing what he sees, and telling the world how it affects him (compare, too, his initial, short speeches, which alternate with the woman's: 1:9–11, 15; 2:2).

His two descriptions of the woman's charms (6:4–10 and 6:13–7:9 [7:1–10 H]) frame a short and rather cryptic first-person narrative about a visit to the nut garden (6:11–12). I treat the entire section 6:4–7:9 [10 H] as a second long speech of the man, though the identity of the speaker in three verses in the middle of it is open to question (6:11, 12, 13 [7:1 H]). Although it is possible that 6:11–12 are the man's speech, more likely they belong to the woman (see below). Regardless of who the speaker is, these verses are only a brief interlude before the man resumes his praise of the woman. Part or all of 6:13 [7:1 H] belongs to a voice, or voices, other than the man's, but we have encountered this phenomenon before: in the man's first long speech and in the woman's second long speech, other voices also made themselves heard (4:16; 5:1; 5:9; 6:1). With 7:9 [10 H], a verse whose meaning is uncertain, the man's long speech comes to an end. It may be that the woman breaks in yet again at this point in a burst of enthusiasm, as she did at the end of the man's first long speech (4:16). In any event, she begins speaking again at some length in 7:10 [11 H].

The man begins and ends this speech with descriptive praise. Each time he first describes his lover's body metaphorically, part by part, and then moves on to extol her perfection in other, more varied ways. He finds her captivatingly beautiful, desirable, and awe-inspiring (6:4–5, 10). He has said all this before (4:1–9), but lovers never tire of saying, or of hearing, familiar words of affection and adoration. He also represents others as sharing his estimate of her, imagining a courtly setting in which queens, concubines, and other women praise her (6:8–10). If 6:11–12 ("I went down to the nut garden") belongs to him, on this occasion he adopts the woman's characteristic way of speaking about love (telling stories), just as she had used his primary mode of speaking about love—looking, and describing the lover's body part by part—in 5:10–16. If, however, these verses are assigned to the woman, then she interrupts his speech at this point to tell of a visit she paid to the garden. She is then called back into the poetic present so that the description of her charms can resume (6:13 [7:1 H]).

This time he begins with her feet and moves up to her head (7:1–5 [2–6 H]), completing, as it were, the picture with which he began, in which he described only her head and face (6:4–7). There are subtle differences in the way he talks about looking each time he launches into descriptive praise of his lover's body. The first time was in his first long speech, where he invited her to share his look, to see herself through his eyes ("Look at you! You are beautiful," 4:1). The second time, here at the beginning of his second long speech, he begins simply with his appraisal of what he sees: "You are beautiful" (6:4). He puts words into the mouths of others—queens, concubines, and numerous women—to praise her perfection, as if to offer objective confirmation. The third and final time— if the first part of 6:13 [7:1 H] belongs to him—he includes others in the act of looking: "Come back, come back, that we may gaze upon you." The woman included others, the women of Jerusalem, in her look at him (5:10–16).

The inventories of body parts are presented for the visual pleasure they offer to the onlookers, who include the poem's readers. The degree to which they objectify the loved one is counterbalanced by the extent to which the lover is affected (and, where readers are concerned, whether looking is experienced as erotic, voyeuristic, or something else; see Introduction, "Erotic Look or Voyeuristic Gaze?" pp. 22–24). The man does not just look. He loses himself in the vision of beauty he sees before him when he surveys the body of the woman he loves. He is overwhelmed by her eyes (6:5) and held captive in her tresses (7:5 [6 H])—overcome by the very features he contemplates (see also under 4:1–5:1). The first description (6:4–10) is an inclusio that foregrounds these feelings. It opens and closes with the depiction of the woman as "awesome in splendor as they" (viz., royal cities of the world, v. 4; celestial bodies,

v. 10), expressing his sense of awe at her aspect. When she looks at him, returning the gaze, he is devastated (6:5; cf. 4:9). Her glance alone inspires awe. "Who
is this that looks forth like the dawn?" (6:10) is either the man's rhetorical question or a question he puts in the mouths of the queens, concubines, and other
women he conjures up to praise his beloved in vv. 8–9. Either way, it expresses
his point of view.

The man's metaphoric description of his lover's body in 7:1–5 [2–6 H] gives
way to a metaphor for his desire when he puts himself into the picture (vv. 6–9
[7–10 H]). He ended his first long speech with a metaphor of the woman as a
garden of erotic delicacies on which he proceeded to glut himself (4:12–5:1);
he ends this one with a metaphor of her as a palm tree that he will possess by
climbing and laying hold of its clusters. He plans to climb the palm tree, and he
expects her breasts to be like vine clusters, the scent of her breath like apples,
and her kisses like fine wine. He does not say that he takes possession of the
tree, for she has not yet asked him to do so. Love, in the Song, may be envisioned by and large as something a man takes and a woman gives, but it is
nonetheless mutual, something the man takes only if his lover offers it. This she
does. In 7:10–13 [11–14 H], she responds to his desire with an invitation to
lovemaking expressing her own desire. Just as she invited him to come to her
garden and eat its choice fruits at the end of his first long speech, she invites
him in 7:10–13 to come with her to the vineyards, which, like the garden, symbolize both the woman herself and the place where the lovers take their pleasure of each other.

The woman had a snippet of dialogue within the man's first long speech. She
speaks within this, his second speech, too, if one or more of the following passages belong to her: the short narrative about the nut garden in 6:11–12, or the
exclamation, "How you gaze upon the Shulammite, as upon the dance of two
camps!" in 6:13 [7:1 H], or the obscure lines about wine flowing smoothly in
7:9bc [10bc H]. He, in contrast, does not intervene in her long speeches; rather,
she quotes him *as if* he were speaking to her on the spot, creating the impression of immediacy. Thus it is the case that each lover speaks within the other's
long speech: he, because she quotes him, and she, because she interrupts him
(that is to say, the poet weaves her speech into his). The dialogue format of
speeches that alternate between the woman and the man is fundamental to the
Song's vision of desire as mutual. By including words of the loved one within
the long speeches of each of the lovers, the poet further ensures that genuine
dialogue is always maintained.

[6:4–7] These verses are like 4:1–5. As in 4:1–5 the man begins with sweep-
ing praise ("you are beautiful," 4:1; 6:4). He then singles out particular attributes for comment. In 4:1–5 he speaks about the woman's eyes, hair, teeth, lips
and mouth, cheeks, neck, and breasts; here in 6:4–7 he also mentions her eyes
first, and then repeats the description of her hair, teeth, and cheeks from 4:1–3.

The description in the present verses is shorter. The absence of the couplet about the lips and mouth, which appeared between the teeth and cheeks in 4:3, is probably due to scribal omission. The description stops with the cheeks rather than continuing downwards to include the neck and breasts, as in 4:4–5. The missing description of the neck and breasts could also be due to a copyist's inadvertent omission, though here one can imagine that the poet might have chosen to stop with the face, since the metaphoric description that follows in 6:13–7:5 [7:1–6 H] will offer a further opportunity to consider the woman's body.

In the commentary on 4:1–5 above, I suggested that in order to come to terms with the overpowering feelings the woman arouses in him, the man distances himself from the object of his desire by processing her body part by part and clothing it in images. The important difference between our verses and the similar description of the woman in 4:1–5, at the beginning of the man's first long speech, is that here in 6:4–5 he loses no time in announcing the devastating effect his lover has on him ("awesome in splendor," "your eyes . . . overwhelm me," 6:4–5). In 4:1–9, in contrast, he built up to it; only after the inventory of body parts did he finally confess "you have captured my heart" (4:9). In 4:1 he exclaimed, "you are beautiful"; here he adds "as awesome in splendor as they [Tirzah and Jerusalem]." In 4:1 he compared her eyes to doves. Here in 6:5 the placid image of dovelike eyes gives way to "turn your eyes away from me, for they overwhelm me" (cf. "you have captured my heart with one glance of your eyes," 4:9).

[6:4] The Song overflows with praise of the countryside. Here the beauty of cities, two royal cities, is used as a metaphor for the woman's beauty. Jerusalem was not only Solomon's capital but has always been the biblical city par excellence, "perfect in beauty, joy of all the earth," "beautiful in elevation, joy of all the earth," "perfection of beauty" (Lam 2:15; Pss 48:2 [3 H]; 50:2). Tirzah became the capital of the Northern Kingdom after Solomon's death and the subsequent division of his kingdom, and remained so for about half a century until Omri moved the capital to Samaria. The mention of Tirzah in parallelism with Jerusalem does not provide evidence for dating the Song, or even this part of it, to the period when Tirzah enjoyed a status comparable to Jerusalem's. Tirzah was perhaps somewhat legendary by the time the Song was composed (Fox). As a fabled royal city, it would be worthy of sharing the stage with Jerusalem in a comparison that suggests the woman's splendor and eminence. "The cities which are the highest ornament of his kingdom serve him as the measure of her beauty" (Delitzsch).

In spite of the parallelism with Jerusalem, LXX, the Syriac, and the Vulgate did not recognize Tirzah as a proper name but rather connected it to the root *rṣh*, "to be pleased with," and understood it in the sense of "pleasing" (cf. Pope, who proposes reading *trṣh* as a verb preceded by asseverative *k*, and translates "verily pleasing"). Perhaps the wordplay had a role in the poet's choice of Tirzah for the comparison.

Like these distinguished cities, both conspicuous for their height, the woman is awe-inspiring. Apart from the appearance of the phrase here translated "as awesome in splendor as they" again in 6:10, the adjective "awesome, terrible, awe-inspiring" (ʾāyōm, ʾăyummâ) occurs only in Hab 1:7, where it describes the awe-inspiring and dreaded Chaldeans, who march through the breadth of the earth, overpowering all who stand in their way. The related noun ʾêmâ is more common, and refers both to something terrifying or awesome and to the feeling of awe or dread it arouses; for example, Deut 32:25 (of war), Ps 55:4 [5 H] (death), Job 39:20; 41:14 [41:6 H] (a monster), Prov 20:2 (a king's anger). God excites terror (Exod 15:16; 23:27; Job 13:21; 33:7), and a theophany, in particular (Gen 15:12), can inspire the dread, veneration, and wonder that are mingled in the sense of awe. That seeing the woman is something like a theophany is suggested in v. 10, when the phrase is again applied to her. Goitein (1965) gives a number of examples of words whose meaning shades over from fear or dread ("terrible") to wonder and reverence ("terrific"); this is, indeed, one of the reasons "awesome" in English is so suitable a translation. Pope remarks that "commentators have been sore abashed to explain the collocation of beauty and terror" (560) and explains what he considers their unusual collocation by recourse to mythological texts featuring a goddess who inspires awe, such as Inanna, Ishtar, and Anat. But it is not unusual at all. The terrible beauty of the loved one and the awe it inspires is a topos in love literature (Gerleman, Murphy; and see, especially, Landy 137–79, on the ambivalence and enigma of beauty in the Song).

The woman is awe-inspiring as *nidgālôt*, a term that has been variously rendered to bring out its connection with *degel*, "banner" (see under 2:4), and *dāgûl*, "distinguished" (see under 5:10). Here, for example, is just a sampling of the fascinating variety of proposals for the phrase ʾăyummâ kannidgālôt in our verse: "awe-inspiring as bannered hosts" (Ginsburg), "more regarded, admired than (celestial) phenomena" (Driver 1954: 231 n. 2), "splendid like the brilliant stars" (Goitein 1965), "majestic as the starry heavens" (NEB for v. 10; it omits the phrase in v. 4), "furchterregend wie Himmelsbilder" [alarming as celestial apparitions] (viz., constellations or signs of the Zodiac, Rudolph), "terrible as an army with banners" (KJV, NRSV), "as awe-inspiring as bannered troops" (NAB), "awesome as bannered hosts" (JPS), "formidable as an army" (NJB), "furchterregend wie die Trugbilder" [alarming as mirages] (Gerleman), "awe-inspiring as/like these great sights"(Gordis), "awesome with trophies" (Pope), "as awesome as the most eminent" (Fox), "awe-inspiring as visions" (Murphy). Krauss argues that *nidgālôt* has no other meaning than that of preeminence (1941–42: 136–37), whereas Byington maintains that it refers to either the aurora borealis or comets (1920: 82).

If we take *nidgālôt* as "bannered (ones)" (from *dgl* I, "lift banners," a verb derived from the noun *degel*, "banner," and meaning in the *niphal* "be bannered"), Ginsburg's translation "awe-inspiring as bannered hosts" has the advantage of suggesting the awesomeness of both military hosts and heavenly hosts. Like KJV "terrible as an army with banners," it is a striking and memorable poetic image that calls up a picture of the two royal cities as strongholds, with troops streaming out of them—an image of power that suggests the woman's "conquering" of the man's heart. It is doubtful, however, that this is what the phrase means. The difficulty this translation encounters is that bannered hosts are nowhere indicated in the rest of our verse, whose subject is the beauty of the cities, not their military might (unless we think of cities as fortresses surrounded by walls with towers, as does Keel, who assigns the metaphor here in v. 4 to the same conceptual field as the metaphor comparing the woman's neck to the tower of David in 4:4).

Since the disputed phrase appears here and in v. 10, where the woman is likened to the dawn, the moon, and the sun, a meaning is required that fits both contexts. Something like "starry heavens" or "constellations" works well in v. 10, but not here in v. 4. Other interpretations more readily suggest themselves. One might take *nidgālôt* with the definite article as a superlative and translate "awesome as the most distinguished" (of things in its class; so Fox), though this translation fails to bring out the connection between the awesomeness of the woman and the cities (and in v. 10 between the woman and the dawn, moon, and sun). The reading I have adopted here, following Gordis, takes the participle *nidgālôt*, used as a noun here and in v. 10, as "distinguished sights" (from *dgl* II, "to look") and understands it as a reference to the cities of Tirzah and Jerusalem (cf. Long 1996). In 5:10 the woman described the man as distinguished among ten thousand; now he describes her as awe-inspiring like the sight of these two great cities (one imagines looking at them, in all their splendor, from a distance). This interpretation fits v. 10 as well, where the woman is described as awe-inspiring like the sight of the dawn breaking, the moon, and the sun.

[6:5ab] Lovers convey their feelings without words through their facial expressions and, particularly, with their eyes. The verb here translated "overwhelm" indicates arousal or agitation of some sort (its other occurrences are in Ps 138:3—in the *hiphil*, as here—and Isa 3:5 and Prov 6:3 [*qal*]). This is how LXX and the Syriac appear to have understood it, but the Vulgate is more dramatic with "they [your eyes] make me flee" (which is one response to anxiety). As in 4:9, the woman's gaze has a profoundly unsettling effect on her lover. This is a topos of love poetry, as, for example, in these lines from Chaucer, "Merciless Beaute": "Your eyen two wol sleye me sodenly / I may the beaute of hem nat susteyne." Stephan (1922: 212) cites the following parallels from modern Palestinian love songs:

Your dark eyes slew me while I was singing (i.e. being without care) . . .

O one clad in citron (yellow garments),
O light of my eyes!

The darkness of your eyes have [*sic*] slain (lit. slaughtered) me,
Embrace me a little.

O one clad in purple clothes, it is worth while falling in love with you,
For your eyes are black and sparkle, and have slain (me) indeed.

Waldman (1970: 216–17) argues that this verse and 4:9 refer to sexual arousal. That may be, but something else is involved as well. The man is overwhelmed by the woman's eyes because he recognizes the look of love in them and the same feelings in himself; otherwise he would have no cause to be perturbed. Of course, he does not really want her to look away; just the opposite! This is lovers' talk. On differences in the way the man and the woman talk about love, see Introduction, "Gendered Love-Talk and the Relation of the Sexes," pp. 13–28. He describes himself as awestruck, she as lovesick.

[6:5c–7] See under 4:1–3. Perhaps the man repeats much of what he said earlier about the woman's face because a person's face is so distinctive (hers recalling the same remarkable images) and conveys so much of their identity (cf. the greater amount of attention his face receives in her description of him, 5:10–16). Her face communicates her particularity, her uniqueness to him, about which he will speak in the following verses (8–10).

[6:8–10] To his own praise, the man adds the praise of others. He compared his lover's beauty to that of royal cities (v. 4); now he focuses in on a scene in the royal court. The women of the court are many—queens, royal wives lower in rank than queens, and countless others—and they might be imagined as the most beautiful and pampered of women, but his lover is one in a million, so to speak (cf. 5:10). "None of them can compare to her, and what's more, even *they* recognize her majesty" (Fox 153). The man attributes to them his own feelings about his lover: she is the pinnacle of perfection, worthy of praise and admiration, and she inspires awe. Compared earlier to thrilling earthly sights, the beautiful cities of Tirzah and Jerusalem, at the end of the description in vv. 4–10 the woman appears as awesome as the very hosts of heaven. Similar sentiments are expressed in an Egyptian love poem, which also includes praise of the woman's physical attributes like that in vv. 4–7 (and also 5:10–16, describing the man).

One alone is (my) sister, having no peer:
     more gracious than all other women.
Behold her, like Sothis rising
     at the beginning of a good year:
shining, precious, white of skin,
     lovely of eyes when gazing.
          (P. Chester Beatty I, Group A,
               No. 31, trans. Fox)

The description here in vv. 8–10 is one of the passages that gives the Song its Solomonic ambiance. The man's royal fiction harks back to the woman's royal fictions in 1:2–4, 1:12, and 3:6–11. The poem began *in medias res* with the woman picturing her lover as a king, desired not only by her but by many women, in a courtly setting suggestive of a harem (1:2–4). Here in vv. 8–10 he pictures her in a courtly setting, where other women, including members of the royal harem, sing her praises. She attributes her feelings to other women, and, interestingly, here he uses other women to demonstrate his feelings too.

[6:8] The sixty queens mentioned here recall the sixty warriors who surround Solomon's litter in the woman's royal fiction in 3:6–11. There are eighty concubines, royal wives of lower rank than queens. This is not a harem of Solomonic proportions (700 wives and 300 concubines according to 1 Kgs 11:3), unless one imagines the "countless women" in this verse to be members of the harem (Murphy) rather than, as seems more likely, women of the court (Keel).

[6:9] The Hebrew has "one is she," which brings out more strongly the comparison with sixty, eighty, and then numberless other women; "unique" conveys the sense better in English. The woman's uniqueness among the others is mirrored in the position of this triplet between references to queens and concubines (Krinetzki). She enjoys a special status with her lover (she is his "perfect one," unique), a status he pictures her having since birth in the eyes of her mother. In another royal fiction (3:6–11), the woman spoke of Solomon's mother and her role in crowning him (cf. the mother's role elsewhere in the poem, 1:6; 3:4; 8:1, 2, 5). The adjective used to describe the woman, *bārâ*, is used in Pss 24:4 and 73:1 of a heart that is pure and in Job 11:4 of Job's moral rectitude or perfection. In Ps 19:8 [9 H] the divine commandment is described as *bārâ* (pure, perfect, resplendent?), enlightening the eyes. The word occurs both here in v. 9 and again in the following verse, where it is applied to the sun, apparently in reference to its intense brightness, its dazzling radiance. As a translation that best fits both contexts I have used "splendid," which in English suggests perfection or excellence in addition to meaning "shining, brilliant." The reference here is to the woman's physical perfection, which the man has been praising, not moral perfection or innocence. The brothers of 1:5–6 are absent in this picture of the woman as her mother's favorite, and the sun, instead of tormenting and darkening her, as in 1:5–6, has met its match in one who is just as radiant (Landy 151).

From the poetic parallelism it is obvious that the women here (where the term is *bānôt*) are the same women as in the previous verse, where the term used is ʿǎlāmôt (as in 1:3). Murphy rightly points out that there is no reason to identify these women with the group called "daughters (*bānôt*) of Jerusalem" ("women of Jerusalem" in my translation; see under 1:5–6). Nevertheless, by using *bānôt* rather than repeating ʿǎlāmôt, the poet invites us to consider this possibility (cf. Müller). If the women of Jerusalem (the audience within the poem) are meant, then the man has drawn them into his fantasy, just as the woman included them in hers in 3:11. There she called upon the women of Jerusalem to come and *see* (*rᵓh*) Solomon on the day of his joy; here in v. 9 the women are among those who *see* (*rᵓh*) the woman and pronounce her fortunate (cf. Munro 47).

[6:10] The question "who (or what) is this?" is used for rhetorical effect three times in the Song (see under 3:6 and 8:5). The woman not only surpasses other women (vv. 8–9), she rivals the sun and the moon in their splendor. For this radiant apparition, the poet uses the poetic terms *lĕbānâ*, "the white one," and *ḥammâ*, "the hot one," for the moon and the sun rather than the more usual *yārēaḥ* and *šemeš*. The combination is found elsewhere in Isa 24:23; 30:26. The designation *lĕbānâ* for the moon recalls *lĕbônâ*, "frankincense," especially the mountains of myrrh and frankincense (4:6), and the mountain peaks of fragrant, far-off Lebanon, together with their associations with the lovers (see under 4:8). On the phrase "as awesome in splendor as they," see under v. 4 above. The sight of his lover produces the same awe, wonder, and reverence in the man as the breaking of the dawn, the beauty of the moon, the sun in its radiance. The hyperbole is elegant; it also holds the loved one at a distance (as when the man distances the woman by clothing her in metaphors; see under 4:1–5; Landy 176, 204).

[6:11–12] These verses are a notorious crux. In v. 12 the MT is hopelessly corrupt, and the ancient versions seem to have translated from a text that was already corrupt as well. It is thus impossible to say with any confidence how these verses are related to the preceding and following verses. Is the man speaking or the woman? And what is he, or she, saying? Verse 11 is clear enough: the speaker goes to the countryside to look for signs of spring (cf. 2:11–13; 7:12 [13 H]). Verse 12 seems to say, literally, "I did not know—my soul—it (feminine, or "she") set me—chariots of—my noble people." If we knew what that meant, we might be in a better position to assign the speech to one or the other of the lovers. Commentators offer various conjectures for what v. 12 might mean (for detailed discussion, see Pope) and, while most allow that the speaker's identity is uncertain, assign these verses accordingly to the man (e.g., Rudolph, Krinetzki, Ringgren, Würthwein, Loretz, Exum 1973: 66; Landy 205, Falk [who, however, omits v. 12 from her translation], Müller, Munro 30, Bloch and Bloch, Barbiero 1997: 177) or the woman (e.g., Ginsburg, Delitzsch, Budde, Meek, Gerleman, Fox, Goulder, Murphy, Snaith, Longman, Garrett). Keel assigns v. 11 to the man and v. 12 to the woman.

Is the man the speaker here? He is the one who goes to the garden. The garden symbolically represents the woman, and its fruits are the pleasures her body offers her lover. The garden is also the place where the lovers retreat to take their fill of love (e.g., 4:16–5:1; 6:2–3). When the woman speaks of going to the garden, it is to invite her lover to it, that is, to her. In 7:11–13 [12–14 H], she does not go by herself to see if the vine has budded and the pomegranates blossomed, as does the speaker here in vv. 11–12; she invites her lover to come with her, which suggests, perhaps, that nature is blossoming wherever the lovers are enjoying love. Perhaps here in vv. 11–12 the man is still talking about the effect the woman has on him: he has gone to the garden to see if its fruits are ripe for the plucking (in v. 2 the woman told us about his visit to the garden, now we have his report of it), and he feels himself transformed by the power of love. In the previous verses (8–10) he made the woman the subject of his royal fantasy but did not explicitly put himself in it (as, e.g., the king to whom the harem and the court belonged). Now he does. He feels regal, which is how she thinks of him (1:4, 12; 3:6–11), transformed perhaps into a princely figure with chariots at his disposal (in 1:9 he also fantasized about chariots, comparing her to a prized horse).

If this is the man's speech, then just as the woman in 5:10–16 shared his principal mode of speaking about love (looking and describing what he sees), he shares hers, storytelling, for there is an incipient story here. But there is an important difference. In her well-developed stories (2:8–3:5; 5:2–6:3) she and he are both characters who speak and act. If this is his "story," it would appear to have only one principal character, the speaker. The potential story here is more like 1:5–6, where the woman's remarks about her brothers' anger, which led to her becoming a vineyard keeper, had the makings of a story.

More likely, these verses belong to the woman. Not only is telling stories her characteristic mode of communicating her feelings but also it is she who later uses the same language as the speaker here about going to see if the vine has budded and the pomegranate blossomed (7:12 [13 H]). LXX bears witness to a Vorlage that had "there I will give you my love" at the end of v. 11 as well as in 7:12 (reading "breasts" in both places, which is how it translates *ddym* throughout the Song). If, indeed, LXX was translating a Hebrew text that had "there I will give you my love," the evidence is even stronger for assigning these verses to the woman (it should be noted, however, that Sinaiticus assigns the words about going down to the nut garden to the man and "there I will give you my breasts" to the woman). If this is her speech, she seems to be imaginatively transformed by desire, transported, as some would have it, into a chariot with her princely lover. And if this is the case, she and he are both characters in this inchoate story.

The strongest argument in favor of assigning these verses to the woman, and viewing her as the one who goes down to the nut garden, is that in the next verse she is asked to "return" (6:13 [7:1 H]). Materializing and dematerializing, conjuring up the beloved and letting the beloved disappear—these are games the lovers play (see Introduction, "Conjuring," pp. 6–7). Having been conjured up by her lover (6:4–10), the woman leaves the scene to visit the nut garden, where love blossoms. She now seems to be the elusive lover, much as he was in 5:6, but, as in 5:6–6:3, going down to the garden intimates that, on the erotic level, the lovers are enjoying each other. The man (or possibly the women of Jerusalem) calls her back—"Come back, come back, O Shulammite!"—so that his description of her can continue, a description by means of which he will conjure her up again (7:1–9 [2–10 H]).

[6:11] The speaker visits a garden where nut-bearing trees grow, and vines and pomegranates can be seen. The word for "nut" (ʾĕgôz) occurs only here, though it is used in postbiblical Hebrew for nuts in general and walnuts in particular. Hebrew ʾĕgôz is often identified as the Persian walnut (*Juglans regia*), which may well have been cultivated in ancient Israel (Zohary 64; Moldenke and Moldenke 119). Nuts may have some special significance, either as a love food or sexual symbol, or simply as a luxury food like fruit (as opposed to dietary staples; see Pope's extensive discussion).

[6:12] Something happens to the speaker in the garden, but what? It seems rather fanciful and fantastic, but that may be simply the result of a defective text. I would have no hesitation emending this verse if any Hebrew variant, versional witness, or conjectural emendation made good sense of it. As it is, I have tried to obtain some sense from the words preserved in MT.

"I did not know": there is something the speaker does not know, and since one would expect the clause to be followed by what it is the speaker did not know, perhaps one should take the following word (*nepeš*, "self") as the object. Thus, "I did not know myself," which as Gordis observes means "to lose one's balance, normal composure" (whether through joy or excitement, as here, or through sorrow, as in Job 9:21). Most critics understand the first half of the verse as expressing a state of confusion and astonishment experienced by the speaker. Pope comments that there is general agreement that "I did not know" here means "Before I knew (it)," but I can find no reason to give it this meaning other than the need to make sense of the verse.

The self or desire or appetite or fancy (NRSV) is involved (*nepeš* can mean all these things). Since "I did not know" needs an object and the following verb, "set me," needs a subject, perhaps *nepeš* should be understood as both. Thus, "I did not know [recognize] myself; it [i.e., myself, the aspect of the self that has taken over to the surprise of the speaker] set [put, transported] me . . ." I have translated in the passive, "carried off," in order to keep *nepeš* as the object in the first colon and avoid repeating it in the second (in the sense of "I lost my composure, my fancy carried me off"; cf. the woman's "I slept but my heart was awake," 5:2). One might expect to hear next where the speaker has been carried off, imaginatively, by his or her fancy.

The presence of two terms, "chariots" and "noble," suggests the continuation of the royal fiction of vv. 8–10. Given the poet's fondness for proper names and unusual, exotic terms, it is tempting to read a proper name here, with LXX and Vg. and a number of moderns; however, although the name Amminadab appears some thirteen times in the Bible, it does not seem to carry any special significance, like other names in the Song. It may be that Amminadab was a well-known figure, who happens to be unknown to us. Gerleman suggests a connection with Prince Mehi of the Egyptian love lyrics, who rides in a chariot attended by an escort, but, as Fox astutely remarks, this hypothesis attempts to explain one obscurity by another, since all the two characters have in common is that they ride in chariots. As Pope says, "Prince Mehy is certainly no *deus ex machina* to deliver us from the problems of this verse" (589).

Perhaps the speaker imagines being carried off amid chariots belonging to nobles or princes. The word *nādîb* can function as an adjective or a noun; cf. 7:2, where the woman is called *bat-nādîb*, "daughter of a noble/prince," i.e., a noble woman. Thus *markĕbôt ʿammî-nādîb* might be translated as "chariots of my noble people" (for *ʿammî hannādîb*, with the definite article omitted; so, e.g., Barbiero 1977: 187). But it is also possible, and seems more likely, that the woman is referring to a specific noble or princely man, her lover; compare Fox ("you've placed me in a chariot with a nobleman"); Longman ("my desire had placed me in a chariot with a noble man"). This is the interpretation I have adopted here, reading *mrkbt* without the *mater lectionis*, as the singular, "chariot," and *ʿm* ("with") for *ʿmy* ("my people").

[6:13 (7:1 H)] The woman is asked to "return" or come back, presumably from the nut garden, and probably not simply, as Murphy proposes, to turn around and face the speaker. Some scholars understand the verb to refer to turning or whirling in a dance, but the verb *šwb* does not have this meaning. J. G. Wetzstein's observations of nineteenth-century Syrian marriage customs, which included a sword dance in which the bride was surrounded by women and men in two groups, led some earlier interpreters to conclude that the woman is here performing a sword dance, but this anachronistic thesis is nowadays rejected (and according to Wetzstein a man might also dance the sword dance; "Remarks on the Song" by Wetzstein can be found in an appendix to Delitzsch's commentary). Pope proposes reading *šĕbî* or *šēbî* for MT *šûbî*, and translates rather unpoetically, "leap, leap," in order to produce a dancing Shulammite. The assumption that 6:13–7:6 [7:1–7 H] describes a dance rests primarily on the obscure phrase *k/bimḥōlat hammaḥănāyim* ("like/in the dance of two camps") at the end of v. 13, for nothing in the following description of the woman indicates that she is dancing or that a group of people is watching her dance.

We encounter here the Song's characteristic blurring of past and present: the story of the visit to the nut garden is recounted as a past event, whereas the woman is called back in the present, so that the description of her begun in 6:4 can continue. The fourfold repetition of *šûbî* and the alliteration, *šûbî šûbî haššûlammît šûbî šûbî wĕneḥĕzeh-bāk*, seems to lend urgency to the request.

This verse presents one of the few instances in the Song where the identity of the speaker is not evident. Is it the man or the women of Jerusalem? In 1:5, the woman spoke to the women of Jerusalem about her appearance. One could see the request to look here in 6:13 as harking back to 1:5 and identify the speakers as the women of Jerusalem, for both this verse and 1:5 raise the issue of the gaze by someone other than the woman's lover. Or one might think of the Jerusalem women as continuing their dialogue with the woman from 5:2–6:3. She has told them that her lover is in his garden, feeding on lilies (6:2–3), and he has praised her beauty (6:4–10). One or both of the lovers are in the garden (6:11–12), and now the women, having heard the man's praises of his lover, call her back so they can look too. The woman responds (or the man) with a comment about their desire to look, the meaning of which is open to question (see below), after which the man continues to sing his lover's praises (7:1–9 [2–10 H]).

I take the man to be the speaker here because in the following verses the woman is seen through his eyes. If the woman imaginatively transported herself to the nut garden in the enigmatic 6:11–12, he calls her back because he has not yet finished looking at her and describing what he sees. The desire to describe, to make the body of the loved one present in words, is the need that impels the man's speech forward. It is through describing his lover metaphorically in the following verses that he conjures her up, as he has done before (see Introduction, "Conjuring," pp. 6–7).

The use of the plural, "we," is significant because it includes in the act of looking both the women of Jerusalem, the audience within the poem, and the readers of the poem, of whom the poet is ever mindful. (And even if the couplet were assigned to the women of Jerusalem, "we" would also include the man, who puts himself in the picture in vv. 7–9 [8–10 H].) How, then, should we understand the nature of the looking here? Is the gaze voyeuristic? Is it unwelcome? Does it make the woman feel embarrassed or uncomfortable? Or is the look erotic? The answer depends largely on whether we understand the reply in the second half of our verse as resistance to the gaze, acceptance of it, or ambivalence toward it, as in 1:5–6—and that, in turn, will be influenced by our understanding of the poem as a whole (see Introduction, "Erotic Look or Voyeuristic Gaze?" pp. 22–24, and the discussion of the gaze under 4:1–5 and 5:10–16).

In this verse, the woman is addressed, for the first and only time in the Song, as *šûlammît*. This is not a personal name, since it appears with the definite article, "*the* Shulammite" in the second half of the verse (here in the first half of the verse, the article is a sign of the vocative, "O Shulammite"). Various proposals have been put forward to explain the meaning of the epithet, which appears only here in the Bible. One view understands Shulammite as a gentilic designating a woman from the town of Shunem (interchanges of *l* and *n* are not uncommon in Semitic). The Vaticanus manuscript of LXX reads Soumaneitis, which is one of the forms LXX uses to render Shunammite, whereas the Alexandrinus manuscript has Soulamitis (cf. Vg. Sulamitis), so there seems to be some early confusion of the epithets. Two Shunammite women are mentioned in the Bible: one, known only as "the Shunammite," was rewarded with the birth of a son for her kindness to the prophet Elisha (2 Kgs 4:8–17), and the other, Abishag, was a beautiful young woman who was brought to attend the aging King David and warm his bed, and who later became a pawn in rival claims to David's kingdom (1 Kgs 1:1–4; 2:13–25). The legendary beauty of Abishag gave rise to some far-fetched speculation identifying her as the woman of the Song of Songs. Budde proposes that Abishag's fame as the most beautiful woman in Israel led to "Shunammite" becoming a byword for a beautiful woman.

A connection with *Šulmânîtu*, a name or epithet of the goddess Ishtar (Albright 1963: 5), seems a remote possibility, but perhaps some listeners would have heard in the epithet Shulammite an allusion to Ishtar, renowned for her dazzling beauty. A hymn to Ishtar praises her not only for her beauty but also for her wisdom and manifold powers:

> She is clothed with pleasure and love.
> She is laden with vitality, charm, and voluptuousness.
> Ishtar is clothed with pleasure and love.
> She is laden with vitality, charm, and voluptuousness.
>
> In lips she is sweet; life is in her mouth.
> At her appearance rejoicing becomes full.
> She is glorious; veils are thrown over her head.
> Her figure is beautiful; her eyes are brilliant.
>
> The goddess—with her there is counsel.
> The fate of everything she holds in her hand.
> At her glance there is created joy,
> Power, magnificence, the protecting deity and guardian spirit . . .
>
> Who—to her greatness who can be equal?
> Strong, exalted, splendid are her decrees.
> Ishtar—to her greatness who can be equal?
> Strong, exalted, splendid are her decrees.
> ("Hymn to Ishtar," trans. Ferris J. Stephens, *ANET* 383)

Some exegetes explain Shulammite as an honorific title, the feminine equivalent of the name "Solomon" (Goodspeed 1934; Rowley 1939, Meek, Rudolph, Müller, Longman; see Rowley for a history of this view). If the man in the Song is Solomon or a type of Solomon, then the woman could be his feminine counterpart. Most likely Shulammite is a derivative of *šlm* (from which both the name Solomon and the word *shalom* are derived), meaning "the perfect one" (Fox). The man has praised his lover as unique and perfect earlier in his speech (6:9, using a different word for "perfect," *tammâ*). I have retained the traditional rendering "Shulammite" because of the allusion, through wordplay, to Solomon and also to *šālôm* ("wholeness, intactness, peace"). In 8:10 the woman refers to herself as one who surrenders to her lover like a city suing for *šālôm* (see under 8:8–10). One also thinks of Jerusalem, called Salem in Ps 76:2 [3 H], and thus it has been suggested that the epithet is the equivalent of "Jerusalemite."

In the reply in 6:13cd the speaker could be either the man, the woman, or the women of Jerusalem. If the women are the speakers who ask to gaze upon the woman in v. 13ab, then perhaps the man responds here in v. 13cd by asking why should they want to gaze as well. But how could they resist, since he has been tantalizing them (and the poem's readers) by cataloguing her charms? More likely, in my opinion, v. 13ab is the man's request to see and v. 13cd is the woman's reply.

But what is the meaning of her reply? The reply begins with an interrogative particle, *mâ*, which normally means "what?" but can occasionally have the sense of English "how" (in the sense of either "in what way?" or "how much, to what extent?"/"how [much]!") or "why?" (see *DCH* V, 150b). "What?" does not fit the context here, where the verb in both halves of the verse is *ḥzh b-*, which means "gaze upon" (cf. Isa 47:13; Mic 4:11; Ps 27:4; Job 36:25). Most English translations (e.g., NRSV, NAB, NJB, JPS) render "why?"; for example, NRSV, "Why should you look upon the Shulammite?" Fox understands *mâ* as a negative imperative ("why would you gaze" in the sense of "do not gaze"; similarly Goulder, Snaith) and sees the reply as a reproach, which, in turn, "suggests that the call in v. 1a was less than completely respectful" (158, following the Hebrew versification). Pope translates, "How will you gaze on Shulamite . . . ?" which he takes to mean that looking is improper or dangerous (i.e., how can you dare to/bear to look?). He draws attention to the danger of looking in 4:9 and 6:5, and one might compare 6:4, 10 and 7:5 [6 H] as well—all cases where the man is deeply, even troublingly (delectably so), affected by the woman's terrible beauty.

I have given *mâ* here the same force as it has in the next verse, "How beautiful are your sandaled feet!"; thus: "How you look upon the Shulammite!" (Meek; cf. NEB, "How you love to gaze on the Shulammite . . . !"); cf. also Gen 38:29; Pss 21:1 [2 H]; 119:97; Job 19:28; Jer 2:33, 36; 22:23; Joel 1:18; *DCH* V, 158a.

One reason the reply is hard to understand is that the comparison to *mĕḥōlat hammaḥănāyim* (here translated "the dance of two camps") is difficult to fathom. If we understood its significance, it would be easier to determine whether the speaker demurs at or approves of the request to look. Will those who look be gazing in awe, as they would at something spectacular? Or will they be looking with curiosity or disdain (so Fox, who revocalizes and sees the reference to "a common dancer who roams the camps of the soldiers"; see also Gerleman)?

Commentators are generally agreed that v. 13cd [7:1cd H] is a comparison, though some read "in the dance" instead of "like the dance," with a number of Hebrew manuscripts (e.g., Bloch and Bloch). A few see "the Mahanaim dance" as the answer to the question, "What would you see . . . ?" (Delitzsch, Krinetzki 1980, Rudolph; so also Ginsburg and Gordis, translating "like a dance to double choirs" and "the counter-dance" respectively), but this involves positing different speakers in 13c and 13d, and nowhere else in the Song is a couplet divided between speakers. Since the phrase begins with *k* ("like") or, in some mss, *b* ("in"), it is difficult to see how it could be the answer to the question. It is preferable to take the entire phrase as a simple comparison (Murphy 1987: 117): "How you gaze upon the Shulammite as you would gaze upon the dance . . . !"

Měḥōlâ is a dance, though it may designate a performance that includes singing and musical accompaniment as well as dancing (Ginsburg). LXX and Vg., both of which render "choruses of camps," may have had instrumental and vocal accompaniment in mind (so Pope), for both Greek *choros* and Latin *chorus* can refer to dancers and singers.

Mahanaim is the name of a town in Gilead near the Jabbok River. David camped there when he fled Absalom's coup (2 Sam 17:24–27; 19:32 [33 H]), but Mahanaim is perhaps most famous as the place where Jacob was met by messengers or angels of God. His exclamation, "This is the camp of gods/God!" provides an etiology for the name Mahanaim (Gen 32:2 [3 H]). Some translations read the name here in our verse (e.g., NIV, "as on the dance of Mahanaim"), but as a place name it does not appear to have any significance for the meaning of the verse. As a common noun, the word refers to an encampment, either a military camp or a company of people (see *DCH* V, 222a). The form in MT is a dual, "two camps" or "a double company." Perhaps *maḥănāyîm*, "a double company," indicates a performance with antiphonal music, dancing, and singing, and possibly ritual games as well (Sasson 1973: 158; see also Pope). The mention of "the dance of two camps" does not mean that the woman is dancing. She does not refer to herself as dancing but rather compares the interest of the onlookers to the interest that the dance of two camps would excite (Murphy 1987: 118). The point of the comparison appears to be that beholding the woman is as mesmerizing as watching a spectacle that arrests one's undivided attention. The woman is elsewhere compared to grand, awe-inspiring sights, such as Jerusalem and Tirzah, the sun, moon, and dawn (6:4, 10).

Munro (31) proposes that the military association of "camp" and the custom of women to dance before warriors (Exod 15:20; Judg 11:34; 1 Sam 18:6–7) sheds light upon the meaning of the phrase, which she, following Gerleman and Fox, emends and translates "as upon a dancer before the camps." She assigns v. 13ab to a male chorus and v. 13cd to the man, who tells them that the Shulammite is not to be looked upon like women who dance in public celebrations of military victory, for she is for his eyes alone. This is an interesting suggestion, but even if one were to accept the reading "as upon a dancer before the camps," there is no reason to take the comparison itself as critical of the gaze. Fox interprets the reply as a rebuke of those who would look upon the woman "disdainfully as if she were a common dancer who roams the camps of the soldiers" (158). But why would the woman, who is not dancing (a point on which Fox agrees), be looked upon as if she were a "common dancer" (in any case, did dancers roam the camps of soldiers?)? There are no biblical examples of women singing and dancing to entertain warriors in a camp. Miriam and the women with her, Jephthah's daughter, and the women who meet Saul and David with music, dancing, and singing are all celebrating victory over Israel's enemies. Such celebrations could be a positive point of comparison: one cannot take one's eyes away from such a captivating sight.

Given that the meaning of the reply in v. 13cd [7:1cd H] is so obscure, is it possible to decide whether it conveys a stance that is critical of the desire to look or one that is accepting of it? The response, "Why will you gaze upon the Shulammite?" could be viewed as expressing the speaker's wish to avoid the gaze because it makes her uncomfortable. Keel comments, "These lines indignantly reject the request to make Shulammite the object of voyeurism" (229; similarly, Weems). If the reply is critical of the gaze, then we might view it as a way of making the reader sensitive to the issue of voyeurism and the reader's complicity in it. I consider it unlikely that the poet has here problematized the gaze in this way, because I see the poem's attitude to the reader differently. Throughout this commentary I have drawn attention to the way the reader is invited to enter the lovers' private garden of eroticism yet is excluded from the most intimate moments (see also Introduction, "The Invitation to the Reader," pp. 7–8). The poem invites the reader to look by presenting inventories of the lovers' bodies, and at the same time it holds the reader off by clothing these bodies in metaphors. When it excludes the reader, it does so without manifestly calling the reader's role into question, for example, by means of the indirection of language and double entendre. It enables the reader not only to look at but, equally important, to overhear the lovers without feeling uneasy about it because there is already an audience within the poem whose presence is both acknowledged and appealed to by the lovers, and with whom the lovers interact. The desire to look here in v. 13 [7:1 H]—a desire expressed in the plural, "that we may gaze"—anticipates the pleasure the reader might take in looking at, and thus knowing, the body (see Introduction, "Erotic Look or Voyeuristic Gaze?" pp. 22–24).

Because in the following verses (7:1–5 [2–6 H]) the looking continues and gives rise to an even more intimate description of the woman—through which we, the readers, see her—I favor taking 6:13cd [7:1cd H] as either (1) a coy way of inviting the gaze: "why will/should you look?" or (2) taking pleasure in it ("how you [love to] look!"), or even possibly (3) suggesting that looking will have an effect on the viewer ("how will you look?" so Pope).

[7:1–6 (2–7 H)] The woman returns through the power of the man's description. Starting with her feet and moving up to her head, he conjures her up, a vision of beauty (vv. 1, 6) clothed in metaphors drawn from artisanship, nature, architecture, and topography. The description he began in 6:4 resumes. He describes her body part by part as he did in 6:4–7, where he concentrated on her face. In the present verses, too, the neck and head receive the greatest attention.

Is the gaze at the woman in vv. 1–6 objectifying? It has been variously described as parodic or comic (Brenner 1993a; Whedbee 1988), grotesque (Black 2000a and 2000b), and pornographic (Boer 1999: 53–70). Brenner sees these verses as a parody of the praise song genre; they poke fun at the woman, whose body parts and proportions are far from perfect: "her belly in dance motion is big and quivering, much like an unstable mound of wheat" (248), "her breasts move fast, much like frolicking fawns" (248), her eyes are turbid, her neck is long, her nose is outsize (250). Not only does Brenner assume that the woman is dancing, she also posits a social setting for the description, for which there is no evidence: a bride is dancing while the audience makes fun of her, perhaps, if female authorship can be claimed for the description, in a parody of male sexual desire (257).

One may allow for an ambivalence toward beauty in the Song (see, especially, Landy 137–79, and the discussion under 4:1–5 above) while still recognizing the individual metaphoric descriptions in these verses as illustrating the summation in v. 6, "How beautiful you are and how pleasing/pleasant!" On the difficulty, in general, of interpreting the Song's body imagery, see Introduction, "Speaking Metaphorically about the Female and Male Body," pp. 17–22. With the outburst praising her beauty in v. 6 the speaker introduces himself into the metaphor; he no longer simply describes, he participates: "I say, I will climb the palm tree . . ." (v. 8). The look in these verses is thus erotic (looking that participates in that which is seen) rather than voyeuristic (looking that intrudes upon that which is seen).

The view that the woman is dancing is widespread but finds little support in these verses. If she were, one might expect at least one of the comparisons to be to something in motion—note that Brenner, whom I quoted above, supplies what the text lacks, an *unstable* mound of wheat, *frolicking* fawns—or some such phrase as "how gracefully your arms move as you turn" or "how your hips sway like grasses in the breeze." But in fact this description of the body, part by part, is no different in this respect from the earlier ones (4:1–5; 5:10–16; 6:4–7), except that, whereas they start at the head and move downward, this one starts at the feet and moves up. None of them indicates what the person described is doing or what the perspective is. Sasson wonders if the perspective here might be from a position level with the woman's feet, looking toward her head while she is reclining on a couch (1987: 737–38). No doubt perspective plays a role in many of the descriptions of the lovers' various body parts, but there remains a question whether or not the perspective of the one doing the looking is constant throughout a description (see also under 4:4).

The description of the woman's body in these verses, at the end of the man's second long speech, is more encompassing than the earlier ones because it progresses all the way from her feet up to her head. It is also more intimate because it deals with parts of the body not normally exposed to view, the navel (which some exegetes see as a euphemism for the vulva), the belly, and the breasts (which the man has described before in the same terms, 4:5). Similarly, in his first speech, the man describes his lover more intimately toward the end, when he compares her to a pleasure garden whose abundance he savors (see under 4:12–5:1). The description here in 7:1–6 is, however, more controlled than the earlier ones. Typically the metaphors consist of two clauses each, whereas his other metaphoric descriptions tend to be more detailed. There is less expansiveness here than in the extended metaphor of the woman as a pleasure garden or, for example, in the descriptions of her hair, teeth, and neck in 4:1–4 and 6:4–7. In terms of its look at the whole body and its apparent intimacy, the man's description of the woman's body here resembles her description of his in 5:10–16.

Some exegetes suppose not only that the woman is dancing but also— because the metaphors describe parts of the body not normally exposed—that she is dancing naked or clothed in diaphanous veils (e.g., Delitzsch, Meek, Ringgren, Gordis, Goulder, Falk 189, Bergant). This is to build one unwarranted assumption on another. Whether or not the speaker pictures the beloved as naked or clothed or partially clothed is a question that also arises in the woman's description of the man in 5:10–16. It is a moot question to ask of the poem (which is a text, not a public spectacle), since the body is clothed in metaphors that obscure as much as they promise to reveal (see Introduction, "Speaking Metaphorically about the Female and Male Body," pp. 17–22).

[7:1 (2 H)] The Septuagint and Vulgate translators may have been influenced by the previous verse to assume a dance. This is, at least, suggested by "your steps" in v. 1 for "your feet" (LXX *diabemata sou*, Vg. *gressus tui*). Also in this verse LXX speaks of the *rhythmoi* of the woman's thighs, which could refer to their rhythm, symmetry, proportion, or arrangement. Hebrew *paʿam* is used in the sense of "foot" or "step" (as well as "occurrence" and "time"). There is no reason to take it as "steps" rather than "feet," unless one thinks of dancing, as, for example, Bloch and Bloch and Bergant, who see *paʿam* as a reference not only to the woman's steps in a dance but also to rhythm and sound. "Steps" does not fit the context: the other descriptions in vv. 1–5 are of parts of the woman's body, and "steps" are not a body part.

The woman's feet are not described by means of simile or metaphor, in contrast to the other parts of her body in vv. 1–5. They are beautiful, and the sandals she wears accent their loveliness. Of Judith, who went to seduce and slay

Holofernes, it is said, "Her sandal devastated his eyes, her beauty captured his soul" (Jdt 16:9).

The woman is addressed as "daughter of a prince/noble" (here translated "noble woman"), which harks back to the royal fiction in 6:8–10 and perhaps 6:12, where the same word, *nādîb* ("noble"), appeared. She is regal in her lover's eyes. The royalty motif, suggested already in the resemblance between the name Shulammite and Solomon in the previous verse, is picked up again at the end of the description, where a king is captured in the locks of her hair (v. 5).

Most commentators agree that v. 1c refers to the curves of the thighs or hips, or perhaps the buttocks (Fox, Keel, Bergant), and not to movement ("turns"; see Textual Note), for the comparison with some ornament or type of jewelry made by an artisan suggests a perfection of shape. Compare NAB, NRSV, JPS "your rounded thighs"; NEB, NJB "the curve/s of your thighs."

[7:2 (3 H)] Hebrew *šōr* (here translated "navel") occurs elsewhere in Ezek 16:4, where it refers to the umbilical cord, and Prov 3:8 in parallelism with "your bones," where either its meaning is more inclusive than "navel" (like *mēʿîm* for the internal organs; see under 5:4 and 5:14) or it is a mistake for *šěʾēr*, "flesh." It could refer to the navel, but, because the bowl to which it is compared is said to contain wine, most commentators take it as a euphemism for the vagina. One cannot argue its meaning from its position between the thighs and the belly in the description, for the praise does not proceed in a strict bottom to top order. The eyes, for example, are not lower than the nose, which is mentioned after them. Some suggest that *šōr* is metonymy for vulva because of its proximity to it and because it resembles an aperture (Krinetzki, Longman; on the interchangeability of navel and vulva in ancient Near Eastern iconography, see Keel, figs. 127, 104–7).

Pope objects to identifying *šōr* with the navel on the grounds that "navels are not notable for their capacity to store or dispense moisture," to which Fox replies that the purpose of the clause, "may it never lack mixed wine," is to praise the bowl and not the navel: "The point is not that the bowl is always full, but that a bowl as lovely as this *deserves* never to lack wine" (italics his). Here Fox is on shaky ground, for surely the point of all the comparisons lies in the total image. The woman's hair, for example, is not like a flock of goats, but like a flock of goats winding down Mount Gilead (4:1; 6:5; see the discussion under 4:1–5). Whatever the point of the comparison may be—and trying to match each image in the Song's metaphorical descriptions of the body to a specific referent takes no account of poetic plurisignificance—the metaphor here in our verse includes both the loveliness of the bowl (well turned, well wrought; see Textual Note) and the wish that the bowl will not lack wine. "Wine" in the image may allude to body fluids, hers or his (Müller). Possibly "mixed wine" suggests their mingling (Snaith), though it may refer simply to the customary mixing of wine with spices—with which the woman's body as pleasure garden is replete, 4:13–14.[1] The woman uses a similarly suggestive wine metaphor in 8:2 when she speaks of offering her lover spiced wine, "the nectar of my pomegranate."

Most commentators suppose that the comparison of the belly to a heap of wheat suggests both shape and color. The point is not that the woman has a big belly. As Fox points out, apart from fertility figurines, Mesopotamian and, particularly, Egyptian art typically portrayed women as slender, and Egyptian women were often depicted with a gently curved belly. Some (e.g., Keel, Murphy, Bergant, Garrett; cf. also Krinetzki) think the grain image connotes fertility; however, the point of the descriptions is to illustrate the woman's beauty, and the Song shows no interest in fertility (though it may be interested in means of preventing contraception, if Brenner is correct that many of the plants mentioned in the Song allude to known, available means of birth control [1997: 87–89]). The image is suggestive of the softness of her belly, as compared to the man's belly, which is described as an ivory bar in 5:14 (Bloch and Bloch).

The stumbling block to interpretation is how the phrase "encircled by lilies" relates to the belly. Like "may it not lack mixed wine" in the first part of the verse, it seems unlikely that "encircled by lilies" is merely a stylistic flourish (so, e.g., Gerleman, Snaith). Commentators frequently mention the practice of surrounding piles of wheat with a thorn hedge to protect it; the significance of the image would then be that the heap to which the woman's belly is compared is so precious that only lilies, and certainly not thorns, could serve this purpose. Or perhaps, if it is surrounded by lilies, the heap is not protected, and the lilies signal the access her lover enjoys, for we know from elsewhere in the Song that he browses among the lilies (2:16; 6:2–3). Some propose that the lilies refer to the decoration of a garment or a belt the woman wears. Those seeking a sexually explicit referent identify the lilies as pubic hair. Pope refers to the belts worn below the navel and above the exposed pubic area by terracotta figurines of goddesses (cf. Keel, figs. 127, 104–7). On "lily," see under 2:1.

[7:3 (4 H)] See under 4:5, where the same comparison appears, followed by the phrase "grazing among the lilies."

[7:4 (5 H)] In 4:4 the woman's neck was compared to the tower of David, bedecked with shields. The image here in v. 4 evokes the gracefulness of a long neck (see under 4:4). According to Keel, the point is not length or size but rather pride and self-confidence. The neck's color and smoothness might also be indicated (Rudolph, Murphy), though perhaps the poet is thinking here, as in 4:4, of a neck adorned with a necklace, in this case a necklace made of pieces of

---

1. There are numerous references to mixed wine in the *Iliad* and the *Odyssey*, usually mixed with water, barley, and even goat's cheese; on mixed wine, see Brown 1969: 153–55. Brown (158) points out that *aggos*, a vessel used for mixing wine (*Odyssey* 16.13), is the same word as *ᵓaggān*, used here in v. 2 for "bowl."

ivory (Fox). Ivory was rare and expensive, like so many of the precious items mentioned in the Song, from metals and gemstones to spices and incense. The ivory palaces or houses referred to in Ps 45:8 [9 H], 1 Kgs 22:39, and Amos 3:15, and the beds of ivory in Amos 6:4 were not made of ivory but inlaid with it. In 5:14 the woman uses "ivory" as a metaphor to describe her lover's body, a measure of just how precious he is in her eyes.

The eyes of one's lover are infinitely fascinating, and each of the lovers speaks amorously of the other's eyes when they describe the features that they find so captivating (see under 1:15–17; 4:1, 9; 5:12; 6:5ab). The comparison of eyes to pools may have seemed natural, since the same Hebrew word, *ᶜayin*, means both "eye" and "spring." It is also a topos in love poetry; "your eyes are limpid pools" is a familiar cliché in English. Lovers often feel that they could drown in the eyes of their beloved. Ringgren imagines the eyes deep and dark like pools, and Würthwein thinks of large eyes. In 5:12 the woman metaphorically linked her lover's eyes with brimming pools (though the word for pools is not the same one used here).

As in 4:1–5, where the woman was a landscape upon which goats and sheep gamboled, gazelles fed, and a decorated tower stood erect, here, too, she is identified with the land and what we might assume to be familiar landmarks. The accumulation of place names in this verse lends concreteness to the comparisons (cf. the tents of Qedar and curtains of Solomon in 1:5). Her eyes are not simply pools, even limpid ones; they are pools in Heshbon, and, more specifically, by the gate of Bath-rabbim. The tower of Lebanon, to which her nose is compared, faces Damascus. At Heshbon, east of Jerusalem, archaeologists have uncovered the remains of a large reservoir, dating from the ninth to eighth centuries BCE (Lawrence T. Geraty, "Heshbon," *ABD* III, 182). Isaiah 16:8–10 speaks of the fertile fields and vineyards of Heshbon (cf. also Jer 48:34–35). As the capital of the legendary ancient kingdom of Sihon king of the Amorites (Num 21:26–30), Heshbon may have had an exotic flavor for our poet (Keel; cf. Bloch and Bloch).

Bath-rabbim is best understood as a place name here, like Heshbon, Lebanon, Damascus, and Carmel, though no place named Bath-rabbim is known to us. LXX and Vg. translate the name, "daughter of many," which makes little sense. The name Bath-rabbim, meaning perhaps "daughter of a multitude" or "daughter of chiefs" (see *rb* II, *HALOT* 1172b), recalls the appellation used of the woman in v. 1 [2 H], *bat-nādîb*, "daughter of a noble/prince." Rashbam explained *bat-rabbîm* as "the populous," "because through it [the gate] a multitude of the inhabitants of the town walk in and out" (Ginsburg; cf. Delitzsch, Rudolph). Drawing on this association, Bergant sees the woman's eyes as deep and open for the refreshment of others, just as the pools offered refreshment to those who approached the busy gate.

Lebanon has a range of associations for the Song (see under 4:8 and 15). Both lovers are associated with the enchantment of Lebanon: its distant, awe-inspiring peaks (4:8); its lofty, scented cedars (4:11; 5:15); its fresh, flowing streams (4:15). A nose like the tower of Lebanon is found by some critics to be out of proportion. Pope proposes that the woman's "towering or mountainous nose" (627) can be better understood if the reference is to a goddess. Delitzsch perceives a good deal in the image: her nose, "without being blunt or flat, formed a straight line from the brow downward, without bending to the right or left (Hitzig), a mark of symmetrical beauty combined with awe-inspiring dignity." Murphy is more reserved: "it is doubtless a compliment" (186). Perhaps "tower" designates simply the way a nose protrudes from the face, and the significance of Lebanon has to do with scent (cf. v. 8 [9 H], "and the scent of your nose like apples").

The tower of Lebanon to which the woman's nose is compared faces toward Damascus, a city located on a high plateau. Subjected to Israelite control under David (2 Sam 8:5–6), Damascus played a shifting role in the affairs of Israel and Judah, sometimes as ally, sometimes as foe, until it was incorporated into the Assyrian Empire in the late eighth century BCE. Insofar as the image of a tower facing Damascus conveys the ideas of pride and military preparedness (Keel), it presents a fitting prelude to 8:10, where the woman describes herself in terms of a well-fortified city, suing her lover for peace. Meyers sees military allusions in all the metaphors in our verse. Not only does the military vantage point of a tower suggest a strategic advantage and power, but also, in her view, the pools in Heshbon[2] most likely refer to artificial pools (reservoirs) constructed for military purposes, and the gate of Bath-rabbim to part of the military defenses of the city (214). Meyers presses the images too far, constructing from them an entire defense network in order to buttress her thesis that, by applying military images from the male world to the female, the Song reverses traditional gender imagery.

[7:5 (6 H)] The woman's association with the land continues. Most commentators suppose the comparison to Mount Carmel, which overlooks the Mediterranean Sea at what is today the modern harbor of Haifa, conveys the stately way she holds her head and carries herself. Isaiah 35:2 speaks of the glory of Lebanon and the majesty of Carmel and Sharon; cf. also Jer 46:18; Amos 1:2. The comparison may connote height; in v. 7 the man will compare her stature to a palm tree. Those who find the imagery problematic see the head as out of proportion. As a common noun, *karmel* means "orchard" or "garden [of fruit trees and vines]" (e.g., Isa 10:18; 16:10; 29:17; 32:15–16; Jer 4:26; 48:33). Carmel thus recalls the image of the woman as a pleasure garden of choice fruits (4:12–5:1). The name of the mountain puns on the name for the color crimson, *karmîl*, which resonates with the following comparison of her

---

2. The original 1986 article mistakenly has "Hebron" for "Heshbon"; this is corrected in the reprinted article in Brenner (ed.) 1993: 197–212 [203].

hair to purple. There is no reason to assume her hair is dyed (Pope, Murphy); shiny black hair has a purple sheen. The hair style suggested by the metaphor, long cascading curls (see Textual Note), is well attested in Egyptian paintings (see Fox, figs. 1, 4, 6, 7). The tresses tumble down from her head, which she bears in a stately fashion like Mount Carmel, just as they cascaded down Mount Gilead (4:1; 6:5). Rich and luxurious hair is also evoked by "purple," for purple has long been the color of royalty. Purple cloth was one of the expensive materials used to decorate Solomon's palanquin (3:10). How fitting, then, that a king is held captive by these tresses! Any king would be captivated, but, of course, the man is speaking about himself in particular. She has already captured his heart with a glance of her eyes and a pendant of her necklace (4:9).

[7:6 (7 H)] The praise of the woman's body does not end in v. 5 with the head; it continues in vv. 7–9 with an extended metaphor about her stature, her breasts, the scent of her nose, and her mouth or kisses. Verse 6 is transitional: it both rounds off the praise of the woman's body from foot to head (vv. 1–5) by praising now her whole person, and it introduces a metaphoric description in which the speaker will include himself. He already included himself, by implication, as the "king" in v. 5. The phrase translated "love with delights" is difficult and emendation is an attractive option. It is unlikely that the abstract noun "love" (ʾahăbâ) is an address to the woman as a personification of love, "O Love" (so LXX, Vg., Syriac, and a number of moderns). But there is reason to think that ʾhbh may refer to her. Vocalizing the consonants to read a passive participle (as suggested by Horst in the apparatus to BHS) and following Aquila and the Syriac in reading bat taʿănûgîm, "daughter of delights," for MT battaʿănûgîm, with a number of commentators, yield a translation, "O loved one, delightful woman!" (cf. NRSV, "O loved one, delectable maiden!"). This is an appealing solution; note the similarity between bat-nādîb (daughter of a noble/prince, i.e., "noble woman"), v. 1, Bath-rabbim, v. 4, and bat taʿănûgîm (daughter of delights, i.e., "delightful woman").

On the other hand, "love" could refer to love itself, the emotion, since that is how it is used elsewhere in the poem (2:4, 5, 7; 3:5; 5:8; 8:4, 6, 7), and that is the meaning reflected in the translation I have adopted. The man praises love itself and its many delights (he would, in any event, have his lover's many wonderful qualities in mind). He is bowled over by her beauty and by the pleasures her body presents, which he will describe in the next verses in terms of fruits—date palm clusters, grape clusters, and apples (as well as wine from the fruit of the vine)—to which she responds with an offer of love's abundant choice fruits, meant only for him (7:13 [14 H]).

[7:7–9 (8–10 H)] He is, we might say, besotted. And so, he pictures himself possessing her with a metaphor that begins with her stature and ends with his desire for kisses like the best wine—a desire that matches hers with which the Song began, "let him kiss me with the kisses of his mouth, for your caresses are better than wine." These verses establish a network of associations across the space of the poem, linking desire and delight in lovemaking with wine and its inebriating effect. Compare also, as part of this associative network, the exclamation in the preceding verse and that in 4:10, where, in summing up his first detailed description of his lover's body, the man exclaimed, "How pleasing are your caresses . . . how much better are your caresses than wine!"

In these verses the man's second long speech comes to a close in much the same way as his first long speech (4:1–5:1). In both speeches he begins by metaphorically describing his lover's body and ends with an extended metaphor suggesting lovemaking—a metaphor that calls for his presence in the picture. In his first speech, the woman was a garden of luscious fruits and exotic fragrances, offering erotic pleasures beyond belief (4:12–5:1). Here, at the end of his second speech, she is a palm tree that he will climb and whose panicles, representing her limbs, he will clasp, seeking the clusters (her breasts) and kisses.

He compares her to the stately date palm, which grows erect and can attain a height of 80–100 feet (Moldenke and Moldenke 170; Zohary 61; Jacob and Jacob 807). Like the preceding comparisons in vv. 4 and 5, "this, your height is like a palm tree" could be considered hyperbolic if one thinks literally in terms of size. The date palm (*Phoenix dactylifera*) is one of the oldest cultivated fruit trees of the ancient Near East. It played an important role in the agriculture, culture, and religion of the region as a source of food and drink, building materials, and—because of its many uses—as a religious and cultural symbol, as is amply witnessed in literature and iconography (see Westenholz 1998: 44–50). *Sansinnîm* (here translated "branches") is a *hapax*. It refers to part of the palm, the upper branches or the date panicle (cf. the variant form *salsillôt* in Jer 6:9 in reference to the branches or tendrils of the vine). On the association of the palm tree with important ancient Near Eastern goddesses, see Keel. These associations would probably have been known to our poet: "Portraying the woman in the Song as a palm is one of those theomorphisms that say she is the best that could be imagined or experienced in the ancient Near East" (Keel 243).

Though the man's two long speeches end similarly, the metaphoric evocation of lovemaking in our verses is less developed than in 4:12–5:1, and consequently lacks their lush sensuousness. Nonetheless it expresses intense desire (Budde, in fact, considers it more tempestuous and meaningful than 4:12–5:1). Like 4:12–5:1, the metaphor here appeals strongly to the senses of sight, touch, smell, and taste, and signifies sexual intimacy. The man intends to enjoy the fruits of love, and, through a series of images, he moves closer to the object of his desire. The tree is tall; he must climb it to reach the enticing clusters that represent his lover's breasts. How much better, then, if the breasts could be like grape clusters, which are more accessible. The move from the palm's date clusters (v. 7) to the vine's grape clusters (v. 8) opens a space for introducing the inebriating effect of wine. From her nose—that is, the scent of her breath—the description moves to her mouth and the taste of her intoxicating kisses. The comparison to apples may be for their fresh scent or for their reputation as a love fruit. The woman asks for apples as a treatment for lovesickness in 2:5, and the man is associated with the apple tree in 2:3 and 8:5 (on the identity of the fruit, see under 2:2–5). *Yên haṭṭôb* is a superlative, wine of the best kind, superior in taste and in its effect.

The second and third cola of v. 9 present a number of problems. If one follows MT, this must be the woman speaking, since its vocalization of *dwdy* as *dôdî* ("my love, my lover") is her pet name for the man. Although she broke in at the climactic moment in the man's first speech, and something similar happens here in his second long speech with the next verse (v. 10 [11 H]), it is extremely unlikely that she interrupts him mid-sentence here in v. 9, for nowhere else in the Song is a speaker interrupted in the middle of a couplet or triplet; that is, before the thought is poetically developed. There is the possibility of reading 7:8c–9a [9c–10a H] as a triplet spoken by the man,

> May your breasts be like vine clusters,
>> and the scent of your breath like apples,
>>> and your mouth like the best wine,

and 9bc [10bc H] as a couplet spoken by the woman,

> Flowing smoothly to my lover,
>> gliding over lips and teeth.

But to have the participle "flowing" in her speech and its antecedent "wine" in his would be a grammatical peculiarity nowhere else attested in the Song. Thus I cannot agree with Fox, who proposes that the man's desire and the woman's are in such harmony that they are uttered in a single sentence. The poet has many ways of expressing the mutuality of the lovers, and antiphonal speech is one of them (e.g., 1:15–16; 2:1–3; 4:16), but a sentence spoken by one of the lovers, while it might be echoed or complemented by the other, is not cut short and unexpectedly completed by the other lover.

The text has certainly suffered corruption. "Flowing" and "gliding" describe the wine to which the man compares his lover's mouth, and the versions bear witness to a text that apparently had the wine gliding over the man's lips and teeth. For want of a better solution to the text as we have it, I have followed Gordis in reading "for lovers" instead of "for my lover" (see Textual Note). This has the advantage of producing a triplet that makes sense in the mouth of the man and also nicely rounds off his speech before the woman breaks in with an invitation to lovemaking in v. 10 [11 H].

MT's "gliding over the lips of sleepers," though "a wonderfully evocative image" (Sasson 1987: 738), makes little sense. It is hard to see why sleepers should be mentioned at this point, or how, if the lovers are asleep, they would be either kissing or drinking wine. In contrast, "lips and teeth" are in keeping with the images of breath (Hebrew *ʾap*, "nose") and kissing (Hebrew *ḥēk*, "palate"). I have therefore opted for emending the MT here (see Textual Note).

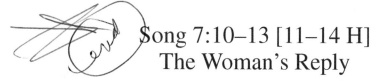

Song 7:10–13 [11–14 H]
The Woman's Reply

<She>

7:10 [11 H] I am my lover's
          and his desire is for me.
11 [12 H] Come, my love, let's go out to the open field,
          spend the night among the henna blossoms.[a]
12 [13 H] Let's go early to the vineyards,
          we'll see if the vine has budded,
       if the grape blossoms have opened,
          if the pomegranates have bloomed.
       There I will give you my love.
13 [14 H] The mandragoras give off fragrance,
          and at our doors are all choice fruits,
       new as well as old.
       I have stored them up for you, my love.

---

a. The word here, *kōper*, is used of henna in 1:14 and 4:13; another word *kōper* (a homonym) is used of a village of the open country in 1 Sam 6:18. A number of modern translations read "villages" here, e.g., NRSV, NAB, NIV, NJB; but cf. NEB ("henna-bushes"), JPS ("henna shrubs"). The setting in vv. 10–13 is outdoors; cf. Pope: "One does not go out to the field in order to lodge in a village."

Once again, the man's long speech gives rise to the woman's invitation to love (see under 4:16). Since 7:10–13 is clearly her reply to his desire for intimacy expressed in vv. 7–9, these verses belong with the preceding. Thus both long speeches of the man (4:1–5:1 and 6:4–7:9) lead to an erotic crescendo, with an invitation to lovemaking alfresco. In this instance, he does not respond to his lover's invitation by eagerly voicing his acceptance, as he did in 5:1, for in 7:8–9 he has already expressed his intention to grasp the opportunity.

I have made vv. 10–13 a separate section for practical purposes; it is a more discrete speech than the woman's invitation in 4:16 and could conceivably be taken on its own. In any case, it has stronger links with the preceding verses than with what follows, for there is a shift in mood and emphasis between 7:13, where the woman invites the man to lovemaking, and 8:1, where she wishes that she could show her love openly. This is the point at which, as the poem moves toward its conclusion, the long, alternating speeches of the lovers yield to a series of shorter speeches, like those with which the poem began (1:2–2:7; see Introduction, "Literary Arrangement and Its Significance," pp. 37–41).

Here in vv. 10–13 the woman acknowledges her lover's desire for her and expresses her own desire by inviting him to enjoy the fruits of love, as she did in 4:16. She adopts the style of 2:10–14, the invitation to enjoy spring that she placed in his mouth, and invites him to go away with her to where blossoms are opening, the air is fragrant, and the choicest fruits are ripe for the plucking. Both here and in 2:10–14, there is the professed intention (let's enjoy nature) and there is the heart of the matter (let's enjoy each other's company); the one enhances the pleasure in the other. Her invitation to love also recalls the visit to the nut garden. She went to the nut garden—if 6:11–12 belongs to her—looking for the same sights of spring she looks for here (vines and pomegranates in bloom) and was called back so that her lover's description of her could continue. Now that he has not only praised her from foot to head but also expressed his intention to possess her, she invites him to the vineyards, where she will give him her love. The love she offers is physical love (*dōday*), and, while it is abundantly clear in the poem that both lovers initiate lovemaking and that their desire is mutual, her invitation reflects a cultural construction of love as something a woman gives and a man takes (cf., e.g., 2:15; 5:1; 7:8 [9 H]; 8:2).

[7:10 (11 H)] This verse is a variation on 2:16 and 6:3. Here, instead of using the mirror statement, "and he is mine," she speaks of his desire. That his desire is for her is evident from his speeches, where he describes how she affects him. The word for desire, *těšûqâ*, appears only two other times in the Bible, Gen 3:16 and 4:7. In Gen 3:16 the woman is told, "your desire shall be for your husband and he shall rule over you." Whereas Genesis connects the woman's desire to her domination by the man, the Song says desire is mutual. Some would see in the Song a kind of return to paradise. Correspondences between the garden story in Genesis 2–3 and the Song of Songs are explored in detail by Trible (1978) and Landy (183–265).

[7:11–13 (12–14 H)] Henna, pomegranates, and choice fruits all grow in the pleasure garden of 4:13, which is both the woman's body and the place for love-making. Spending the night among the henna blossoms and going to the vineyards recalls 1:13–14, where the woman likened her lover to a sachet of myrrh lying all night between her breasts and a cluster of henna blossoms in vineyards. On pomegranates as a love fruit, see under 4:13. In a decidedly suggestive erotic image in 8:2, the woman speaks of offering her lover "the nectar of my pomegranate."

Mandragoras, or mandrakes (*Mandragora officinarum*), also known as "love apples," are native to the Mediterranean area. Their Hebrew name, *dûdāʾîm*, recalls the word for "caresses," *d(w)dym* in 1:2, 4; 4:10 and 5:1, as well as the term of endearment the woman uses for the man, *dôdî*, "my lover." Perhaps because the root of the plant resembles a human figure and possesses narcotic properties, mandrakes in various cultures were used as aphrodisiacs (see, further, the discussion in Pope, and Keel, figs. 149–51). They were believed to aid conception. Elsewhere in the Bible mandrakes appear in the story of Rachel's offering Leah a night with Jacob in exchange for mandrakes that Leah's son Reuben had found (Gen 30:14–16). The mandrake's large, wrinkled leaves grow in a rosette. In winter it bears small bluish-violet bell-shaped flowers. Its plum-sized yellowish-red fruits ripen in spring and sometimes remain in the field until early summer (Zohary 188–89; Moldenke and Moldenke 137; Jacob and Jacob 812). Here in v. 13, the mandrakes, in giving their fragrance for the lovers' pleasure, mirror and participate in the woman's gift of love.

The phrase translated "at our doors" is literally "at our openings." Some readers have seen here a sexual allusion (cf. *ptḥ*, "open," as a sexual innuendo in 5:2–6; cf. also Müller). Others connect the reference to doors to the house in 8:2 (e.g., Murphy, Gerleman, Keel). This is possible but not necessary. Nature too provides an abode for the lovers, as in 1:17, where "the beams of our house are cedars." The fruits the woman offers are the choice fruits of her garden (4:13, 16). "New as well as old" includes the whole spectrum of delights, known to lovers who appreciate how new the familiar can be.

Song 8:1–14
A Dialogue about Love

<She>

8:1   If only you were like a brother to me,
       who had nursed at my mother's breasts!
    I would find you in the street and kiss you,
       and no one would disdain me.

2   I will lead you, bring you to my mother's house,
       to the chamber of her who conceived me.[a]
    I'll have you drink spiced wine,
       the nectar of my pomegranate.[b]

3   His left hand is under my head,
       and his right hand caresses me.

4   I place you under oath, women of Jerusalem,
      not to rouse or awaken love
      until it wishes.

<Women of Jerusalem>

5   Who is this coming up from the wilderness,
      leaning on her lover?

<She>

      Under the apple tree I awakened you;
        there your mother conceived[c] you,
        there she who bore you[d] conceived.

6   Place me like a seal on your heart,
        like a seal on your arm,
      for love is strong as death,
        jealousy as adamant as Sheol.
      Its flames are flames of fire,
        an almighty flame.

7   Floods cannot quench love,
        nor rivers sweep it away.
      Should a man offer all his wealth[e] for love,
        it would be utterly disdained.

8   We have a little sister
        who has no breasts.
      What shall we do for our sister
        on the day she is spoken for?

9   If she is a wall,
        we will build upon it a silver tier.[f]
      And if she is a door,
        we will panel[g] it in cedar.

10 I am a wall,
        and my breasts are like towers.
      So I have become in his eyes
        like one who brings[h] peace.

<He>

11 Solomon had a vineyard in Baal-hamon;
        he gave the vineyard to keepers.
      For its fruit one would give
        a thousand silver pieces.

12 My own vineyard is before me;
        the thousand for you, Solomon,[i]
        and two hundred for the keepers of its fruit.

13 You who dwell in the gardens,
        companions listen for your voice.
      Let me hear it!

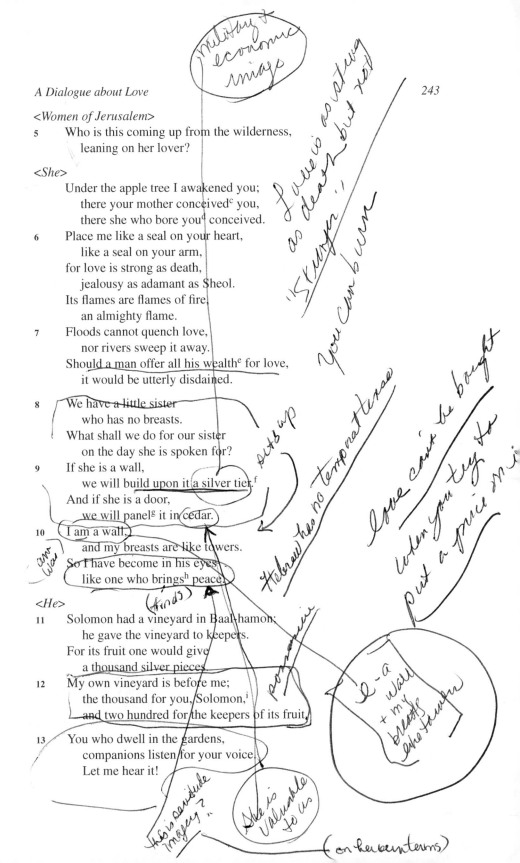

<She>

14   Take flight,[j] my love, and be like a gazelle
       or young deer
       upon the mountains of spices.

a. Reading with LXX and Syriac, against MT "she/you will teach me."

b. Or read plural "pomegranates" in place of MT "my pomegranate," with a number of Hebrew mss, the Targum, LXX, and Vg.

c. There is some debate whether the verb *ḥbl* means "conceive" or "give birth" (the noun *ḥēbel* refers to labor pains). The progression in Ps 7:14 [15 H]—the only other appearance of what *DCH* identifies as *ḥbl* III (*DCH* III, 150), *HALOT* as *ḥbl* IV (*HALOT* 286a)—supports the translation "conceive": "See, he conceives iniquity, is pregnant with trouble, gives birth to falsehood."

d. Perhaps "there she conceived, gave birth to you" or "There she who conceived you gave you birth." The verb *yĕlādatĕkā* in MT is a perfect, "she bore you"; LXX, however, reads a participle; see the Commentary.

e. Literally, "all the wealth of his house."

f. The meaning of the term is debated; see the Commentary. The versions read plural; LXX translates *epalxeis*, denoting fortifications; similarly Vg. *propugnacula*, "bulwarks."

g. Either *ṣwr* I, "to bind, fasten" (JPS) or, more likely, *ṣwr* III, "to fashion, shape."

h. The form *mwṣʾt* could be either the *qal* active participle of *mṣʾ*, "one who finds," or the *hiphil* of *yṣʾ*, "one who brings"; see the Commentary.

i. I have rendered this line rather literally to retain the cryptic style of the verse and the parallelism with "for the keepers"; the sense is "You can keep the thousand, Solomon."

j. "Flee" (so LXX *pheuge*, Vg. *fuge*; cf. NJB, "haste away"), not, as most translations have it, "make haste" (KJV, NRSV), "be swift" (NAB), "come away" (NIV), "hurry" (JPS).

The woman and the man have each had two long speeches, in which the poet portrays them speaking in distinctive ways about their mutual desire and infatuation. In this way the poet presents a vision of love that includes both points of view, a woman's and a man's. Now the Song returns to the mode in which it began, with a series of shorter speeches, where the voices of the woman, the man, and the women of Jerusalem intermingle, and the transitions from one topic to another are more abrupt. Like 1:2–2:7, these verses are a kind of montage, with alternating voices expressing various aspects of love: its determination to express itself (vv. 1–4), its arousal (v. 5cde), its urgency and profundity (vv. 6–7), its playfulness and its worth (vv. 8–12), its endless eager anticipation of gratified desire (vv. 13–14). There is no need for another, third cycle of long speeches in which the woman speaks and then the man, for what would it be but yet another variation on their previous speeches? (Compare the way the second speech of each of the lovers plays variations on their first speech.) Although the poem is coming to an end, significantly it does not end with a sense of closure. Instead, the man's request to hear his lover's voice (v. 13) and her reply, in which she sends him away and allusively calls him to her at the same time (v. 14), take us back to the beginning. Only when the woman seems to send her lover away can the poem begin again with longing and the quest to gratify desire (see Introduction, "Love Forever in Progress," pp. 11–13).

The affirmation that love is strong as death in vv. 6–7 is the climax of the poem and its raison d'être. Now at last we hear expressed, in a few vivid images, what the poet has been showing us all along by means of what I call the Song's controlling poetic strategies: the illusion of immediacy that makes it seem as though the action takes place in the present; conjuring, whereby the lovers materialize and dematerialize in an ongoing game of seeking and finding; the invitation to the reader to enter the lovers' intimate world of eroticism, facilitated by the presence of the women of Jerusalem as an audience within the poem; the blurring of distinctions between anticipation, enjoyment of love's delights, and satisfaction; the lovers as representing all lovers, speaking here in vv. 6–7 on behalf of love itself (see Introduction, "Controlling Poetic Strategies," pp. 3–13). By means of these strategies—particularly the dialogue format, which gives the impression that we are overhearing the lovers as they speak—the poet seeks to make the lovers present through language and thereby to immortalize a vision of mutual desire, sensual pleasure and sensory delight, where love is experienced as astonishing, overwhelming, confident, undeterred, deep, and strong as death. The Song's resistance to closure, the way it circles back upon itself, is a defense against mortality, against the silence of the text that would betoken the death of desiring. It is surely no accident that the Song of Songs opens *in medias res* and concludes without closure. Without beginning and without end, the poem, like the love it celebrates, strives to be everlasting.

The woman's petition in v. 6, "Place me like a seal on your heart, like a seal on your arm," draws attention to the signifying process by which lovers' bodies become textual bodies. As literary creations, the lovers already belong to the realm of the semiotic. Here in v. 6 the woman takes on the status of a seal, a sign of love's permanence. A seal worn on the body, over the heart or on the arm or finger, inscribes the body with meaning. The particle *kî* ("for" in "for love is strong as death") is not a particle of affirmation best left untranslated (Murphy; see also Murphy 1997: 118). Quite the contrary; it explains the reason for wearing the seal and its significance: it makes the body a signifying body—signifying love's refusal to die. Throughout the Song, the body is the object of desire; for example, in the metaphoric descriptions in which the lovers praise each other's physical charms, and in the mutual longing for and seeking of the loved one (as when he comes to court her, or she seeks him in the streets). The body is also the object of the poem's desire—the poem seeks to make present what is absent, to embody the lovers in language. Addressed to its readers throughout time, the Song relies on our act of reading to enable the lovers to conjure each other up again and again, and so live on to give voice to the poet's vision of love.

[8:1–4] Previously (7:11–13 [12–14 H]) the woman was exuberant and eager for lovemaking, as she invited her beloved to a tryst in the countryside. Now in v. 1 the mood suddenly changes, and she wishes she could show her affection openly in the city streets. Wishing, however, readily gives way to what seems to be anticipation or fulfillment or both, for in these verses we encounter again the Song's characteristic blurring of distinctions between wishing for, anticipating, and experiencing erotic satisfaction (see under 2:6, and Introduction, "Blurring Distinctions between Anticipation and Enjoyment of Love," pp. 9–11). A number of commentators and translations maintain an optative (wishing) mode throughout these verses; cf., e.g., NRSV: "O that you were like a brother to me. . . . I would kiss you. . . . I would lead you. . . . I would give you spiced wine. . . . O that his left hand were under my head and that his right hand embraced me!" However, although the woman begins with a wish in v. 1 ("If only you were like a brother to me . . . !"), we cannot be sure where wishing ends and plans for lovemaking, or even sexual union itself, begins, for there is no clear indication that vv. 2 and 3 are also wishes.

The woman wishes her lover were like a brother so that she could kiss him openly in the street without censure. This awareness of social constraints allows the real world to intrude briefly into the world of the lovers. But in v. 2 she tells him of her desire—or intention, since the verb is "I will cause you to drink," not "I will offer you to drink"—to feed him the sweet wine of her pomegranate. One hardly needs to know that in the Song the imagery of choice fruits, including pomegranates, is used of the sexual pleasures the woman's body offers, and that drinking wine is associated with the intoxication of lovemaking, to recognize the sexual innuendo here. "Cause you to drink," *ʾašqĕkā*, puns on "kiss," *ʾeššāqĕkā*, a wordplay implied in 1:2. There is a slippage from imagining kissing, as one might openly kiss a brother, to picturing sexual intimacy that would not take place between sister and brother. Perhaps she says "like a brother," rather than, "if only you were my brother," because it is not really a brother that she wants (LXX and Vg., however, bear witness to a Vorlage that omitted the particle *k*, "like," so perhaps one should not make too much of this subtlety). I have signaled both the shift from the kissing that might take place in the open to the intimacy that will take place in the mother's house, as well as the blurring of anticipation and satisfaction, by translating v. 1 as a wish, v. 2 as future tense, and v. 3 as present.

Finding her lover in the street and bringing him to her mother's house is what the woman does in 3:1–5. When she gets him there, she places the women of Jerusalem under oath not to rouse love, as she does here (3:5; 8:4). The watchmen of 3:3 who patrol the streets (and represent societal constraints; see 5:7) are replaced in our verses by a more general, internalized sense of society's attitudes to amorous behavior. Following each of these episodes, something new is heralded by the question, "What/Who is this coming up from the wilderness?" (3:6; 8:5).

Verses 1–4 also resonate strongly with 2:4–7. In both cases, the countryside as the setting for lovemaking (1:16–17; 7:11–13 [12–14 H]) yields to the house as the place for intimacy. In 2:4, the man brings his beloved to the house of wine; here in 8:2 she brings him to her mother's house. Spiced wine and pomegranate nectar (v. 2), like apples and raisin-cakes in 2:5, feed the lovers' desire. In both contexts she describes his embrace (2:6 and 8:3) and places the women of Jerusalem under oath not to rouse love until it wishes (2:7; 8:4).

[8:1–2] These verses are only incidentally about social reality. To be sure, they reveal that it would not be fitting for a young unmarried woman to display her love in public. But it would also be unacceptable for her to bring her beloved to her mother's house for love play. So while there is a contrast between the street as public and the house as private, there is also a shift from the world in which social expectations influence behavior (v. 1) to the world the lovers inhabit throughout most of the poem, where they are so completely wrapped up in each other that they give little thought to convention (v. 2). The woman might kiss a brother openly and bring him home with her, but this is where the comparison ends. Beginning with the second half of v. 2, she imagines lovemaking with her lover, who is not "like a brother" in this respect, and the erotic imagery continues through v. 4.

[8:1] On fantasizing the lover as a sibling, see under 4:9.

[8:2] I follow the LXX and the Syriac in v. 2b in rendering "to the chamber of her who conceived me," which is also the poetic complement to "to my mother's house" in 3:4. This reading is accepted by a number of commentators (so also NRSV). Omitting the *m* of MT *tlmdny*, one could read simply *tldny*, "who bore me" (Kuhn 1926: 555, followed by Rudolph, Würthwein). MT has a verbal form with a suffix that means either "she [i.e., the mother] will teach me" or "you [the man] will teach me," neither of which makes much sense. A reference to teaching seems out of place (*pace* Sasson 1987: 738, who proposes that "the poet here has chosen a verb which shifts the focus from the world of siblings, wherein brothers and sisters mingle without dishonor, to one in which lovers teach each other the ways of love"). Some understand "she would teach me" as foregrounding the mother's role in instructing her daughter in the art of love (e.g., Bloch and Bloch; cf. Landy, who sees the male lover assimilated to the figure of the mother [100]). Although the mother plays a distinctive role in the Song (1:6; 3:4, 11; 6:9; 8:1, 2, 5), it is hard to see how this interpretation can be supported exegetically (if the reference is to education that took place in the past [Müller, Garrett], it seems an odd point to make). By this stage in the poem the lovers hardly seem to be in need of any lessons in the ways of love.

Moreover, the idea of love play as something to be taught or learned does not feature elsewhere in the poet's vision of love.

The word here translated "nectar" (*ʿāsîs*) ordinarily refers to wine (cf. its other occurrences in Isa 49:26; Joel 1:5; 3:18 [4:18 H]; Amos 9:13), and the parallelism with "spiced wine" indicates that an intoxicating brew is meant. In 4:13, using similarly suggestive imagery, the man describes his lover as a pleasure garden of pomegranates with choice fruits. In this resonant and mellifluous imagery, some exegetes see specific referents; for example, Fox, followed by Snaith, takes "pomegranate" as figurative for "breast" and spiced wine as alluding to kisses. Allusion and suggestiveness can, however, evoke an even wider range of associations, and are more tantalizing than explicitness.

[8:3] See under 2:6.

[8:4] Love, as it is spoken of here, seems to have a will of its own (see under 2:7; 3:5). The oath formula here differs slightly from that in 2:7 and 3:5: there is no mention of the gazelles or does of the open field (though some ancient witnesses supply it), and *mâ*, as a particle of negation, replaces *ʾim*. Some think these differences make the injunction stronger and more urgent (Pope, Longman), but it is questionable whether one should read so much into what may be only a stylistic variation. On the other hand, perhaps there is a subtle difference in this, the last adjuration before the climactic affirmation of love in vv. 6–7. If we understand *mâ* in the sense of "why?" (see *DCH* V, 150b), then "why should you rouse or awaken love before it wishes?" becomes a rhetorical question, whose implied answer is: there is no need to since, when it is ready to be roused, love overwhelms with its force. This is something the woman has herself experienced, that is to say, something the poet shows us through the lovers' words and actions. And the universal lesson she draws from it—when she speaks on behalf of the poet about the strength and tenacity of love in the following verses (vv. 6–7)—is precisely what she has been leading up to in placing the women under this oath.

[8:5ab] The question "Who is this coming up from the wilderness?" recalls 3:6, where the woman watched, and we watched with her, as a palanquin bearing her lover in his Solomonic guise approached from the wilderness. Here the woman and her lover come up from the wilderness together. This question is thus best assigned to the women of Jerusalem, the only other speakers in the Song. As in 3:6, the question dramatically focuses our attention on the scene unfolding before us, but here the scene is not developed. The participle *mitrappeqet*, "leaning" or "reclining," is a *hapax*. Perhaps the lovers are walking together, but to the extent that the question transports us back to the scene in 3:6–11, we might imagine them reclining together in a royal palanquin. By having the women of Jerusalem speak at this point, the poet once again reminds us of the presence of an audience, onlookers who participate in the unfolding of the lovers' relationship, and so encourages the readers' involvement. We not only look, with them, to see the lovers approaching from the steppe, we also listen.

[8:5c–7] What we hear is a paean to the power of love. The woman speaks of love's arousal (v. 5cde) and then makes the Song's only didactic pronouncement (vv. 6–7). Although the poem's readers are its ultimate audience, within the world of the poem this succinct credo on the subject of love is spoken by the woman to her lover, for the poet is too subtle, and too good a poet, to preach or teach, and never addresses the reader directly. The woman does not speak specifically about her love or their love, as she does elsewhere, but about love itself. What she says here about love is of paramount importance, and everything in the poem, indeed the Song's very existence, serves to illustrate it. Love in these verses is virtually personified as a force that contends with cosmic powers. This personalizing of love is also found in the adjuration refrain in 2:7, 3:5, and 8:4, where love is spoken of as having a will of its own. The affirmation of love's power here thus sheds light on the meaning of the oath the woman places upon the women of Jerusalem: the injunction not to awaken love is rhetorical, for why seek to rouse love, since love cannot be denied when it wishes to be roused (see under 2:7)?

[8:5cde] Having just admonished the women of Jerusalem for the third time not to rouse or awaken love before it wishes (v. 4; cf. 2:7; 3:5), the woman speaks to her lover about the time she awakened him. This allusion to the awakening of their love—love that has already, since the beginning of the Song, been pleased to be roused—serves as a prelude to her request for a permanent sign of their love in v. 6. An erotic understanding of the arousal of love to which she refers is encouraged by the fact that it was also in just such a setting that the man's mother enjoyed sexual intimacy (mention is twice made to his conception "there"). The apple tree has erotic associations in the Song (e.g., 2:3, where the woman compares her lover to an apple tree whose shade and fruit she enjoys), and love under the trees is a familiar motif in love poetry. The woman calls for apples to treat her lovesickness (2:5), and the man longs for his lover's apple-scented breath (7:8 [9 H]). On the identity of the tree, see under 2:3.

The woman associates the place where she and he enjoy intimacy with his conception, that is, the prior sexual intimacy that has made her own pleasure possible, and specifically with his mother's sexual pleasure, which must have been something like her own. Like the woman, the man's mother spent time dallying in the countryside. Some exegetes have suggested that the woman may be exercising poetic license by imagining her lover having been born under the apple tree (see Textual Note; Pope, Bloch and Bloch); however, it is difficult to see the relevance of such an assertion (Fox), though birth under a special tree is an ancient mythological motif (Pope).

The Syriac reads the pronominal suffixes in this verse as feminine, so that it is the man who awakens the woman here and the woman's mother who conceived her. Some commentators have followed suit. No strong reason exists to question the MT here, and, as a prelude to her request for a binding sign of love, the address to the beloved here in v. 5cde fits best in the mouth of the woman. The masculine suffixes present a problem for the allegorical interpretation of the Song in which God is represented by the male lover, since the male lover is not only awakened by the woman but is pictured as having been conceived and having a mother, hardly an acceptable portrayal of the deity. The fact that the MT vocalization of the suffixes as masculine was preserved through centuries of allegorical interpretation indicates that it was a well-established tradition (Pope).

[8:6] In the context of sexual union, through which life continues (v. 5), the woman now proceeds to set love against death. There is an urgency in her plea, "place me" or "make me like a seal." Here the Song's erotic imperative—its call to love by means of imperatives and other grammatical forms that give the impression of the lovers' presence at the moment of utterance—reaches its most fervent pitch as the preface to the affirmation of love's power. The term used here, *ḥôtām*, refers to the seal itself, not the impression it makes in the clay. The woman is not asking to be stamped on her lover's heart or arm but to be to him *like* a seal, a mark of his identity. In other words, she longs to be as close to him, as intimately bound up with his identity, as his seal might be. Seals often served as a mark of ownership or identity. Jezebel sends letters in Ahab's name by sealing them with his seal (1 Kgs 21:8), and Judah leaves his seal with Tamar as a pledge, which she later uses to identify him (Gen 38:18). The idea of wearing someone like a seal is expressed in the same words in Hag 2:23, where Zerubbabel is God's chosen one: "I will make you like a seal because I have chosen you" (cf. Jer 22:24).

Seals were of two types: a cylinder, drilled through the center and engraved around its circumference, and a stamp, a flat incised surface. Made of precious or semiprecious metal or stone, and thus highly valued, they could bear a design or inscription or both. Engraving names and inscriptions on seals is mentioned in Exod 28:11, 21, 36; 39:6, 14, 30. Seals were carved in mirror-writing so that the impression they made would appear in positive form (except for votive seals, which frequently were designed to be read from the seals and not from their impressions [Hallo 1985]).

"On your heart" and "on your arm" refer to where seals could be worn. A cylinder seal or a stamp seal could be hung on a necklace, so that it rested on the chest (over the heart), or on a bracelet for the wrist or upper arm. A cylinder seal was most commonly mounted on a pin and hung from a necklace, and a stamp seal could be worn as a signet ring on the finger (Hag 2:23; Jer 22:24). If the seal is on the heart itself, perhaps there is, after all, a suggestion that the woman wants to inscribe herself on the very core of her lover's being. Deuteronomy 11:18 speaks of placing words in or on one's heart and soul, as well as binding them as a sign on the hand; and loyalty, faithfulness, and teachings can be written on the tablet of the heart (Prov 3:3; 7:3, where "write them on the tablet of your heart" parallels "bind them on your fingers"). The Zohar, a medieval Jewish mystical text, takes the idea of inscription to its logical conclusion: "For as the imprint of the seal is to be discerned even after the seal is withdrawn, so I shall cling to you."[1]

Love and death have something in common besides their strength: the dissolution of the self (Landy 1983:123, Müller). Losing oneself in another in the act of love can also seem like a transcending of mortality. Perhaps this is the meaning of these lines from the Gilgamesh epic: "the fine young man, the beautiful girl when making love, together they confront death" (cf. Watson 1997: 386). But above all, love and death are adversaries. The woman affirms that love is strong as death, not that it is stronger (contra Longman). Death is as strong as love, and lovers, flesh-and-blood ones, do not live forever. The Song is acutely aware of this fact, but rather than mourn the transience of love, in an act of resistance to it, the Song seeks to immortalize love by celebrating love in the here and now—not the love of two individuals, for the Song's lovers stand for all lovers, but the enduring vision of desire they embody.

The parallelism of the couplet "for love is strong as death, jealousy as adamant as Sheol" indicates that "love" and "jealousy" are synonymous (love/ strong/death // jealousy/adamant/Sheol). What is implicit in the first line is explicit in the second, which repeats the thought of the first and renders it more specific. That love and death are indeed involved in a struggle is vividly illustrated in the rivalry between their counterparts, *qinʾâ* (jealousy) and Sheol (the netherworld, the abode of the dead), each seeking to possess the same object, the loved one. Jealousy here is an aspect of love, not a negative force in opposition to it (contra Landy 1983: 125–26, who sees jealousy as love in the service of death).

Nevertheless, translations of *qinʾâ* as "passion" or "ardor" are misleading. English "jealousy," though it may seem rather narrow and negative to pair with "love" in what is the Song's crowning proclamation, better expresses the sense of the Hebrew. *Qinʾâ* is a violent emotion, usually aroused when a rival, specific or nebulous, is felt to threaten an exclusive relationship. Frequently destructive in its ferocity, it is often associated with anger (*ʾap*, Deut 29:20 [19 H]; Ezek 5:13; 35:11; Zeph 3:8; *ʾnp*, Ps 79:5; *ḥēmâ,* Num 25:11; Ezek 5:13; 16:38, 42; 23:25; Zech 8:2) and other such strong, negative reactions (e.g., Isa 11:13; 26:11; 42:13; 59:17; Ezek 38:19; Zeph 1:18). Jealousy can drive a man to put his wife through a harrowing ordeal if he suspects her of unfaithfulness (Num 5:14–30); it can drive a man to kill his rival (Prov 6:34). It can prompt God to heap punishment on Israel (e.g., Num 25:11; Deut 29:20 [19 H]; Ezek

---

1. Gershom G. Scholem, *Zohar: The Book of Splendor* (New York: Schocken Books, 1949), 70.

5:13; Ps 79:5). Sometimes jealous fury is directed against the rival (as in Prov 6:34; Ezek 36:5, 6; 38:19; Zech 1:14; 8:2), sometimes against the other partner in the relationship, seen as a possession, as in the case of the suspected wife in Numbers 5, or of Israel, pictured metaphorically as God's unfaithful wife in Ezek 16:38, 42; 23:25. *Ḥēmâ* and *ʾap*, both terms for anger, appear together with *qinʾâ* in Prov 27:4, a passage that, like our verse, pictures jealousy as a force that cannot be withstood: "Wrath is cruel, anger is overwhelming, but who can stand before jealousy?"

In our verse both jealousy and Sheol are described as *qāšâ*, "hard," which is equivalent to "strong" (cf. also Gen 49:7) and has here the sense of hard to withstand or (too) hard to prevail against. A battle that is "hard," for example, leads to the defeat of one of the combatants (Judg 4:24; 2 Sam 2:17); God wields a "hard" and great and strong sword against which the sea monster Leviathan cannot prevail (Isa 27:1); and none can stand against the force of the powerful ("hard") wind sent by God (Isa 27: 8). In 2 Sam 19:43 [44 H] the words of the Judahites are described as "harder" than the words of the Israelites, which is to say that the Israelites could not prevail against them. Similarly, Job complains of God, "Who has hardened himself against him and succeeded?" (Job 9:4).

Like death, Sheol, the netherworld, cannot be withstood or resisted. It is too strong: "What man can live and never see death, save his life from the hand of Sheol?" (Ps 89:48 [49 H]). Death and Sheol are often paired (e.g., Isa 28:15, 18; Pss 6:5 [6 H]; 18:5 [6 H]; 116:3; Prov 5:5; 7:27), and sometimes personified: "For Sheol cannot thank you, Death cannot praise you" (Isa 38:18); "They open their throats wide as Sheol; like Death they never have enough" (Hab 2:5); "O Death, where are your plagues? O Sheol, where is your destruction?" (Hos 13:14); "Like sheep they are appointed for Sheol; Death shall be their shepherd" (Ps 49:14 [15 H]). Here in the Song the poet comes close to personifying them, which makes it seem as if the struggle between death and Sheol, on the one hand, and love and its fiercely possessive counterpart, jealousy, on the other, takes place on a more personal level, as a lover might experience it (thus my translation "adamant," which attributes to Sheol, like love, a will of its own).

Any potential rival to its exclusivity arouses *qinʾâ*. God is described as a jealous god because he brooks no rivals (Exod 20:5; 34:14; Deut 4:24; 5:9; 6:15; the adjective in these cases, *qannāʾ*, is used only with reference to God). Deuteronomy 4:23–24, which enjoins Israel not to make graven images because God is "a devouring fire, a jealous god," uses images similar to those in our verse. What rival might the poet of the Song have in mind here in v. 6? The woman shows no jealousy of other women and finds it only natural that they should adore her lover (1:3–4). Moreover, she speaks here not about any jealousy of her own but about jealous love in general. (There are, as it happens, no biblical examples of a woman exhibiting jealous wrath, only envy [Gen 30:1], which is understandable in a patriarchal society where wives did not have the same exclusive rights as husbands). Nor is it likely that, in our verse, love's rival is anything that might interfere with the happiness of lovers, such as family members (1:6), or city watchmen (5:7), or society in general, with its mores and standards of propriety (Fox). Nothing in the poem has suggested that these things pose a real threat to love. There is no sense of insecurity about love in the Song. What, then, could threaten the powerful bond between lovers that the poet portrays? For the Song of Songs, love's ultimate rival is mortality. In the face of death's ineluctable claim on the loved one, the woman audaciously declares, on behalf of the poet, that love—and specifically love in its violently possessive form, *qin'â* —is just as unyielding, just as adamant in its refusal to let go of the object of its desire, as its rival, death.

The assertion in the last couplet of our verse, "its flames are flames of fire," could refer to the flames of jealousy or of love, but it amounts to much the same thing. Love is the subject of vv. 6–7 (where it appears three times), which suggests that the flames mentioned here are love's flames. Poets often speak of love as a raging fire or inextinguishable flame. Though the precise meaning of *rešep* is uncertain, it appears to designate flashes of lightning, sparks, or flames (Ps 78:48; Job 5:7). A number of the terms in vv. 6–7 recall names of deities and cosmic powers. Like Mot (Death), the Canaanite god Resheph was a chthonic figure. Not a great deal is known about him, though he seems to be related to the Mesopotamian god of the underworld, Nergal, and the Greek and Roman god Apollo. He is mentioned in connection with arrows (lightning?) (cf. Ps 76:3 [4 H], which speaks of *rišpê qāšet,* "fiery arrows"), and pestilence ("pestilence" is one of the meanings of *rešep* in Hebrew as well [Deut 32:24; Hab 3:5]). The connection between plague and divine arrows is widespread; cf. *Iliad* I.9–12, 49–61, where the arrows of Apollo bring pestilence.

Love's flames are further described as *šalhebetyâ.* Commentators are divided over whether this word is an intensive form of the word *šalhebet,* "flame" (Ezek 20:47 [21:3 H]; Job 15:30)—and thus means something like "mighty flame" (Gerleman; see *HALOT* 1504a)—or whether *yh,* the final letters of the word, represent an explicit reference to the name of God, Yhwh— thus, "flame of Yah." In one of the major manuscripts of the Masoretic tradition, the Ben Asher, *yh* forms part of the word, which suggests it was probably not understood as an explicit reference to God. The Ben Naphtali tradition, however, which reads two words, *šlhbt yh,* with a *mappiq* in the *h,* seems to have understood *yh* as the divine name. The Ben Asher writing is supported by LXX and Vg., neither of which attached any particular significance to the affix. LXX appears to have had a Vorlage with one word, which it rendered "its flames" (presumably taking *yh* as a third-person fem. sing. pronominal suffix referring to love); similarly, Vg. *atque flammarum,* "and of flames." Some find this line too short. Given the repetition in the previous line ("its flashes are flashes of fire" or, as translated here, "its flames are flames of fire"), it is possible that the text has suffered haplography and originally read "its flames are the flames of Yah" (so Horst in the apparatus to BHS, Budde, Rudolph, Ringgren, Würthwein; Pope proposes ignoring the word as a gloss). Some exegetes see no theological significance in the choice of this expression, while others find in it a basis for linking human love and divine love. The poet is suggestive at best, as in the other allusions to cosmic powers in vv. 6–7; thus my translation, "almighty flame."

[8:7] Love is a consuming, almighty fire that no waters can quench, not even the mightiest. The phrase here translated "floods," *mayim rabbîm* (literally "mighty waters"), is used of abundant waters, flood waters, mighty rivers, or the raging waters of the sea. It provides yet another cosmic allusion, this time to the waters of chaos that only God can subdue (Pss 24:2; 77:19 [20 H]; 93:4; Isa 51:10; see May 1955; Murphy 1987). Hebrew *nāhār* is a common word for "river," but here in v. 7 one might be reminded of the Canaanite deity Yam, who was also called Prince Nahar (Prince River). This may be another allusion to the primeval chaotic waters, though some take it more specifically as the rivers of the underworld (Pope, Keel; cf. Ezek 31:15; Pss 24:2; 93:3; Hab 3:9). The numerous allusions to chthonic and cosmic powers in vv. 6–7—Mot (Death), Sheol, Resheph, flames of Yah, cosmic waters, and Nahar—lend cosmic proportions to the struggle between love and death.

At the end of this paean to love, society's attitudes again come into play (both 8:1 and our verse mention public scorn or disdain). Verse 7cd shows that the notion money cannot buy love is an ancient one. Whether the second line in this couplet should be translated "it would be scorned" or "he would be scorned" is debated, but the meaning is virtually the same in both cases: either the offer will be scorned or the man will be scorned for making such an offer.

[8:8–14] In the previous verses the poet placed a profound declaration of love in the mouth of the woman. Saying more on the topic of the strength of love would risk allowing the poem to slip into sentimentality—and the poet knows well that showing is better than telling. In vv. 8–12 the woman and man offer further affirmations of love (vv. 10, 12), but the tone becomes lighter.

There is considerable debate over the meaning of the two vignettes in vv. 8–10 and vv. 11–12 and over the identity of the speaker in vv. 8–9 and 11–12 (it is generally agreed that the speaker of v. 10 is the woman). If we take as our cue the formal correspondences between these two vignettes, or similitudes (to use Landy's term for the second [153]), vv. 8–14 can be most readily understood as a dialogue between the lovers in which, first, they each tell a story in which they speak metaphorically about themselves and their beloved (the woman in vv. 8–10 and the man in vv. 11–12). Then, in a passionately serious vein, they express once again their desire for each other: he, by asking to hear her voice (v. 13), and she, by answering in a way that does not allow the dialogue to end, though the poem comes to its close (v. 14). Her speech thus moves from an urgent appeal to him ("Place me like a seal on your heart . . . for love is strong as death," vv. 6–7) to similitude (vv. 8–10), and his from similitude (vv. 11–12) to an urgent appeal to her ("let me hear," v. 13). The fact that they do not address each other as "you" in vv. 8–12 is no obstacle to seeing these verses as dialogue. They are always speaking to each other even when they speak about each other in the third person (cf. "Like a lily among thistles, so is my friend among women. Like an apple tree among the trees of the forest, so is my lover among men," 2:2–3).

As it nears its end, the Song reverts to themes and motifs from the beginning. The sexually suggestive talk of vineyards and vineyard keepers in vv. 11–12 is reminiscent of 1:6, and the man's "my own vineyard is before me" (v. 12) provides a counterpoint to the woman's "my own vineyard I have not kept" (1:6). Solomon, who figures importantly in the man's vignette, was mentioned in 1:5, and the implicit reference to Solomon's harem in vv. 11–12 resonates with 1:2–4, where the setting could be a royal harem. Companions (v. 13) have been mentioned only once before, in 1:7. If the poet has the same companions in mind, they now listen for the voice of the woman, who earlier wished to avoid them. Hers is the voice the man wants to hear. His "Let me hear it!" has the same urgency about it as her "Let him kiss me . . . !" (1:2). His wish to hear her voice is granted in v. 14.

[8:8–12] The two similitudes in vv. 8–10 and vv. 11–12 are formally quite similar. Both begin as a story that seems to be irrelevant: "We have a little sister . . ."; "Solomon had a vineyard . . ." The woman is not the "little sister," as most commentators think, nor is she putting words into her brothers' mouths, as many assume. She is the narrator of this vignette, and the little sister of whom she speaks is fictive in the same way that Solomon's vineyard in Baal-hamon is. Both the sister and Solomon's vineyard are foils that allow the speakers to say something about themselves. They say it metaphorically, and poetic metaphor is by its very nature plurisignificant, but the thrust is fairly clear. She says that, unlike the girl in her example, for whom preparations will be made when she reaches marriageable age, she needs no such attention, since she (a fortified city) has already surrendered to her lover. He says that his vineyard (the woman) is worth more than Solomon's and he alone will tend it.

Both vignettes have an enigmatic quality, as if the speakers wished to engage the audience in solving a puzzle (cf. Müller on 8:8–10). And both seem to have marriage arrangements as their backdrop, in a way that is lighthearted but leading up to serious avowals of commitment. In what appears to be a detached, playful manner—detached because social conventions are pushed aside by the overwhelming power of love (vv. 6–7, though v. 1 and v. 7 deal with society's attitudes)—the woman speaks about preparations made when a girl reaches marriageable age, the time when she will be "spoken for" (vv. 8–9). As far as she herself is concerned, it is a moot question. She has already reached womanhood and surrendered herself to her lover (v. 10); in a sense, she has been spoken for (not necessarily formally, since that is not really the issue). The man confirms their mutual commitment by declaring that she belongs to him: she is his very own vineyard, worth more than any vineyard a king might possess (v. 12). As elsewhere in the Song, they speak along gender-determined lines. She deals with a subject that can only have been of great concern for women. In a society where women were under the control of their fathers or other male relatives before marriage, where marriages were usually arranged, and where the virginity of the bride was an important issue, what role do matters of the heart play? He thinks in terms of competition with other men and the imagery he draws upon—vineyards, hired workers to tend them, and payment for the produce—belongs to the sphere of economic livelihood.

In these vignettes, as in 3:6–11 and 2:15–16, marriage, as far as the Song's lovers are concerned, is only indirectly alluded to (see the general discussion under 3:6–11). Perhaps there is an implicit criticism of the practice of paying a bride price (Rudolph, Krinetzki), but it is only partially true to conclude that society's values are not the Song's values (see the discussion in Landy 152–76). Rather, when desire burns like a raging flame (8:6), when it pleases love to be roused (2:7; 3:5; 8:4), social expectations and values are irrelevant.

[8:8–10] Most interpreters assign vv. 8–9 to the woman's brothers of 1:6 and identify the woman as the little sister spoken of here. The brothers, they assume, are still concerned with their sister's chastity and speak about their measures to protect it. Since it would be surprising to hear the brothers speak directly now, for the first time in the poem, many suppose that the woman is quoting words her brothers spoke in the past (e.g., Budde, Rudolph, Krinetzki, Gerleman, Würthwein, Murphy, Munro 33–34, 77, Longman). Assigning the speech to some time in the past also explains the discrepancy between the brothers' claim that their sister has no breasts and hers that they are like towers, clearly observable: she has, in the meantime, grown up. The problem with this view is that it appeals to a "story" that lies outside the poem in order to account for what is being said; it invents a plot where none exists. The woman's brothers appear in only one verse of the Song. Not only do they never speak, they are never spoken to. To assign to them a speaking part, even in the form of a quoted speech, is to give them an important role in the Song that the text does not warrant.

Another view, that the woman is speaking about *her* little sister (Landy 160; cf. Cook 1968: 149), seems even less likely. As Rudolph observes, the mention of another sister is without interest and has no point. It also involves one in supplying a context, another plot of sorts, in which the woman's family includes a little sister (whom we hear of for the first time), and in which the woman speaks in the plural ("we") on behalf of the family. Other proposals for identifying the speakers of vv. 8–9—all of which involve either bringing hitherto unidentified characters onto the scene or rather arbitrarily carving up this speech, or both—include a group of suitors (e.g., Gordis), the woman in v. 8 and the brothers in

v. 9 (Delitzsch), the brothers in v. 8 and suitors in v. 9 (Ringgren, Rudolph, though they observe that v. 9 may also belong to the brothers), one brother in v. 8 and another in v. 9 (Ginsburg), older siblings (including sisters) of a girl who has not yet reached puberty, quoted by one of the sisters (Keel), the woman, putting words in the mouths of those who scorn one who would offer wealth for love (Goulder, looking back to v. 7).

Whereas the woman's brothers are incidental, like the watchmen (3:3–4) or queens and concubines (6:8–9), the women of Jerusalem are not, and, as the only speakers in the poem besides the lovers, theirs could be the voice we hear here (so Meek; Exum 1973: 75–76; Garrett). All the speakers in the poem have a function: the female and male voices allow the poet to portray love from both a woman's and a man's point of view; the women of Jerusalem provide an audience with whom the lovers interact. Viewed as a dialogue between these women (vv. 8–9) and the woman (v. 10), these verses are reminiscent of the banter in 1:7–8 between the woman and someone else (perhaps also the Jerusalem women; see under 1:8). If vv. 8–9 are attributed to the women of Jerusalem, there is no reason to assume that they are talking about the woman. They could be speaking, hypothetically as it were, about a girl who has not reached sexual maturity, referring to her as their "little sister." The woman's reply in v. 10 contrasts her situation with that of the young girl—and the discrepancy between "she has no breasts" and "my breasts are like towers" no longer requires explanation (viz., the reference is to the past [so most commentators], or the speakers are teasing [Fox]).

That the women of Jerusalem should speak now—at the very point when the poem has reached its climax in the affirmation of the strength of love (vv. 6–7)—is very much in keeping with the way they function elsewhere: to remind us, by their presence, that the poem is addressed to us. However, despite the advantage that it does not require having someone speak who has neither spoken before nor been spoken to before in the Song, assigning vv. 8–9 to the women of Jerusalem is not altogether satisfactory. It seems a curious, and wholly unanticipated, exchange for them to be holding with the woman at this point in the poem. That they should speak now is less likely than the suggestion put forward above that all three verses belong to the woman, and that the little sister is a hypothetical example rather than the woman herself. Not only does taking vv. 8–10 as the woman's speech require the least amount of reading between the lines, it is also supported by the formal and thematic parallels with the man's vignette in vv. 11–12.

The woman's similitude here in vv. 8–10 is enigmatic. The issue appears to be the girl's chastity, since vv. 8–9 are about her person and the context is betrothal (cf. 1 Sam 25:39). If "wall" and "door" are metaphors for the girl's chastity, are they antithetical (being a wall is good but being a door is bad) or complementary (parts of one and the same image, a walled city)? The wall metaphor suggests inaccessibility. The nature of the edifice to be built upon it is not entirely clear. The word here translated "tier" (*tîrâ*) refers to encampments in Gen 25:16; Num 31:10; Ezek 25:4; Ps 69:25 [26 H]; and 1 Chr 6:54 [39 H]. Perhaps originally it referred to rows of stones used to mark off an encampment; see the discussion in Pope. In Ezek 46:23 it is applied to rows of masonry. The idea seems to be a course or tier decorated in silver crowning the wall, although it could be a structural feature; compare "parapet" (REB, NAB), "turret" (Ginsburg, Gordis, Landy 160, Fox, Falk), "battlement" (NRSV, NJB, JPS).

Building a tier decorated in silver upon the wall might be a measure to strengthen it, but the use of silver suggests that the edifice is for show, an adornment, which, in terms of the image, presumably would enhance the young woman's appeal to potential suitors. The door, on the other hand, since it can be either closed or open, represents either inaccessibility or accessibility or both. The door is an important part of the metaphor in v. 9 for precisely this reason. Here the idea seems to be that it is closed: the word used is *delet*, the door itself, whose function is normally to bar entry, rather than *petah*, the doorway, which allows it (Fox, Keel, Garrett). To panel it in precious cedar wood would be a costly way to reinforce it but a most impressive form of ornamentation. It is difficult to think of this speech as anything other than playful; its cryptic, question-and-answer style makes it seem almost like a riddle. A moral lesson about the rewards of chastity and the punishment for sexual freedom, as some interpreters read it, or, worse, a warning or threat, would be out of place after the climactic paean to love in vv. 6–7, for if torrents cannot threaten the flame of love, how can social restrictions intimidate it?

Verses 8–9 use architectural and military imagery—a young woman as a walled city, fortified and decorated. In v. 10 the woman takes up the wall image and applies it to herself. She is a wall, but in contrast to the aforementioned little sister, she requires neither reinforcement to protect her from suitors nor ornamentation to attract one. She possesses her own enhancement, an erotic one, her breasts. The phrase *kĕmôṣᵊ̄ēt šālôm* in v. 10d is difficult. It is reasonable to assume that the comparison, "*like* one who brings/finds peace," because it too is a metaphor, continues the metaphor of the walled city, and that, like the rest of the imagery in vv. 8–10, this phrase too has a sexual significance. The woman is (like) a wall, her breasts are (like) towers, and she is like one who brings, or finds, peace (*shalom* is her answer to the military allusion). Whether one takes *mwṣᵊt* as the *hiphil* of *yṣᵊ*, "one who brings," or as the *qal* active participle of *mṣᵊ*, "one who finds," makes little difference. In the context of a city under siege, to bring peace signifies surrender, and to find peace is to have the offer of surrender accepted (e.g., Deut 20:10–11; Josh 9:15; 11:19). The significance of the door in v. 9, which could be opened or closed, now becomes clear. A city that surrenders does not have its walls besieged, since it opens its doors. The woman is both a wall and a door (like the little sister in v. 9), but in her case the door has been opened so that her lover can take possession of the city.

"In his eyes" can refer only to her lover. She speaks here about his perspective, the way he sees her. Keeping in mind that vv. 8–14 are dialogue, "in his eyes" conjures him up, allowing us to imagine that he is present and might even be looking at her as she speaks, just as "my own vineyard is before me" in v. 12 suggests that she is in his presence. Throughout the Song he has been talking about how he sees her; it is his characteristic mode of speaking (e.g., 4:1–7; 6:4–10; 7:1–7 [2–8 H]; see Introduction, "Different Ways of Speaking about Love," pp. 14–15). Here in v. 10 she describes how she thinks he perceives her: like a magnificent fortified city offering peace, that is, as surrendering to him. There is a rather nice irony here because, whereas earlier he spoke of being captured by her (4:9; 7:5 [6 H]), she speaks now of surrender to him. The woman's similitude complements the momentous affirmation of the power of love in vv. 6–7; compare Gerleman 219: "As in the previous poem [8:6–7] here too the theme is the power of love."

The expression "find *šālôm* in his eyes" is evocative of the idiom "to find favor (*ḥēn*) in someone's eyes," that is, to please them (for a woman pleasing a man, see Ruth 2:2, 10, 13; Esth 5:8; 7:3; Deut 24:1). This is how JPS translates: "So I became in his eyes / As one who finds favor," which seems to mean that, now that she is sexually developed, she is *like* someone who pleases him—and not that she *is* one who pleases him, for JPS has retained the *kaph*, "as"; similarly KJV, "as one that found favour." This seems an odd thing to say. Delitzsch suggests that *šālôm* is used instead of *ḥēn* in order to form a wordplay on the name Solomon, which is an interesting suggestion but one that does not justify his inference that she has found *šālôm* (which he takes to mean inward agreement, confidence, friendship) with *šĕlōmōh* (Solomon). He does, however, propose a way of dealing with the *kaph* on *kĕmôṣᵊʾēt*, "*like* one who finds," that, in effect, enables him to ignore it. He takes it as the *kaph veritatis*, indicating exact similitude or equality (cf. Joüon-Muraoka §133g). Murphy also appeals to the *kaph veritatis* and interprets along the same lines, concluding that "the man's loving acceptance of her . . . has brought peace, well-being, and fulfillment" (193; similarly, Longman). This is to strain the sense of the verse. Even if the *kaph veritatis* does exist—and in my view all the examples can be explained without recourse to it—to say that her lover perceives her as pleasing him, or even "worthy to find peace with him," is not the same thing as saying that she finds well-being or fulfillment or a relationship of affection with him. She is not speaking about her feelings here. The perspective indicated by "in his eyes" needs to be taken seriously, as does the metaphorical force of the *kaph*. To introduce a nonmetaphorical statement about the lovers' relationship in v. 10d would wreck the metaphor of the walled city that governs vv. 8–10, in which the woman is described in terms of a city suing for peace, and would take us outside the fictive world of the similitudes in vv. 8–12.

[8:11–12] Now it is the man's turn to affirm the bond between them, in a way that also illustrates the theme of love's supreme value (vv. 6–7). His lover has just described the way she imagines he perceives her: like a fortified city suing for peace. Now he describes how he perceives her: like a vineyard to be tended by him alone. "Vineyard" in v. 12 is a metaphor for the woman (see the discussion under 1:6, 2:15, and 4:16). The phrase "my own vineyard," literally "my vineyard which is mine," appears in 1:6, where it is spoken by the woman, which leads some critics to conclude that the woman is the speaker here (e.g., Ginsburg, Delitzsch, Landy 154, Munro 41–42). But the context, where the speaker's vineyard is preferred over Solomon's vineyard, makes it more likely that the man speaks here. Moreover, the vineyard is "before me." I take the phrase literally to mean that the woman is in the presence of her lover as he speaks these words (others stress various aspects of the preposition; e.g., Pope, "at my disposal," as in Gen 13:9; 20:15; 24:51; 34:10; 47:6; 1 Sam 16:16; Fox "near at hand," i.e., in his care, in the center of his attention, as in Prov 4:3; Isa 53:2; Gen 17:18). In 1:6 she announces "my own vineyard I have not kept," which, among other things, may suggest that she has given herself to her lover or that she needs tending (see under 1:6). Now the man declares that this vineyard belongs to him; he will tend it.

His speech takes the form of a similitude or parable, as is indicated by such features as its setting in an indeterminate time, its semilegendary protagonist, its formulaic opening, and its apparent triviality (Landy 1983:153). Its enigmatic nature is part of its appeal; what does it illustrate? Since "vineyard" is a loaded term in the Song, we may suspect that Solomon's vineyard is something more than a collection of grapevines in a place called Baal-hamon. No such place is known (for attempts to locate it, see the discussion in Pope), and meanings of the name, "owner of wealth" and "husband of a multitude," suggest that it was chosen to emphasize Solomon's affluence—his vast riches, his holdings of land, his many wives. Proper names lend specificity, concreteness, and sometimes exoticism to the poetry; compare, for example, tents of Qedar (1:5), vineyards of En-gedi (1:14), David's tower (4:4), pools in Heshbon, gate of Bath-rabbim, tower of Lebanon (7:4 [5 H]). Two things are noteworthy about this vineyard: Solomon does not tend it himself, and its produce is very valuable. I take the second couplet in v. 11 in a general sense to mean its produce is worth a thousand silver pieces, a substantial sum (cf. Isa 7:23, where a vineyard with a thousand vines is worth a thousand shekels of silver). The alternative ("each [i.e., the keepers] would bring for its fruit a thousand silver pieces") seems less likely, both because it leaves one with a more complicated business transaction to explain (the keepers pay Solomon a thousand silver pieces; he then pays them two hundred) and because in v. 12 the speaker tells Solomon he can keep his thousand (not a thousand from each keeper, though that could be implied).

In v. 12, the man compares his vineyard to Solomon's, and here the sexual referent of "vineyard" becomes explicit. He prefers his own vineyard (his lover) to Solomon's vineyard, which because it belongs to the king must be a very fine one, and because it needs keepers must be extensive. If Solomon's vineyard is his harem, v. 12 ("you can have the thousand, Solomon") may hint at its legendary size, a thousand women (1 Kgs 11:3). The man's vineyard means more to him than a royal harem. His vineyard is priceless; no other woman can compare with her (cf. 6:8–10). What is more, he has his vineyard to himself, unlike Solomon, who relies on vineyard keepers to tend his.

Because Solomon's vineyard operates on two levels, literal and metaphorical, whereas the man's is clearly metaphorical (the woman), one should perhaps not expect the correspondences between the two vineyards to work completely. The motif of vineyard keepers allows the man to illustrate indirectly his sole responsibility for his vineyard. But whereas vineyard keepers could allude to harem guards (cf. Esth 2:3), for whose upkeep Solomon would have had to provide ("two hundred [silver pieces] for the keepers of its fruit"), they do not tend Solomon's vineyard in the way the man tends his vineyard (unless this is a sexual joke at Solomon's expense).

Does this vignette make fun of Solomon, who "possessed so many women that he could not keep their 'fruit' to himself" (Fox; cf. Keel)? Might it be critical? Falk thinks these verses reject a view of woman as sexual object or sexual property (the relationship of Solomon to his harem) and advocate the kind of loving relationship the man has with his beloved. Longman proposes that the lovers' exclusive relationship is implicitly favored over Solomon's polygamy. If Solomon is the butt of a joke or the object of criticism, then we would have here a very different treatment of Solomon and royalty from what we find elsewhere in the Song, where King Solomon is portrayed positively (3:6–11) and the man assumes a royal guise as "the king" (1:4, 12; 7:5 [6 H]).

[8:13–14] The Song ends, as it began, with the erotic imperative, the call to love addressed directly, and urgently, to the beloved. First the man, then the woman, speaks. The lovers' exhortations are juxtaposed: his *hašmîʿînî* ("let me hear!") is followed directly by her *bĕraḥ* ("take flight!"). Far from being anticlimactic or mystifying as a conclusion, as many critics have observed, these verses provide an inspired ending to the Song. Rather than bringing the poem to closure, they lead us back into it.

[8:13] From the woman as his very own vineyard, the man turns to thoughts of his garden (cf. "my garden," 5:1). The garden (or gardens; cf. 6:2) is both the woman, and often specifically her sexuality, and a place to delight the senses, where the woman and man enjoy erotic pleasures (on the theme of love in the garden, see Fox 283–87). She dwells in the gardens; he goes down to the gardens to graze among lilies (6:2; cf. 2:16) and to eat its choice fruits (4:16; 5:1). The garden blooms for their eyes and flourishes in the light of their love. It is secluded ("a garden locked," 4:12), but lovers everywhere know the way to it and are welcome there ("Eat, friends, drink yourselves drunk on caresses!" 5:1).

One could divide this verse differently, with the Vulgate (so, e.g., Meek, Krinetzki, Gordis, Pope, Fox, Murphy, Longman), but it makes little difference to the meaning:

> You who dwell in the gardens,
>   companions are listening.
>   Let me hear your voice!

Reading with the MT accentuation (followed by LXX), as I have done, "let me hear [it]"—one word, *hašmî'înî*, in the Hebrew—stands alone and is thus all the more emphatic. "Companions" are listening (the word appears without the definite article "the" or a pronominal suffix "my"). Who are they? The man's companions have been mentioned before (1:7). Here companions function like the women of Jerusalem, as an audience within the poem whose participation invites ours. Once again the Song invites its readers into the lovers' private world—like the companions, we are listening for her voice—and it keeps us out when the lovers want to be alone ("let *me* hear it," the man says). The listening (a participle) takes place now, in the present, creating the illusion of immediacy. We are listening. The voice we listen for is the poet's. And the tension between the voice and silence is also that between love and death (Landy 113).

[8:14] The last words of the Song, like the first, are the woman's (so most commentators; a minority view holds that the man tells the woman the words he wants to hear her say, a view that goes back to Ibn Ezra; e.g., Gerleman, Gordis, Müller). They are the same words she used in 2:17 to answer the man's request to hear her voice (2:14), except that "mountains of spices" replaces the obscure "cleft mountains," and, unlike the ambiguous imperative "turn" in 2:17, the verb here is *brḥ*, which indicates movement away from someone or something. Is she then sending her lover away? Not if "mountains of spices" refer to her. Most translations and commentators smooth over the difficulty of the injunction "take flight" and translate "make haste" or "hurry," as though the woman is calling the man to her. Some suppose that the woman is telling her lover to flee from his companions and come to her (Fox, Krinetzki, Garrett). Keel proposes that she uses double entendre so that the man's nosy companions will think she is sending him away, but he will understand that she wants him to come to her (obviously the companions are not very clever). More likely, the ambiguity is part of the meaning. The contradictory impulses observable in 2:17 are even stronger here: "take flight . . . upon the mountains of spices" signals both the lovers' separation and their union (see under 2:17). "Mountains of spices" is a double entendre for the woman herself. She is a mountain of myrrh and hill of frankincense in 4:6 and a pleasure garden of spices in 4:13–14.

The ambiguity of "take flight . . . to me" is the dynamic of the Song, the seeking latent in finding and the finding latent in seeking, the separation prerequi-